We Spared Not the Capital of America

We Spared Not the Capital of America

WAR BETWEEN BRITAIN AND THE UNITED STATES 1812-15

Tony Maclachlan

authorHOUSE®

AuthorHouse™
1663 Liberty Drive
Bloomington, IN 47403
www.authorhouse.com
Phone: 1-800-839-8640

© 2011 by Tony Maclachlan. All rights reserved.

No part of this book may be reproduced, stored in a retrieval system, or transmitted by any means without the written permission of the author.

First published by AuthorHouse 09/14/2011

ISBN: 978-1-4567-8185-9 (sc)
ISBN: 978-1-4567-8186-6 (ebk)

Printed in the United States of America

Any people depicted in stock imagery provided by Thinkstock are models, and such images are being used for illustrative purposes only.

Certain stock imagery © Thinkstock.

This book is printed on acid-free paper.

Because of the dynamic nature of the Internet, any web addresses or links contained in this book may have changed since publication and may no longer be valid. The views expressed in this work are solely those of the author and do not necessarily reflect the views of the publisher, and the publisher hereby disclaims any responsibility for them.

CONTENTS

MAPS

Key: British forces and their movements are shown in black.
American forces and their movements are shown in grey.
All maps are orientated with north point at top unless otherwise stated

By the same author:

'The Civil War in Wiltshire'

(Rowan Books 1997)

'The Civil War in Hampshire'

(Rowanvale Books 2000)

The author would like to credit the London Statesman newspaper for use of the title of this book, but has been unable to find any organization existing today that might be given credit.

PREFACE

The 1812-14 war between Britain and the United States was, until fairly recently, one of the forgotten wars, regarded as insignificant, militarily valueless and largely inconsequential. Perhaps this was because it was overshadowed by events in Europe, when the fate of that continent's people was far from clear. Events, battles and sieges in Spain and Russia were far more momentous, exhilarating and fast moving. European warfare for centuries had involved movements of vast armies, the occupation of conquered territory and the spoliation of the countryside. Invariably the treaties that followed long 'years' of war involved territorial adjustments that altered the political map of Europe, solved little and seeded beds of resentment that inevitably led to further wars. At the time, the Napoleonic Wars might have been seen as climactic by contemporaries—the 'war to end' wars, but, seen from our later viewpoint, these wars turned out to be just part of the sequence and merely continued the tradition.

The war in America, however, was not set in this military mould. It is, for this reason, that recent military historians have found it a subject of particular interest. Territories, when invaded, were promptly abandoned and reverted to their former owners. This was clearly a war which had no real causes, no clear objectives and no long-term consequences. No frontiers were altered and no wrongs were righted. The present relationship between Great Britain and the United States would have been much the same if this war had never been fought. The Treaty of Ghent, which ended the war, was, as one contemporary Frenchman claimed, a 'Treaty of Omissions.' It was also a 'war without enemies'—a war between people of the same linguistic and cultural background. Men living near the border between Canada and the

United States would not necessarily choose to join the forces of the nation in which they dwelt. Many crossed that frontier to enlist in the ranks of their homeland's opponent. No battle honours had been awarded in the American War of Independence a few years previously because King George's ministers in London had regarded this war as a civil war. Only reluctantly were those arrogant politicians forced to accept that the war of 1812 was an international conflict and not an internecine struggle between factions within the national family.

The small-scale nature of the war also makes it appealing as a subject of study. More than half the skirmishes (the term 'battle' is often inappropriate) involved forces numbering less than one thousand men on each side. For this reason, it makes it easier to see the protagonists as individual human beings with blood, fears and emotions rather than as minute components in an impersonal military machine.

In this book, I have attempted to convey some of the emotions, the tragedies and the dislocating impact of war upon a young nation nurturing valuable notions of freedom and self assertion. I have also attempted to consider that war from the viewpoint of the imperialists in London and Canada, while simultaneously outlining in some detail the campaigning that took place. Whether I have succeeded or not will be for others to decide.

ACKNOWLEDGEMENTS

No author can ever really claim *all* the credit for the production of a work of non-fiction. Just as the director of a Broadway show will pay tribute to the tireless individuals who work behind the scenes, so, too, an author must recognise the contributions of all those who produced the scenario upon which the book is based. These, in a work about war and politics, include the generals, social commentators, politicians and the occasional eye witness—the men or women of the time whose thoughts and actions have been recorded by themselves or by others, and whose writings now fill the pages of dusty volumes in academic libraries. I pay tribute to all such people. Without their quarrels and contributions, there would have been no material for this book.

Those who have left no literary footprints must also be thanked: The quayside merchant, the uniformed soldier, the sweating sailor manning the guns of a sea going schooner—and even those who tried to remain uninvolved. To each of these, I express my gratitude. Their pain and suffering is the material on which I have fed.

Yet, of course, I must pay a greater acknowledgement to the two members of my family who have helped me more directly. My son Tim and daughter Catherine, both computer wizards, have taken my rough maps and translated them into something more presentable. It is also prudent for husbands to pay tribute to wives. I would, therefore, like to thank my wife, Eileen, for not complaining too much when I have chosen to research and write rather than attend to essential gardening and household repairs.

CHAPTER 1

'We consider the whole Gulf Stream as of our water'

Three crewmen were killed when the rigging came down. Fifteen more were injured. Three of these later had limbs amputated. A box, lashed to the deck, was split open, disgorging its contents of coloured feathers. His Majesty's ship 'Leopard' maintained her fire for fifteen minutes, her gunners instructed to aim their shots at the masts and sails of the 'Chesapeake', the newest frigate in the Congressional Navy. The American ship, its decks covered with splintered wood and the tangle of rigging, managed to return just one shot, achieved when an officer brought hot coals from the galley to one of the guns.

The two nations were not even at war—and would not become officially embroiled in hostilities for a further five years. Many similar incidents occurred in that tense interval before the formal start of war, mostly caused by Britain's provocative attitude and seeming determination to limit the young republic's national independence. Less than a generation after the signing of the Treaty of Paris in 1783, which had ended the War of Independence and had aspired to remove '*all past misunderstandings and differences that have unhappily interrupted the good correspondence and friendship between the two nations,*' the guns were firing again and bayonets were coated with blood. Simon Myer, a resident of the Mohawk River valley in New York State and an ardent Hanoverian loyalist in the earlier war, would be one of those who enlisted in the army of the United States in 1812. Fighting in the Champlain Valley a year after the war's start, he came face to face with an Ontario farmer standing in the British ranks. A moment's hesitation followed, both men raised their weapons, and Myer fell to the ground with a ball through his heart. The two men had worked together in a boatyard before the war. Myer, in fact, had apparently saved the other man's life during a brawl in Albany.

In the twenty or so years of nationhood since she had won her independence, the young United States had begun to forge a concept of nationhood, something distinct from the fervid patriotism that had led her to victory in her struggle for independence. In addition, the youthful nation had formulated the concept of 'Manifest Destiny', an emotive driving force that would take its people, in the following half century, to the Rockies and beyond.

In those same few years the fighting 'sons of freedom' had gained graceful old age. From their rocking chairs on summer verandahs, they could now recount stories of heroic fighting to their attentive grandsons, stories which helped to infuse pride of nation into this new generation. And, in those same few years, a national capital had been established on the banks of the Potomac, a constitution developed and the first presidents elected.

The search for a national identity had required painful decisions and painful consequences. Europe had been involved in a political earthquake, triggered by the revolution in France. King Louis XVI, the 'friend' of the revolution and republicans in America, had been toppled and executed by republicanism bred in France. The newly independent nation had now to adopt a stance towards this apparently trouble-seeking nation in Europe and to the crowned heads of state who would be antagonized by republican France.

The United States took on a neutral hue, vowing officially to remain uninvolved. On 22nd April 1793 President George Washington and his ministers proclaimed the nation's neutrality, hoping, by this gesture, to win no favours and make no enemies. The proclamation was followed in June 1794 by a Neutrality act, which prohibited American citizens from enlisting in the services of a foreign power and the fitting out of foreign naval vessels in U.S. ports. All of this took place during a period when political parties were emerging, the Federalists crystallizing around Alexander Hamilton, the Treasury Secretary, and the Democratic republicans of Thomas Jefferson, the latter a general pro-France grouping and the champion of the sovereignty of the individual states of the Union.

It had thus been a promising start, ten or so years of emerging democracy, healthy debate and some economic progress. Friction had occurred, debtors against creditors, town conflicting with the country folk, sometimes spilling into uprisings, recriminations and bloodshed. But the western boundary seemed limitless, providing countless opportunities for the hardy and the enterprising. Every problem faced by the nation appeared to have a solution.

In the fall of 1794, a treaty with the colonial mother seemed likely to remove some of the causes of dispute. King George's government, despite the 1782 agreement, had failed to evacuate the forts of the north-west [1], justifying the tardiness on the grounds that some pre-revolutionary debt owed to British subjects remained unpaid. This left the lucrative fur trade of the region squarely in British hands or in the hands of the Ontario Canadians. And there were those in the Ohio area who believed that his Britannic Majesty's agents were insidiously encouraging the Indian tribes to indulge in the periodic massacre of white settlers. In an attempt to remove these causes of friction, John Jay, the Chief Justice, was sent to London as special envoy, but was instructed to make no commitment which might violate any agreements with France and so compromise the policy of strict neutrality. Determined to succeed, Jay engineered an agreement by which Great Britain would withdraw from the still occupied posts within two years and would permit U.S. vessels to participate in trade with the British West Indies, on the condition that the U.S. renounced her self-claimed right to carry certain staple products. Within the framework of this treaty, an agreement was made to refer to an appointed commission the issue of all the outstanding debts owed to British merchants.

Those who thought that Jay's Treaty might pave the way to long-term amity with Britain, however, were soon to be disillusioned. The fact remained that the ex-parent of the colonies had never accepted the wayward child's departure from home and still considered that she could discipline, chastise and control. In the following twenty years, the areas of conflict grew larger and far more bitter.

Two particular issues lay at the heart of the discord, both maritime. Impressment, the forced enlistment of men into military service, had

---

1 Forts Oswego, Oswegotchie, Pte au Fer, Detroit, Miami, Niagara and Michilimackinac

been standard practice in Great Britain for well over one hundred years. Desertions from the Royal Navy averaged 2500 men per annum during the 1790's, causing a shortage of manpower in the fleet at a time of almost incessant war. Many of those deserting ended up on American ships. British vessels cruising off the North American coast frequently stopped and searched American vessels and seized any crew member suspected of being a deserter from His Majesty's fighting ships. Those taken often claimed to be American citizens. But the frequency of such claims caused the British captains to ask for proof of their citizenship. Large numbers of those who managed to prove their non-British status were still seized and unwillingly enlisted into the ranks of the Royal Navy. Perhaps 6000 sailors a year were taken this way, almost every one of these snatched from unarmed vessels engaged in peaceful trade.

American politicians, angered by this practice, would identify another issue, more odious even than impressment and just as difficult for the British to justify. Attempts to control and restrict American trade should have been laid to rest by the Paris Peace Treaty and the subsequent 1794 treaty negotiated by Chief Justice Jay. The Navigation laws of earlier decades, arrogantly applied by Britain on the spurious claim that she ruled the seas, had alienated European maritime nations and had contributed to America's desire for early independence. Complacent, self-centred Britain had not learned from her high-handed application of her laws, and was determined to continue with the practice.

Yet it was to be disagreements with France that clouded the horizon in the last two years of the century. The republican government of France, angered by Jay's treaty with the British, refused to receive an American ambassador. Further irritations followed, culminating in French threats and the exchange of canon fire between the warships of the two nations. Full-scale war, however, was avoided through the careful diplomacy of President John Adams, who sent the golden-mouthed William Vans Murray to settle grievances. France, becoming more compliant when she found the armies of Europe's major powers standing on her frontiers, was suddenly prepared to talk. Men hoped that the Treaty of Morfontaine, signed in September 1800, would herald a period of more peaceful relations.

Such hopes were immediately dashed. Rumours that Spain was about to cede the vast area of Louisiana to France revived those years of distrust and the war hawks were heard again. President Jefferson, writing to his ambassador in Paris in 1802, sums up the national feeling at the time: '*There is on the globe one single spot the possessor of which is our natural and habitual enemy. It is New Orleans, through which the produce of three-eighths of our territory must pass to market . . . . France, placing herself in that door, assumes to us the attitude of defiance; . . . . The day that France takes possession of New Orleans fixes the sentence which is to restrain her forever within her low-watermark . . . . From that moment we must marry ourselves to the British fleet and nation.*' Sabre rattling, however, ceased the following year; the United States purchased the entire region from France for 60,000 francs and so acquired unrestricted access to the Mississippi and the vital port of New Orleans.

Relationships with Britain, by contrast, continued to deteriorate. The underlying concept which aggravated the dispute with the English in the first decade of the nineteenth century was the 'Rule of 1756', a maxim that prohibited any ship, during time of war, from engaging in trade forbidden to it in time of peace. When war re-emerged in Europe in 1793, France, in a gesture to win American favour, granted American ships the right to trade with the French colonies, something which had previously been France's exclusive preserve. Initially Britain made no real fuss about this. In a test case, the Admiralty judge, Sir William Scott, even conceded that the 'Polly', an American vessel which loaded cargo in a French colonial port and then unloaded in the U.S.A. before reloading and setting out for a French mainland port, was not actually involved in 'direct' trade and therefore had not violated the sacred rule of 1756. The judgement, although soothing affairs at official level, enraged Great Britain's merchants. They stormed the Admiralty in protest. Poor Scott felt obliged to consult his law books again and, in a more publicised case in 1805, he reversed his decision. The 'Essex', involved in exactly the same pattern of 'indirect' trade, was deemed to be in violation of the rule and subject to seizure, just as if she had been an enemy vessel. British policy had been blown off-course by the winds of public opinion. It was now the turn of American merchants to swell with anger, convinced that Britain was still trying to dictate the tenor and pattern of American trade. Congress reacted almost too casually, appointing William Pinkney to assist James Monroe, the American minister in London, to undertake fresh negotiations with the Crown.

The year 1806 was to be a particularly thorny one. Thomas Jefferson, elected president in 1804, was attuned to public opinion and vociferous in his denunciation of British interference in the affairs of America. Anglophobia now became fashionable and served as a tonic to boost patriotism and provide Americans with their distinctiveness. It helped, also, to define U.S. foreign policy, a belief that the destiny of the New World lay in American hands—and perhaps the ocean, too, that separated the two continents. '*We begin to broach the idea that we consider the whole Gulf Stream as of our waters,*' Jefferson had declared in 1805, at a time when relations with Britain were not yet beyond repair.

On 6th May 1806 British Orders in Council set up a blockade of the European coast from Brest to the Elbe with the overt purpose of strangling French overseas trade. The ships of neutral countries were liable to seizure—and their crews impressed. The twin grievances of impressments and interference in the trading rights of a sovereign country were thus brought together to create a situation in the United States that men considered intolerable.

Pinkney and Monroe demanded the cessation of the twin practices. Fox was conciliatory but firm, bending in both directions in a way that could settle nothing. '*His Majesty's Government, animated by an earnest desire to remove every cause of dissatisfaction, has directed His Majesty's Commissioners to give to Mr. Monroe and to Mr. Pinkney the most positive assurance that instructions have been given . . . for the observance of the greatest caution in the impressing of British seamen, and that the strictest care shall be taken to preserve the citizens of the United States from any molestation or injury and that immediate and prompt redress shall be offered upon any representation or injury sustained by them . . .*'

Charles James Fox died soon after giving this anodyne re-assurance and was succeeded as Secretary for Foreign Affairs by Lord Howick. The two Americans, hoodwinked by British affability, accepted Britain's promise on 31st December 1806, signing a treaty, despite the fact that London had not yet agreed to abandon the right to search or impress, and had made no commitment to pay damages for stopping ships at sea. Moreover, in a partial amelioration of the Orders, U.S. vessels would be permitted to carry goods from French and Spanish colonies to their mother countries, but only on payment to the U.S. customs of a tax not less than 2% of the value of the goods. This concession effectively implied that Britain felt that she could dictate the commercial and taxation policies of a now independent nation.

King George's government could have turned Napoleon's Berlin Decrees to her advantage. Designed to counter Great Britain's May orders, this imperial ruling, proclaimed on 21st November 1806 called for a complete blockade of Britain, prohibiting all trade with the emperor's most defiant enemy. Any ship sailing directly from a British port or from one of her colonies would be liable to seizure. Instead of stoking the rage in America that surely should have arisen against France, Britain chose to warn the United States that, unless Washington refused to recognize the decrees from Berlin, Britain would not ratify the recent treaty. Jefferson, on receiving a copy of the treaty, refused to present it to the Senate and merely filed it away. Napoleon, by clever timing, had deftly exploited the friction that was pulling the two English speaking nations apart. And, to assuage any nascent francophobia that might be developing across the Atlantic, M.Decres, the French Minister of Marine, assured America that the decrees did not apply to her.

1807 took the two nations even closer to war. On 7th January another order in council reinforced the earlier prohibition of trade with France or with any ports from which British ships were barred. Then, on 18th March, the Whig government of Lord Grenville was replaced by a Tory ministry under Portland. Untried George Canning was hoisted to the post of Foreign Secretary at a time of growing crisis. His skills of diplomacy were to be tested a few months later by two incidents which, probably more than any others in this sequence of blunders, directly contributed to war.

In June 1807 several British warships lay off Lynnhaven Bay, Virginia. Amongst them was the 36 gun 'Melampus' and the 50 gun 'Leopard'. Several sailors were reported to have left the first named boat, rowed to Norfolk and enlisted in the navy of the United States. These deserters then apparently paraded through the streets of the town, watched, it is said, by some of their former officers. Vice-Admiral George Berkeley, in command at Halifax, Nova Scotia, hearing of the desertions, ordered the squadron off Lynnhaven to search for the deserters and remove them from the ship on which they now served.

On the 19th the 'Chesapeake', the newest frigate in the American navy, put into Norfolk to take on a crew and provisions before sailing to the Mediterranean. When the young ship sailed out, none of her guns fully mounted, the 'Leopard' followed her. Just outside the three mile limit, the captain of the British vessel hailed her and requested permission to search the ship. Commodore James Barron of the U.S. Navy chose to refuse. The immediate consequences of the American commodore's lack of co-operation have been mentioned at the start of this chapter. Barron, despite being injured during the bombardment, offered to surrender. Captain Humphreys, commander of the 'Leopard', declined and insisted on searching the ship. Four suspected deserters were found; three immediately claimed to be Americans who had been earlier impressed into British service. The fourth, a Briton named Ratford,(or Wilson) was later hanged.

America, not just its president, was enraged. Federalist and Republicans, two parties with normally divergent views, united in an explosion of anger. '*At that moment',* Jefferson later declared, '*I had the issue of peace or war in my hand,'* In fitful and immediate retaliation, he issued a ruling on 2nd July, forbidding all British warships from entering U.S. ports. Poor Barron was court-martialled and retired from naval service without pay for five years. Some claimed that his punishment was for his failure to prepare his ship rather than for his weak defiance of the British.

Monroe dropped a formal protest on Canning's desk. The Foreign Secretary, seemingly prepared to apologise for the boarding of the 'Chesapeake', was far less willing to forgive the Americans' counter-action. In a note to Monroe, he was ruthlessly forthright: *'I am . . . . to inquire whether you are authorized to withdraw the proclamation on the knowledge of His Majesty's disavowal of the act which occasioned its publication.'*

The stand-off continued. In April 1806 Congress passed a measure prohibiting the importation from Britain of a long list of articles including flax, hemp, tin and brass. Held in abeyance during the ongoing negotiations, the measure would be re-installed as a weapon of diplomacy in December 1807. Canning promised to send a commissioner to Washington to discuss the matter, but made it clear that the man's brief would not include discussion of impressments. That issue, Canning made clear, was closed. Public opinion in the US would have taken the country to war at this moment, but the matter-of-fact president remained statesmanlike and conciliatory despite his people's anger. '*No two countries upon earth have so many points of common interest and friendship; and their rulers must be great bunglers, indeed, if with such dispositions they break asunder.*' But, as a clear warning to England, Jefferson added, '*We have the seamen and materials for fifty ships-of-the-line and half that number of frigates . . . . they would give to England serious proofs of the stock from which they are sprung and the school in which they have been taught.*' On 11th November 1807 Britain issued a fresh set of orders, re-asserting the blockade of all ports from which her ships were excluded. But, starved of some of her pre-war imports normally obtained from the continent of Europe now within the grip of Napoleon, London issued an additional order which would permit the ships of neutral nations to transport goods from a French dominated port to Britain on payment of duties to the British Crown. George Rose, the commissioner sent out to America by Canning to discuss the 'Chesapeake' incident, had clearly not been briefed by the Foreign Secretary and had been given no liberty to concede or barter. Laying the British case on the table, he almost demanded that the ban on British warships should be lifted prior to any discussion of reparations for the damage to the 'Chesapeake'. Canning, becoming less conciliatory as time went on, was soon insisting on the punishment of Barron as a pre-condition for any talks.

It is difficult to construe Britain's maritime reasoning and see it as anything other than vindictive. But Britain's long-term dominance on the high seas had fed her a false sense of pride and a culture of arrogance which the young nation across the ocean was bound to despise. The war lying on the horizon was provoked entirely by British false pride.

Napoleon responded to Britain's November orders with a new set of decrees of his own issued from Milan on 17th December. Any ship complying with Britain's orders and paying the required duty to King George's exchequer would be regarded as British property and consequently seized. American ships, whatever they did, would be seized by either France or Britain and her overseas trade would be annihilated. Jefferson, as president, would be obliged to search for a sharp retaliatory weapon.

The Embargo Act was the result. Passed just as the first effects of the two European countries' measures began to bite at the commercial life of America, this measure prohibited all US vessels from leaving their home ports and, more pointedly, forbade all foreign ships from entering American ports. Trade, likely to be upset by the Emperor's edict, would now, as a result of Jefferson's Act of Embargo, be brought to a standstill. Designed to punish other nations, the measure would prove disastrous to American mercantile trade. Within days of the passing of the legislation, American port life began to congeal, warehouses filled with unmoved goods, and it is estimated that 55,000 seamen and 100,000 dock workers were thrown into idleness. The prices of basic commodities, unable to find an overseas market, fell. Tobacco planters, so reliant upon the European trade, still had to support their productive infrastructures—and it was frequently the slaves who suffered most. Sailors and port workers, without jobs, sought employment on the decks and rigging of Royal Navy warships, temporarily dulling the issue of impressments. The measure whipped up a storm of political opposition, particularly dangerous in an election year. Some relied on hackneyed verse in their attempts to bring the measure down:

'Curse of our nation, source of countless woes,
From whose dark womb unreckoned misery flows,
The Embargo rages, like a sweeping wind-
Fear lowers before, and Famine stalks behind.'

William Cullen Bryant wrote over-dramatically. The second verse of a rhyme, which quickly became popular, was deliciously whimsical.

'What a fuss we have made,
About rights and free trade,
And swore we'd not let our own share go,
Now we can't for our souls,
Bring a hake from the shouls,
'Tis a breach of the Twentieth Embargo'

A handbill appearing on tavern doors was more vociferous and punchy: *'Let every man who holds the name of America dear to him stretch forth his hand and put this accursed thing—the Embargo—from him. Be resolute, act like the sons of liberty, of God, and of our country. Nerve your arms with vengeance against the Despot who would wrest the inestimable gem of your independence from you, and you shall be conquerors.'*

Those supporting the measure, however, felt that the storm of anger would soon blow over and sunnier times would come again. The warring nations of Europe, dependent upon American raw materials, would cry for forgiveness and offer to withdraw their savage measures. Pinkney, writing to Jefferson in the Spring of 1808, painted a picture of British hardship caused by the effects of the Embargo. '*The Embargo and loss of our trade are deeply felt here, and will be felt with more severity every day. The wheat harvest is likely to be alarmingly short, and the state of the continent will augment the evil. The discontents among the manufacturers are only quieted for a moment.*'

Napoleon's act of retaliation against the Embargo was just as savage as anything that Britain might have concocted. His Bayonne decree, issued on 17th April 1808, laid orders for the seizure of all American vessels and cargoes that might still lie in French controlled ports. To justify this order, he applied a logical and almost irrefutable argument. All US vessels in French ports must be there in violation of the Embargo and the Washington government should be grateful to him for seizing the ships and so enforcing American law! Such an argument, however, did not appeal in the emotive real world, and France was now perceived to be almost as much an irritant as Britain.

But few clamoured for war against Napoleon. Memories of French assistance less than thirty years previously remained strong, despite the more recent tussle on the seas, and French diplomats were more conciliatory when talking to the Americans. How many times were the men of Paris to explain that their harsh measures had been forced upon them by Britain? And just occasionally a senior French minister would declare that none of the Emperor's decrees applied to America anyway.

James Madison, despite the governing Democratic Republicans' deep unpopularity, won the autumn presidential election vote with 122 electoral college votes to 47 for the Federalist candidate, Charles Cotesworth Pinckney, whose party had opposed the measure from the start. The new president chose to take a fresh look at the effects of the Embargo, and on 27th February 1809 the hated Act was repealed. In unbiased recognition of the mischief caused to American trade by the malicious duo, Britain and France, Congress passed a Non-Intercourse Act instead, by which the commerce and ports of the United States were laid open to every nation on earth, with the exception, that is, of England and France.

One of the most undiplomatic attempts at diplomacy in the long drawn out sequence of blunders that eventually triggered war was now to occur. David Erskine, son of Britain's Lord Chancellor, was sent to the United States to smooth out ruffled feathers. He informed newly elected President Madison that the 1807 Orders in Council would be withdrawn in June 1809, a year hence. Immediately the President announced that American ports would be opened on that date to British ships, and bilateral trade would resume again. Madison, and even Britain, was toasted in celebration parties, and merchants began to dream again of fatter wallets and larger villas. Warehouse doors were re-opened and dust swept off the quayside walks. But this balloon of euphoria was quickly burst. Erskine had exceeded his brief, and Britain repudiated the agreement. Poor little Madison, riding a crest wave of popularity, was politically capsized and accused of a terrible blunder. The United Kingdom and the United States drifted further apart.

In Britain, a change of government in December 1809 put Spencer Perceval in the Prime Minister's seat and Richard Wellesley in the office of the Foreign Secretary. This new ministry, no keener than its predecessor to secure rapport with America but prepared to play lip service to the concept, sent Francis Jackson to America to keep discussions flowing. This man was totally unsuitable for the role. Used to dining with monarchs and to being entertained by diamond-encrusted women, he arrived in Washington with a coach and four and a retinue of personal servants. Poor, pedestrian Washington was no place for this man of lace and fancy, and he quickly alienated his hosts with his superior airs and over-haughty manner. Madison requested his recall. 'Copenhagen' Jackson, so named because he had presented the ultimatum to the Danish admirals in 1801, returned with his coach and four to the far more appropriate circles of London society.

Negotiations with France would prove to be just as fruitless. M. de Champigny, official mouthpiece for the Imperial government, informed General John Armstrong, the American minister in Paris, that, if Great Britain withdrew all her pernicious orders, France would withdraw the Berlin decree. This gesture produced a minor thaw in the iced-up relationship between Paris and Washington, but, of course, it would remain a mere gesture unless Britain responded. The thaw froze over a few weeks later when Napoleon issued yet another decree, this time from Rambouillet, in which he ordered the sale of all American vessels seized under the Bayonne ruling.

America had now to re-consider. Non-intercourse was proving to be as ineffective as the embargo in forcing concessions from either European nation. Congress consequently repealed this short-lived regulation and replaced it with the uncomfortably named 'Macon's no. 2 Act'. This stipulated that, if either of the European duo revoked her irritating trade restrictions, then the United States would revive non-intercourse against the other.

Here was the opportunity for which Napoleon sought. On 5th August 1810 he informed General Armstrong that the Berlin and Milan decrees had been revoked, knowing full well that Britain would not withdraw the offending orders. France suddenly soared in America's estimation in contrast with the dark and satanic island across the Channel. On 2nd October Madison revived non-intercourse against Great Britain only. Pinckney, sensing that any further attempts at negotiation would be pointless, left London soon afterwards. Great Britain had shown no willingness to concede anything and was still impressing sailors from American merchant ships. A mist of mistrust had enveloped the men of both sides, and the most innocuous of events would be open to misinterpretation.

The arrival of Augustus John Foster on 15th February 1811 as the new British agent in America was, therefore, a hollow gesture, containing no substance and as vaporous as the winter air. Those winter mists had hardly dispersed when two maritime duels propelled the United States and Britain to the very threshold of war. On 1st May 1811 the frigate 'Guerriere' halted the American merchantman 'Spitfire' and impressed one of her crew. Just five days later, on the 6th, the crew of the 44 gun American frigate, the 'President', resting at anchor off Annapolis, received instructions from Washington to investigate an unidentified British ship lying off New York. Commodore John Rodgers, the frigate's commanding officer, was on his estate 70 miles away and was not expected back for several days.Midshipman Matthew Perry, reluctant to respond until his captain was at the helm, lowered one of the frigate's boats and, taking a few crewmen, rode to the commodore's home, a journey of 23 hours of non-stop rowing and very little rest. Eventually the boat was pulled up on shore, and

Perry leaped out to report to the commodore. The officer returned with them to the waiting ship. The round trip had taken 39 hours. The journey by road from Annapolis to Havre de Grace would have taken just 10 hours!

Five days later the 'President' set sail. Passing around the capes on the 16th, she spotted a mast to the east and hurried to intercept. Rodgers hailed the vessel in the standard matter of the time and awaited the courtesy of a formal reply. The only response was a crashing shot from the stranger, direct enough to splinter a mast. Within minutes, both ships were dueling, the gunners too busy to pause and wonder why. Soon the unidentified ship fell silent, out gunned and outclassed. She turned out to be His Majesty's 18 gun ship 'Little Belt'. Damaged, with 9 of her crew dead and 23 wounded, she limped off to Halifax for repairs where, no doubt, Captain A. Bingham would tell tales of the unprovoked attack by the American, his version of events probably dissimilar to that recounted by Rodgers.

And, of course, it rekindled the glowing crisis of relationships. Foster, now settled in his Washington post, wanted to know why a 44 gun frigate had fired upon a small friendly vessel. America divided over the issue. Madison's Democratic Republicans, dominating Virginia and the south, clamoured for war. But Federalist New England was still coloured with a more pacifist hue, seeing all of the disadvantages and few of the advantages from adopting a belligerent tone. Many here felt that the 'Chesapeake' incident had now been avenged and so persuaded their congressional representatives to try to temper the war talk of the southerners. Geographically and politically America was in danger of dividing into two over the issue of war, a dichotomy which distinguished the pacific Federalists from the governing party more keenly than any divergences of opinion concerning the constitution or state rights.

Britain, too, called for reprisals. So, while Madison congratulated Rodgers, the London 'Courier' wrote: *'the hostile conduct of the American was unprovoked . . . there is but one course left to us . . . the blood of our murdered countrymen must be avenged and WAR MUST ENSUE. The conduct of America leaves us no alternative . . .'*

This London war talk was reported in the American press and construed as indicating an imminent attack. *'A squadron of ships under the command of Rear-Admiral Sir Joseph York, consisting of four vessels of 74 guns and 2 frigates, has been dispatched for our coast, and may be daily expected. Some of the London newspapers say the Admiral has orders to commence immediate hostilities unless our government shall disavow the conduct of Commodore Rodgers,'* the Weekly register of Baltimore reported in its issue on 5th September.

Trouble with Indian warriors in the vast expanse of Indiana, triggered by American expansion westwards, would be cunningly embroidered into another reason for war with Britain. In the vast expanse of Indiana territory, established in 1800 and covering today's states of Indiana, Wisconsin and Illinois, 25,000 pioneers had settled, living precariously alongside the Creeks and Shawnees. By treaties with these tribes and others, mainly through the provision of liquor, the white settlers had already acquired the titles to over 40,000 acres of land and were busily negotiating for more. Encroachment on tribal lands threatened tribal survival and inevitably stirred up resittance. Two Indians of remarkable personality emerged at this moment, two brothers, the sons of a Creek mother and a Shawnee father. Tecumseh was a man of distinguished appearance and great courage. His brother, Tenskwatawa, known as the 'Prophet', was far less striking, his features made more menacing through the lack of an eye. *'Tecumseh furnished the brains, the Prophet the mysticism. The latter conversed with the Great Spirit and attributed to himself the power of performing miracles.'* The two men established a farming community at Tippecanoe on the Wabash, a well ordered society where liquor was banned. And, from there they called for a great federation of all the tribes, Choctaw, Creek, Chickasaw, and Cherokee, to resist the white man's greed for land.

For four or five years, settlers and Indians lived in relative harmony, but under the white man's laws. But in mid 1809, the Baltimore 'Weekly Register' had reported that, *'at a meeting held in Vincennes . . . it was agreed . . . that the persons and property of this frontier can never be secured, but by breaking up of the combination formed by the Shawnee prophet on the Wabash.'* Of far greater relevance for any account of the causes of war with Britain, the newspaper went on to indirectly blame the British for some recent atrocities. *' . . . It is generally believed in the western country that the outrages committed by the Indians are brought about by British influence.'*

The powder keg's emotional fuse was lit on 30th September 1809 when Governor William Henry Harrison, the 29 year old governor of the territory, concluded a deal with several tribes to acquire 3 million acres of land on the Wabash. The forward looking Tecumseh and the one-eyed prophet were the only Indians to see the likely outcome. *'How can we have confidence in the white people? When Jesus Christ appeared on earth, you nailed him to a cross,'* he was quoted as remarking in testimony to his lack of faith in the settlers' words.

Harrison initially played the diplomat, and one can never really accuse him of duplicity. In fact, he had a deep respect for Tecumseh. *'If it were not for the vicinity of the United States, he would perhaps be founder of an Empire that would rival in glory that of Mexico and Peru,'* he had generously remarked. Yet, despite this accolade, Harrison eventually assembled a force of about 900 men and led them towards Tippecanoe, determined to smash the influence of the two brothers and any confederation that they might create.

The details of the Indian attack on Harrison's camp before dawn on 7th November 1811 are not particularly relevant. Tenskawata was probably responsible for inciting the Indians to attack, although one of the Indians later testified that two Englishmen had urged them to strike. The Prophet had apparently managed to convince his disciples that he had charmed the white men's bullets so that they could cause no harm. In the fighting that followed the Indians' late night attack, Harrison lost 62 killed and 126 wounded, almost one-quarter of his force. The attackers lost more than 200. Harrison had a remarkable escape, protected during the battle by the hand of God. He had been mounted on a white horse the previous day, and the Indians had been instructed to search that evening for a man on a snow white mount. But the animal had broken its tether during the night and Harrison had been forced to borrow another officer's horse. A much more junior officer, riding a white horse, was felled by the bullets intended for the governor. Throughout the fight, the Prophet stood on a high rock and continued to chant his spells.

The following day, a scouting party found that Tippecanoe had been abandoned. In a day of vengeance, the army torched the buildings, reducing Tecumseh's little empire to a mass of ashes. Amongst the ruins were found weapons manufactured in Britain, enough, it was believed, to justify the claims of the Baltimore newspaper. The Prophet's followers, having expected no deaths, turned on their master. He saved himself by claiming that his wife had touched some of his talismans while menstruating and had consequently reduced the power of his spells. Tecumseh, who had probably had no part in this pre-dawn attack, later stood amongst the ruins and vowed eternal enmity to the white man.

A battle on the western margins of civilisation, this fight might be dismissed as insignificant in the build-up to the war between Great Britain and the United States of America. Yet it is often regarded as the opening battle of the war of 1812. The discovery of British made weapons in the burning township finally convinced all good American patriots of Britain's role in stirring up Indian hostility. Furthermore, it persuaded Tecumseh and his adherents, despite his recent oath, into an alliance with Britain. Much would happen in the remaining months before the two nations drew their rapiers and went to war.

CHAPTER 2

'Frigates With Strips of Bunting, Manned by Sons of Bitches and Outlaws'

Many of these events would be political in character. In November 1811 Congress met after a Republican landslide in the congressional elections. Dominant amongst the triumphant congressmen were people like Henry Clay and John Calhoun, a breed of demagogues who could conceive of no compromise with Britain. Swayed by their rhetoric, the newly constituted Committee of Foreign Affairs claimed that '*if it be our duty to encourage the fair and legitimate commerce of this country by protecting the property of the merchant; then, indeed, by as much as if life and liberty are more estimable than ships and goods, so much more impressive is the duty to shield the persons of our seamen.*' Impressment, a long-standing issue, had become more a pretext for war than a cause, something at which these Republican 'hawks' chose to grasp in order to justify their stance.

The powerful oratory of men like Congressman John Randolph failed to over awe the belligerents of the House or halt the accelerating rush to war. In December 1811, in the frenzied debates that followed the Republican landslide, Randolph's was the only voice raised in opposition to the 'hawks'. '*The question is one of peace or war . . . a war not of defense, but of conquest, of aggrandisement, of ambition, a war foreign to the interests of this country, to the interests of humanity itself,*' he declared in a speech that lasted for more than two hours, his gaze fixing on the leaders of the war party. And, in response to Peter Porter's suggestion that an invasion of Canada and the destruction of the Newfoundland fisheries might be the quickest and surest way of bringing proud Britain to her knees, the shrill-voiced representative from Roanoke exploded. '*I know not how gentlemen calling themselves republicans could advocate such a war. To whom will you confide the charge of leading the flower of our youth to the Heights of Abraham? . . . . You have taken Quebec. Have you conquered England? Will you seek for the deep foundations of her power in the frozen deserts of Labrador?*' Henry Clay, in his response, was just as eloquent, neutralising the impact that Randolph might have had on his audience. Clay poured deep scorn on Great Britain. '*She* (Britain) *sickens at your prosperity; she is jealous of you, she dreads your rivalship on the ocean. She saw in your numberless ships, whose sails spread on every sea; she perceived in your hundred and twenty thousand gallant tars the needs of a naval force which, in thirty years, would rival her on her own element,*' he prophetically declared in a speech of almost equal length.

And so Congress turned to the task of preparing militarily for the conflict. An army and navy of sufficient numbers would need to be hurriedly developed to hold off the onslaught of the force that Britain would attempt to place on the North American continent. In 1808, Congress, in its state of semi-preparedness, had increased the numbers of the regular army from 3068 to 9311 men—and this during a period when fears of a standing army were still voiced. Now, in late 1811, Secretary for War, William Eustis, called for an additional 10,000 regulars and 50.000 volunteers, together with a programme of repair for naval vessels and the arming of merchant ships. Despite considerable opposition, the necessary legislation was pushed through the Houses and, by the Spring of 1812, the army consisted of 35, 925 regulars, 50,000 volunteers and 100,000 militiamen.

Expansion of the navy was hamstrung by ideological opposition. The more moderate Republicans, the followers of Jefferson, regarded a navy as a tool of imperialism. Even Madison was accused of being lukewarm about the need for a strong naval arm. As late as 27th January 1812 the wary House of Representatives defeated by 61 votes to 59 a proposal to build any additional frigates to those already in service. Only the ravages of the early weeks of warfare could persuade the House to reluctantly embark on a programme of modest naval expansion. At the start of 1812, the navy's entire strength consisted of just 6 frigates, 9 other sea-going warships and 200 gunboats. The Times of London, contemptuously eyeing up the strength of the opposing fleet, dismissed this paltry fleet as a '*few fir built frigates with strips of bunting, manned by sons of bitches and outlaws.*' Use and distribution of the available warships, however, was felt to be more important than numbers. Commodore Rodgers, asked by Secretary of the Navy, Paul Hamilton, in May 1812, to suggest how the handful of frigates might best be deployed in the coming war, felt that a mere three frigates and an accompanying sloop situated off the coasts of Great Britain might do more destruction to Britain's web of commerce than any larger naval force concentrated in American seas.

44 gun frigates:	United States	Constitution	President	
38 gun frigate:	Congress			
32 gun frigate:	Essex			
28 gun frigate:	John Adams			
Sloops (12-18 guns)	Hornet	Wasp	Argus	Syren
	Nautilus	Viper	Oneida	Vixen
	Enterprise			

The 15 ships in service at the start of war in 1812

In addition, 5 frigates were laid up in Ordinary (Reserve): *Constellation, Adams, Chesapeake, Boston* and *New York*

Supporting these larger vessels were 165 gunboats, of which 62 were in commission.

Personnel: approximately 5230 seamen, of whom 2346 were assigned to sea going vessels. The rest served in shore establishments or on the vessels on the Great Lakes.

Note: the 6 frigates actually carried more than the armoury quoted above. The 'United States', for example, carried more than 50 and so was equivalent to a British 5th rate.

Warships of the American navy at the start of war in 1812

The question of how to finance this war was only now asked. Albert Gallatin, Secretary to the Treasury, gloomily reminded Congress that taxation and the excise from the customs would be insufficient to finance the required expansion in the fighting forces or the costs of supplies and provisions, particularly after the non-importation measure had reduced the take from import duties to virtually nothing. He advocated the raising of internal duties, a tax on auctions and carriages and a loan of $10,000,000. Congress, after considerable debate, authorised a loan of $11,000,000 at 6%, but refrained from reliance upon duties or additional taxation, a fiscal policy that only the Federalists would normally have been likely to propose.

New Englanders, those from whom Congress expected to borrow the money, were reluctant to finance a war of which they disapproved. '*Our merchants constitute an honorable, high-minded, intelligent and independent class of citizens. They feel the oppression, injury and mockery with which they are treated by their government. They will lend them money to retrace their steps, but none to persevere in their present course.'* The Boston Gazette, mouthpiece of the Federalists and industrialists, stormed. Faced by such intransigence, the Administration managed to obtain only $6.1 million—and so had to rely upon an issue of short-term Treasury notes to fill the gap.

A dose of French mischief, at this juncture, threatened to upset the inexorable roll towards war with Britain. Congress had the motive, and possibly now the finance, to fight Great Britain. Washington's politicians had done their best to play down an ever-present francophobia and avoid war with the French. The prospect of fighting two nations simultaneously had been real, but somehow too ridiculous to contemplate, given that the two European nations were foes of one another and could never combine in a common cause against America. Yet the burning of two American ships by a French squadron in mid-Atlantic, as reported by the master of the U.S. brig 'Thames', resurrected that fanciful prospect and heightened tension in Washington. The French commodore informed the commander of the 'Thames' that he was acting under orders to destroy all American ships leaving or entering enemy ports. The war minded press bristled with indignation, and Monroe made his protests. Reality, however, took hold; America was psychologically and politically committed to a war with Britain. Irritation at the Frenchman's perfidy was a distraction that had to be ignored. Napoleon's 'treachery' was allowed to go unpunished. And an election, which Madison hoped to win, was on the not too distant horizon.

But, by the start of 1812, he and the party 'hawks' needed something new to rekindle the cooling passions for war. Impressment had become an inescapable fact of life, something which non-maritime Americans were prepared to accept or ignore, and Britain's continuing arrogance was hardly likely to whip every American farmer or his wife into an uncontrollable frenzy. Public opinion in this young democracy mattered: Madison wished to ensure that opinion was on his side.

Fortunately something occurred to feed this flagging appetite for war. Sir James Craig, Governor-General of neighbouring Canada, wanted to discover the true state of feelings in America and so contracted a Mr. John Henry to visit New England and assess the depth of war fervour in the leafy streets of Boston and surrounding countryside. The man did as he was asked and returned to Canada to make his report and claim his pay. Craig baulked at the price, and the indignant agent sailed to England to claim his reward from the Foreign Office instead. Failing in his attempt to gain satisfactory remuneration, he sold his information instead to a young Frenchman in return for the latter's title to an estate on the Spanish border. The sequel, a story of deception and false dealings, had a political significance as well. The Frenchman turned out to be an impostor and had sold a worthless scrap of paper to Mr. Henry. But, arriving at Washington with the information about New England's attitude to the war, the Frenchman sold the package to Monroe for $50,000 and then disappeared without trace.

The information collected by Henry, although of little value in itself, would now be used to further discredit Great Britain. Madison submitted the papers to Congress on 9th March 1812, claiming that the London government had employed an agent to engage in espionage and foment disaffection within New England. Exploited cleverly, the suggestion that Great Britain was guilty of such a heinous offence was enough to restoke the fires of anger.

An additional issue now arose to hasten the drift to war. East and West Florida, part of the Spanish empire, had long been 'eyed' by the young republic, intent on achieving its dream of the Manifest Destiny. The opportunity for formal annexation was delivered in 1810 when the citizens of Baton Rouge in W. Florida rose up against Spanish rule, declared themselves an independent state and applied to the United States government for protection. The latter responded by claiming the district as part of the Louisiana Purchase and sent in troops to enforce their spurious claim.

Movement of these troops took place at a time when Britain was bolstering Spanish resistance to Napoleon's occupation of that nation. And, as protector, Great Britain felt that she also stood as guardian of Spain's overseas possessions. American activities in the Floridas consequently aroused British alarm. Equally, British interest in those lands gave rise to a belief in America that London would formally annex the whole of Madrid's North American empire. The resolution passed by Congress in January 1811 that '*the United States; under the peculiar circumstances of the existing crisis, cannot . . . . see any part of the said territory pass into the hands of any foreign power,*' far from being a new issue to muddy further the international conflict, was merely part of the sequence of deteriorating relationships with the government of the United Kingdom. In a sequel, that was as provocative as anything issued by Great Britain in this stormy pre-war period, the government of the United States threatened that, if any foreign power tried to take possession of the Floridas, or if the citizens of the provinces declared a desire to be annexed, then Washington would take formal possession.

By Spring 1811 Federal troops had occupied almost all of West Florida. The United States had less pretext for the occupation of Eastern Florida, which followed soon after. Naval forces were sent to the St. Mary's River area in an apparent attempt to persuade the locals that they would be better off as subjects of the United States. The move prompted British minister Foster to protest. His government, he claimed, was '*still willing to hope that the American government has not been urged to this step by ambitious motives or by a desire of foreign conquest and territorial aggrandizement,*' which would be '*so injurious to the alliance between His Majesty and the Spanish nation.*' Letters flowed between Secretary of State Monroe and Foster. Monroe politely pointed out that Great Britain had no right to interfere in any dispute between the Federal Republic and Spain. Foster, on his part, expressed shock and sadness at the Washington government's dishonorable behaviour.

News of happenings in Florida only slowly crossed the Atlantic. In Britain the Parliamentary debates still centred on the issues that had been driving the two nations apart since before 1800. A few of the more outspoken, people like Samuel Whitbread, Alexander Baring and George Canning questioned the wisdom of pushing America too far, while those with an eye on Britain's financial position pointed out the likely cost of hostilities. But the intransigent attitudes of the Prince Regent and Prime Minister Perceval drowned out these softer voices of conciliation, and the national press seemed hell bent on war. '*If anything was wanting to prove the inflexible determination of the present Ministry to persevere in the orders in council, without modification or relaxation, the declarations of leading members of the administration on these measures must place it beyond the possibility of doubt,*' Jonathan Russell, American minister in London, wrote to Monroe in March 1812. Outside Westminster, however, opinion was far less disposed to war. The rioting and machine breaking that occurred in the north of England was partly atttributable to the effects of non-intercourse. Those suffering, if asked, would probably have favoured resumption of trade with America and the withdrawal of any threat of war.

Madison and his Cabinet now embarked on the final preparations for hostilities. To protect his merchant ships, a source of privateers in any extended sea war, he applied a ninety day embargo from 4th April to keep them in port. Unfortunately reports of the intended embargo leaked out before the day of application, and a frenzy of activity occurred in New England to get cargoes and ships to sea before the legislation took effect. For one week in April, the quaysides of New England, Baltimore and Philadelphia buzzed with over-activity as masters and dockers laboured to load their waiting vessels. Fifteen million dollars worth of flour and grain alone cleared the ports in just five days, destined for British markets. America's men of commerce had shown that they were more interested in fattening their wallets than in playing the roles of patriots.

While New England's merchants undermined their government's war preparations, William Eustis and his departmental staff appointed the officers who would command the nation's armies. It had been thirty-one years since America had last fought a war, and only silver-haired gentlemen could boast that they had the necessary military experience. Henry Dearborn, hoisted to the highest command, claimed unflawed Republican credentials and a medical qualification, and it was probably his political purity that secured him the senior post. He had fought at Bunker Hill, Saratoga and Monmouth Court House, but had never commanded in the field. Thomas Pinckney, his deputy, was sixty-three years old, a year senior to Dearborn, and, like his superior, had limited military experience. A period of guerilla fighting under Sumter in the Carolinas seemed enough to satisfy the War department that he was fit for an executive military role.

The two Secretaries, War and Navy, were not even in the same league of experience as the two generals. William Eustis had, like Dearborn, practised medicine before moving into politics. Paul Hamilton, at the Navy Department, was a plantation owner who had never been to sea! Both staunch Republicans, however, they were deemed to have all the qualifications needed for a high administrative role. Eustis was reported as spending his working day '*reading the ads of petty retailing merchants to find where he might purchase 100 shoes or hats,*' while Hamilton was frequently found drunk at his desk. Neither man inspired the confidence of politicians or staff. Randolph was highly dismissive of both. '*I do verily believe, and I have grounds to believe it to be the opinion of the House, that he (the Secretary of War) is at least as competent for the exercise of his duties as is his colleague who presides over the Marine.*'

The naval officers appointed, however, would not be tarred with the same brush of inexperience. Since independence, the U.S. marine had fought a brittle war on the ocean against buccaneers from North Africa. Consequently young men had gained worthy experience in battle-like conditions. Commodore Rodgers, the most senior appointment, was only forty.

Britain, of course, could choose its officers from a deeper reservoir of experience. Nearly twenty years of warfare with France had honed redcoated soldiers to virtual perfection. By the spring of 1812, many of these men might conceivably be released from their European commitments. The Royal Navy was equally blessed; Trafalgar had left battle scars on seamen's arms and a stockpile of expertise that only the French could match. Moreover, Sweden and Russia had recently resumed full trade with Britain, allowing the latter to transfer warships from the Baltic to Atlantic waters. On the American station, based at Halifax and Jamaica, were five ships of the line, nineteen frigates and fifty-seven other fighting vessels. In addition, a small squadron sailed the Great Lakes. This impressive enough armada could be augmented within weeks by warships released from European service. America's fifteen ships and two hundred poorly built gunboats could be no match for the Goliath-like force that Britain could present.

On the very eve of war, Britain lost her Prime Minister. On 11th May the deranged John Bellingham shot dead Spencer Perceval. Into Perceval's shoes stepped Robert Banks Jenkinson, the 2nd Earl of Liverpool, a man more moderate in his views towards America than his murdered predecessor. Responsibility for conducting the war fell upon Henry, Earl Bathurst, a man as well-tempered as his political master in his attitude to the United States.

But the change in political attitude towards America had come too late to slow down the rush to war with Britain. On 11th May 1812 Napoleon had at last revoked his hated decrees, softening the latent francophobia that still haunted the corridors of Washington. On 1st June President Madison delivered his war speech to Congress, in which he alleged British incitement of the frontier Indians and criticised the unwillingness of Britain to do anything more than talk. Two days later Calhoun tabled a motion demanding an immediate declaration of war. On the 4th the proposal was carried by seventy-nine votes to forty-nine. Thirty-four of New England's Congressmen votes against the declaration while the south voted by a similar ratio in favour. Nothing had cemented over the regional differences in opinion. The geographical and sectarian rift, on the eve of war, remained as wide as ever. On 18th June the Senate, too, voted for war, this time by nineteen votes to thirteen and with a division along exactly the same geographical fault lines. A simultaneous proposal for war against France was defeated by just two votes!

The public attitude was geographical as well. While the south rejoiced with bonfires, bunting and bands, the north went into mourning. Church bells tolled and flags flew at half-mast. Cullent Bryant, in a lament for the pre-war days, wrote:

Lo! Where our ardent rulers
For fierce assault prepare,
While eager 'Ate' awaits their beck
To 'ship the dogs of war'.
In vain against the dire design
Exclaims the indignant land.
The unbidden blade they haste to bare,
And light the unhallowed brand.
Proceed! Another year shall wrest
The sceptre from your hand!

Ironically, on the 16th, only two days prior to the declaration of war, Castlereagh, Britain's new Foreign Secretary, in a spirit of conciliation, announced that the orders in council had been withdrawn. But word of the repeal of the Orders did not reach Madison until 12th August, fifty days later. Confirmation of the American declaration of war only arrived in London on 29th July! Slowness of communication and America's justifiable frustration with British intransigence had brought on an unnecessary war.

CHAPTER 3

'They Might Have Passed For The Spectres of The Wilds'

Canada, its waters and its fisheries, had long been identified as America's prime target. Her population, standing at about 500,000, was less than one twelfth of that of the United States and so was vulnerable to even the most feeble of attacks. The governors of Upper and Lower Canada saw possible salvation in an alliance with the two provinces' Indians and in a buffer state separating Canada from its war-keen neighbour.

Britain's land forces stationed in Canada totaled little more than 8000 men, 6000 of whom were regulars, mainly the men of the 41st, 49th and 100th Regiments of Foot. Amongst the most elitist of the home-bred units was the 600 strong Glengary Light Infantry, recruited almost exclusively from the Scotsmen of Nova Scotia. Governing Canada since Sir James Craig's departure in the summer of 1811 was forty-four year old Sir George Prevost, son of the distinguished Swiss—born major—general in the British army, who had fought in America's war for independence. A fastidious dresser, he expected all others to dress equally carefully. Just as fussy in his eye for detail and correctness in administration, he enjoyed generally good relationships with the legislatures of both Upper and Lower Canada. When he heard of Washington's declaration of war, he placed a battalion south of Montréal and moved his own post of command from Québec to Montréal in order to be closer to operations.

Neither Prevost in Canada, nor the imperial government in London had any clear idea about the strategy that they should employ. Prevost's approach was largely defensive: protection of the St. Lawrence and a 'wait and see' attitude. London, fully occupied with Napoleon, had ignored the threat from America and clearly had little idea how to proceed. And of course, the assumption had long prevailed that America would never actually dare to fight. Nor had she any need to do so. The hated Orders had been revoked, and the new ministers in London were anxious to refrain from passing any further measures injurious to American interests

Confirmation of the American declaration of war, arriving in Whitehall at the end of July 1812, came at a time when ministers would have preferred to think of summer pastimes. The European war was far from over, although Wellington' successes in Spain had recently given it a more favourable hue. Now a strategy for fighting two wars would have to be forged. No-one at the Cabinet table initially had any perception of how to proceed. Two opposing proposals were eventually placed on Lord Liverpool's polished table. The more forceful called for a hammer-like blow that should instantly annihilate America's commercial power and her potential to develop as a future trade rival. For this, a blockade of ports would be insufficient; only an invasion of her territory would secure this aim.

But this bullish strategy would be welcomed by Paris and would benefit France more than Britain. Britain and America would destroy each other's commerce and war-waging capabilities, allowing France to dominate the Continent of Europe, the sea lanes of commerce and possibly even America itself. It was probably this, rather than any reluctance to push the Americans too far, that persuaded the government of the new Prime Minister to favour the less harsh alternative—and, in this, Prevost largely concurred. The only offensive ingredient would be a robust defence of the Canadian border and a limited naval blockade of American ports, sustained for long enough to strangle her trade and ability to fight. Britain's full reservoir of resources would not need to be tapped and would remain available for the struggle against France.

Prevost and his officers would therefore have a crucial role to play. The Lieutenant-General was determined that Britain should dominate the Great Lakes and so seal off the potential invasion routes into the two British provinces. He occupied Carleton Island, which dominated the head of the St. Lawrence, and stationed militia men in pairs along the northern shore of Lake Ontario. With nearly 5000 regulars positioned down river from Montréal, he felt reasonably prepared to deal with any semi-spirited attack that America might care to launch. The four-man garrison on Carleton Island was instantly overpowered, even before the declaration of war. But Colonel Robert Lethbridge, commander of the post at Kingston, retaliated by destroying the small United States naval base and its flimsy gunboats at Sackets Harbor.

Madison, Eustis and Dearborn, the senior triumvirate of the nation, had already recognized the advantages to be gained from an early drive into Canada. They proposed a three-prong incursion: the main thrust would move along the course of the Detroit River while another force would simultaneously strike along the Niagara River. A third would advance in support along the Lake Champlain lowland towards Montréal. '*You will make a diversion . . .. at Niagara and at Kingston as soon as practicable,*' Eustis had ordered Dearborn in an almost dismissive manner, somehow believing that the resources for this would materialise without any arrangements being made. In the event, neither of these two men seemed to take much interest in the project, and General William Hull, the Governor of Michigan Territory and the man personally chosen by the President to command the Detroit expedition, became the victim of their indifference. Eustis assumed that Dearborn would take full responsibility for obtaining supplies and giving orders. Hull, still at Boston, seemed to be in the dark about the extent of his duties. It was not a promising start.

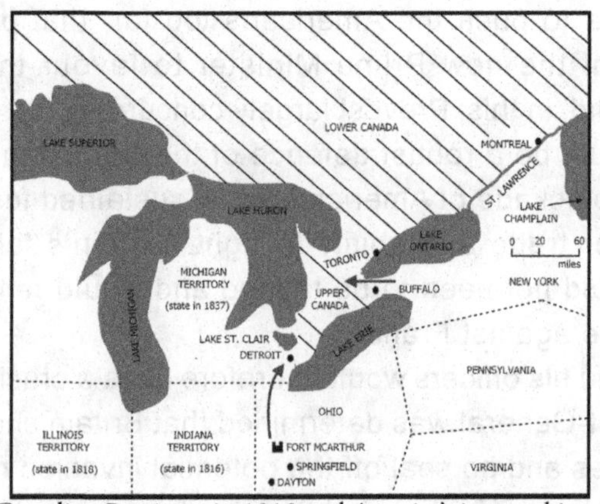

The Canadian Provinces in 1812 and America's intented invasion routes

The entire Washington establishment, not just the President, seem to have believed in Hull. He had served with distinction during the Revolutionary War, and his image as a commander who never retreated was indelibly stamped on the minds of those who now gave him high command. Time, however, had not been kind. Now 58 years of age, he looked more like 70 and chewed tobacco incessantly. To his men, he appeared constantly uneasy. He accepted the honour reluctantly, hoping that his brief would be purely to save Detroit and let others take responsibility for the drive into Canada.

But the orders eventually delivered to William Hull by the President would demand hardship and sacrifice along the way. It required an advance through the wilderness of the 'Black Swamp' and the uncertainties of the frontier territory of Lake Erie. The area to be traversed was occupied by Indians, and the lake itself was controlled by a British squadron. Most of the men under his command were Ohio militia men, unruly individuals unwilling to accept discipline and with almost no military experience. Formed into three infantry regiments [2] and one company of dragoons, they had assembled at Dayton in May, even before the declaration of war or the formal appointment of Hull as their commander.

In the absence of any federal provision of supplies, Governor Jonathan Meigs of Ohio called upon each family in the state to provide one blanket and as much food as they could spare. Hull himself arrived at Dayton on 25th May and, in a showy ceremony, took over the command of the 1200 men selected for the expedition. On 1st June the column left the town and advanced through Staunton to Urbana, where it was joined by the 450 men of the 4th Regiment of Regulars under Lieutenant-Colonel James Miller, the men who had fought at Tippecanoe. Their first task was to cut a road from Urbana to Detroit, a distance of 200 miles through pure swamp and in the heat of growing summer. For two whole weeks, the militia and regulars sweated, advancing the road by three miles a day, taking the track as far as Kenton. Then, on the eve of the war's actual declaration, the rains began to fall and the swamp's mosquitoes attacked. Morale dipped, men cursed and fell ill, and progress slowed.

---

2 1st, 2nd and 3rd Regts. of Ohio Volunteers under Cols. Duncan McArthur, James Findlay and Lewis Cass respectively

On 24th June Hull, stagnating in the swamp, received a despatch from Washington. It urged him to speed his step but, on the subject of the expected declaration of war, it made no mention, and Hull, still unsure whether his country was formally at war, was left to ponder on what stance he should take towards the British. On the 30th his weary party reached the rapids of the Maumee River and here he found the schooner 'Cuyahoga' waiting for him. Upon her decks were placed the sick, those who had succumbed to the biting flies, and the heavier supplies, all the encumbrances, in fact, that would slow him down. On 1st July the boat headed downstream for the waters of Lake Erie, allowing the unburdened land force to proceed overland to a planned rendezvous with the schooner at Detroit. On board the ship, apparently loaded mistakenly, were Hull's personal papers with details of the size of his force and the purpose of his mission.

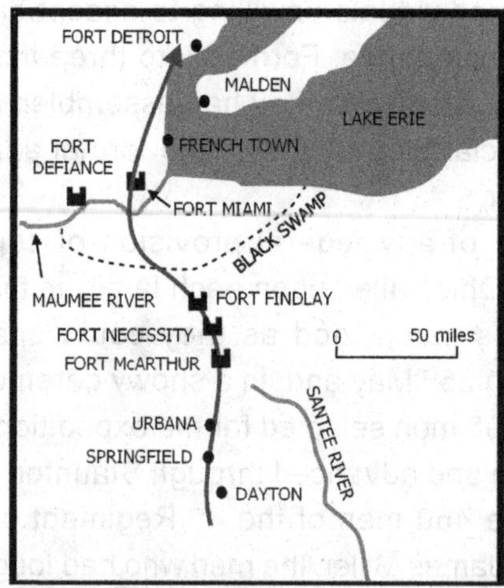

Hull's advance towards Detroit

On that same day, Hull, at last, heard that his country was at war with Britain. But he was unable to inform the master of the 'Cuyahoga', in time, and soon the crew would be approaching the guns of Fort Malden on the Canadian side of the Detroit River, unaware that those guns would not remain passive. General Hull hurriedly sent a messenger racing along the Maumee's bank in the hope of warning the crew in time. The messenger returned the following day with reports of the ship's capture. An armed vessel from the fort had intercepted the 'Cuyahoga'.

The British officer in command had informed the surprised crew and passengers that they were now prisoners of war. Hull's papers and official orders fell into redcoat hands.

4th U.S.Infantry, 1st, 2nd and 3rd Ohio Militia
The units of General Hull's army

On 5th July, William Hull and his force reached Detroit, a tiny garrisoned settlement of less than one thousand souls. The enemy commanders in the area deemed that the American force was too large and abandoned Sandwich, the garrisoned outpost on the opposing side of the Detroit River. On 12th July, a Sunday, Hull crossed the river near Sandwich, despite the fact that many of the Ohio men refused to accompany him, insisting that they were obliged to defend their home state and nothing more. Colonel Lewis Cass was the first to leap from the boats and so gained the honour of being the first American soldier to set foot on Canadian soil. Sandwich was a picturesque village, full of neat gardens and small orchards—all now in American hands! After ceremoniously unfurling the Stars and Stripes, Hull took up residence in the Baby mansion, the villages's most imposing dwelling, and, projecting himself into the role of liberator, he issued a proclamation of freedom and protection to the citizens of Canada, emancipating them from '*Tyranny and oppression and* (restoring them) *to the dignified station of freemen.'* It is reported that, as a result, most of the garrison of Fort Malden joined him, leaving Colonel T. St. George, the fort's commander, with less than 500 men. America's first invasion of American soil seemed to have been flawlessly executed.

On the 16th, Colonel Cass, supported by another enthusiast for action, Colonel James Miller, scouted to the south, as far as the River aux Canards, a sluggish stream just three miles above the British post at Fort Malden. Here they found a detachment of the 41st Foot and supporting Indians guarding the narrow bridge. The two colonels, sensing that they could be the victors in what was probably the first engagement of the war, were determined to attack. Miller remained in place to assault frontally while Cass looked for a crossing place up river, intending to fall on the British flank. Aware of the danger, the British force retired, leaving just a small rearguard to slow the American advance.

James Hancock and John Dean of the 41st Foot became the first British casualties of the war. Standing on the bridge, both men fought in a manner normally only expected of Hollywood's heroes. Swinging their rifles about their heads, they brought down a dozen or more men until both fell wounded and were taken captives. The youthful Americans at aux Canards had never seen British regulars in action, the 'scum of the Earth,' as Wellington chose to call them, and even Miller's semi-regulars must have begun to doubt their chances of ever outclassing the men in red. Yet, these same red lines had awakened a sense of revulsion in an earlier generation of Americans. These had learned to regard the professional British soldier as little more than a soldier of fortune, semi-robotic, motivated only by his wages and with no political ideals at all. This same perception would gradually be infused by the younger members of the republic, and the awe which Miller's men felt today would soon evaporate.

Cass and Miller personally felt none of these inhibitions. In possession of the bridge, they were anxious to move against Fort Malden, eighteen miles south of Sandwich. Hull, however, was the proverbial pessimist, a man who forecast disaster from the mildest of military setbacks. He had just been informed of an American disaster at Michilimackinac (or Mackinac) on the northern shore of Lake Huron, and this had convinced him that swarms of Indians would now be free to descend, like locusts, upon the Detroit region and devour him and his troops. The report of the arrival of Captain Proctor and the British 41st Regiment of Foot at Malden landed on his lap at the same time as news of the setback on Lake Huron and drained away what remained of his fighting spirit. Moreover, the two 24 pounder guns and 3 howitzers that he planned to use were too heavy to cross the wooden bridge, and he was having serious doubts about Washington's commitment to the war. Personal distrust of Cass and Miller probably undermined his resolution, too. Sensing that both men were sitting in judgement of him and would clearly like to be wearing his uniform, he dithered, held back and then did nothing The presence of the 18 gun vessel, the 'Queen Charlotte', which had anchored in the river close to Malden, convinced the Michigan governor that attacking Malden would be an act of folly. On 21st July he returned to Detroit, leaving Robert Lucas and his Ohio militiamen to tentatively hold the bridge near Malden, and arousing suspicions that he was either a coward or traitor.

The incident that had so dispirited Hull was actually an insignificant affair and of no importance at all in deciding the direction that the war might take. Far to the north, just beyond the tip of Lake Huron, Captain Charles Roberts held the fort of St. Joseph for Britain. Warily eyeing the Americans in Mackinac (or Michilimackinac), an island lying in the straits between Huron and Michigan, he had asked Isaac Brock, the Governor of Upper Canada, for permission to assault this island position. Lieutenant-Colonel Isaac Brock had long nurtured a desire to prise Fort Mackinac from America and had hoped to recruit the Indians of the west for this purpose. His chosen agent was Robert Dickson, a Scotsman married to an Indian, a man who held an almost mystical control over the tribes. The Dakota called him 'Mascotapeh', 'the Red-Haired Man'. In February 1812, long before the war's start, Brock had managed to send an appeal to him, couched almost in the language of a 21st Century business man.

'*As it is probable that war may result from the present state of affairs, it is very desirable to ascertain the degree of co-operation that you and your friends might be able to furnish . . . You will be pleased to report . . . . upon the following matters.'* Amongst those listed was a request for estimates of the number of Indians who might fight for the British Crown and '*their disposition towards us.'* Dickson wasted no time in responding. On 30th June, at the head of 130 Sioux and Winnebago, he set off from his base in the heart of the Wisconsin country and moved north-east towards Green Bay and a planned union with Roberts' men at the fort on tiny St. Joseph's Island.

Captain Roberts, meanwhile, had received Brock's permission to move against the American garrison. With him at St.Joseph's, a semi-ruined blockhouse, were 44 men of the 10th Royal Veteran Battalion, regulars of the British Army, but now regarded by Brock as too old to fight. On 15th July, these men embarked on the North-West Company's gunboat 'Caledonia'. Behind followed a string of ten boats, filled with 180 volunteers, and then Dickson's Indians in their canoes. One hundred miles to the west lay the arrow-shaped Michilimackinac Island, surrounded by steep cliffs of grey stone. Somewhere off the coast, the flotilla of invasion met a lone canoeist, a man sent by Lieutenant Porter Hanks, the commander of Fort Mackinac, to watch the waters of the lake.

The disloyal man, knowing the island intimately, agreed to assist and, in the early hours of the 17th, the British landed near the northern end of the island. With difficulty, the two brass six-pounder guns, which had accompanied the party, were dragged across the terrain of boulders, past the 300 foot high Sugar Loaf Rock, and placed in a position from which they could threaten the fort. Poor Lieutenant Porter Hanks, the American commander, had not even realised that a state of war existed and, with less than 60 men in his ranks, would have found it impossible to hold out anyway. He wisely surrendered without further delay

Lieutenant-Colonel Thomas Bligh St. George, commanding at Fort Malden (or Amherstburg), had, so far, done everything that his king in London could reasonably have expected him to do. Under his command, he had about 300 men of the 41st Regt. of Foot, an indeterminate number of militiamen and perhaps 400 Indians. Three vessels patrolled his water frontier—the sloop 'Queen Charlotte', the schooner 'Lady Prevost' and a brig, the 'General Hunter', each adding considerable fire power to his land-based batteries. Critics might have questioned his reasons for not defending Sandwich, but his decision to establish his front line along the river Aux Canards made good sense, given the paucity of his numbers. From here he could control the north shore of Lake Erie and maintain his vital line of communications with the town of York.

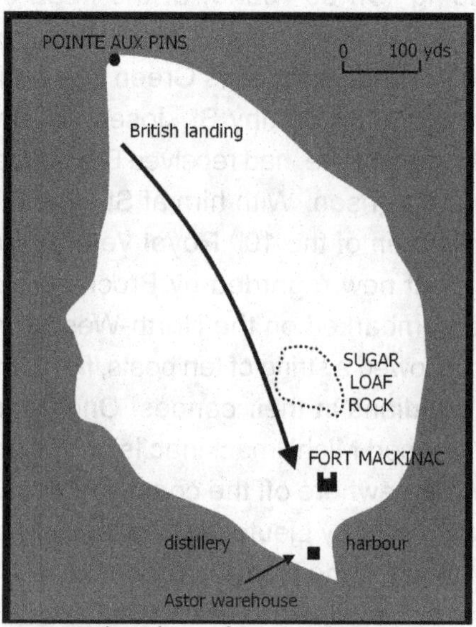

The Taking of Fort Mackinac

Sir George Prevost and Sir Isaac Brock, together responsible for the defence of Canada, were in danger of pulling in different directions. Prevost, the politician, was already finding it necessary to curb the enthusiasm of Brock, the soldier. Sir George, faced by the threat of invasion from Albany as well as on the Detroit River, had recently moved his offices from Québec to Montréal in order to personally oversee the defence and, if necessary, rein in his subordinate. Fearing that Brock might rashly undertake his own invasion of America, he had decided to restrict the number of men under Brock's command and ordered Sir Isaac to confine his efforts to the relief of Fort Malden and nothing more.

Hull's failure to move against the fort seemed inexplicable to both British commanders. A smaller force than the one at the American general's disposal could have undoubtedly taken the stronghold. The northern shore of Lake Erie might then have been overrun and Upper Canada snatched from the British hold. Despite such favourable prospects, it is not difficult to understand Hull's sudden loss of fibre. Neither Eustis nor Dearborn had shown any personal commitment to his needs, and the supporting thrusts into Canada further east had not materialised. The trail back to Urbana, punctuated by the occasional blockhouse on route, could be cut at almost any place by bands of Indians in the employment of the British. Complacency and administrative incompetence elsewhere had made the ageing American general even more cautious. In desperation, he called upon Governor Return Meigs of Ohio to keep the valuable trail open and augment his dwindling force. Two hundred Ohio men volunteered in just one hour to serve as a relieving force, women sewed all the needed uniforms in a single day, and the very old and very young made cartridges for the weapons. Two hundred cattle and 70 pack horses, each of the latter carrying 200 lbs. of flower, were also corralled and prepared for the trail northward through the Black Swamp to Detroit.

This force of men and animals had been placed under the command of Captain Henry Brush. On 1st August, the expedition reached the River Raisin, just thirty-three miles from Detroit. The captain, infected by the same caution that slowed everyone's steps, called upon Hull to provide guides and an escort. Hull, receiving the request, sent out Major Thomas Van Horne and 200 men to meet Brush's party and lead them north.

Unfortunately, Van Horne's movement was reported to Colonel Henry Proctor, now in command at Fort Malden. He immediately instructed reliable Major Adam Muir to lead 100 regulars, some militia and a handful of Indians under Tecumseh across the Detroit River and fall upon van Horne. A cocktail of secondary events was about to bring on the campaign's first clash.

In the early hours of the 4th, Van Horne's men rode through the deserted Wyandot village of Magagua towards Brownstown Creek. The only possible ford across the stream passed through a narrow gorge flanked by thick bush land. Directly ahead, Tecumseh, with one white man and 24 Indians, lay waiting in a landscape of summer silence. Although outnumbering the ambushing party by 20 to 1, Van Horne's men were dislocated by the sudden piercing yells and well-aimed gunfire. Finding themselves confronting shadows, few men remained to fight. Most flung down their weapons and fled, pursued by the taunting yells of the Indians, who had achieved so much with so few men. They left behind 18 men dead in the gorge—and the mailbags full of letters from Hull's soldiers to their loved ones further south. Major Muir arrived too late to take any part in the fighting, later rather grandly described as the 'Battle of Brownstown.'

He had arrived, however, in time to witness the ritualistic slaughter of one of the prisoners. '. . .. *under the circumstances, what could we do?'* Thomas de Boucherville, one of Muir's party asked when criticism of the British employment of Indians was voiced. '*The government had desperate need of these Indian allies. Our garrison was weak and these warriors were numerous enough to impose their will upon us.'* Poor Brush, unaware of the fate of Van Horne, was waiting with his cattle train and volunteers in a clearing beside the River Raisin. Every sound from the river or bush played upon their over-fertile minds, freezing inactive men with dread of the approach of Indians, those wild men who scalped or mutilated for amusement or revenge.

Hull in Detroit was equally afraid of shadows. Daily he expected hordes of warriors in British pay to pounce, and every avenue that he might pursue, back towards Ohio or forward to Amherstburg was, in his mind, full of men with war paint and tomahawks. Then, on the 7th, his scouts reported that boats loaded with British troops had been seen on Lake Erie heading for Amherstburg. Any briefly held idea that he might have floated during the previous week of advancing towards the British fort was shot down by this report. The following morning, to the disgust of Cass and Miller, he ordered back the troops from the Canadian side of the river. They had been there for just thirty days and had done nothing apart from distributing copies of Hull's wordy proclamation.

Meanwhile, Brush was still immobilised on the banks of the River Raisin. More out of a desire to reduce the mutterings of condemnation amongst his senior officers than out of any real concern for Brush's predicament, Hull sent out a relief party to rescue man and beast from the mud and dangers of the Raisin swampland. Under the command of James Miller, this force consisted of the bulk of the 4th U.S. regiment, 200 Ohio riflemen and another 100 volunteers, triple the size of the previous rescuing party. Infused with memories of Tippecanoe, the 300 men of the 4th were anxious for the chance of revenge and the settling of scores with Tecumseh. Hull was keen to keep his critic busy.

Muir's troops were still on the American side of the Detroit River, but it was Tecumseh, not he, who was to be the architect of the ambush laid. John Richardson, just fifteen years old at the time, described the scene many years later. '*No other sound than the measured step of the troops interrupted the solitude of the scene, rendered more imposing by the wild appearance of the warriors, whose bodies, stained and painted in the most frightful manner for the occasion, glided by us with almost noiseless velocity. Uttering no sound, ... they might have passed for the spectres of the wilds, the ruthless demons which War had unchained for the punishment and oppression of man.*'

The site chosen for ambush was a low ridge about three miles from Maguaga. The British and Canadian volunteers lay concealed behind hastily collected brushwood while Tecumseh's Indian bands formed up noislessly on left and right. The Americans, suspecting little, were marching in column with drummers at their front, hardly the appropriate tactics for warfare against shadows.

They reacted surprisingly quickly to the sudden danger, and the trap intended for them was never really sprung. Throwing down their knapsacks when the first shots rang out and hurriedly forming in line, Miller's infantry forced back Tecumseh's Indians on the flanks and then charged the brushwood barricades behind which Muir's men crouched. Miller's men on the right were instantly successful, but Van Horne, responsible for attacking at the other end of the breastworks, was not as fortunate and called for assistance. Miller moved a detachment of troops from the right and, in so doing, provided the British with a chance to withdraw.

Confusion thereafter stalked the British lines. At some point, a reinforcing detachment of grenadiers and light infantry from Amherstburg joined Muir. Trying to make sense of what was going on, they spotted half-concealed figures on their right and assumed that they were Americans. The new arrivals fought blindly—and brought down a dozen or so of Tecumseh's Indians. The enraged warriors fired back, and the internecine fighting which ensued served only to accelerate the final disintegration of the British lines. Soon the soldiers of the 41st Foot were hurrying for their boats and seeking the shelter of Fort Malden's walls. They had become men again, as emotionally frail and human as any man who considers the prospect of death.

It had, in its later stages, become almost a conventional battle, with Tecumseh's Indians playing only a secondary role. Miller had lost 18 men killed and 64 wounded, the British had lost far less, perhaps a third of that number. The Battle of Magagua gained nothing for either side: Brush was still immobilised on the River Raisin and the British could re-cross into America.

General Hull pulled Miller back to Detroit soon afterwards. Deterred by the enemy and by the logistics involved in trying to keep open a two hundred mile communications road, he had all but despaired of success. He had recognised the ease with which the British and their Indian allies had been able to threaten his escape route south. The pattern of warfare in this area was not to his liking. Set against a background of swamps, biting insects, elusive Indians and a growing fear of shadows, such warfare was likely to be indecisive or even impossible to wage.

Brock arrived at Fort Malden on the 13th and immediately engaged in efforts to limit the potential of Hull's widely distributed proclamation. Something of a master of propaganda, he appealed to the Canadians' sense of loyalty and patriotism and commented acidly on America's '*unprovoked declaration of war.*' Then, in a colourful whim of fancy, he claimed that the United States, if victorious, would hand Canada over to Napoleon as a reward for France's help during the recent war for independence. '*. . . it is but obvious that . . . . you must be reannexed to the dominion of France . . . . Are you prepared, Inhabitants of Upper Canada, to become willing subjects or rather slaves to the Despot who rules the nations of Europe with a rod of Iron? If not, arise in a Body, exert your energies, co-operate cordially with the King's regular forces to repel the invader, and do not give cause to your children when groaning under the oppression of a foreign Master to reproach you with having too easily parted with the richest Inheritance on Earth.*'

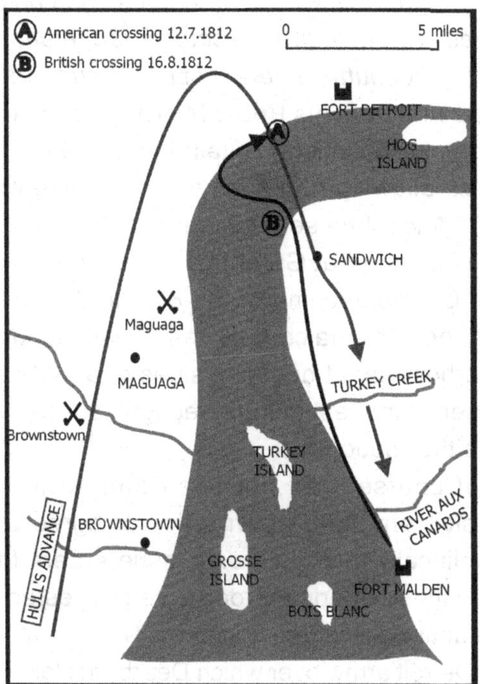

The Detroit River campaign

The image of Bonaparte the monster, used tellingly to frighten children in Britain into immediate obedience (or even sleep), cast a similar shadow of terror over Canadian fireside hearths. Brock, in using such imagery, was adopting the style of rhetoric, which would be used by Winston Churchill 130 years later.

And he also enjoyed a valuable advantage. In possession of Hull's orders, Brock must have known as much about the Americans as they knew about themselves. He also knew their weaknesses. Playing cruelly on Hull's fears, he dressed militiamen in the red tunics of the regulars and positioned them where they could most impress the enemy. He then wrote a letter and allowed it to fall into American hands. Purporting to be from Colonel Henry Proctor, the writer requested that no more Indians be sent, as he already had 5000!

Prevost, however, was still trying to pull in the opposite direction. While Brock was sharpening his blades of war, Sir George, still the diplomat, was attempting to plough a more peaceful furrow. '*Your Lordship may rest assured that unless the safety of the Provinces entrusted to my charge should require them, no measures shall be adopted by me to impede a speedy return to those accustomed relations of amity and goodwill which it is the mutual interest of both countries to cherish and preserve,*' he had written to his Prime Minister during the summer. He had some reasons for optimism; Britain had revoked the provocative Orders in Council, allowing American ships to trade without any fear of seizure. On 2nd August he sent Lieutenant-Colonel Edward Baynes to negotiate with Dearborn at Greenbush, the latter's headquarters in New York State. On the evening of the 8th, the day that Hull's orders for a withdrawal from Canada caused near mutiny amongst his troops, Baynes and Dearborn sat at opposite sides of a table and, according to one aide present, unquestioningly recognised that war was not in the interests of either nation.

Dearborn, of course, had not been endowed by Washington with powers to sign any form of armistice or agree concrete terms. Straitjacketed politically, he could only issue orders for a temporary cessation of hostilities. American troops, he suggested, would remain on the defensive until Washington had formally pronounced—all, that is, apart from Hull's Detroit army, over which Dearborn claimed to have been given no authority. Documents were exchanged, but no promises were made—and Baynes departed with a feeling of hope and self-importance. Both sides would be free to recruit, organise and supply without fear of attack, and a state of war would presumably still exist.

His journey back to Montréal took him along the eastern shore of Lake Champlain, through a peaceful, unhurrying landscape of small hamlets where no visible sign of war was evident. Attempting to interpret every sign, nuance or comment heard, he concluded that there existed '*in the United States the greatest contempt and repugnance to the restraint and discipline of a military life . . . . few gentlemen of respectability are willing to become officers but prefer the militia where they obtain high ranks without serving.'* But many of the officers of the militia, he was also able to observe, were lowly types, inkeepers, sadlers and tradesmen, and it was men such as these who would be held in such contempt by Britain's serving officers, most of whom were members of a social elite. Surely, Baynes and others probably concluded, the United States could never hope to launch a successful invasion of Canada with officers such as these.

None of America's more senior command showed any more promise. While Hull conjured up visions of hostile Indians, Dearborn was caught up in a spider web of poor organisation, for which Washington was largely to blame, myopic strategic thinking, for which he must take some responsibility, and a failure to control his subordinates. On 9th August, Dearborn wrote to Hull, informing him of the truce and permitting him to decide for himself whether he wished to observe its terms. And this was on the very day that Hull began his withdrawal from Canada! Hull, in being given an independent command, seemed to assume that this would exonerate him from any obligation to keep the High Command informed of his intentions.

Brock was also waging his own private war. It is, of course, possible that Prevost had failed to inform the soldier of the commitment made at Greenbush to refrain from aggressive moves. But Brock was the counterpart to Hull; independent in mind and motion like Hull, but assertive where the American was cautious. Within days of his arrival at Fort Malden, he had constructed a 3 gun battery opposite Fort Detroit, repaired the bridge over the Aux Canards River and moved all of his available men to Sandwich. On the night of the 14th, Procter's 18 and 15 pounder guns opened fire. On the following day, having paraded his war painted Indians in full view of the enemy, Brock sent Hull a demand for the surrender of Detroit, graphically reminding the American general of the consequences of a refusal. *'It is far from my intention to join in a war of extirmination; but you must be aware that the numerous body of Indians who have attached themselves to my troops will be beyond my control the moment the contest commences . . . .'*

The demand had the medicinal effect of reviving the fighting spirit that Hull was known to possess, and he suddenly found the sinew to refuse. The force at his disposal, however, had been dangerously depleted the day before. Responding to a fresh appeal from Henry Brush, who claimed to have discovered an indirect but less hazardous route back to Detroit, he had ordered out Cass, Miller and 350 men to serve as an escort for the cattle and supply train that Brush had somehow managed to keep intact. At midday on the 14th, only hours before the British heavy guns spoke out, the two colonels had ridden out of Detroit and swung westward to avoid any contact with Fort Amherstburg's mobile patrols.

Soon a messenger was sent racing after Cass and Miller, calling them back to assist in the defence. The man departed during a heavy bombardment from across the nearly mile wide river. Hull's battery of 24 pounders had eagerly replied, directed energetically by their young commander, Lieutenant James Dalliba, who had insisted on standing on the highest and most exposed rampart to search for targets. A large pear tree obstructed his view, and the lieutenant ordered a soldier to find an axe and cut the tree down. A chance shot from across the water, however, was far more effective, removing tree and branches far quicker than any lumberjack could ever do. A metal fragment from a passing British shell tore the clay pipe out of the mouth of one of the town's residents. The man, furious at the destruction of his favourite pipe picked up his musket, waded into the river and fired across the water until he and his ammunition were exhausted. A mortar shell fell through the roof of a house and destroyed the table around which a family had just gathered for dinner. They escaped unhurt, just seconds before the bomb exploded. Tales of near misses abound, poignantly colouring the story of this minor war. Some justification can be attached to the claim that the war for independence and this, its sequel, marked the transition from the traditional set-piece battle war, involving few civilians, and determined more by the push and shove of armies on the field, to the more modern style of warfare, which today is often labelled 'total'. Non—combatants suffered horribly in both American conflicts, either during bombardments, or as result of reprisals taken against those unfortunate enough to cross the path of the merciless and unforgiving.

The story of Detroit, however, now unfolds conventionally. At 10 p.m. that evening, Britain's guns ceased firing. The silence that followed seemed almost unnatural. During the twilight of that summer night, the

'Queen Charlotte' and 'Hunter' anchored off Sandwich, indicating that something was about to happen. Few in Detroit, and certainly not Hull, would have slept that night. The more vigilant might have detected the activity on the Sandwich shore as Brock's party began to embark. First to paddle across were Tecumseh's warriors in their canoes, followed by the regulars of the 41st Foot and the four recently raised regiments of militia from the Lakes peninsula—[3] all four of which arrived at the fort with Brock. The general had 700 soldiers and 600 Indians in his command—enough, he believed, to expel the Americans from Fort Detroit.

By dawn, the Indians were all across and were already creeping through the forest and cornfields. The soldiers disembarked at Spring Wells, a little higher up than the Indians, their passage screened by the guns of the Sandwich battery. The two forces, Indian and white men, operated independently, but moved in parallel, Brock closest to the river and the Indians still on the fringes of the forest. The soldiers advanced in column, with intervals separating the various units in an attempt to make the column appear longer.

One of the war's more unique characteristics is illustrated now. Farmers, bent over hoe or spade, seeing the soldiers passing, seemed indifferent rather than hostile. People living on the artificial and only recently established political border were not all fervent patriots. The demands of the seasons were of greater importance than any invasion by fellow English speakers. Those who did stop their labours to watch Brock's marching soldiers did so more out of curiosity than concern. British Canadians were perhaps more patriotic, and an American invasion across the border would be likely to ignite a little more passion. Yet Brock's reliance upon an almost pulpit like denunciation of the enemy and his exaggeration of the consequences of an American success revealed something of the calmness of mind that the citizens of Upper Canada felt towards an American takeover of their lands. Further east, where Québec and the lands that had once been New France touched the newly independent states of America, an atavistic anglophobia and a feeling of affinity with the American republican spirit held greater sway. The French settlers on the border frequently welcomed the American invading forces. Yet, any attempt to generalise on the complexity of passions and feelings that existed

---

3 The two Norfolk regiments and the Oxford and Middlesex regiments

is bound to be simplistic and ignores the fact that people nowhere welcome the disturbances to daily life that any invasion must entail. None of this, however, applied to areas at distance from the border. In the heartland of the United States, patriotism's beat was loud. When, in 1814, British forces advanced on Washington, the full venom of the proud republican spirit was unleashed. Canada would not experience any such far reaching invasion by American forces, and the extent of patriotism consequently remained unmeasured.

Those who saw the Indians on the flanks of the British, however, would not have remained so calm or dispassionate. For everyone, American or British, fear of the 'Redmen' was overarching. Even as allies, the very presence of Indians in fearful war paint would have watered down the composure of even the most rocklike of men. Those who employed the warriors were viewed by the other side as employers of the Devil. The ethics of using North America's native tribes as allies would be long debated. The fact remains, however, that they were generally felt to be too valuable to discard.

Four hundred militiamen, with two 24 pounder guns loaded with grapeshot, had been placed in position outside Detroit. Alerted by the glint of sunlight on bayonet blades, the gun crews stood by their weapons with lighted matches in their hands. Behind stood the fort itself, held by an equal number of men and enclosed by an 11 foot high parapet and 6 foot deep ditch. And somewhere in Brock's rear, Cass's recalled detachment was only three miles behind. Despite the British general's careful preparations, he found himself in a less than favourable situation.

The battery at Sandwich was still firing and the aim was more accurate than previously. A single well-placed shot from any one of those heated barrels would have been capable of knocking down 20 or more of Hull's closely packed men. The British ranks were advancing, too, precise, tidy and almost mechanical in their discipline. Detroit's volunteer warriors, watching their approach and used only to raising a gun against an errant animal or cook pot prey, no longer felt comfortable in their new role as the nation's defenders. Two companies of Michigan infantry promptly deserted, leaving a gap in Hull's line. A well aimed shot from across the water passed through a narrow window of the fort and exploded in the officers' quarters, killing 4 men, amongst them Lieutenant Porter Hanks, the man who had commanded at Fort

Mackinac. The odds, stacked minutes before in America's favour, had swung in Britain's direction.

About a mile from the fort, just beyond musket range, Brock ordered his marching column to wheel to the left and form into line. He now elected to re-employ his psychological weapon, repeating his earlier strategy of parading his Indian bands in full view of their adversary. Briefly he deployed them in a line, before sending them back into the forest and out again.

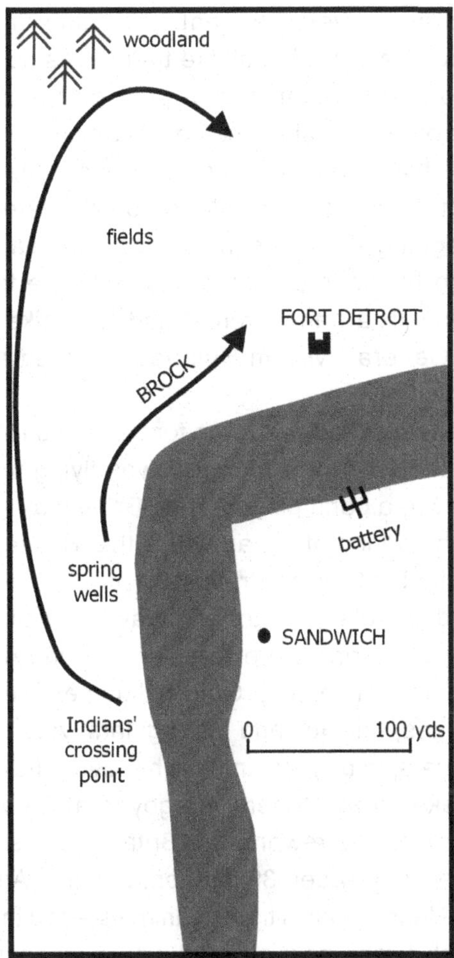

The Taking of Detroit

Three times they repeated this movement, giving the impression of an endless and uncountable number of warriors. And, in further shock tactics, his militia men, dressed in red, were deliberately placed in the enemy's line of vision. General Brock seemed to be enjoying his day.

General Hull, by contrast, was not. One of his officers found him half-crouching on the canvas of a half-folded tent and frantically chewing tobacco. He seemed completely unable to grasp the situation in which he now found himself. Better commanders than he have been comatosed at the very moment when they most need to be sharp and decisive—and Hull, just like them, was no invincible deity with the ability to hurl thunderbolts or perform the miraculous. The consequences of offering resistance haunted him, too; a chance shot had already carried off several of his officers, while the thought of what the Indians might do was too terrible to contemplate. With so much weighing on his ageing shoulders, he decided upon an unspectacular surrender. Calling his lines of militia back into the fort, he sent out his son Abraham with a handkerchief tied to a pike to obtain what terms he could. General William Hull had not fired a single shot in defence of the town.

The ceremony which followed was formal and subdued. By 7 p.m. on that evening, the 16th, the Union flag was flying from the flagpole and, across the river, a band played 'Rule Britannia'—and all this had occurred during the period of the armistice that Baynes and Dearborn had negotiated with Sir George Prevost.

Brock relished his role as victor and played it well. Included in the haul of troops surrendering were Cass's returning detachment and the lost men on the Raisin. The Ohio militiamen were permitted to return to their homes, but Hull and his regulars were taken by boat to Montréal as prisoners, to be held until exchanged. The brasses that the Americans had taken from General Burgoyne at Saratoga were sent in triumph to Québec. The rewards for Britain were staggering: 2500 muskets, 40 barrels of powder, 39 cannon, the brig 'Adams' (promptly renamed Detroit), Henry Brush's train of animals—and the entire territory of Michigan, which Brock now claimed would *'henceforth be part of Britain.'* The troops involved in the victory were well rewarded—each receiving at least £4, the equivalent of twenty weeks' wages, paid out to every soldier present on that day.

Hull was portrayed in his homeland as either victim or villain, depending upon the slant of opinion. Those who felt that his task had been made impossible due to a clear lack of War Department support were inclined to be generous in their assessments. But their hesitant voices were drowned by those who called for his punishment and public humiliation. *'Never was there a more Patriotic army—neither was there ever an army that had it more completely in their power to have accomplished every object of their Desire than the Present, and must now be sunk into Disgrace for want of a General at their head . . .* Robert Lucas, one of Hull's most senior officers had written in his diary before the surrender. Some burned his effigy, others cold-shouldered him in public, and comparisons were made with Benedict Arnold. His life as a social outcast began.

Nearly two years later, in March 1814, a court-martial sat to hear his case. Cruelly, it was presided over by Dearborn, whose lack of support had done so much to undermine Hull's prospects of success. The defendant was cleared of the charges of treason and cowardice, but the court condemned him to be shot for neglect of duty. In a more humane mood, the members of the tribunal later recommended clemency on grounds of his age and his past war record. President Madison supported the recommendation, and the disgraced man lived on. He died in 1825, in his eighties, still trying to save his name from perpetual damnation.

The loss of Detroit was followed by disaster at Chicago. Fort Dearborn, a small strongpoint on the Chicago River and now in the heart of the city, was held by Captain Nathan Heald and 54 men. Here they had lived in comfortable harmony with the neighbouring Indians, even in the dark days after Tippecanoe. But, on 7th August, when Hull retired from Detroit, he sent the captain instructions to evacuate the riverside fort and withdraw to Fort Wayne on the Maumee. Most of the garrison wanted to remain within the fort's protective stockade, aware that the attitude of the Indian tribes outside had changed since the start of hostilities with Britain. Heald, however, a man used to obeying orders, unquestioningly complied with Hull's instructions. The fort's whiskey supply was poured into the river and the surplus guns and ammunition destroyed before the exodus began. On 15th August the small garrison, their wives and children, left the fort and headed south for an unrecorded destination. With them was a group of Miamis serving as an escort.

The route to apparent safety took the party through sand hills on the shores of Lake Michigan. Only miles from the fort, they were attacked by Pottawattomies. A dozen children and two-thirds of the party were killed or wounded—and many were scalped. One of the officers, admired for his manliness, was singled out for an even more gruesome fate. Believing that they would be infused with his leonine spirit, the warriors cut out his heart and ate it raw. With the loss of Detroit and Fort Dearborn, the Americans had only three garrisoned posts north of the Ohio river; Forts Wayne, Harrison and Madison.

But Britain's sharp campaigning sword was now in danger of being blunted by differences of opinion in the high command. Prevost, still anxious to explore paths to peace, had locked horns with his over-energetic subordinate, who, having conquered Detroit with ease, was keen to cross the Niagara River at the very earliest opportunity. '*I am really placed in a most awkward predicament,*' Brock wrote to a friend when he received Prevost's veto on his request to attack Fort Niagara. '*My instructions oblige me to adopt defensive measures, and I have evinced greater forbearance than was ever practised on any former occasion. It is thought that, without the aid of the sword, the American people may be brought to a full sense of their own interests. I firmly believe that I could at this moment sweep everything before me from Fort Niagara to Buffalo.*'

On the Niagara front, Dearborn's brief armistice and Dr. Eustis's lethargy had caused the intended movements to stagnate. A few desultory raids across Lake Ontario and the St. Lawrence had occurred, matched by similar Canadian efforts in the vicinity of Ogdensburg. Through no fault of his own, General Stephen Van Rensselaer, the designated commander on the Niagara front, still had less than 700 men under his jurisdiction at Lewiston in September. None were uniformed, many were shoeless, rations were inadequate and not a man had been paid. But Van Rensselaer was a Federalist, a lone fish in a military sea of Republican generals and brigadiers. The government party machine of the day consequently chose to blame him for this unacceptable situation at the front. Dearborn, who, probably more than Eustis, was responsible for inaction, made some honourable gestures and offered lame excuses in an effort to exonerate the officer. The later build-up in Van Rensselaer's army was triggered by public shock at the loss of Detroit and a wave of emotion that eventually forced Dearborn to act.

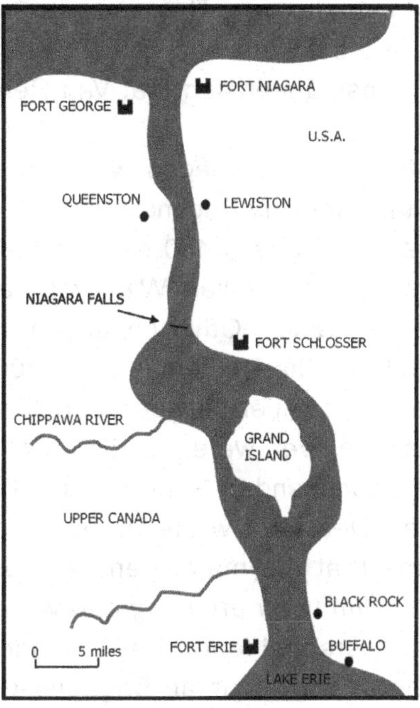

The Niagara River Front

Van Rensselaer was faced with a task just as formidable as that faced by Hull. The frontier that he was required to defend stretched for 36 miles and separated Lake Erie from its northerly sister, Ontario. At the southern end of the Niagara River, which dissected this neck of land, lay British held Fort Erie, its guns largely neutralised by the American batteries at Black Rock and Buffalo on the opposite bank. At the northern end, where the river met Lake Ontario, the garrisons of Fort George and Fort Niagara, rivals in war, glared at each other across the water, little more than a mile apart. Between these points, the river flowed through a bluff-flanked channel, widening mid-way to encircle Grand Island. Creeks flowed into the Niagara from left and right, some wide enough to form obstacles for forces moving north or south, but generally the terrain of this region afforded few problems.

From Lewiston, the site of Van Rensselaer's headquarters, the river could be crossed in ten minutes. Queenston lay on the opposite bank, close enough for a musket ball fired from Lewiston to penetrate British flesh. Halfway up the heights behind Queenston, a V-shaped redan housed an 18 pounder gun. This was mirrored by an American battery at Lewiston. But the Canadian village was known to be lightly held—and it was against Queenston that Van Rensselaer proposed to launch his attack.

The build-up of forces, once it began, was rapid. In September the 5th and 13th United States Infantry Regiments, a total of 1650 men, were despatched to Buffalo, along with 400 newly recruited militia. In the same week Brigadier-General William Wadsworth arrived at Lewiston with 1700 New York militiamen. Other contingents joined in the next few days; by 10th October the Dutchman had 6300 troops stretched along the thirty-five mile frontier between Fort Niagara and Buffalo. Opposing him across the river, were just 2200 British troops, regular and militia, under the command of General R.H. Sheafe.

In early October, Dearborn wrote to his Niagara commander, expressing the hope that the major-general would '*embrace the first practicable opportunity for effecting a forward movement.*' But, as so often happens, personal feuds played a hand in reducing this advantage of numbers. The Virginian Brigadier-General Alexander Smyth, commander of the 5th and 13th regiments, refused to report in person to a mere major-general of New York militia and wrote to him instead. He then proposed a plan of attack that ran contrary to the planned attack on Queenston advocated by Van Rensslaer. '*From the description I have had of the river below the Falls (*Niagara*) the view of the shore below Fort Erie, and the information received as to the preparations of the enemy, I am of opinion that our crossing should be effected between Fort Erie and Chippewa. It has, therefore, seemed to me proper to encamp the United States troops near Buffalo, there to prepare for offensive operations . . . .*' When invited to a council of war, Smyth made no effort to attend or even reply. And, by this time, Brock had arrived at the Niagara front to take personal command.

General Rensselaer, aware that the vocal Republican press would howl in derision if he failed in his attack, modified his original plans by suggesting a two-pronged attack on a wider front. One of these would cross the Niagara river and attack Fort George from the rear while the other force would cross from Lewiston and assault the British positions in Queenston and the precipitous heights that lay just behind.

Two ships anchored on Lake Erie—the 'Caledonia', the boat that had been used to transport British troops to Fort Mackinnac, and the 'Adams', the ship so recently scooped up in the haul of prizes taken by the British at Detroit, threatened the security of the Fort George party, and American minds were hurriedly employed in working out how the two ships could be neutralized. The resulting action on the night of 9th October, the evening before the proposed invasion, could easily provide the setting for a story in an adventure book for boys. Soon after midnight, two longboats, each carrying about 50 men, put out from Black Rock with silent oars, hoping to take the British crewmen by complete surprise. Rowing up close to the stern of the 'Caledonia' to avoid early detection, the sailors headed for the 'Detroit', considered to be the more desirable of the two ships. Lookouts, however, saw the approaching silhouettes against the glassy, moon-strewn lake, and fired. Others on board joined in, pouring a rain of musket shot, stilling for ever the heartbeats of many young Americans. But the familiar shape of the warship that had once been theirs spirited the survivors forward and upward—and the coveted 'Detroit' was soon in their hands. British guns on shore opened up, sending 12 pound balls across the water. The boat's new owners replied, touching the powder of the warship's 6 pounders with lighted candles brought with them for the purpose.

The 'Caledonia' was taken in pure pirate fashion. Men with cutlasses in their mouths clambered up ropes to overpower the 12 man crew assembled on the open deck. Under fire from Fort George, the captors raised anchor and sails and stole away—and soon the 'Caledonia' lay safely anchored under the protection of American guns at Black Rock; she later became the nucleus of an American flotilla on the lake. In her holds were quantities of salted pork—and the prisoners taken at Fort Mackinac. The Americans on board the 'Detroit', however, found escape far less easy and, despite their efforts, the unfortunate vessel grounded off Squaw Island. The ensuing struggle for ownership ended when the sailors of the United States abandoned the ship and set her on fire to prevent her recapture.

The American attack on Queenston was launched on the night of 11th October, after a violent storm. Only 600 men were assembled for the attempt. Thirteen large boats had been brought down from the north by wagon during the previous evening and placed under the supervision of a Lieutenant called Sims. This officer was the first to row out, moving out into the darkness on his own and calling on the others to follow. Still wet from the heavy rain, the soldiers pulled their boats into the water, but then discovered that they had no oars. Sims had taken them all! The man never returned; his boat was later found tied to a tree. Whether he was a traitor or merely a coward has never been established.

Colonel Solomon Van Rensselaer, the general's nephew, had been placed in charge of the attack on Queenston. On the night of the 12th a second attempt was made. Lieutenant-Colonel John Christie, commanding the 300 men of the 13th US infantry based at Four Mile Creek, asked for his regiment to be allowed to participate. Receiving Van Rensselaer's consent, he marched his regiment down to Lewiston, choosing a road south that would conceal his movements from the British. And, late that day, the 2nd Artillery regiment arrived under the command of Lieutenant-Colonel Winfield Scott, a man who would later feature prominently in the nation's military hall of fame.

The ineptitude of the Americans proved to be something of a blessing in disguise. British troops had watched the farce and could not believe that the near-comedy on the other side of the river could possibly represent a genuine effort to cross and attack. In the opinion of the spectators, this must be a 'feint', a light-hearted attempt to distract the watchers while the real attack went in thirty miles to the north near Fort George. Generals Brock and Sheafe consequently made no effort to reinforce their force at Queenston. On the day of the American attack, it consisted of a company of Canadian militia, 60 grenadiers of the 41st Regiment of foot and a handful of Indians.

At about 3 a.m. on the 13th, 600 men crowded into the boats and, protected by Scott's artillery, struck out for the Canadian shore. Ten of the thirteen boats crossed within a quarter of an hour, carrying 300 regulars to the enemy's beaches. The remaining boats, one of them carrying Christie, were swept downstream, and command of the 13th regiment devolved temporarily upon youthful Captain John Wool, a man with no military experience but, as it turned out, endowed with the heart of a lion. With difficulty, Wool led his men from the beach and up the steep banks to the plateau, all the time under fire from the British battery on the heights. Three hundred more Americans, militiamen under Solomon Rensselaer's command, landed within the next hour. Men hardly dared fire—for the flash from their musket barrels allowed the British to find the small crouching targets, and the casualty toll on the beach and heights began to rise. In those strained minutes under fire, Wool received a bullet through his thighs, and Solomon was wounded in five places. Dawn was already born, lighting the river behind the attackers and filtering away the darkness on the beach. The captain, clutching his damaged thigh, and his men were compelled to retreat, shelter beneath the high bluffs and try to hold onto their valuable beachhead. Van Rensselaer, too badly wounded to stay, was taken back across the river, leaving young Wool in full command.

And so Wool made his first battlefield decision and brought on the Battle of Queenston. Retreat to the river would be as hazardous as attack—and far less attractive. Determined to silence the 18 pound gun in the redan on the heights, he took his men up instead, ordering them to climb the steep 300 foot scarp that took them to the plateau top of Queenston. In a movement reminiscent of Wolfe's achievement at Quebec, men scrambled, slipped and swore, holding onto roots and branches and pulling themselves over the loose earth. They reached the top, scratched and breathless, but still an even greater danger lay ahead. Just below them, the gun in the British redan roared out, some shots still targeting the boats on the river and the far bank,

On the night before the crossing from Lewiston, Brock at Fort George, in far less sanguine mood than previously, penned a slightly confusing letter to Sir George Prevost . . . '*The vast number of troops which have been added this day to the strong force collected on the opposite side convinces me . . . . that an attack is not far distant . . . . I have in consequence directed every exertion to be made to complete the militia to two thousand men, but I fear I shall not be able to effect my object with willing, well-disposed characters. Were it not for the number of Americans in our own ranks, we might defy all their efforts against this part of the province.'*

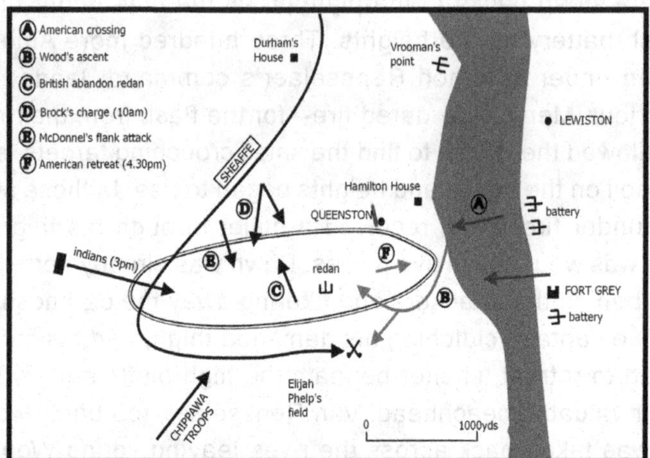

The Battle of Queenston

Five hours later, awakened by an aide knocking frantically on his door, or possibly by the sound of guns to the south, he was in his saddle, anxious to be in personal command of Canada's defensive efforts. In the pre-dawn mist, he galloped south, leaving the men of the 49th Foot and the York volunteers, the latter stationed at Brown's Point, to follow. At Vrooman's Point, a lone 24 pounder was firing across the river, the gunners firing through the semi-light at anything that moved. He arrived on the battlefield, 7 miles to the south of Fort George, just as the last of the American landing craft had left the Lewiston shore. Another few miles to the south, the waters of the Niagara were tipping themselves over the great falls, little heeding the activity that was taking place on the shoreline further north.

General Alexander Smyth's Brigade: 5th U.S., 6th U.S, 13th U.S. and 23rd U.S. Infantry

General William Wadsworth's Brigade: 16th and 17th New York Militia

Colonel James Miller's Brigade: 18th, 19th and 20th New York Militia

The Army of the United States at the Battle of Queenston

41st and 49th Foot, 1st, 2nd and 3rd York Militia, 1st Essex Militia, 4th and 5th Lincoln Militia

British forces at the Battle of Queenston

Wool, despite his youth and lack of experience, was about to prove that he equaled the British commander's battlefield skills. Just as Brock, still mounted on his horse, rode up to the battery to give fresh orders to the troops assembled there, the American captain on the ridge above ordered the men of the 13th U.S. infantry to charge.There was very little the men of the British 49th Foot could do: within minutes the Americans were swarming all over the redan, hacking and stabbing at all those unfortunates who remained in the way. Isaac Brock ordered his troops to retire towards Queenston, trusting that the rest of the 49th would arrive in time to enable him to arrange a counter-charge.

But shame and impatience got the better of him. Brock, who had outwitted 63 year old General Hull, was galled when he realized that he was being outclassed by a raw and inexperienced captain. Observing a steady flow of Americans moving up the heights from the beach, he was quick to realise that an immediate counter-attack would have to be launched if he were to retain any chance of regaining his self-esteem and forcing the enemy from those strategically vital heights. His first counter-charge uphill was thrown back by the intensity of the fire from Wool's men, now sheltering in the redan. '*This is the first time I have ever seen the 49th turn their backs,*' he was heard to exclaim.

These were almost his last words. His life would end shortly afterwards. Riding at the head of his men, the six feet tall officer in full dress uniform made an attractive and easy target. The second charge took the British to within 50 metres of the American line. At the moment the redcoat line halted to fix bayonets, the general slumped from his horse with a musket ball in his chest. The reign of his successor Lieutenant-Colonel John Macdonnel was short-lived.

He, too, fell mortally wounded a few minutes later. At 7 a.m. the British attack ended, demoralized by the death of two of their senior officers. The Stars and Stripes flew over a field littered with the fallen. Brock had died just three days after his elevation to the Knighthood of the Bath, his reward for victory at Detroit, an honour that he never knew that he had received. Wool's enjoyment of his success and command would be brief. Within an hour he would be outranked by his superiors, Stephen Van Rensselaer, Wadsworth and Scott, who crossed the river in the coat tails of the American success. At this moment, America had only 1000 men on Canadian soil. Many of these, unnerved by their first experience of warfare, remained cowering on the river's shore and refused to ascend the heights.

The work of entrenching lasted all afternoon, supervised by Colonel Scott. [4] Aware that the rest of the 49th Foot and other regulars were moving down from Fort George under the command of Major-General Roger Sheaffe, Scott positioned his men, now dangerously short of ammunition, to face west with their backs to the village of Queenston and with their left flank hanging on the edge of the scarp. Fortune, the weather, Providence or the skills of the new British commander would probably dictate how long the Americans would remain.

A less expected factor, however, shaped the next stage of the Battle of Queenston. At about 2 p.m. a war band of Mohawk Indians appeared from the woods to the west and began to work its way around the American left. Intimidated by the bizarre face paint and curdling cries, the militiamen on this flank, never likely to be more than mere human beings, crumbled and fled without firing a shot. Regulars in the redan desperately tried to bring the captured 18 pound gun into action, but it had been spiked by the retreating British and was as useless as a log of wood. Winfield Scott himself led the counter move that halted the warriors' advance. By 3 p.m. the Indians had withdrawn, the field fell silent, and the second stage in this battle of great variety had ended.

But a third stage was about to be unveiled. A British battery on the lawns of Hamilton House, a villa at the northern end of the village, had just opened fire to prevent any further American troops from crossing the river. And Scott's men on the hill, looking towards Vrooman's Point, only a mile from Queenston, now saw a column of redcoats, 800 strong, advancing

4 Van Rensselaer had returned to the American shore

from Fort George. Scott, in sole command after Rensselaer's return to the American shore, had only about 600 men on the hill. A sizeable number of militia men, who had originally crossed into Canada, had recently deserted, knowing that they could never be forced to serve in a foreign country. And British guns at Vrooman's Point and Hamilton House still commanded the crossing points, making any further forays across the river extremely hazardous. Captain James Dennis, assuming command of the survivors of the battle on the heights after the fall of the two more senior officers, had withdrawn to Vrooman's Point to await Sheaffe's arrival. More alarming and potentially demoralizing for the soldier folk on the hill was the message that Scott and Wadsworth had just received from Van Rensselaer. *'I have passed through my camp; not a regiment, not a company is willing to join you. Save yourselves by a retreat if you can.'* The words employed by a commander during battle can contribute to defeat or victory almost as much as any action on the field.

Boston born Major-General Sir Roger Sheaffe, although lacking the showmanship and dash of Brock, would turn out to be just the kind of officer most needed in the circumstances. He had actively served the King during the war for independence and, like so many other loyalists, he had withdrawn to Canada at the war's end. Cautious and ploddingly methodical in his reasoning, he was quick to appreciate that a frontal assault up hill against an enemy well entrenched on high land would be an act of unpardonable folly. Instead of advancing directly against the heights, he decided, therefore, to take his force on a detour to the west towards the village of St. David's, and gain the heights without a fight. Passing Durham's House, where Macdonnel lay dying, on the afternoon of that long, eventful day, his mixed force of professionals, militia and Indians hauled in Dennis's blooded force at Vrooman's Point on the way. Crossing the ridge well to the west of where the Americans were entrenched, he met up on the other side with a detachment of 150 militia that had been based at Chippawa under the command of Captain Richard Bullock. At 4 p.m., Sir Roger Sheaffe, carrying the expectations and hopes of his country on his epauletted shoulders, deployed his men in line across Elizah Phelp's newly ploughed field, effectively obliging the enemy to descend from the heights and fight. With Bullock forming on his right and the survivors of the morning fight boosting his centre, Sheafe had more than 1000 men in line. Britain's redcoats moved forward, advancing in perfect order with their polished bayonets fixed. Behind were the supporting militia, almost as disciplined as the regulars On the flanks, partially concealed by woods, were the Indians. And two grasshopper guns were firing now, aiming at the very centre of the American line. Sheaffe expected little opposition.

He would be largely correct in his assessment. Scott, standing on a stump, tried to reassure his men and rekindle the fighting spirit that they had previously shown. A few muskets were raised, a volley or two was fired, but the sight of the Indians with tomahawks in their hands, and the clockwork steadiness of Britain's regulars dissolved any chance of a stand. Sheafe's ranks were deploying against the American flanks, known to be the weakest points, and the Indians had now left the cover of the trees. Scottish born Adam Waters, a true American by inclination, pulled a portrait of his sweetheart from his coat. A musket ball hit the casing and was deflected past his head and saved him from certain injury. He married the young lady on his return to Albany. The invaders of Canada were soon scurrying for safety, the instinct to survive proving far stronger than any patriotic or regimental glue that might keep the fighting units together. Seized by fear, men sought concealment in crevices, tumbled over rocks, bushes and roots, or leaped to their deaths from the cliff tops' edges. Tomahawks became blooded in the moments following and despatched to God's keeping those unlucky few who remained too long.

Tall Winfield Scott, America's hero in a later international war, narrowly avoided becoming one of the victims. Tying a white cravat to the point of his sword when he saw his army had almost evaporated, he stepped out in the open to offer America's unconditional surrender. Savaged by two Indians, who did not recognise the white man's signal of capitulation, or else choosing to ignore the pleas, he was only saved by the timely arrival of a party of British soldiers.

Only about 250 Americans had actually been in action that afternoon, but the haul of captives topped 900, far more than Scott believed to be present on the Canadian shore. The militiamen, as at Detroit, were paroled while the Regulars were impounded. Amongst the former was a 64 year old who, far from permanently laying down his musket, as his captors demanded, appeared again in America's fighting ranks at the later Battle of New Orleans. The Mohawk warriors would have preferred to slaughter the captives on the spot, but Sheaffe, displaying impressive qualities of dominance, managed to hold them off. It was just half-past four; the battle for Queenston had lasted intermittently for more than twelve hours.

The counting of the casualties then began. The Americans had lost 90 killed and 100 wounded in the day's three actions. The British had lost 14 killed and 84 wounded, a relatively small number, but overshadowed in most people's reckoning by the loss of Brock. The dead, apart from the most senior officers, remained on the field of battle that night. Soon after midnight, it snowed, the first fall of the season. By the time the burial parties arrived in the morning to perform their duties, sympathetic nature had already covered the bodies in shrouds of her own.

General Isaac Brock lay in state for three days. On the 16th, he and McDonnel received a formal but simple funeral, attended by 5000 soldiers resting on reversed arms, and both were then buried in the York bastion of Fort George. Across the river, American guns fired a salute of respect for their enemy. He (Brock) '*would have ordered the same*' for a fallen American general, the grief-choked Sheaffe was heard to say when he heard America's guns.

Brock's epitaph was written many times—in stone at the place where he fell, in books, letters and in the hearts of his admirers. One, with no known author, reflects well the over-florid and sentimental styles of the time:

No tongue shall blazon forth their fame-
The cheers that stir that sacred hill
Are but the promptings of the will.
That conquered then, that conquers still.
And generations shall thrill
At Brock's remembered name.

Conjecturally, if America had repulsed Sheaffe, what might the nation have achieved? A further advance inland into a near empty interior and, at best, the taking of Fort George? But limited successes like this would never have caused Britain to sue for peace. Only a hearty strike at Canada's commercial or political capitals would have been noticed by Britain. Tiny bridgeheads on a long frontier might have caused a ripple of national self-approval in Washington, but would be hardly likely to raise even an eyebrow of the politicians of London.

Comparisons were made with Napoleon's advance on Moscow, taking place at that very moment. He, too, would gain very little from an invasion of foreign soils.

That day America also learned the limitations of the militia. '*They have disgraced the nation,'* General Alexander Smyth retorted the day after the battle. The regulars were perceived to be only a little better. The 14th U.S. regiment was dismissed by a high ranking officer as '*possibly even worse*' than the militiamen alongside which the regiment had just fought.

The disgrace at Queenston brought about a change of personalities at the top. The bombastic Smyth and Van Rensselaer had sparred indecorously before the battle. Military failure fueled Smyth, who had remained in his tent throughout the action into further verbal assaults on his superior. ' . . . *the nation has been unfortunate in the selection of some of those directing it. One army has been disgracefully surrendered and lost, another has been sacrificed by a precipitate attempt to pass it over at the strongest point of the enemy" lines* '. He savagely wrote in a letter that mudded Hull as well for his failures at Detroit. Van Rensselaer reminded his critics that the brigadier-general had refused to co-operate, and he now asked to be relieved. On 16th October the self-opinionated Smyth took over command on the Niagaran front, clearly believing that he was the best man for the job. '*In a few days, the troops under my command will plant the American standard in Canada. They are men accustomed to obedience, silence and steadiness. They will conquer or they will die,'* he boasted, choosing to ignore that this description of the American soldiers' valour was completely at variance with his earlier denigration of the militiaman's lack of courage under fire. And then, in a further touch of self-grandeur, he added: '*Where I command, the vanquished and peaceful man, the child, the maid and the matron shall be secure from wrong. If we conquer, we will conquer but to save.'* General Van Rensselaer, before his resignation, had negotiated a month's truce with the British, giving the new man time to reorganise his forces and plan his alternative campaign.

Henry Dearborn probably felt that some of the bombast's remarks were aimed at him as well. His energies in the aftermath of the setbacks at Detroit and Queenston were pronounced. Within days he had established a communication system that would enable messages to be passed between headquarters near Albany and the Niagara within forty-two hours. Smyth then made appeals to the men folk of New York State to enlist, proclaiming, in florid, almost hectoring tones, that posterity would honour those who responded. '*Men of New York, . . . have you not a wish for fame? Then seize the present moment. If you do not you will regret it and say 'the valiant have bled in vain. The friends of my country fell and I was not there.'*

The clarion tones were far from discordant. They came in droves. Within a month, his Niagara force topped 4500. The men of New York, Baltimore and Pennsylvania were there: farmers, bachelors, tradesmen and even convicts. Some remembered the dark days when the redcoats had cast shadows over their lives, others came from a spirit of adventure. Now they would need to be honed into a cohesive military unit. Demoralisation, however, soon stalked the ranks of the army at Bufflalo, causing the barrack block mutiny of two of the regular regiments and insubordination amongst the militia. Dysentry and measles stalked, too, placing men in hospital or in graves, and the cemetery behind the camp, where men were buried four to a grave, was nearly doubled in size during November. And still Smyth, son of a parish rector, continued in high-flown language to speak of the glory that he and the more stout-hearted would sculpt. '*The regular soldiers of the enemy are generally old men, whose best years have been spent in the sickly climate of the West Indies . . . . come on, my heroes! And when you attack the enemy's batteries, let your rallying word be: The cannon lost at Detroit or Death.*' On 9th November, he publicly announced his intention to attack Canada before the end of the month. Every word of his announcement was heard on the opposite shore. But of the strategy to be adopted, nothing was discovered, and not even Eustis, Madison or Dearborn were aware of the details of his plans. Dearborn, the most involved of the trio, urged his general not to cross with less than 3000 men, reminding him of the fact that many of those now assembled at Black Rock, would feel little commitment to serve across the border.

Sheaffe, in an attempt to blunt Smyth's still scabbarded sword, struck first. On 17th November, even before the termination of the month long truce, he bombarded Smyth's quarters at Black Rock, destroying the magazine and a pile of furs kept in storage nearby. On the 21st he commenced a furious bombardment of Fort Niagara, pouring 2000 rounds of red-hot shot into the fort during the day; the Americans probably sent back almost as much in return.

This, probably more than any criticism Washington, goaded Smyth into launching the action that he had so long promised. Under cover of darkness on the night of the 27th, two assault columns of the 14th and 15th U.S. regiment under the command of Lieutenant-Colonel Charles Boerstler and 220 men of the 12th and 13th U.S. regiment under Colonel William Winder assembled under a shroud of silence on the banks of the river at Black Rock. Winder's 130 men had been charged with the responsibility of silencing the batteries at the Red House on the opposite shore, while Boerstler and his 200 men simultaneously set out to destroy the bridge across Frenchman's Creek and cut the enemy's communication route between Forts Erie and George as preliminaries to the crossing of the main American force.

Winder's men achieved more than might have been expected, given the scale of the preparations for their reception on the opposite shore. Several boats were sunk or lost, and others were carried downstream during an operation that was bound to be logistically hazardous. Despite the keen opposition of Sheaffe's gunners and the loss of men and boats, the American party spilled ashore, spiked the coastal artillery and then drove back two companies of militia and a detachment of the 49th Foot positioned in support. Most of the party then returned to their nation's shores, taking with them 30 prisoners, and told their tales of the day's thrilling skirmishes. A small group, intent on further mischief, continued down river under the direction of Captain William King, but were forced to lay down their arms when confronted by a much larger force moving up from Fort Erie.

Boerstler's column, composed of men of the U.S. 14th Regiment, would be able to tell similar tales. Locating the mouth of Frenchman's Creek, they had seen the low silhouette of the simple wooden bridge a little way upstream. The bridge, however, would survive intact, too well protected by militia forces and the force from Fort Erie. Undaunted, a few of the American party managed to row to within a few hundred yards of the bridge and then creep almost unnoticed to the timbers of the structure, only to discover that they had left their axes in the boats. When morning's light took over from the night, those that survived were seen rowing frantically back towards America's shores under fire from the muskets of the British. All through the period of action on the Canadian shore, and for the rest of the day, the men of Smyth's main force waited in ice-coated boats, cold, wet, inactive and impatient, hands gripping the boat sides and the soldiers questioning whether this self-praising man could ever be the nation's messiah. And, while the Americans waited, shivered and complained, the British and Canadian forces assembled in strength along the most threatened three mile stretch of the river. Yet, despite the inactivity and the failure to make any attempt to cross, Smyth sent a messenger across with a demand for the surrender of Fort Erie. It was, of course, promptly disregarded by Lieutenant-Colonel Cecil Bisshop, commandant at the fort. Nobody, British or American, now took Smyth seriously. And then came the order to disembark. Smyth, it appeared, had neither the nerve nor the men to launch his promised invasion.

On the 30th he re-assembled his troops again, identifying the following day as the definite day for action. '*Neither rain, snow or frost will prevent the embarkation,*' he loudly declared during another bout of empty rhetoric . . . '*The landing will be effected despite cannon. The whole army has seen that cannon is to be little dreaded. Tomorrow will be memorable in the annals of the United States.*' Smyth's senior officers were rocked with incredulity. The distinct shapes of soldiers on the opposite shore showed the extent of the enemy's preparations and the folly of a frontal assault. They remonstrated with him for hours and eventually persuaded him to change his angle of approach. Instead of rowing into the hail of fire directly opposite, the American boats, he ordained, would slip unnoticed down river and land just above Chippawa. The rain kept falling and the bands played martial airs. And nobody—apart, perhaps from Smyth himself—really believed that the Stars and Stripes would soon be fluttering on the misty shore opposite.

At 3 a.m. on the following morning, the embarkation began again. But only the regulars, less than 900 men in total, 100 or so men of the militia and 506 volunteers appeared at the water's edge. More than 1500 Pennsylvanians, the men who had responded so enthusiastically to the appeals to patriotism, had announced their refusal to cross and went home instead, claiming those same constitutional rights which had caused Hull's invasion to miscarry. The decision was made again to abort operations, the men disembarked, and the waiting British guns felt no need to open fire.

Smyth's camp broke into bedlam. Officers broke their swords in anger while his men, some disappointed, others relieved, brawled like schoolboys at the end of term. Muskets were discharged and emotions unleashed. General Smyth, who had promised so much but delivered very little, felt under threat, and a double guard was placed outside his tent to protect him from the indiscipline of the day.

Brigadier Peter Porter, a New York congressman, was justifiably scornful of Smyth's poor leadership and provoked the general so much that on 12th December Smyth challenged him to a duel. They exchanged shots at twelve paces but missed. *'You will hardly believe me when I tell you that our two doughty generals, Smyth and Porter, got into a boat yesterday with something like 20 men, and . . . . went over to Grand Island, burnt a charge of powder at each other, shook hands, and came back again without staining the ground with even one drop of their precious blood.'* Cyrenius Chapin, a former river trader now turned soldier, wrote. Honour still intact, Smyth sought retirement in his native Virginia. He was mobbed at Buffalo, shot at in Pennsylvania and spat at near his home. Dropped from the army's rolls, he never quite faded into the background. He continued to fire the occasional loose cannon in defence of his record. *'The affair at Queenston is a caution against relying on crowds who, if they are disappointed, break their muskets; or if they are without rations for a day desert,'* he asserted from his lawn-decked home. Nobody, however, considered that his opinions had any validity, but his powerful eloquence eventually ensured his election to Congress.

The third prong of America's trident of invasion proved to be even blunter. Dearborn had stated his personal reputation on a drive through the Lake Champlain lowlands towards Montréal. Colonel Edward Baynes had estimated that there were no more than 2000 men in camp at Plattsburgh and Albany. Having digested this information, Prevost did not feel unduly concerned about this eastern front, particularly as America did not seem yet to be making any threatening movements.

Apart, that is, from a few disconnected raids. On 21st September a company of the 1st U.S. Rifle regiment under the command of Captain Benjamin Forsyth advanced down the St. Lawrence from Sackets Harbor and landed at Gananogue on the 24th, about twenty miles below Kingston. This insignificant settlement, under the protection that day of the Leeds militia regiment, served as the last convoy staging point on the river between the Kingston naval base and Montréal; its capture, therefore, would have been calamitous. The raiders, however, seemed content with their haul of 60 muskets, some ammunition and a sack load or two of food. Poor Mrs. Stone, the wife of Joel Stone, the militia commander, unwisely came to the door when the raiders appeared outside her house; she was shot in the hip by a stray musket ball and so became the only recorded casualty of the day. Mischievously burning a small storehouse, the entire party withdrew and so lost an opportunity of seriously dislocating Prevost's war strategy and communications. In apparent retaliation, Colonel Robert Lethbridge, commanding on the Canadian shore, set out on October 4th to attack Ogdensburg. Initially landing at Briton's Point, where they burned down an American blockhouse, the party moved on to Ogdensburg. Under cover of a battery of guns, he sent 750 men across the river, but most of his 25 boats were sunk or repelled by American gunfire, few even managing to reach the half-way point. Prevost, who had forbidden any visits to enemy territory without his prior consent, relieved Lethbridge of his responsibilities and consigned him to a more junior post in Montréal. Lethbridge, however, had influential friends and, within less than a year, received a major-generalship.

This petty tit for tat warfare continued into the period when heavy snow covered the ground. On 21st October, two hundred members of the New York militia under the command of daredevil Major Guildford Young attacked Saint-Régis, a tiny settlement situated on the international boundary. Snatching the Union flag and a few prisoners, they, too, pulled back and ceremoniously paraded the captured flag in Albany. Clearly not part of Dearborn's strategy, these minor raids seemed to serve no military or diplomatic purpose at all.

By November, however, Baynes' earlier estimates of the size of the enemy forces in the area of Lake Champlain would have been widely inaccurate. Surprisingly, Dearborn had now assembled the largest of all the forces, greater in number than Hull's Detroit force and larger than Smyth's Buffalo army. The staunch Democrat Brigadier-General Joseph Bloomfeld commanded here. At Albany and supporting points, he had 2500 regulars and about 3000 militiamen from Vermont and New York, together with an impressive array of artillery. And Dearborn was entertaining more ambitious projects than previously, nothing less than the capture of the city of Montréal itself. There were those in his entourage who believed that he might now actually be about to deliver on his promises.

But Dearborn was made of the same fragile clay as Hull and Smyth and just as capable of freezing mentally. On 8th November, intending to synchronise his advance on Montréal with Smyth's attack on the Niagara, he informed Eustis that he was about to move north to join Bloomfield at Troy and Plattsburgh as a preliminary to the attack on Canada's prime city. Rheumatism, however, held him at Albany for a further ten days. When he finally reached Plattsburgh on the 19th, he found Bloomfield on his back in bed, laid low by fever and far too unwell to take on any command in the field. Many of the soldiers he met were similarly infected.

An epidemic of measles had swept through the Plattsburg camps, reducing the available fighting force by one-third. Typhus had joined forces with the measles and had more than decimated a supporting force based at Burlington. Eustis and Dearborn, for once, could not be blamed.

In such circumstances, Dearborn felt that he would have to be satisfied with an attempt to cut the lines of communication between Montréal and the border, and reap the psychological benefits of showing his flag in Canadian territory. To do this, he split his available force into two independent columns, each about 650 strong and sent them out to tease the British border posts towards the St. Lawrence.

Major Charles-Michel d'Irumberry de Salaberry, commander of the Voltigeurs, the Provincial Corps of Light Infantry and the man responsible for defending the line of threatened posts, was kept fully informed of America's moves. Detecting the first forward movements of the Americans, he sent two companies of the Voltigeurs under Captain Joseph-François Perrault, and a party of Indians to reinforce the post at Lacolle, the British forward position that seemed most endangered. Dearborn's two columns advanced in parallel columns, exchanging periodic fire with a mobile force of British regulars and militiamen, who had felled trees and piled stones across the route way north. Numerically inferior, this screening force generally managed to keep just beyond his reach and remained as nebulous as the forests that lay around.

On the 20th November, one of the columns reached the Lacolle River, probably unaware that 300 Voltigeurs and 230 Mohawks had developed defensive positions around a blockhhouse on the far side of the river. America was again to be plagued by the same problem that had destroyed Hull and Smyth. Two-thirds of the advancing army halted about a mile short of the Ontario border and refused to step across, leaving the regulars to advance on their own During the early winter darkness, the first American unit to arrive, commanded by Colonel Zebulon Pike, crossed the stream and surrounded the blockhouse, expecting to find it occupied. The defenders, however, had recently left, pulling back to consolidate their strength. Muddle then followed. Pike and his men had just taken possession of the tiny building when the regulars of Dearborn's other column arrived. The latter, assuming that those within were Canadian, opened fire. A tense nocturnal fight ensued between the two American forces, and fifty men died or were wounded before the error was discovered.

Canada struck back a few days later. On 23rd November, Captain Alex Roxburgh led the Glengarry Light Infantry and Stormont Militia against Major Young's position at French Mills on the Salmon River. Referred to as the Battle of French Mills or the First Battle of the Salmon River, the hour long engagement resulted in the capture of 47 of the 50 Americans present and the taking of bateaux, weapons and supplies. There were apparently no casualties on the victorious side.

And so Dearborn's dream invasion evaporated. The man, still about a mile and a half from the frontier, cursed, pulled back to Plattsburg and began to pen his excuses. *'I had anticipated disappointment and misfortune in the commencement of the war, but I did by no means apprehend such a deficiency of regular troops and such a series of disasters as we have witnessed.'*

All of America's border forces were soon in winter camps, conditioning themselves to a long season of near inactivity, and talked of farms and peacetime occupations instead. They possessed an unndeveloped sense of patriotism that would rally them to the defence of their country, but nothing more. The pulse of the frontier campaign, which had been slow from the start, had faded now. Thomas Jefferson, looking out at the snows from the comfort of his Monticello home, must have rued his earlier careless words: *'The acquisition of Canada this year as far as the neighbourhood of Québec, will be a mere matter of marching.'*

CHAPTER 4

'Where He Would Have The Pleasure To Break His Own Sword Over His Damned Head'

The sporting contests on the seas and rivers were to prove more rewarding than any theatricals on land. Never likely to do much more than stir up currents of patriotic satisfaction, the actions between the frigates of the tiny United States navy and the king's ships required more individualistic skills and resourcefulness, and generally fewer protagonists than any land based battle.

America was fortunately blessed with a handful of men accustomed to the force of the wind and the cutting salt sprays. Mindful of the fact that the causes of this unnecessary war had been largely maritime in origin, the members of the Administration were determined that Britain's naval presence should be neutralised, and her ships prevented from blockading the nation's premier ports. Ambitious hearts in the administration hoped for a little more; the disruption of British commercial life and the sinking of convoys at sea. And so the sound of lathe and saw grew louder when war was declared. America was aiming to find the resources needed to beat Britain at sea.

The Republic did not have to wait long to test nerves and timber. On 22nd June, soon after war was declared, Commodore John Rodgers, flying his flag on the 44 gun frigate 'President', and accompanied by the similarly armed 'United States', the 38 gun frigate 'Congress', the

'Hornet' and the 16 gun 'Argus', set sail from New York in an almost piratical mood, endeavouring to search out and destroy the ships of the West Indies fleet. In the early hours of the following morning, at 4.40 a.m., while about 100 miles south of the Nantucket Shoals, according to one of the logs, lookouts on the 'President' spotted sails on the horizon. Rodgers, in no doubt that the sails were British, gave chase, applying every straining yard of sail to close the distance.

Soon after 11.30 in the morning, the 'President', having identified the intruder as the 36 gun H.M.S. 'Belvidera', aimed her guns, and the first ship-launched shot of the war sent a ball through the stern of the British ship. Another two shots followed, equally devastating in effect—but no reply came back from the enemy. The gunners prepared to fire again, watched by the commodore and his officers. Another shot or two like this would suffice, Rodgers mused, after which he could surely claim his prize. Minutes later, Rodgers lay sprawling on the deck, his leg broken. Around him lay the blooded corpses of several of his men. Others lay groaning, clothing torn and blackened. But this had not been the work of the enemy, for the 'Belvidera' did not seem to have replied. One of Rodgers' bow guns had blown up, spewing metal, powder and timber. Twenty-two crewmen were killed or injured. The 'Belvidera' began firing back. Captain Richard Byron, RN, commanding the Englishman, sent a few shots from his stern guns and then, jettisoning excess stores, pulled away. Rodgers, nursing his shattered leg, looked around for his companion ships. In the chase, he had outsailed all three.

No laurels were won that day. The 'Belvidera' escaped to Halifax, and the merchant convoy, which the 'Belvidera' had been accompanying, lay well to the south. All day Rodgers searched for his missing ships. Unable to find them, he decided to hunt alone. During the following days at sea, he crossed the Atlantic and sailed almost within sight of Britain's west coast, still searching for the Jamaica convoy. Turning south, he headed for Madeira, another promising hunting ground, and here he captured seven British merchantmen, their cargoes and their crew. In early September, after seventy days at sea, he returned to New York with several tales to tell.

His name was already on the lips of the senior Royal Navy officers based at Halifax. Rear-Admiral Herbert Sawyer, commander of the station, organised a squadron to sail in search of the American. Commanding this seven ship squadron was Captain Sir Philip Broke accommodated on board the 38 gun 'Shannon'. Richard Byron, itching for revenge, sailed in support. Most powerful of the companion ships was the 64 gun 'Africa', still, at that time, the largest British ship in American waters. Captain James Dacres, commander of the 'Guerriere', also saw his chance for avenging his earlier humiliation. The 32 gun 'Aeolus', the captured U.S.brig 'Nautilus' [5] and a schooner made up the squadron's number.

But it would not be Rodgers that they caught in their far flung net. Isaac Hull, nephew of the unfortunate general, was also at sea. Having left Annapolis on 12th July in the frigate 'Constitution' to search for merchant prey off New England, he spotted a mast on the evening of the 17th and sailed closer to investigate. Morning's light revealed three sails on his starboard and four on his stern; he had unwittingly taken up the bait intended for Rodgers, and would now have to find a way of extricating himself from an obvious disaster.

His frigate could outsail even the fastest of the British ships, but a sudden calm deflated his sails and those of his rivals. Eight vessels sat impassively in the waters off North America, sails flapping, and with very little power of movement. For the British, this must have been particularly frustrating: the 'Constitution' lay just out of range. Officers paced their decks, crewmen pointed excitedly, orders were given and gun crews prepared. Eyes looked upwards to detect the first breath of wind that would fill the sails and bring the action on. And meanwhile the target lay teasingly beyond reach, the stars and stripes boldly flying from a mast that no British gun could hope to fell.

Crew men on the British ships then saw that the American was moving. Hull had lowered his rowing boats, run out hawsers to each and ordered his sailors to row. At the same time he removed two 18 pounder guns from his main deck and placed them at the cabin window to shoot astern. Broke's crews responded in similar fashion, towing their becalmed ships in an attempt to close the range. The naval war had generated into a contest of muscle and speed. It is doubtful whether

5 captured on 16th July off New York by the blockading squadron. She was the first American loss of the war.

the stories of naval war had ever carried a similar incident—fully-rigged warships hauled by rowing boats in a race that would last for hours.

Concerned that the leading ship, the 'Shannon', was gaining on him, Hull resorted to another seldom used stratagem. Casting a small anchor some distance ahead, the 'Constitution' was hauled by winching the anchor lines on a capstan, a process known as 'kedging'. Periodic gusts of wind sometimes gave hope, but died almost as quickly. All that day and throughout the following night, the rowing and the kedging continued, a remarkable feat of physical and mental endurance, neither side giving in, and few men failing to perform what was expected of them. By dawn three of the Royal Navy's frigates had clearly gained, creeping within cannon shot range. Hull, in desperation to remain beyond their reach, offloaded some provisions, hoping that this would inch the ship forwards a little faster. Another day of pursuit followed. But enemy guns were being run out, the range calculated, and punishment seemed imminent.

God, the provider of winds, turned out to be American. For, just as hope of escape must have evaporated and physical exhaustion finally overcame his crewmen, a Providential breeze was born—at about 11 p.m. according to his log. By the morning of the 20th, Hull had lost his hunters, and clear blue water lay all around. Hull, unlike his terrestrial uncle, had handled the situation with calmness and skill; he and his sweating crewmen were the newest heroes of the nation.

Captain Isaac Hull met one of the disappointed Englishmen on its own a few weeks later. On 2nd August the 'Constitution again left port, aiming to search for merchantmen operating on Britain's trade routes. On the 9th, in mid-Atlantic, the 'Guerriere' found her, hoisted colours in the usual pre-battle manner, and fired an opening broadside of grapeshot. Then, turning about, she prepared to deliver a second broadside with the guns of her other side. Hull, this time with a full wind filling his sails, which might have enabled him to escape, welcomed the opportunity of a contest between equals. Instead of straining sails and crew in an effort to escape, he adopted the same tack and ordered his crew to run out the guns and load them with both grape and solid shot. For a while, the firing was one-sided, the 'Guerriere' pouring continuous broadsides while Hull's ship remained silent. Damage mounted, blood flowed, and still the 'Constitution' did not fire back.

At 6.05 p.m., two hours after the first encounter, when the American had drawn abeam, Isaac Hull at last gave the order to fire. The very first broadside sent the Englishman's mizzen mast crashing over board. A second broadside toppled her mainsail. Spars and rigging fell to the decks—and still the guns of the 'Constitution' fired on, literally tearing her adversary to pieces.

For a brief moment, the two ships touched, and men on both sides prepared to board. Providence again intervened, filling the sails of the U.S. frigate and allowing her to pull ahead. Crossing the bows of the 'Guerriere', Hull's ship raked her adversary's decks, leaving her mastless and with gunports taking water. Dacres, unable to believe the fate that had overtaken his ship, hauled down her colours and surrendered. Hull had lost 14 men killed or wounded; Dacres had lost 79.

Throughout that night, the two ships rode alongside each other while Hull's surgeons assisted the British wounded, and his carpenters laboured to keep the British warship afloat. In the early hours of morning, however, the latter task was abandoned. A torch was applied to the wreckage and the warship consigned to her grave. Her magazines soon exploded and, watched by her crew, now aboard the 'Constitution', the outclassed ship settled below the waves. In a combat of equals, an American built ship had proved superior to her British-built rival. The order would soon go out from the Admiralty in London for British ships to avoid single combat with enemy frigates and hunt in packs instead. The loss of the 'Guerriere' was played down in Britain for fear of an adverse public reaction and the exposure of weaknesses in warship design and skills of gunnery.

Isaac Hull re-entered Boston on 30th August and was given a hero's welcome. But, for personal reasons, he stepped down from the command of the 'Constitution', and William Bainbridge occupied the captain's cabin in his place. Anxious for a sedentary job on land, Hull took over Bainbridge's role as commandant of the naval yard in Charleston. The latter had been in Russia in the Spring of 1812. Anxious to secure a senior naval posting, he had set out by land across Siberia. His subsequent exploits in command of the 'Constitution' would fully justify the naval department's faith in his abilities.

Captain David Porter, commanding the frigate 'Essex', was another of those who soon glowed in the early U.S. successes at sea. In the early weeks of war, however, he was engaged in a verbal war with the British rather than dueling with cannons. Having heard that Porter had mistreated a British subject serving in his crew, Sir James Yeo, commanding the British ship 'Southampton',

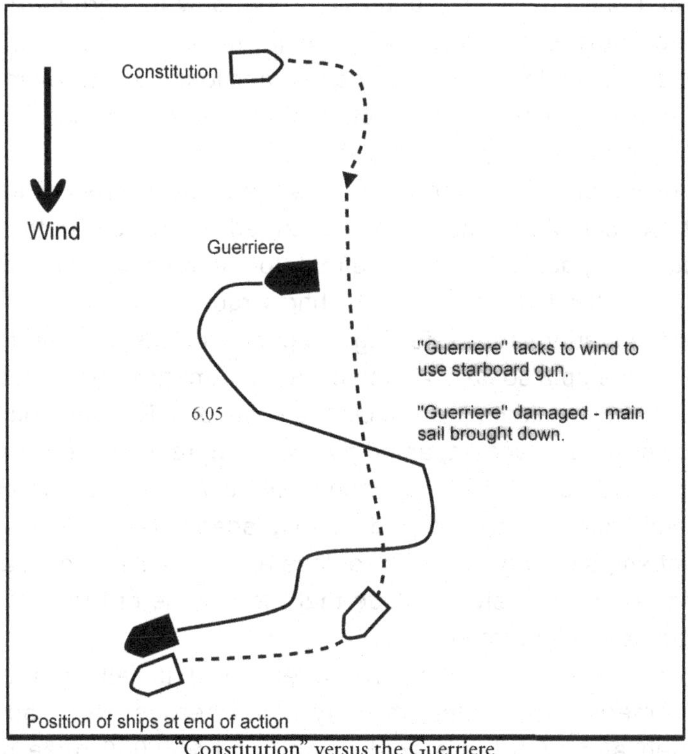

"Constitution" versus the Guerriere

wrote a letter to an American newspaper in which he challenged Porter to a duel. '*Would he be so glad to have a tête-à-tête anywhere between the Capes of Delaware and the Havanna, where he would have the pleasure to break his own sword over his damned head and put him down forward in irons.'* The two never met, and Porter was eventually to take the 'Essex' on a voyage around the world.

But first he had to prove his worth in homeland waters. Setting out for sea on 9th July 1812, he captured seven merchant men during the summer of 1812, most off the banks of Newfoundland and Nova Scotia. On 13th August he saw an unidentified warship, and, assuming it might be Yeo's 'Southampton', he eagerly sought out

Yeo's retributive sword. At 11.30 a.m. the enemy ship, now almost within pistol shot range, ran up her colours and revealed herself as the 22 gun brig 'Alert'.

The ensuing fight, not surprisingly, was short and one-sided. Outgunned and outclassed, and raked from bow to stern by Porter's guns, the 'Alert' surrendered within eight minutes. The first British warship to surrender to the Americans, her loss caused even more dismay in Britain than the destruction of the 'Guerriere', whose crew, at least, had put up a spirited resistance.

On 8th October, Stephen Decatur, a man whose pre-war exploits against Tripoli's pirates had been described by Nelson as the '*most bold and daring acts of the age,'* left Boston at the same time with the 44 gun frigate 'United States' and the brig 'Argus' on an intended cruise towards the Caribbean. Preferring to operate on his own, he left the 'Argus' to take up a solitary station off South America and headed out into the Atlantic's middle waters. On the same day, Rodgers, on board the 'President' and accompanied by the 'Congress', sailed from the same port. But, unlike Decatur, who would confront and defeat a 38 gun warship a few days later, Rodgers managed to take only two small merchant ships during his 30 or so days at sea—a haul so small that it led him to erroneously conclude that the volume of British Atlantic trade had been overstated.

While Britain struggled to come to terms with its failing reputation at sea, America applauded its early naval heroes. Hull had been banqueted and awarded a gold medal, and $50,000 prize money had been shared by the crew. Soon every captain, returning from a spell of duty at sea, would be expected to have achieved similar maritime success.

Yet it would be some time before further banquets were arranged. Britain, a little over cautious of exposing her frigates to American anger, was less provocative and would now try to keep her ships out of danger. One of His Majesty's ships, however, was far out to sea and well beyond the reach of Admiralty orders. On 18th October Captain Jacob Jones and the 18 gun sloop 'Wasp', sailed out from the Delaware to harass the attractive West Indian trade. Just north of Bermuda, in heavy post-gale seas, he found the similarly armed sloop 'Frolic' undertaking repairs to her rigging. When the American failed to respond to the Englishman's signals, Commander Thomas Whinyates, captain of the 'Frolic', ran up Spanish colours to confuse his opponent. The coming contest would consequently depend upon seamanship and fighting skills and it would be hard to distinguish between the relative qualities of the men of both sides.

By 11.32, in still heavy seas, the two brigs sailed parallel to one another about sixty yards apart. In the early rounds of gunfire, the crew of the 'Frolic' showed marked superiority, firing perhaps three balls to every two discharged by the 'Wasp'. And, choosing to fire as the vessel rolled upwards, Whinyates could target the upper masts and rigging of the U.S. ship. In less than twenty minutes of dueling, he brought down the American's topmast and much of her essential rigging.

Jones, by contrast, fired from the trough of the waves, a position that allowed him to hole the hull of the 'Frolic', and spread death and injury to the crew within. The 'Wasp' eventually pulled ahead and cut across the bows of the enemy, a process known as 'crossing the T', and giving her the opportunity of raking the Englishman's decks from bow to stern. Then the two boats entangled, timber slammed against timber, rigging and bowsprits became entwined, and the broadsides of the 14 pounder guns was forced to stop.

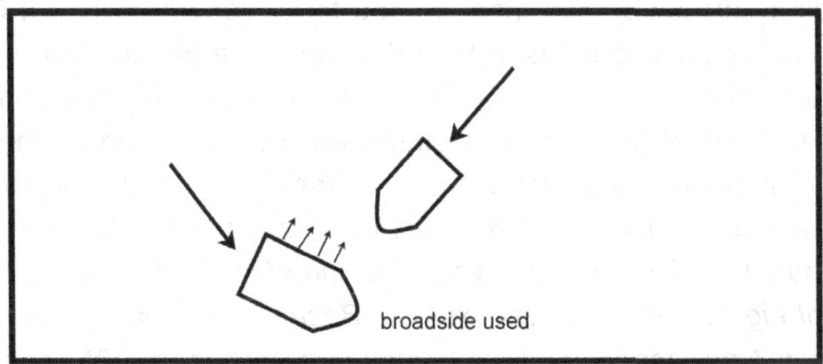

"Crossing the T" Crossing

The command to board was given instead. This was a moment of dread for some, the time when the less dexterous at the art of hand-to hand fighting would feel the penetrating point of steel and probable slow death. For others, it might have been a time of exhilaration and accomplishment and the chance to show their fighting superiority. Such men dealt death to others and felt no later pangs of remorse. Brandishing cutlasses and axes, the Americans crossed to the 'Frolic' and set about showing what the Republic's fighting seamen could do in close combat. But only the officers of the 'Frolic' remained on deck—and the helmsman at the wheel. Offering no resistance, the British officers handed over their swords and surrendered the vessel. The reasons for swift surrender soon became clear. In the forty-five minutes of engagement, more than 90 of the 135 crewmen of the 'Frolic' had been killed or wounded; the Americans had lost 10! Jones had his victory and could look forward to a banquet and bunting when he returned to port.

For a while, Jones and his crew would be denied the thronging crowds of praise. The next day a sail appeared on the horizon and quickly grew in size. This was no sloop, brig or frigate; the silhouette and distant bulk indicated that she was a ship-of-the-line, a warship that Jones could never hope to beat. Jones wisely attempted to escape but, handicapped by damage, he could not make full sail. And the giant was growing more formidable, her three gun decks became clearly visible and the colours of the King of England were being raised. Only yards away now, the gunports of the 74 gun H.M.S. 'Poictiers' loomed over the low decks of the 'Wasp'. Captain Jones, overawed, offered immediate surrender. His men supped that evening on Royal Navy rations in the grim confines of the orlop deck of a British man-of-war. '*They were the finest—looking fellows I think I ever saw,'* Midshipman Charles Loftus of the 'Poictiers' observed. His admiration remained undulled in the days afterwards, following the discovery of a plot to take over the ship. '*I cannot blame them*', he said,' *for it would have been a glorious thing for them to have taken one of His Britannic Majesty's ships of eighty guns into New York or Boston.'* The Wasp was taken into Royal Navy service and renamed 'Loup Cervier'. In 1813 she was renamed yet again, this time as the 'Peacock'. Her subsequent eventful life ended in the summer of 1814 when she foundered off America's southern coast.

Yet ultimately, Jones received his reward. Landed at Bermuda, he and his men were permitted to return home. Despite the loss of his ship and prize, Captain Jacob Jones was presented with a sword by the citizens of New York, and his crew shared prize money totaling some $25,000.

That October continued to be eventful in the Atlantic's seas. On 25th Stephen Decatur, was sailing close to the Azores in search of prey and caught sight of an approaching enemy frigate. The vessel in view was the 'Macedonian', with just 38 guns, and her light weight armoury of 18 pounders would probably provide no match for the 24 pounders on board the American ship.

Captain John Carden, RN, however, enjoyed the advantage of the windward position and the greater manoeuvrability that this provided. Afraid of losing the weather gauge, he hauled into the wind in an effort to slow his approach and avoid passing to leeward of Decatur's ship. At 9 a.m. the 'United States' fired a broadside, but the shots fell short. Carden, still holding to windward, replied, but, approaching too close, received several shots through the hull and rigging. For two long hours, the duo hammered at each other—and again superior American gunnery, combined with the warship's heavier armament, began to take a toll on the Englishman.

The mizzenmast fell first, the tops of the others followed, and a hundred or more shots had already pierced the wooden hull of the 'Macedonian'. Too crippled to sail away, the English warship struck her colours, and Captain Carden duly offered his sword to the captors. Decatur, ever the gentleman, refused. '*Sir,*' he said, '*I cannot receive the sword of a man who so bravely defended his ship. But I will receive your hand.*' He had lost only 7 men in the action; Carden had lost 36. Captors and captured drank together that night. *'All idea that we had been trying to shoot out each other's brains so shortly before seemed forgotten . . . . a perfect union of ideas, feelings and purposes seemed to exist among all hands.'* Samuel Leech, one of the crewmen of the 'Macedonia', reported. Britain's battered frigate was taken as a prize into New York's harbour, the first captured warship to actually reach an American port. She was valued at $200,000, and this was distributed to the crew. The 'Macedonian' sailed thereafter under American colours and the command was given to Jacob Jones, recently exchanged for a British captive.

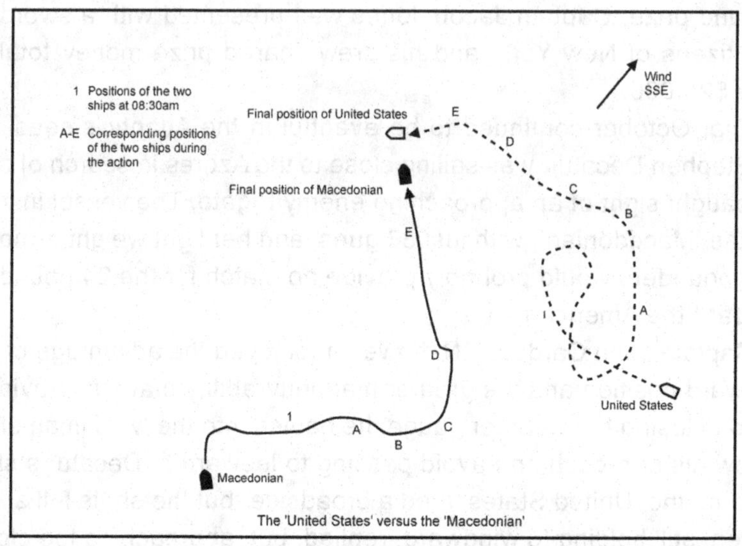

The 'United States' versus the 'Macedonian'

Before the year's end, the 'Constitution' had again reaped laurels, this time under the command of the capable William Bainbridge. Leaving Boston on 26th October with the sloop 'Hornet' as companion, he first cruised near the Cape Verde Islands and then headed west to take up station off Brazil on 13th December, watching, like a predatory insect, for any British sail, merchant or warship that might chance to venture into his extensive layer. On the 16th, the two vessels encountered the British sloop 'Bonne Citoyenne', a ship believed to be carrying £500,000 worth of specie. Leaving the 'Hornet' to deal with the sloop, Bainbridge sailed out to sea again and at midday on the 26th, he met His Majesty's frigate 'Java', carrying 38 guns, off Bahia. Feeling that it would be injudicious to fight within Portuguese waters, he sailed seaward for two hours, hoping, no doubt, that the Britisher would follow.

The resulting struggle turned out to be the most elaborate of the three great frigate actions. The 'Java', a superior sailor, quickly overhauled the American and at 2 p.m., the 'Constitution', fearing that the British ship would attempt to cross her bows, fired the first broadside of the action across the 'Java's bows. Both ships then wore away from the wind in tandem, less than half a mile apart, trading broadsides for half an hour and bringing down each other's rigging.

At 2.30, or thereabouts, a crippling British broadside carried away the wheel and the head of an unfortunate American sailor, and so gave the British ship an advantage, which she was quick to exploit. Passing astern, she raked the American ship throughout her length, bringing down the majority of those still on deck, but causing little hurt to masts or rigging. Bainbridge quickly regained control of his undamaged ship, and soon the two combatants were duelling again, each trying to snatch the weather gauge in a wind that comfortably filled the two vessels' sails.

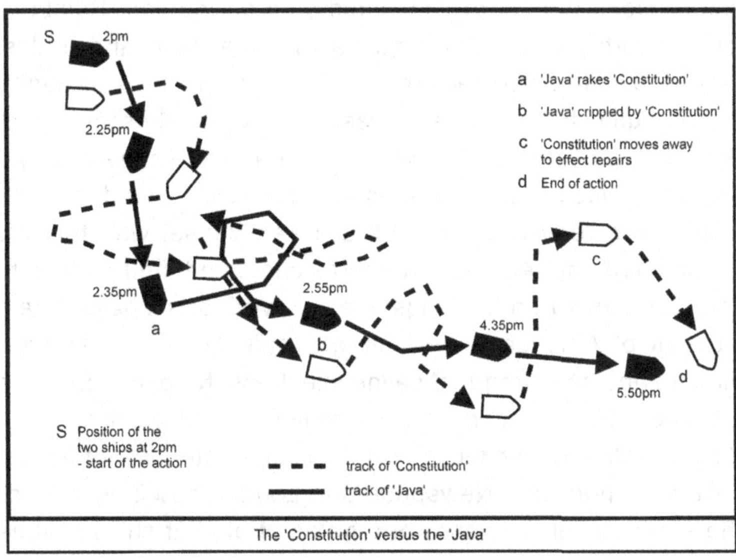

The 'Constitution' versus the 'Java'

Just before 3 p.m., the contest of near equals ended. For, at that moment, the jib boom and bowsprit of the 'Java' were shot away and the vessel lost her ability to wear and tack. The 'Constitution' now began to sail around her crippled opponent, alternating with port and starboard guns. The Englishman's fore and mainmasts were quickly felled, leaving Captain Henry Lambert, commander of the 'Java' to feel that boarding his enemy was his only remaining option.

In his clumsy efforts to close, however, the bowsprit stump became entangled with her adversary's mizzen rigging, obliging the 'Constitution' to break free. Further punishment from the hard hitting American now brought down the main topmast and worse still, Lambert fell mortally wounded. The 'Java' was now mastless, but, until 4.35, her guns continued to blaze. At that late afternoon hour, Bainbridge, confident that his enemy had no chance to escape, pulled away to repair some of the damage to his ship. An hour later, according to his log, he took up position across the 'Java's bows, planning to administer his final blow.

The 'Java', however, no longer had the will to resist and soon struck her colours. Her two most senior officers lay bleeding, and 150 of her crew were either dead or wounded. The engagement had lasted for three hours and had cost 14 American lives and 44 wounded, a higher effusion of blood than in any previous duel on the sea. Bainbridge's deliberate efforts to bring down the masts of the 'Java' and so destroy her abilities to manoeuvre had probably been the single most significant factor contributing to America's success. His 24 pounders, fired at close range into the stricken Englishman's hull, had sealed the victory.

The 'Java' was too badly damaged to be saved. The dying captain and crew were removed, and the stricken vessel was torched. A musket ball had entered poor Lambert's chest and the resulting bone splinters had punctured his lungs. He survived for six days, attended continuously by American surgeons, who pulled out the splinters with their fingers and gave frequent saline injections. No one in Britain held him in blame. Four American victories, coming in such quick succession, would suggest that British tactics or the physical inferiority of the British boats were responsible. Newspapers in London now began to claim that the American ships were not frigates at all, but ships-of-the-line in disguise.

America's little navy, fighting a series of single-ship actions, had severely blunted Britain's sharp naval pride. Since the start of war, the ships of the United States had captured or sunk British warships totaling 4330 tons in weight, and had taken 3108 men and 216 merchant ships. Britain's Admiralty, humbled by failure, increased her naval force off America—another 4 ships of the line, 5 sloops and 10 frigates. It was hoped that this would compensate for the perceived physical superiority of American-built hulls.

The war on the Lakes, restricted by the dimensions of these waters, was a microcosm of that fought on the open sea, but just as intense. At the outbreak of war, the Navy Department had placed 40 year old Captain Isaac Chauncy in command of the lakes flotillas. He had served in the nation's navy since 1799, and was an experienced man of oceans and tides, but had never been under fire.

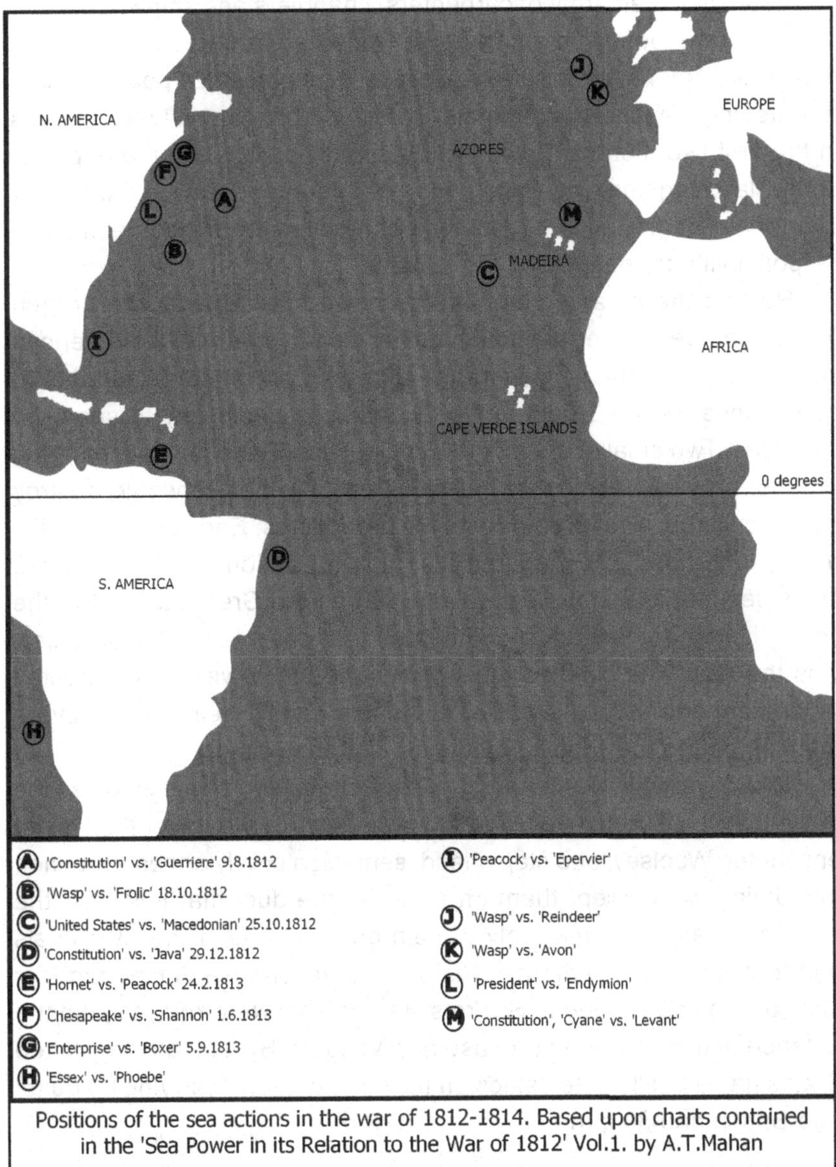

Positions of the sea actions in the war of 1812-1814. Based upon charts contained in the 'Sea Power in its Relation to the War of 1812' Vol.1. by A.T.Mahan

He quickly proved himself to be an able administrator. He installed a courier system, which could carry messages between New York and

Sackets Harbor, the navy base on Lake Ontario, in three days. And here, on the vulnerable eastern shore of the lake, by late September, he had established an army of carpenters, chandlers and shipwrights and a depot of weapons and ammunition From there prowled the 'Oneida', the largest American warship on the lake, its eighteen 24 pounder guns threatening the lake's commercial traffic and bringing in two fat prizes in the first two months of war. Thirty-six miles away, on the opposite shore, lay Kingston, the British base of operations, where the elderly Lieutenant Hugh Earle, in command of naval matters, had been given responsibility for destroying the 'Oneida'.

He had the means. Heading his powerful fleet was the 24 gun 'Royal George', powerful enough on her own to deal with the American ship. Supporting this ship were the 22 gun 'Earl of Moira' and the 16 gun 'Prince Regent', built in North America specifically to serve on the lakes. Two smaller ships, the 'Simcoe' and 'Seneca', both carrying 8 guns, provided additional muscle. Boasting that he would destroy Sackets Harbor and its ships with his broadsides, Earle positioned his quintet off shore and prepared his guns for action. On 29th July the two sides met in the earliest naval clash on the Great Lakes. But the young lieutenant in charge of the base that day, Melanthon Woolsey, was the man who claimed the victory. The place was well protected by artillery and this, in Woolsey's capable hands, delivered a severe mauling before the British could even find their range.

Two days later, Earle sought his revenge. Two of his ships sailed down the St. Lawrence to Ogdensburg to destroy whatever they might encounter. Woolsey, one step ahead, sent out a poorly armed schooner, the 'Julia', to intercept them on route. In the duel that followed, the tiny American boat, with only 3 main guns, outfought her two rivals and forced them to withdraw. His brilliant actions purchased time for Chauncy, newly arrived in Sackets Harbor from New York, to plan the defence of the lake and purchase new vessels. By late fall, the United States had a flotilla of ten ships on the lake, together carrying 63 guns. The British had 88 guns.

British ships (guns)	Armament details	American ships	Armament details
RoyalGeorge (22)	Inc.32pdr. carronade	Oneida (18)	18x 24 pdr
Earl of Moira (24)	18x9pdr, 4x6pdr	Julia (3)	1 x32 pdr, 2x 6pdr
Prince Regent (16)	16 x 9 pdr	Conquest (6)	2x 32 pdr, 4x 6pdr
Gloucester (10)	unspecified	Gov. Tomkins (5)	1x 32pdr, 4x 6 pdr
Seneca (8)	unspecified	Hamilton (1)	1x 32 pdr carronade

Simcoe (8)	unspecified	Fair American (5)	1x32 pdr, 4x 6 pdr
		Ontario (5)	1x 32 pdr, 4x 6 pdr
		Pert (2)	2x 24 pdr carronades
		Growler (8)	unspecified
		Scourge (6)	6x 6 pdr

The rival fleets on Lake Ontario in the autumn of 1812

In the weeks of shortening daylight which followed, America continued to mock Britain's feeble efforts. Two or three times, during November, Chauncy hovered off Kingston, looking for suitable targets to attack. Each time the 'Royal George' refrained from approaching and allowed him to continue his mischief unhindered. On 8th November Chauncy dealt the cheekiest blow of all. Spotting the enemy flagship without escorts, the 'Oneida', supported by the sloops 'Conquest', 'Julia', 'Pert' and 'Growler', forced her into Kingston and, on the 9th, bombarded the ship and harbour facilities until the onset of dusk.

The following day his ships returned again, hoping to complete the destruction of Britain's largest ship on the lake. But the wind was now unfavourable and prevented the American executioners from delivering their killing blows. Reluctantly Chauncy withdrew; unaware that the 'Royal George', far from being savaged almost to death, had only sustained light injuries to her rigging and topmast. It was to be the only occasion in the entire war when the U.S. navy actually entered the harbour of Kingston. Chauncy's vessels captured a further 4 vessels before the year's end—and not a single American ship was molested. Adapted for use as fighting ships, these four bolstered his strength and shifted the balance of advantage back in the young republic's favour. This would be further improved a fortnight later when a new corvette, the 'Madison' with twenty-four 32 pounder guns, was launched on the lake and made ready for immediate service.

Winter ice should have stopped all warfare on the lakes, leaving time for commanders to plan, scheme and anticipate the enemy's springtime moves. Chauncy retired to Buffalo to arrange the building of additional ships. Britain, too, took the opportunity to build. Three new ships were built in the shipyards of York and Kingston, all three to be ready by the time of the spring thaw.

Warfare on Lakes Huron and Erie did not assume such frantic proportions. America had virtually nothing to throw against the six powerful ships [6] that sailed Lake Erie, and America's officers had no delusions

6 Queen Charlotte (20 guns), Detroit (14 guns—the ex-American 'Adams'), Caledonian (8 guns), Hunter (10 guns), Prevost (14 guns) and Nancy (8 guns)

about their ability to resist. The easy capture of the 'Caledonia' in October gave the United States some additional naval muscle, but a string of British outposts on Erie's northern shore made the captured ship almost powerless. Lake Huron, from where the waters of the Detroit river tipped south into Erie remained a placid backwater, its surface hardly rippled by the movement of oar or sail in anger. During the winter, forest trees near the two lakes' edges were felled and, under the direction of Jesse Elliott, the man who had masterminded the expedition which had captured the 'Caledonia', two 20 gun brigs and three gunboats were constructed at Black Rock, within range of General Isaac Brock's guns on the opposite shore of the Niagara River. Eagerly eyeing the boats' construction, the redcoat frequently fired at the shipyards, but failed to prevent the boats' completion. When ready, the vessels were moved to a new base of operations at Presque Isle, well beyond the range of British guns.

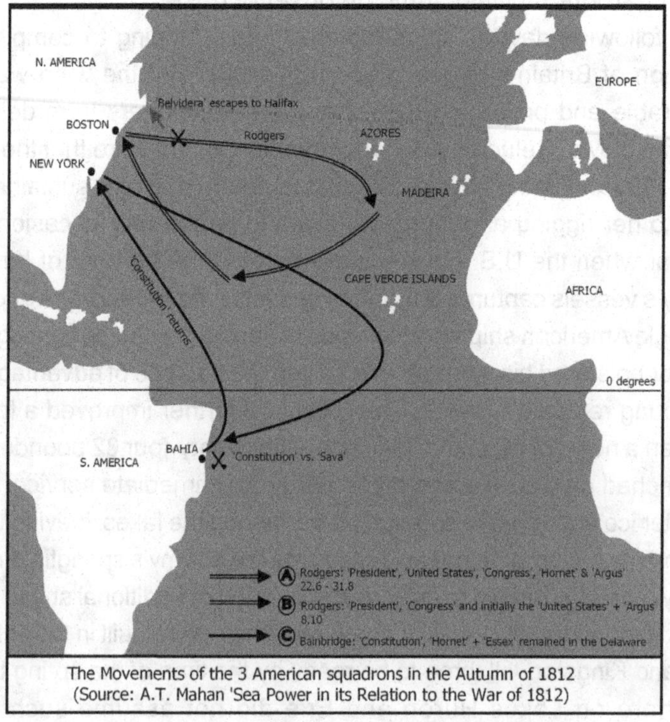

The Movements of the 3 American squadrons in the Autumn of 1812
(Source: A.T. Mahan 'Sea Power in its Relation to the War of 1812)

Finger shaped Lake Champlain, projecting deep into the territory of the Uninted States and flanked by a wilderness of dense forest and untamed countryside, was America's most vulnerable waterway. A flotilla of two gunboats and six supporting vessels, under the command of Lieutenant Thomas Macdonough supported Joseph Bloomfield's land based forces, deterring, for 1812 at least, any water-borne invasion of the United States. No betting man would have been wise to place much money on what might happen here.

CHAPTER 5

'They had the air of men to whom cleanliness was a virtue unknown'

The immediate future would hardly suggest any more promise either, despite these signal American successes at sea. Britain's distraction in Europe, the territorial ambition of Napoleon, was crumbling rapidly. Congressmen in Washington had received with dismay reports of the Emperor's retreat from Moscow and the British victories in Spain, and now realised that the time when Great Britain would be able to throw all her resources into the trans-Atlantic war was rapidly approaching.

The United States administration sought to re-energise her efforts on the Canadian front. This required a massive investment in personnel, a build-up of forces along the frontier and a hammer-blow across the frontier. Demographically America had a huge advantage, and the nation should have no trouble in finding the manpower needed for such positive action. But, of course, this is to ignore the logistical problems that beset the government in 1812. Men had been sent to the battlefield without adequate supplies of essential equipment. Politicians like Governor-elect Isaac Shelby of Kentucky and his predecessor, Charles Scott, had found no problem in attracting short-term volunteers, but each had exhausted himself trying to find the provisions and incentives to keep men in service. Charismatic men, the sort of person who could somehow circumvent such limitations, as well as rallying men by passionate appeal, were also in short supply. One possible man was fortunately emerging. William Henry Harrison, the putative hero of Tippecanoe, had been an officer in the army between 1791 and 1798 and, as already recorded, had been appointed governor of Indiana territory in 1801. In August 1812, after lobbying Washington, he had been commissioned as brigadier-general and had received instructions to co-operate with General Hull in Detroit.

But then came the surrender of the town, and the reverberations from that disaster would take time to subside. In the aftermath of the surrender, the Administration had appointed Brigadier-General James Winchester to succeed Hull in the command of the western army This man, a veteran of the Revolution, was sixty-one years old, in the same age bracket as most of the other high-ranking officers. Harrison, by contrast, was just forty-one when he accepted his commission. Two potential rivals stood untested in the west. Bitterly worded notes passed between the two men, each man parading his qualifications in front of the other. In the resulting locking of antlers, other men, politicians and generals, joined in. For, while Winchester had been chosen by Eustis to command the region's army, Harrison had the backing of Isaac Shelby and the leaders of Kentucky, all of whom contended that Harrison should be hoisted to the highest command. '*If you will carry your recollection back to the Age of the Crusades and of some of the most distinguished leaders of these expeditions, you will have a picture of the enthusiasm existing in this country for the expedition to Canada and for Harrison as the commander,'* Shelby wrote to Secretary of State Monroe in August. Then, to fortify his view, he appointed Harrison as a major-general of Kentucky militia and gave him the command of two regiments of infantry.

Henry Procter, in the aftermath of victory at Detroit, had grown restless. Convinced that the American commander, whoever that might be, would not make an attempt to recover Detroit until the Spring, he had taken possession of the American camp at Frenchtown on the north bank of the River Raisin and sent out reconnaissance parties as far as the Maumee. Then, largely to feed the Indians' taste for blood, he had either instructed, or merely allowed, Tecumseh and his warriors to strike out at the enemy's forts in the west. Fort Madison, near St. Louis, was visited on 4th September and Fort Harrison on the Wabash a day later. Both places withstood prolonged assault, the first during a three day attack and the latter, under the command of Zachary Taylor, holding out for thirteen days until a relief column under Colonel William Russell arrived on 16th September and scattered the besieging force.

Taylor, a future president of the nation, in command of a garrison of only 50 men, later received a commendation for holding out against a party of several hundred Indians.

Fort Wayne, held by James Rhea and 80 men, followed next. The appeal for assistance sent out by Rhea, when he anticipated an attack, allowed Harrison to become the hero of the hour. Hauling in a force of more than 2000 militiamen and an old cast iron 4 pounder gun at Cincinnati on 28th August, he set out for the Maumee, barely announcing his intentions to Winchester as he departed. From Cincinnati, he advanced through Dayton and Piqua. Here, standing on a wagon, he made an appeal to those who had accompanied him. '*If there is any man under my command who lacks the patriotism to rush to the rescue, he, by paying back the money received from the government, shall receive a discharge.*' Apparently, only one man chose to leave. He was given a ducking in the river by the soldiers for his decision.

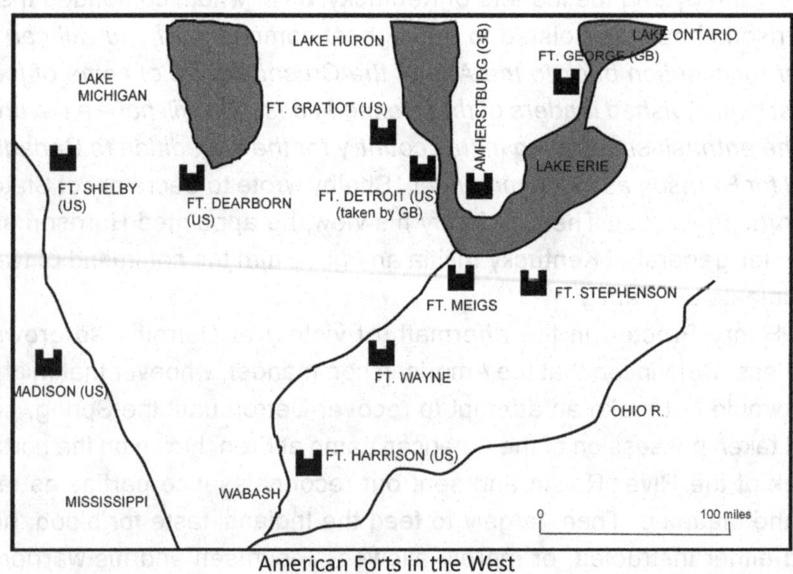

American Forts in the West

Harrison's force reached Fort Wayne on 12th September The fort had been under semi-siege by 600 Indians for 6 days. Tecumseh, working more for himself than his English allies, had disguised logs as guns in an attempt to persuade the defenders that he had a formidable battery at his disposal. Rhea, however, had stubbornly held out, sensing that the method of death meted out by the Indians after surrender would be less humane than any death incurred in battle. The Americans relieved the fort with hardly a shot fired in the process. Only one man was killed—in error by one of Rhea's sentinels. Tecumseh's Indians melted away far more rapidly than they had arrived.

Left—wing (Brigadier-General James Winchester):
Kentucky Militia Brigade (Brigadier-General John Payne): 1st, 4th, 5th Kentucky Regiments and 10th Kentucky Rifle Regiments
17th U.S. Infantry and a detachment of the 19th U.S.Infantry
Centre (Brigadier-General Edward Tupper):
Mounted militia of Kentucky and the Kentucky Mounted Regiment
Right-wing (Brigadier-General William Harrison):
Ohio Militia Regiment, the Virginia Brigade, Kentucky Dragoons, U.S. 2nd Light Dragoons, a detachment of the 19th U.S.Infantry, 2nd Pennsylvania Infantry Brigade and the Pittsburgh Blues Volunteers

The North-Western Army of the United States (Brigadier-General William Harrison)

Hide and seek warfare was the type of fighting that Harrison most enjoyed. In the days following, his columns moved in every direction, determined to crush all Indian resistance and to convert the frontier country into a wasteland which would deny the fugitives both food and shelter. Such a policy, however, was bound to be counter-productive, for it merely swept the fleeing Miami and Potawatomi into the camps of the British and instilled in the warriors a deep desire for revenge. In support of Harrison's purge, Brigadier-General Samuel Hopkins, a Kentucky man, headed west from Fort Harrison with 2000 volunteers towards the Kickapoo settlement on the Illinois River. His quarry, however, set the grassland on fire, and the riflemen, fearing hunger and fire more than they feared the Indians, retired. Ninian Edwards, Governor of the Territory of Illinois, adopted a similarly punitive stance towards the Indians. Swooping down on the settlements of the Peoria Lakes on the Illinois River, he destroyed every encampment in the area, claiming that the safety of the settlers in his charge justified such draconian action.

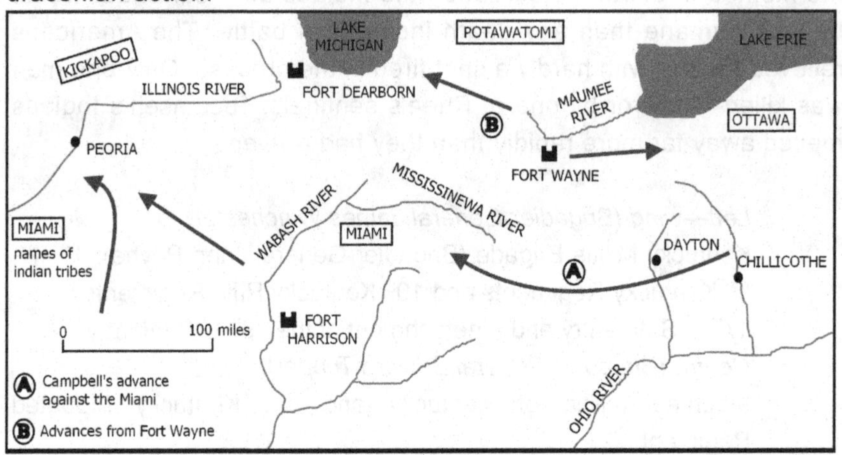

Punishing the Indians

Winchester, of course, was anxious to deny Harrison any of the glory. He consequently set out with 2500 of the regular infantry to take over responsibility on the Maumee. On 18th September he reached Fort Wayne at almost the moment that Procter, incensed by reports of Harrison's activities, had sent out Major Adam Muir with 600 British regulars and almost the same number of Indians on an undefined mission. Quite what Muir was expected to do is far from certain, but it is probable that Fort Wayne was his target. The British force sailed up the Maumee but, experiencing abnormally low water, the men disembarked at dilapidated Fort Defiance on the 23rd and continued their journey on foot towards Fort Wayne. On the 25th Muir's scouts discovered that Winchester's force was only two miles distant. Muir, aware that he was outnumbered by nearly 2 to 1, retreated, his men melting, Indian style, into the forest when the Americans approached. He reassembled in a strong defensive position on the far side of a ford on the Maumee and prayed that the Americans would try to cross the river at this point.

Wilkinson failed to oblige. Muir then chose to withdraw to Fort Defiance, took up another defensive posture and prayed again that his adversary would follow. But the American had secured his main objective, the Maumee frontier, and developed Fort Wayne as his frontier command post. Consequently he felt no need to advance any further. Muir, with nothing further to achieve, decided on withdrawal and headed back on his boats to Fort Amherstburg. He had spent three weeks on the Maumee and not seen a single American soldier.

The reasons for Winchester's reluctance to take action on the frontier were not entirely military in origin. The Kentuckians in his command refused to take orders from him. Worse still, the poor old soldier had become the butt of practical jokes. At one camp, a porcupine skin was placed on a pole over the latrine pit. The general suffered an indignity when he used the pit and fell in. His crime? Only his age, lack of vigour and a reluctance to socialise with the troops. Soon afterwards, Eustis bowed to pressure and raised Harrison to command of the army in place of Winchester. *Exercise your own discretion,'* Eustis wrote in his order to the Governor of Indiana, '*and act in all cases according to your own judgement.'* The newly elected officer recognised the burden that now lay on his shoulders. '*I am fully sensible of the responsibility invested in me. I accepted it with full confidence of being able to effect the wishes of the President, or to show unequivocally their impracticability,'* he wrote to Secretary Eustis on 13th October.

Governor Shelby of Kentucky now began to argue that the responsibility for the campaign should be shared between several men and should not depend upon the aptitude of just one man. Even after his favourite's appointment, he proposed that a Board of War, made up of '*respectable characters,*' should be appointed by the President to mastermind the campaign. This idea, however, found little favour, and probably did not even land on President Madison's desk. Harrison remained in sole charge, gambling his past glorious reputation for a future career where success was far from certain.

The annexation of Michigan territory by the British after the capture of Detroit was something of a blessing—for it reduced the length of frontier which Harrison needed to guard. Instead of the four hundred or so miles of water frontier along Lakes Michigan and Huron, he now had only to consider the two hundred mile front along the northern edges of Ohio and the adjacent territory of Indiana. Yet to guard even this limited frontier required most of the manpower at his disposal. Few troops, perhaps 4000 at most, would be available for any planned incursion into Canada—and most of these were of untested quality. Eustis, therefore, called upon the governors of the four nearest states to provide Harrison with an additional 10,000 men. 6500 men only had materialised by late October, half of them Pennsylvanian volunteers and none of them regulars. But such numbers would be rendered ineffective without weapons and provisions—and no-one, and certainly not Eustis, seemed willing to accept responsibility for feeding or equipping this disparate and inexperienced army.

The logistics of invasion were no easier to solve. Winter weather, the treacherous Black Swamp, poor roads and the uncertain movements of Tecumseh's Indians were imponderables which made detailed military planning difficult to implement. '*I am not able to fix any period for the advance of the troops to Detroit,*' Harrison wrote to Eustis on 22nd October. '*It is pretty evident that it cannot be done upon proper principle until the frost shall become so severe as to enable us to use the rivers and the margin of the lake for transportation of the baggage and artillery upon the ice.*' Yet soon afterwards he was writing to James Monroe, who had taken over the reins of the War Office following Eustis's sudden resignation, requesting that all offensive operations should be postponed until the spring!

Perhaps he had little appreciation of exactly how vulnerable the British felt at that moment. Colonel Henry Procter had only about 2000 British soldiers and Indians at Amherstburg and Detroit, but almost no units to protect recently annexed Michigan. But, while protection of this territory caused Proctor considerable concern, news of the territory's capture had caused delight in London. '*This news is a great relief to me,*' Lord Liverpool wrote to the Duke of Wellington. '*After the strong representation which I had received of the inadequacy of the force in those American settlements, I know not how I should have withstood the attack against me for having sent reinforcements to Spain instead of sending them for the defence of British possessions.*'

Harrison himself seems personally to have told Winchester of his displacement at the top. General Winchester briefly considered resigning, but he accepted his downgrading in good grace and agreed to serve as deputy. Harrison, to placate the ageing warrior, gave him command of the army's left flank and named a new fort being built nearby in his honour. And, to the demoralised troops who had made their camp in the ruins of crumbling Fort Defiance, Harrison spoke firmly but reassuringly: '*Harrison, with a look, can awe and convince—where some would be refractory. All are afraid and unwilling to meet his censure.*'

General Harrison's instructions from Washington were almost identical to those issued to Hull, Rennselaer and Smyth, all failed men. He was, first, to reclaim Detroit for the United States and then penetrate Canada '*as far as the force under your command will, in your judgement, justify.*' His plans were soon unwrapped. It required the concerted movements of three columns, each with a distinct task and with a need for effective communications. The most westerly column, commanded by Winchester was instructed to complete construction of Fort Winchester and then advance down the Maumee River to rendezvous with the other two at the river's rapids.

The centre column, 1200 men, formed at Urbana under the command of Brigadier-General Edward Tupper, was given the task of protecting the roadway built by Hull. The most easterly column, under General Simon Perkins and Harrison, built from Virginia and Pennsylvania volunteers, was to move up from Wooster in Ohio, take up position at Upper Sandusky and await further instructions.

Harrison, reviewing the situation at the end of October, seemed satisfied with all these arrangements. He felt at last that he had the resources to protect the frontier and launch the invasion of Canada that Washington demanded. His quartermaster, William Morrison, however, did not agree. He argued that the number of administrative staff and costs were excessive, and the arrangements for the procurement of provisions were unreliable. And some of the individuals contracted to supply these provisions preferred profit to patriotism and charged prices that were extortionately high. And just as frustrating was Winchester's near refusal to move without first obtaining everything that he needed.

The hero general now began to vacillate, torn between a winter campaign or a delay until the Spring, when the weather might be more favourable. Arguments with suppliers, political considerations and a failure to clear away the Indian threat on his left flank finally persuaded him to postpone his efforts and concentrate instead on neutralizing the tribes and removing the misgivings of men like Morrison. It would be better, he asserted, to first win dominance on Lake Erie, control of which would oblige the British to give up Detroit and their other posts in the west. Monroe ratified Harrison's decision, and the west of the international frontier began to quieten down for the winter. Winchester's column, having come no further than the edge of the Black Swamp and the Maumee, put down its roots, slowly sliding into a winter lethargy and way of life in which even basic hygiene would be neglected. Within weeks, lack of provisions as well as poor hygiene would bring misery to the troops. Many soldiers still wore their summer clothes; medicines were in short supply and sanitation almost non-existent. '*They had the air of men to whom cleanliness was a virtue unknown . . . their clothes . . . had undergone every change of season,'* an officer reported in disgust.

Morale plummeted with the temperatures, the snow kept falling and no pay arrived. Men were discharged, many died, other deserted, and indiscipline, as well as fever, stalked the camp. Flour supplies failed to arrive, and men tried to survive on salted beef and boiled hickory roots.

Winchester, visiting his soldiers, responded with both gentleness and hard-faced discipline. A sentry, sleeping on duty, was sentenced to be shot. Blindfolded, the young man was forced to kneel. Then, at the moment the execution party raised their muskets, a reprieve was called. The general shared the same touches of compassion that all men experience. Lesser punishments, however, were meted out. 'Riding the wooden horse' was a favourite. The offender, usually naked, sat astride a bent sappling, and was then subjected to joltings. Painful for the victim, it was a source of great amusement to the spectators, and, because it entertained bored and frustrated men, punishments like this became frequent. Harrison, in whose camp conditions became just as bad, preferred to encourage rather than punish. He habitually sat with his troops in the mud beside flimsy fires and ate the same meager rations. He laughed at their jokes and entertained them with stories of his own. Other officers, less charismatic or inspirational, would disapprove of his demagogic ways and would insist on maintaining a touch of luxury in their winter tents. But, like him, they would mendaciously assure their men that blankets, food and supplies were on their way.

Hostile Indians lay on Winchester's flank. The desire to remove the threat drained away the energies that might have made campaigning against the British more effective. Samuel Hopkins, nettled by his earlier failure, soon tried again. Collecting three Kentucky militia regiments, a company of regulars and some rangers, more than 1200 men, he set out from Fort Harrison on 11th November and wiped out the viperous village of Prophetstown and a larger settlement of the Kickapoos.

Colonel John Campbell's assault on the Miamis and Potawatomies in Indiana, culminating in the so-called 'Battle of Mississinewa, was less one-sided. William Henry Harrison felt able to justify giving permission to Campbell on the grounds that these tribes were in a strong position to intercept the movement of supplies to his new depot on the Maumee River. Campbell was certainly given the means to achieve his mission: a regiment of Kentucky dragoons, a company of the 19th U.S. regulars, the Pittsburgh 'Blues', a squadron of the U.S. 2nd Dragoons and a company of Pennsylvanian riflemen, 600 men in all. The force left Franklinton (now Columbus) on 25th November and marched through Springfield, Xenia and Dayton to Fort Greenville. Bitterly cold when they left, it became still colder, clear skies at night with only a teasing touch of comforting sun by day. On 14th December the column marched out of Fort Greenville. Each man carried twelve days' rations. The cold became even more intense. '*A great many of the boys got frost bitten, by getting off their horses and walking, in order to warm themselves. The fatigue of walking would put them in a perspiration and, mounting again, would chill off, and frost bite in a very little time,'* one of the survivors later recollected. Numbed and exhausted, the men reached the first of the villages at 4 a.m. on the 17th, and were immediately ordered into battle positions for an early assault on the sleeping inhabitants. Not all were asleep, however, and the white man's intentions were discovered. The alarm was promptly given, and the furious dragoons instantly charged. '*What few warriors there were in the town made their escape, leaving the old and feeble, with the women and children to fall into our hands,'* the same eye witness source reports. Campbell nervously made an encampment for the night, knowing that at least 500 warriors were encamped at Mississinewa, just twenty miles downstream. His frost bitten men lay down to rest, trying to interpret the wild sounds of the night and what they might signify.

At 4.a.m. the lieutenant-colonel felt that he could no longer afford to let his men continue their fitful sleep and so ordered reveille. They were alerted only just in time. The south-west corner, were the 19th U.S. regiment were defending, was soon under attack. The Indians had the cover of woods and darkness, and the position was quickly breached. The light Dragoons fell back, but the line was stabilized by the Pittsburgh 'Blues'. Effective American firing gradually forced the attackers back and the Indians dispersed. The whole fight had lasted about one hour. Ten men had been killed, 48 wounded and over 300 had been incapacitated by frostbite and gangrene.

The retreat to Greenville took seven days. Men hobbled, slid and swore, their passage made a little easier by iced rivers and bright moonlight that made night almost as light as day. The Mississinewa expedition had not been a success. The troops had stopped twenty miles short of their intended target and the alleged threat to Harrison's flank remained.

Christmas revealed Harrison's army to be in a desperate plight. Winchester's left wing was glued to the junction of the Maumee and the Au Glaze, starved of supplies. Elias Darnell, one of the victims, wrote in his journal that '*obstacles had emerged in the path to victory, which must have appeared insurmountable to every person endowed with common sense. The distance to Canada, the unpreparedness of the army, the scarcity of provisions, and the badness of the weather, show that Malden cannot be taken in the remaining part of our time . . . . Our sufferings at this place have been greater than if we had been in a severe battle.*'

The politicians of Washington, for their own reasons, suddenly forced an end to Harrison's inactivity and pressured Harrison into action in the snow. On Christmas Day, perhaps irritated by criticism, Harrison ordered Winchester to move forward to the Rapids of the Maumee as soon as provisions were delivered. Two days later, flour, salt and winter clothing arrived, and Winchester's 1300 men were suddenly in motion. The force that moved out, however, hardly provoked the image of an army in expectation of victory. It appeared more like a throng of displaced refugees, faced bowed, but nevertheless glad to be abandoning the hell that their insanitary camp had become. Few had winter protection, most were ragged and their hair knotted and uncombed. Horse drawn sleds conveyed the provisions and supplies, one sled to each company of men. The winter landscape ahead, however, was not one of seasonal promise or comfort, and the men expected to soon become mired in the mud and misery of yet another awful camp. For three days they slouched forward, camping at night in knee-deep snow and kindling fires from soaking wood that refused to burn.

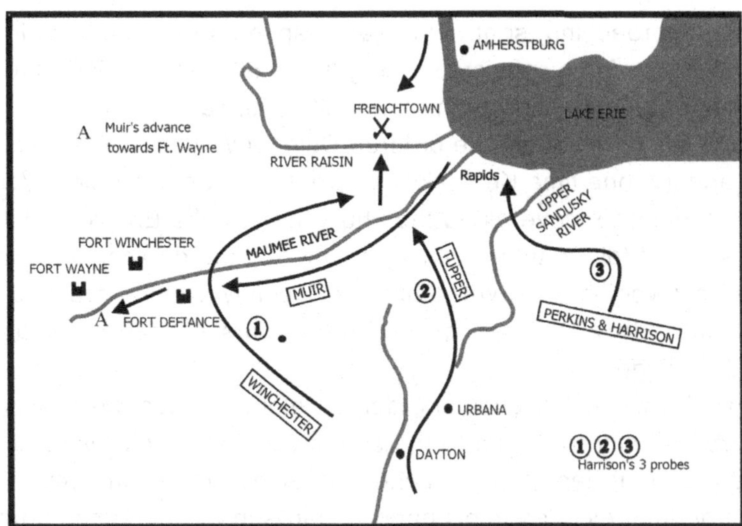

The Winter campaign on the Erie frontier

Then, on 1st January 1813 an order arrived from Harrison to turn back. The general had received reports of a growing Indian presence in the area and felt it unwise to proceed. Winchester chose to ignore the command. A wish to shine in the eyes of the nation, while Harrison wallowed in the shadows, must have motivated this insubordination. And so he continued towards the Maumee Rapids, little knowing what Fate might hand him there.

Procter was watching his enemy's movements like a hawk—and reacted as quickly as the bird. Two supporting strategies unveiled themselves, both of which would minimise the casualty rate amongst his forces. First he sent out Major Ebenezer Reynolds and two companies of the Essex County Militia to support a Potawatomi visit to Frenchtown, the tiny settlement which some of the British had occupied during the autumn. Secondly, in an effort to halt the sleds, hooves and feet of Winchester's slowly advancing troops, he embarked on a scorched earth policy, destroying any food and shelter that lay along the path of advance.

Reynolds' orders were simple but inhumane—to destroy the village and eject the settlers, mainly Frenchmen, who, Procter suspected, would be likely to assist the Americans. The settlers, seeing Reynolds and his men approaching, sent out a frantic appeal to Harrison, claiming that the British force consisted of only about 50 men and 100 Indians. Winchester, again acting on his own initiative, saw this as promising territory. On 13th January, he ordered Colonel William Lewis and 400 men, and the one time Kentucky gubernatorial candidate John Allen, with 150 men, to move along the shoreline of Lake Erie and restore the displaced folk to their homes. On the 18th the detachment, warm in the new woolen underwear that had recently arrived, reached the Raisin and, after a fight lasting two or three hours, ejected the intruders from the village.

Two days later, Winchester ordered Colonel Samuel Wells and the 17th U.S. Infantry to march to the support of Lewis and Allen. At the moment of their departure, Winchester decided to accompany them. He set out that evening in his cariole. Harrison, at his camp 65 miles away, received reports of Winchester's unauthorised move and quickly boiled with anger. The advance to Frenchtown was, he maintained, '*opposed to a principle by which I have ever been governed in Indian warfare i.e. never to make a detachment but under the most urgent circumstances.*' He, too, decided to visit Frenchtown and set out in a sleigh. Two generals, rivals in theory and in practice, were riding to the same spot in vehicles suitable for the season.

On the night of the 20th, the American force at Frenchtown numbered about 1000. Frenchtown was paradise and the soldiers dined well that night. Apple orchards surrounded the village, and, in the barns were barrels of cider as well as supplies of sugar, whiskey and fresh vegetables. By the time that Winchester arrived, men were already drunk and quarrelsome. Soldiering and the instinct for security and self-preservation were forgotten, even by the general. No entrenchments were dug and no pickets or patrols were sent out to watch for movements of the British. North and west of the village was a wooden fence, palisaded in parts, offering protection from the wind and rain but providing only a scant shield against attack. The exposed eastern flank was held by the regulars of the 17th Infantry, who slept and dined with no protection at all. Winchester chose for himself a pleasant cottage on the opposite side of the river and dismissed every suggestion that his subordinates put forward to improve the defensive capabilties of this forward position. The general, a wealthy plantation owner for over twenty years, had missed the luxuries to which he was accustomed. Accommodated in a spacious room at the front of the house, he would allow himself to dream that those comfortable times had returned.

Procter, by contrast, would never allow himself to dream of times gone by. Leaving a detachment of militia to hold the valued points at Detroit and Amherstburg, he called into active service every able-bodied man—sailor, regular, volunteer or militia member, and ordered them to be ready to cross the Erie River as soon as he snapped a command. 600 men were soon assembled, many with no military training at all, but all with muskets in their hands and with a willingness to shoot. In addition, nearly 600 Miami, Potawatomi and Wyandot hurried in, seizing the God-given opportunity of extracting vengeance for Harrison's recent harassment of the tribes.

John Richardson, the future author and then just 15 years old, converts the dark shades of war into rugged colour in his description of the crossing of the frozen Erie from Amherstburg to Brownstown on the 19th: *'It was the depth of winter, and the river we crossed being four miles in breadth, the deep rumbling noise of the guns prolonging their reverberations like the roar of distant thunder, as they moved along the ice, mingled with the wild cries of the Indians, seemed to threaten some convulsion of nature, while the appearance of the troops winding along the road, ... their polished arms glittering in the sun beams, gave an air of romantic grandeur to the scene.'*

From Brownstown, Procter moved to Stony Creek, four miles short of the River Raisin, and prepared. He enjoyed every advantage that nature could bestow at that time—soft snow to dull the sounds of his approach, frozen ground over which to travel, and the possibility of launching a surprise attack while the Americans were still wrapped in their blankets. He chose, unfortunately, to adopt the conventional tactics for attack, drawing up his men in 3 divisions, with artillery and regulars in the centre, the set-piece layout for European land battles. Too cautious by far, he spent ages inspecting the sites for his guns, and was spotted by a Kentucky sentinel. A soldier of the British 41st regiment fell, shot through the head by the vigilant American. The bullet passed through one ear and out at the other. Those moments of delay had lost Proctor one of the most precious commodities that can be enjoyed by any commander—the advantage of surprise.

It was still dark. The Canadians, advancing from the north in line, could just make out the outlines of shapes beyond and fired their first volley at this target. But the indistinct line held firm. When dawn's light broke, the immovable line turned out to be the fence posts behind which the defenders, shaken from their sleep, were waiting.

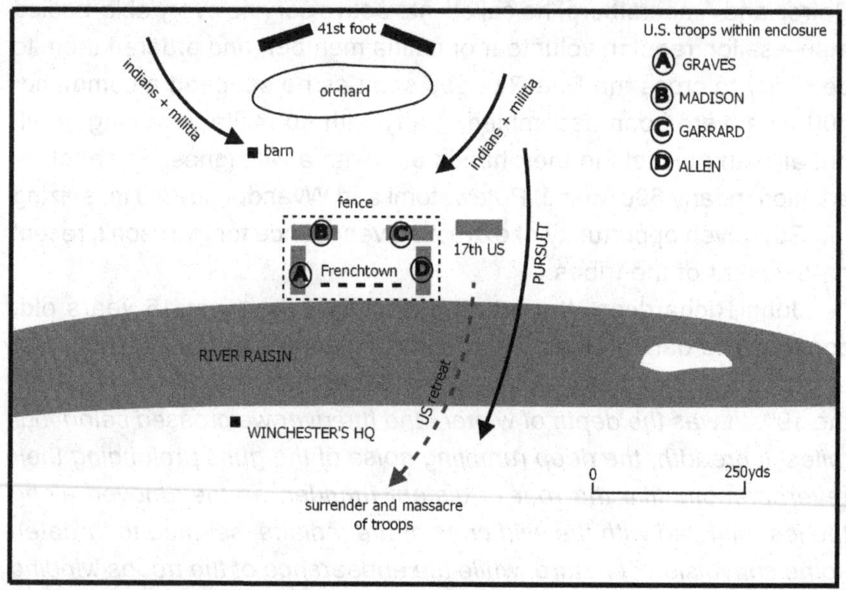

The Battle of Frenchtown

The Battle of Frenchtown continued in the conventional manner in which it had been started—apart from the irregular movements of the Indians placed on both Canadian flanks. The irregulars, crouching behind the wooden fencing north of the village, had some protection, but the men of the 17th U.S. regiment, exposed beyond the fencing on the right of the American line, were savaged by the militia and Indians on this flank, the latter under the petulant Chief Roundhead, and half the regiment were soon in need of graves. Those that survived the onslaught fell back to the Raisin; the entire American right was on the point of disintegrating. Lewis and Allen, commanding in the centre, rushed over with two companies of militia to stabilise the position, but Allen was scalped in the carnage that followed. Shot in the thigh and, unable to stem the retreat, he had limped painfully towards the river. Unable to go any further, he had sat on a log to await his fate.

Winchester, having risen from his bed when the attack started, was taken prisoner. Stripped of his cocked hat, coat and epaulette, he was found to be wearing nothing but his silk night shirt.

The battle still raged. Major George Madison, commanding the troops inside the palisade, was concerned that the attackers might seize a barn just yards beyond the perimeter fencing. William O'Brien volunteered to set it alight. Vaulting over the fence, he threw a flaming torch into the hay and ran back. His was a charmed life. In later life, he would stand as a candidate for the governorship of Kentucky.

Madison's spirited resistance might still have snatched victory for the Americans, despite the collapse of the right flank. The British guns had almost run out of ammunition and the gunners' hands were numbed by cold. Procter, sensing that the defence was too strong, was on the point of pulling his troops back when Winchester issued an order to surrender. Madison was mortified by this and refused to capitulate. '*It has been customary for the Indians to massacre the wounded and prisoners after a surrender. I shall therefore not agree to any capitulation which General Winchester may direct, unless the safety and protection of all the prisoners shall be stipulated. We prefer to sell our lives as dearly as possible rather than be massacred in cold blood,*' he replied in a message to Procter. The British general then agreed to guarantee the safety of all those who lay down their weapons.

About 200 Americans had been killed or wounded; another 700 were taken prisoner, amongst whom were Winchester and Lewis. Only 33 found their way back to the Maumee Rapids. One ingeniously pulled off his boots and ran through the snow in stockinged feet in order to leave tracks that resembled moccasins. Procter withdrew to Brownstown. He had lost about 180 men and felt that he had too few men to advance towards the Maumee while simultaneously guarding his haul of captives. He left only a veneer of forces to guard the American wounded. An American officer, asking for medical supplies with which to treat the wounded, was told that '*the Indians are excellent doctors.*'

And that was exactly what they soon proved to be. That night the Wyandots in Proctor's force returned to Frenchtown and smashed open the doors of the small shacks where 27 of the day's wounded lay. Those that were fit enough to walk were taken away for ransom; the less fortunate were dragged outside and despatched with a single tomahawk blow. One, hoping to purchase his life, offered his boots to the would-be executioner. The Indian accepted the bribe, put on the soldier's boots and sunk a tomahawk in the man's skull.

The victims of the night's atrocity remained where they had fallen, trapped in their last moments of agony and with their skulls disfigured. They had been sons, brothers and fathers, all unique during their lives, but had shared the same gruesome fate. Days after the battle, the village's inhabitants witnessed the ghastliest spectacle possible. Hogs, having fed on the remains, passed through the village with bits of human torso hanging from their mouths. Harrison, delayed at Uppér Sandusky until after the battle ended, never saw the passionless eyes of the American dead or the blood drenched victims of the Indian tomahawks. Sending only a small detachment into the village to search for survivors, he turned back, ordering all his detachments to withdraw south of the Portage River. For the time being, he abandoned all thoughts of an advance upon Detroit. The retreat, however, did his image no harm. He had proved to be a man of action, and Winchester's folly was not placed on his shoulders. And it gave America a new rallying cry; '*Remember the Raisin,*' the massacre at Frenchtown had somehow to be avenged.

From his prison in Fort Malden, General Winchester wrote to the Secretary of War to exonerate himself. '*However unfortunate may seem the affair of yesterday, I am flattered by a belief that no material error is chargeable upon myself, and that still less censure is deserved by the troops I had the honor of commanding.*' Opinion split on where to pass the blame; some chose to censor Harrison for allowing his subordinate a free hand.

America, particularly Harrison, learned from the mistakes that Winchester had just made, even if Winchester himself felt no shame. To Harrison, maintenance of the Maumee River line was vital and, for this, a position closer to Amherstburg seemed essential. He consequently moved his headquarters to a point just below the Maumee Rapids and began the construction of a new defensive point to be called Fort Meigs.

This would involve the labour of most of his men for the remaining weeks of winter. He felt able, however, to detach a number to raid the naval base at Amherstburg where, he had been informed, the

Canadians had just laid the keel of a new warship. The American party planned to move across the ice of Lake Erie and hit the infant ship from offshore. When the troops reached the lake's shores, however, they saw moving water and so abandoned the mission. This January raid achieved nothing, cost nothing, and only served to remind the men in the Canadian fort that the war still showed signs of life, even in the midst of a North American winter.

The opportunity of avenging the slaughter at the Raisin would not be likely to present itself for some time. Harrison's army in February shrank from more than 6000 to only 2000 when most of his short-term enlistments melted away with the thawing snow. Many of those remaining were due to return to their homes in April, so depriving Harrison of any real chance of a forward movement. Instead, he employed his men in building up the defences at the rapids on the Maumee and watching the border for movements of the enemy. Just before the first green shoots pushed their way through the thawing ground, General John Armstrong, who had served as his country's minister in France, replaced Monroe as Secretary of War. From the start, he seemed to show little confidence in Harrison's ability to deliver victory. In March the new Secretary ordered the general to abandon any thoughts of campaigning until the navy had gained full control of the waters of Lake Erie.

Harrison clearly felt that this was an affront on his self-esteem. Worse still, his promotion to a major-generalship failed to come through, leaving some of those he commanded superior in rank to him. In frustration, he wrote in March to Armstrong, offering his resignation. '*. . . . if I have manifested either neglect or incapacity, a fair opportunity for another selection is offered by the tender of my commission as a brigadier . . . In this event I should retire from the Regular Service. But so deeply impressed on my mind are the injuries which our country has received, from the nation with which we are at war . . . . that I am determined to continue to serve if I can get a regiment or even a company of volunteers to follow me.*'

Washington's response ruffled his feathers still further. In an act of reorganization, the Department created the Eighth Military District, consisting of the states and territories over which he held command. Although leaving him in overall authority, the action, political more than military, placed much of the responsibility in the laps of Washington's officials, and so did nothing to sharpen the decision making process in the field.

Days later, Harrison received word from Armstrong that the government intended to limit the amount paid out for the employment of militia units. Henceforth Harrison would have to rely upon the services of seven regiments of regulars, 7000 men in total when fully recruited. The general, of course, was indignant and argued that the defence of depots and supply lines required many more troops. He disregarded the Minister's orders, appealed to the state governors to supply him with fresh units and then took brief leave to visit his family in Cincinnati. The officer he left in charge to supervise the building of the fort was incompetent and lax; construction of Fort Meigs almost halted. The period of service of the men involved was about to end. Caring little about the future of the fort or the wellbeing of those who would be left behind to garrison it, they took on a holiday-like mood and played cards instead. With their departure, only 500 men remained in the still incomplete fort.

Procter had been watching the slow progress. The Indians on his payroll had also been watching. The general had promised them all the lands north of the Ohio River—and the time for redeeming that promise, they believed, had come. To Procter, holding newly-won Michigan was worth the shedding of a little more blood. A strike at the fort before its wooden walls were completed became his late-winter priority—and every sinew was directed towards developing a force strong enough to sweep away America's flimsy presence on the Maumee. But putting together a force for the purpose took longer than he had hoped. By the time he had the men required, a nine acre potato shaped fort with four large batteries had emerged on the Maumee, and the chance for an easy reduction had passed.

The weather, never inclined to ally permanently with either side, unfortunately had done very little to assist Procter. The spring of 1813 was unusually wet. The British troops were forced to entertain themselves for weeks in raid sodden tents and barrack blocks, barely motivated by the pay they received, and certainly seeing little reason for fighting a war against an enemy who had made few threats. By 1st April 1813 Procter had the 520 regulars of the overworked 41st Foot, about 450 militiamen, mainly the corps of the Select Embodied Militia,

1500 Indians and two supporting gunboats. The bad weather, probably aided by a touch of ineptitude, delayed the army's embarkation at Amherstburg until 23rd April. By this time, Harrison's defending force at Meigs had swollen to more than 1100, brought up to strength by patriotic appeals to the governors of the adjacent states.

Canada's troops disembarked at the mouth of the Maumee on the 26th. From here they dragged themselves westward along a mud-defined river path that would eventually lead them to Fort Meigs. Wagons and cannon, some of them captured at Detroit, sunk to their axles or tipped on their sides. Men, knee deep in mud, strained to pull them out. Only the iron cage of discipline kept the ranks together and carried them forward. The two gunboats, each carrying a single 9 pounder gun, kept abreast of the slow movement, reluctant to outpace the advance and face American firepower on their own. On the 28th the mud-caked troops set up camp near deserted Fort Miami and began the construction of two gun emplacements, each holding 5 guns, opposite Fort Meigs. And meanwhile, Harrison, alerted by a messenger, was racing back from his family home in Cincinnati to supervise the defence.

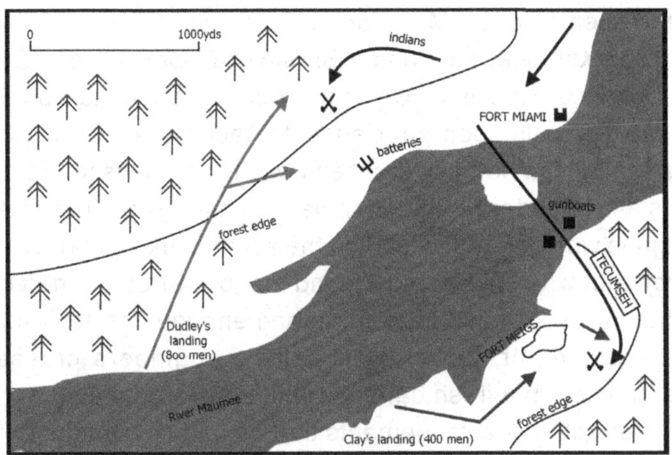

The Attack on Fort Meigs

On 1st May, in heavy rain, Procter's batteries on the north bank began a bombardment of the fort while a detachment of troops and Indians under Tecumseh's leadership crossed the river to attack the fort from the rear.For four days, the bombardment was ceaseless. It was supported by small arms fire from the detachment to the south, whose sharpshooters picked on any unfortunate who rashly exposed head or limbs on the fort's upper parapets. Abel Richards had his flute shot from his hand. He had been carefully putting it away in his bag after giving an evening recital.

Captain Eleazer Wood, taking over from his lethargic predecessor in March and commanding at the fort on the day of attack, had shielded the works in the north with a stout mound of dirt, and most of Procter's raining shot bored harmlessly into the soft earth. He had also constructed a traverse and works around the landward side of the fort, providing some additional protection against any frontal assault from the south. Two more British batteries were installed on the north bank and, for a couple of days, the quartet continued to spew out an ineffective punishment. Because ammunition was scarce, Harrison, who had arrived just as the bombardment started, offered the men a gill of whisky for each solid shot recovered. In very little time, one thousand rounds had been collected, and these were sparingly fired back towards the British positions. An unfortunate pig, scavenging in the woodland, had its tail shot off; the distressed animal's squeaks were apparently heard on the river's north bank.

On the evening of 2nd May Harrison received a report that a relief force of 1200 Kentucky men under Brigadier-General Green Clay had left Fort Defiance, 30 miles away to the west, by boat and would arrive outside Meig's walls soon after sunset. Harrison sent a messenger hurrying through the hours of darkness with instructions to Clay to land one of his two brigades on the north bank to engage the batteries. The other brigade was ordered to land on the south bank and break through the cordon that was developing around the fort. Strengthened by their arrival, the garrison would then sortie and engage Procter's forces.

That same night, however, Procter's engineers crossed the Maumee and set up a fresh battery within 250 yards of the rear of the fort. Satisfied with the arrangements that he had now made, but sadly unaware of Clay's approach, the British general sent out a demand for surrender on the 4th, backing it up with dire warnings about the consequences of a refusal. Harrison, of course, rejected the invitation and tersely suggested that the British would gain far more glory if they took the fort by assault.

Colonel William Dudley, commander of the brigade which had been given the task of silencing the north bank guns, was a self-opinionated man with little sense of caution. Obedient to his orders, he landed his 800 men and had little trouble taking the guns. But, instead of crossing to the fort as he had been instructed, he allowed his men to set off in pursuit of the fleeing gunners and the small party of supporting Indians. His rashness brought on a quite unnecessary disaster. Procter reacted with quicksilver speed to the sudden appearance of new players on his flanks. Calling back Tecumseh's Indians from the south shore, he also despatched Major Adam Muir with the Newfoundland regiment and a detachment of the 41st to regain the guns and halt Dudley's advance.

Muir and Tecumseh fell on Dudley's deeply fragmented force in thick woodland. Without the cohesion necessary for survival, the Americans were slaughtered where they stood, some barely having time to raise their weapons in retaliation. Eighty men were killed, amongst them Dudley, and 300 severely wounded in the ambush, a greater casualty rate than that experienced at the Raisin. Only about 150 of the 800 who had landed so confidently on the Maumee's north bank escaped the crushing blow of tomahawks and returned to their boats. Tecumseh's Indians again washed themselves in white men's blood in a massacre after the battle that was as merciless as the earlier incident on the River Raisin.

Clay's brigade on the southern bank fortunately fared better. Playing to an appreciative audience in the fort, the 400 men overran the newly established battery and scattered the small group of infantry and Indians left here after Tecumseh's recall. Formed into two parties and assisted by gunfire from the fort, the rescuers fought their way through to the fort, receiving a cheer of approval from the soldiers inside. 50 men were killed or were maimed in this struggle in the clearing. A white flag was hoisted from the fort's pole at the end of that day of the double skirmish. But General Harrison was purchasing time, not selling his men, and he had no intention of agreeing to terms. For the next two days, the guns remained silent. Piecemeal negotiations, never serious in purpose, took place, largely for the release of prisoners and the repatriation of the wounded.

On the 7th Procter announced his intention of renewing his attack on Fort Meigs. But the unnecessary scalping in cold blood of prisoners sickened Procter and his officers and had led them to question the morality of relying upon such bloodthirsty allies. Other, more compelling reasons, however, crowded the general's thoughts and induced him to call back his men and guns.

His militia men, most of whom were farming folk, wished to return to their farms to attend to their crops, the neglect of which could create a severe shortage of food in the coming summer. And even the Indians seemed satisfied with the harvest of scalps they had collected and were anxious to return to their homes to boast of their successes. With some reluctance, therefore, the redcoat general pulled back from the fort and retired to Fort Amherstburg. He had lost 15 men dead and 47 wounded, far fewer than the Americans, but he had only a loss of face to show for all his efforts.

Employment of Indian mercenaries would be an issue haunting every British general. Tecumseh, to do him justice, had never condoned the taking of scalps, and it is unlikely that any of the scalp removals took place when he was present. But Indians went to war, not out of sympathy for the white man's cause, but because that is what warriors were expected to do. Trophies were proof of manliness in battle, a vital attribute for any warrior who wished to find a squaw. Tecumseh's warriors would just as willingly have removed the scalps of the British. Preservation of homelands was, of course, a major factor in helping the tribes to decide which side to support. But, with both sides promising to respect those ancient territorial rights, the choice of which side to support depended largely upon who would pay most and offer most in material rewards. Britain, in winning the support of Indian tomahawks, had let a potentially unmanageable genie out of the bottle and would find herself without the means of forcing it back.

General William Harrison must now have felt that the cross he carried was becoming too heavy to bear. In the aftermath of Procter's withdrawal, he was confronted by the resentments of the men of Ohio. 3000 men from the state had voluntarily enlisted to serve under his command. But the general, believing that the maintenance of large forces on the Maumee was no longer necessary, and perhaps recalling Armstrong's injunction to minimize the use of militia, instructed them to disband, offering few words of gratitude in the process. Ohio's sons regarded this as a snub. Kentucky men, fighting at Frenchtown, had just saved Ohio from invasion, a fact which caused humiliation in every farm and village in the state. Seen from their viewpoint, it appeared that Harrison had actively welcomed the assistance of the Kentuckians, but had chosen to rebuff similar offers of help from Ohio.

His enemy was also afflicted by personal rivalries and friction. Major-General Francis de Rottenburg, Procter's superior, had, so Procter felt, deliberately deprived him of men and supplies, arguing that the British centre and east in Ontario was far more important. Procter had been left with only the overworked 41st Regiment of Foot and the Kent and Essex Militia, far too few with which to undertake an offensive. Appealing directly to the adjutant-general in Sir George Prevost's office, he wrote that *'if his Excellency (*Prevost*) does not interfere, I shall be kept so weak as to tempt the enemy forward. If Sir George's intentions had been fulfilled, I could venture to ensure the safety of this flank for some months at least.'* It was at this juncture that Proctor advocated the creation of a specially formed corps of full-time rangers to take the place of the militia, who, however hard they might fight on the day, would always expect to be given seasonal leave to attend to their farms.

Yet it was not only troops for which Sir Henry felt a need. He was short of just about everything—from bedding and pots to clothing and food. A further bout of letter writing ensued; intentionally bypassing de Rottenburg and all aimed at Prevost's desk. *'The want of meat does operate much against us. As does the want of Indian arms and goods. In short, our wants are so serious that the enemy must derive great advantage from them alone.'* De Rottenburg got wind of the flavour of these complaints, puffed in anger, and wrote acidly to Procter. Only Prevost's diplomacy prevented a very public rift. Relationships were fouled even further when, in one of his letters, De Rottenburg instructed Procter to be ready to abandon his position in Upper Canada and fall back as far as Lake Superior.

Abandonment of the British army's right flank had, in fact, been under consideration for some time. Ninian Edwards, governor of the Territory of Illinois, had built defensive positions at Prairie du Chien, Fort Madison and on the Rock River, and a fleet of warships was on the point of being completed at the American shipyard of Presque Isle on the southern shore of Lake Erie. Regarding these as threats to the stability of their positions in western Canada, almost every British general eyed these developments with concern and feared a reversal of fortunes in this region. Procter alone seemed to retain any strand of hope. As late as 11th July, he was still trying to persuade Prevost to permit him to attack the American shipyards at Sandusky and Presque Isle and destroy the nearly completed vessels before their keels touched the water.

He had the resources necessary. Outside the walls of Fort Malden, several thousand Indian warriors were camped, clamouring for something to do after so many months of inactivity. And he had the larger than life Tecumseh at his side, a man who would always advocate offensive action even in the most disheartening of situations. The Shawnee now proposed a second attempt at Fort Meigs, tempting Procter with a delightful vision of success that the redcoat found impossible to resist, despite his lingering misgivings about employing Indians as allies. In accepting the Shawnee's proposal, however, Procter was in danger of casting the charismatic warrior as the puppet master in virtual control of the strings of British military strategy in the west. But any reservations that Procter might have entertained about the wisdom of such an assault on a robust fort were dispelled by Tecumseh's warning that his warriors were baying for white men's blood and might, if unfed, turn on the British instead.

The plan devised by Tecumseh was devious and subtle. Procter and the Shawnee chief would move up river and, within earshot of Meigs, would then engage in sham battle. Colonel Clay, Tecumseh hoped, would assume that an American force, presumably advancing at Harrison's orders from Fort Stephenson, was being attacked and would sortie to the column's assistance.

On 20th July, Procter and the Indians, supported by about 400 regulars and militiamen, complying with every aspect of the plan, indulged in a mock battle where the road from Lower Sandusky crossed the Maumee River. Cannons roared, muskets were fired and war cries loosed. John Richardson was one of the sham belligerents waiting for the fort's gates to open. '*We were all instantly, although noislessly, upon the alert, but in vain did we look for any movement from the fort. Many of the garrison lined the ramparts in the rear, and seemed to look out anxiously in the direction of the firing, but they gave not the slightest indication of a design to leave the fort . . . . Either they had obtained information of our presence, or they suspected the nature and object of the ruse, and we had the mortification to find ourselves utterly foiled in the grand design of the expedition*'. The fort's doors remained shut. Clay had not been deceived. He well knew that no American forces were on the move—for Harrison had recently written to him to inform him that he felt the fort robust enough to withstand attack. But, in something of a shielding movement, Harrison withdrew from his base at Lower Sandusky to Seneca Town further up the Sandusky River, from where he could move in support of either Meigs or Fort Stephenson, if the need arose. Procter and Tecumseh, in the circumstances, could do nothing and so again withdrew to Canada on the 28th. But the genie remained uncorked, and, sooner or later, Procter would have to find the unsatisfied Indians an alternative avenue in which to spill blood.

America, by midsummer, had consolidated in three places: at Fort Stephenson, where youthful Major George Croghan commanded a garrison of 160 regulars, at Clay's Fort Meigs and at Seneca Town, Harrison's command post. Together, the three points housed about 1000 men, probably sufficient for a purely defensive role, but of questionable size if required to mount any sort of attack.

Fort Stephenson on the Sandusky seemed to be the most vulnerable of the three. And it was against this point that Procter struck next. Collecting up 385 regulars and an unspecified number of warriors, the British general sailed up the Sandusky on 31st July against Croghan's untested strongpoint. Only two days previously, Harrison, feeling that the fort would be very vulnerable to artillery fire, had ordered Croghan to evacuate the place, set it on fire and return to Seneca if the British approached. The 22 year old major, a veteran of Tippecanoe, saw no valid reason to abandon the place and wrote back: *'We have determined to maintain this place and, by heavens, we can.'* Harrison, seeing his orders disregarded, relieved the insubordinate youth of his command and ordered him to report to Seneca. But before the youngster could comply, Procter's guns opened on the fort and the assault commenced.

Fort Stephenson's defences were nearly as impressive as those of its companion on the Maumee. The stockade, 16 feet high and about 100 yards long and 50 yards wide, was encircled by an eight foot deep ditch with pointed logs beyond. A relic from the Revolutionary War, 'Old Betsey', a six pounder, Croghan's only gun, guarded the fort's northwest angle, the weakest point, and was well positioned to rake the ditch in front.

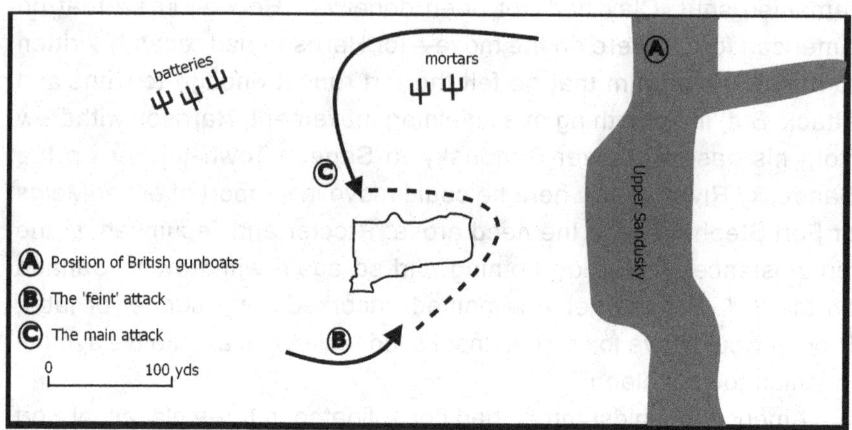

The Attack on Fort Stephenson

On August 1st, Procter's two gunboats swept up the Sandusky River and his troops landed in a protected cove, less than a mile from the fort. The general, twice disappointed at Meigs, planned to splinter the wooden palisades with his three six-pounder guns and two 5.5 inch howitzers, and then throw the 500 regulars of the 41st and 700 Indians into the breach that he hoped to form. Hidden in the woods between Fort Meigs and Seneca Town were Tecumseh and 2000 of his warriors, guarding the approaches in an effort to prevent any assistance reaching Croghhan and his men. Satisfied with his dispositions, the general sent in a demand for the fort's formal surrender, colourfully describing in his letter to the young man how the Indians dealt with their victims. Croghan, however, refused, and, at about 4 p.m. that afternoon, the British guns began their bombardment. 'Old Betsey' responded intermittently—for Croghan had very little ammunition and was anxious to husband his supplies. Then, in an effort to give the impression that he had a larger armoury at his disposal, he ordered the gun to be periodically moved to different points of the perimeter.

At 5 p.m., hoping that he had softened the fort's defences, Procter decided on a change of tactics. Forming his men in three columns of assault, he ordered his second-in-command, Lieutenant—Colonel Augustus Warburton, to sweep around the fort and launch a feint attack from the south. The other two columns, under the field command of Lieutenant-Colonel William Shortt, moved forward behind the smoke screen provided by the artillery and advanced against the fort's weakest point, the north-west corner, from where 'Old Betsey' had recently been firing bits of broken crockery. Croghhan, expecting the attack at this sector, had massed most of his men here, from where he could obtain a clear view of the field, and he could now wait until the attackers were within a comfortable range before giving the orders to fire.

Distant rumbles of thunder backed the British infantry's advance towards the ditch. For a while, there was no response from the fort, and the redcoated party quickly gained the ditch. But Shortt's men had no scaling ladders and their axes were blunt so that the chances of mounting or hacking away the parapet were less than minimal. Procter, usually so practical in his assessment of fortunes, showed strategic flaws that day. The frustrations of rebuttal at Meigs and his feelings of security as a commander probably combined to cause this dose of uncharacteristic rashness.

Then, when British soldiers had massed in the ditch, just 50 metres from the fort, they were met by a shower of musket balls and grapeshot from 'Old Betsey'. The effect was devastating: shot embedded itself in clothing and skin, men writhed in pain and stumbled and gaps opened in the British line. And then another scattering of grapeshot at equally short rage, followed by a further fall of blooded men. When the gun's smoke cleared, 100 redcoats or more lay in the ditch. The Indians had no heart or stomach for this type of warfare and retreated into the woods to watch. Shortt and his deputy, calling on their men, reached the ditch, but here met instant death. Behind, lower ranked officers, urged the survivors forward. But the barrel of the six pounder gun, now hot to touch, was full again, and Procter's soldiers feared to go on. Iron discipline, threats or bribes, failed to induce them forward. They had become frail mortals again, realizing, before it is too late, that life is too precious to lose. They cringed, cowered and ultimately pulled back. A cheer came from the American lines, a spontaneous whoop of jubilation. The defenders had lost just one man—a drunkard who had insisted on climbing to the top of the palisade and was shot through the head. Britain's highly trained warriors had been reduced to rubble by a single six pounder gun and the unsophisticated ranks of a few Kentucky farmers.

The two actions, Meigs and Stephenson, do not project Procter in a favourable light. It is difficult to determine what he was really trying to achieve—apart from giving the Indians a chance for a little killing.

He, of course, looked for scapegoats and pointed a finger at Tecumseh for suggesting that the attack should be made! Prevost accepted the man's pathetic attempt at self-exoneration, but admonished his junior in words that must have cut him to the quick: *'I cannot refrain from expressing my regret at your having allowed the clamour of the Indians to induce you to commit a part of your valuable force in an unequal and hopeless conflict.'*

Many of the British wounded lay in the ditch all night, sustained by the defenders, who lowered buckets of water to them. Those who were able crawled or limped away in the morning, their wounds infested with flies—and it took nearly a week to clear the dead. The overworked 41st Foot had been sacrificed by one man's craving to bathe in glory.

The 22 year-old guardian of the fort became a national hero overnight. The general had no alternative but to re-instate the young man, adding, almost humbly, in his muted praise for the youngster. '*It will not be amongst the least of General Procter's mortifications to find that he has been baffled by a youth who has just passed his twenty-first year.'* Croghan received a gold medal from Congress and, perhaps more importantly to him, a sword and praise from the admiring ladies of Ohio. Harrison, by contrast, received criticism and was faced by a call for his removal. He had been in command in the west for nearly eight months, had spent thousands of dollars on equipment, but had not set one single foot on Canadian soil. Personal criticism is just as hurtful to pride as any setback or defeat on the field of battle.

CHAPTER 6

'Still shall it be said we died like brave men.'

The miasma of strategic confusion and uncertainty that had enveloped America's politicians and generals since the start of the war had still not dispersed. Like an avaricious predator, the mist had devoured failed generals and had then vomited defeat and dead men upon Canadian soil. And it had created widows and fatherless children, left to cry at night with nothing but the memories of earlier family life and their broad-shouldered men folk, who now lay interred near where they had fallen. No wonder why many, and not just in New England questioned the wisdom of this war. Had it just been national pride and a vanity that had taken the nation into a conflict which did not actually threaten America's existence?

Yet through that swirling mist, the grey waters of Lake Erie remained definable, reminding yet again those confused men at the pinnacle of America's command that a successful invasion of Canada could never occur until the navy had gained undisputed control of Erie's waters. This would place the major burden on Commodore Isaac Chauncey. Throughout the winter just gone, he had supervised the building of gunboats at Presque Isle and Black Rock, sometimes insisting on modifications, often cajoling, but always maintaining a sense of reality and urgency that inspired the confidence of his superiors.

Those building the boats had been living in wretched conditions. The men at Black Rock, dwelling in fragile shacks on the edge of an ice-bound stream, were constantly shelled by British guns across the water. Moved by their plight, the commodore arranged for the construction of a blockhouse to protect the boats and accommodate the men. Satisfied with progress, he returned to Sackets Harbor, the American navy base on Lake Ontario. In mid-February 1813 he traveled to Albany to consult Dearborn and plan the details of a Spring campaign to sweep both lakes clear of the British.

Dynamic personnel would be needed to undertake the purge of Erie's waters. On 8th February the Navy Department appointed the 27 year old Commodore Oliver Hazard Perry as commander on this lake, junior to Chauncey, but, in skill and determination, clearly his equal. Perry reached Sackets Harbor on 3rd March and then moved to Presque Isle on the 27th. He immediately ordered the acceleration of the ship building programme and searched for ways to make the construction yards even safer from attack. Five hundred militiamen from Pennsylvania arrived to serve as a force of defence and 4 artillery pieces were moved up from Pittsburg. Ahead lay the nearly impossible task of outbuilding the British. In early May, three of the new gunboats were launched, followed on the 27th by the commissioning of two brigs, the 'Laurence' and the 'Niagara'. The 'Caledonia', held until this point in the Niagara River by the power of British guns, slipped past the enemy fleet in a fog and joined the Presque Isle flotilla, giving Perry a powerful arm with which to challenge the British. Nine ships sailed under his command. As well as the two new 20 gun brigs and the 'Caledonia', he was supported by the sloop 'Trippe' and the schooners 'Ariel', 'Scorpion', 'Tigress', 'Ohio' and 'Porcupine'.

Britain had been building, too, and had assembled a 6 ship fleet at Fort Malden. The 17 gun brig 'Detroit', the intended flagship, had not yet been completed, and so the burden would fall on the supporting ships, the 17 gun 'Queen Charlotte', the 13 gun schooner 'Lady Prevost', and three smaller vessels, the 'Hunter', 'Little Belt' and 'Chippewa'. In number of ships, the U.S. fleet was only slightly inferior, but in broadside power, Perry's ships could fire twice the weight, 896 pounds to 459.

Early testing of these vessels, however, would not occur. Secretary of War John Armstrong placed a quietening hand on the western field of war, restraining Harrison on land and Perry on the lake from any offensive action. The battle lights over the Ontario front were switched on instead. At his first attendance at Cabinet in January 1813, the new Secretary advocated an attack on York and Kingston, Upper Canada's most vital cities and the nest of Canada's Ontario fleet. Britain's ships had been contained during the winter by ice and American vigilance, but the lake's waters were expected to be free of ice by the start of April. The American assault force, Armstrong argued, should be ready by that date. Accordingly he ordered Dearborn to concentrate 3000 men at Buffalo and 4000 men at Sackets Harbor. 1500 of these were selected for the task and lodged in rough accommodation to wait for the change in season. While this attack was taking place, the remaining troops, most of whom were now based at Black Rock, would strike at Forts Erie and Chippewa. If these two were taken, American vessels would be able to pass freely between Lakes Erie and Ontario. Chauncey, whose co-operation would be vital for such an operation, requested a brevet military rank so that he would not feel outranked by the army officers involved.

In late February, however, Armstrong was informed that the spring thaw would be later than expected. He consequently modified his orders and instructed Dearborn to launch an almost immediate attack on Kingston before the ice had melted. The plan was strategically simple and potentially flawless. The Sackets Harbor contingent were to cross the ice to Kingston, destroy the ice-encased warships in the town's harbour and then press on to launch a similar offensive against York (now Toronto). Chosen to lead this grand offensive was Montgomery Zebulon Pike, the nation's newest brigadier-general and one—time explorer. A peak in the Rockies bears his name, but it was for his exploits at York that his name has been included in the lists of the slightly famous. A stickler for discipline, he lectured his men on the evils of drink, but somehow gained their respect and a touch of distant admiration.

Dearborn's solid enthusiasm for the project, however, was melted by reports of British activity and a build-up of forces at both the chosen targets. March turned to April, and still the forces did not move. In fact, York and Kingston were actually only lightly garrisoned, no more than 1000 in either place, but frequent movement of these defending forces had given Dearborn the impression of far larger numbers. General Dearborn remained in comfortable quarters at Plattsburg and passed up an early opportunity of baiting the British in their lairs.

Yet the attraction of attacking both these places continued to sparkle in the weeks that followed. However, there would be less chance of success in the future; veteran redcoat regiments released from the European war were even now known to be landing in Halifax and would soon be unpacking their kit in the barrack blocks of Ontario. Royalty was also imposing its views; George, the Prince Regent, had recently taken a personal interest in the war across the ocean. He had declared that the Royal Navy should take responsibility for the naval establishment on the lakes. The Admiralty had then appointed Sir James Lucas Yeo, the man who, when commanding the 'Southampton', had issued the challenge to David Porter of the 'Essex', as commander of the Great lakes fleet. Britain, it was believed, would soon have a fleet too formidable for the Americans to tackle.

Armstrong was, therefore, forced to reconsider his timetable and revert to his original plan for a water borne crossing. But Isaac Chauncey felt that York, rather than Kingston, should be visited first and he successfully managed to persuade the two men to accept his naval line of reasoning. Throughout March and April 1813, America's commanders prepared for the attack on York. By April 1st forty-eight transports had been assembled at Sackets Harbor and nearly twice that number at Oswego. Previously used to convey salt, the vessels could accommodate up to 100 men. The 4 regiments, the 6th, 15th, 16th and 21st regiments, about 1700 men, selected for the expedition, embarked in 14 of the larger vessels on the 22nd, expecting a quick and easy crossing of the lake. After a violent storm, which had forced the boats back to port on the 24th, the invasion group tried again on the 25th. '*If success attends my ships,*' Zebulon Pike colourfully wrote on the eve of departure, '*honor and glory await my name . . . . if defeat, still shall it be said we died like brave men . . . if we are destined to fall, may my fall be like Wolfe's—to sleep in the arms of victory.*' On the 27th the transports, accompanied by all of America's available fighting ships, three sloops and 14 schooners rounded Gibraltar Point and appeared off York. The wind, still lively after the storm of three days previously, blew from the east, forcing the ships to seek an anchorage well to the west of the town's harbour.

York was not one of Canada's most formidably defended points, boasting nothing stronger than a blockhouse and a ditch. Major-General Roger Sheaffe had made elaborate preparations to protect the town, even constructing a concealed mine beneath the approaches. Manning the town's defencess were two companies of the 8th Regiment of Foot and detachments of the Glengarry Light Infantry, Royal Newfoundland Regiment and the still assembling men of the York Militia, about 800 men in all. Supporting these troops were countless numbers of Indians, usually reliable when conditions were favourable, but prone to desertion when events turned nasty. Having spent the day giving orders, moving troops and writing letters, Sheaffe sat down for a hearty meal and then went to bed, trusting that the invaders would attempt nothing to the morrow.

At 8 a.m. on the 27th, Pike's troops went in, half-swimming the last few yards to the beach near the old French fort. Sheaffe, wondering until the last minute where the invading force would land, had spread his defenders along a ten mile beach front. First to confront the Americans was the grenadier company of the 8th, the King's Regiment of Foot, under Captain Neal McNeale, a few Indians and, a little further behind, the Newfoudland 'Fencibles'. They reached the flanking woodland just as Major Benjamin Forsyth's riflemen, the spearhead of the invading force, touched shore.

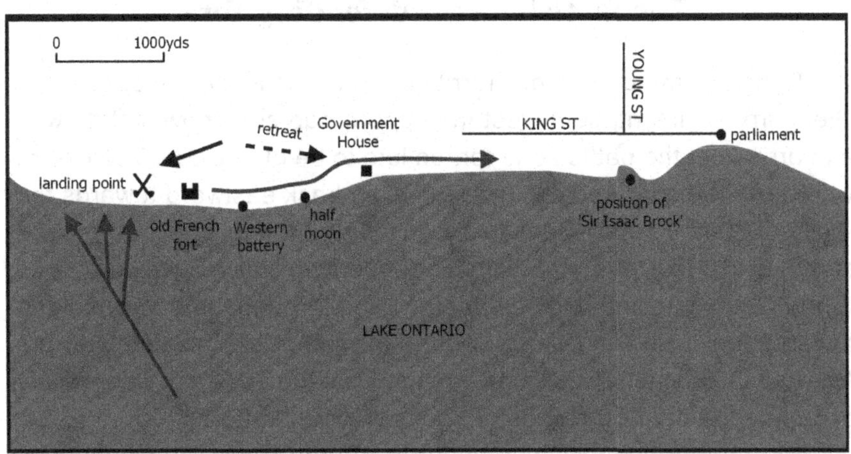

The American attack on York

But any attempt to prevent the establishment of a beachhead was hindered by gunfire from the six American warships. Pike's infantry regiments were now coming ashore on both sides of the riflemen, widening the landing zone and making it even more difficult for the grenadiers to blunt the invasion. The redcoats, in heroic spirit, now decided to risk all in a bayonet charge down the beach. McNeale fell in the first minute of the battle on the beach. So, too, did Donald McLean, Clerk of the Upper Canada House of Assembly. Only 30 of the 119 redcoat grenadiers who charged that day survived the carnage on the beach. The Newfoundlanders, arriving in support, suffered just as badly, cut down by fire from the warships and the American regulars on their flanks.

One company of 3rd regiment of U.S.Artillery, One company of U.S. 1st Rifle Regiment, detachments of 5th, 14th and 29th U.S. Infantry Regiments, 6th, 15th, 16th, 21st, 22nd and 23rd U.S.Infantry Regiments.

The United States forces involved in the attack on York

8th Foot, Glengarry Light Infantry, Royal Newfoundland Regiment, 1st Lincoln Militia, 1st and 3rd York Militia Regiments

The British forces defending York

Things continued to go horribly wrong for Roger Sheaffe. The Glengarry regiment, sent west in support, had somehow lost its way and arrived at the battle zone far too late to be of any use. The British were now in disordered retreat, stumbling back eastward towards the Western Battery, where Sheaffe hoped to rally his men and make a solid stand. By 10 a.m. every participating American was now ashore. Pike formed them into line and sent them rolling through the thin woodland towards the town. At 11 a.m., after intermittent skirmishing with the Newfoundland men, Pike's men emerged into the open and were halted at last by the fire of the guns of York's western battery.

But another calamity was about to rob the British commander of the comforting fire of these well-positioned guns. The six American warships, with no target left near the old French fort, considered the British battery to be an attractive alternative and threw more than 200 pounds of iron in a single volley. The ships, however, could not take credit for what happened next. One of the sweating British gunners accidentally dropped a lighted match in the magazine. A dozen men were killed in the resulting explosion and the guns were torn from their mountings. A score of badly scorched men lay nearby, screaming in uncontrollable pain. Sheaffe was almost a mile away, preparing his final stand within York's main defences. Without his steadying hand or any word of encouragement from officers on the spot, the defenders '*began now visibly to melt away; there was no person to animate them, nor to tell them when they were to make a stand, their officers knew nothing of what was to be done, each was asking of another . . . . In the meantime the General walked backwards and forwards on the road . . . . more than half a mile from the troops.*'

Pike must have believed that God was fighting for America. He unhesitatingly ordered his men to advance towards the next obstacle, the Half-moon battery, while his bandsmen played 'Yankee Doodle' on fife and drum. The British had employed music as a weapon of intimidation during the Revolutionary War. Pike, a colourless and fairly unimaginative man, hoped that it might do the same for him.

The Half-moon battery remained strangely silent as the Americans moved within range. But, having never been furnished with guns, it remained no more than a mound of earth. The only obstacle now impeding complete American success was the still untested Government House battery and a possible stand of the regulars. Ahead, in the open clearing, disordered strands of retreating British militia were hurrying in no particular direction; no orders had been given, no lies of stubborn red congealed—and Sheaffe seemed to have vanished from this world. The American warships had opened up again, plying the defences of Government House with grapeshot and national anger. Within minutes, this last British battery had been silenced. Stories later circulated that the guns had only been supplied with round shot—suitable for use against warships, but of little use against human targets.

Sheaffe, despite his absence from the area where he was needed most, was still giving instructions and weighing up the odds. Aware that retention of York had become impossible now that the outer defences had been shot away, he ordered the defenders to retire to Kingston and permit the invaders to take quiet possession of Upper Canada's prime city. But he felt reluctant to surrender the huge stockpiles of gunpowder, cartridges and shells that lay buried near the shore of the lake and, before evacuating, he sent out an instruction to blow up the entire magazine and underground vault.

Zebulon Montgomery Pike was within 400 yards of the magazine when it exploded shortly after midday. He had been in the act of interrogating a prisoner when boulders, earth and masonry rained down. Several British soldiers and civilians, amongst them Sheaffe's pastry cook, were killed outright, but the death toll among the Americans was far higher. Amongst the 52 who died was General Pike, crushed by an enormous stone before he had time to run. 180 more were injured; the euphoria of the previous hours suffocated in the thick billowing smoke.

Pike lived long enough to see the Stars and Stripes flying above York's roofline. Sheaffe, however, had departed before that event, leaving behind a musical box and his personal papers in his anxiety to be gone. However, he would probably have seen the smoke rising from the partially completed warship, the 'Sir Isaac Brock'. Still on its stocks in the boatyard, it had been set on fire at his orders. At the very moment that he rode east past the provincial parliament buildings, Pike, his head resting on the captured British flag, expired.

Colonel Cromwell Pearce succeeded him in command. Under his direction, the Americans moved towards the undefended town. At 4 p.m. the first of the American soldiers vaulted a fence and entered the streets of York. A musket ball nearly removed his head. Fired by one of the last rearguard defenders to leave the town, it was probably the final shot in the battle for York.

The subsequent fighting was fought largely with words, not weapons. Sheaffe had left Lieutenant-Colonel William Chewett, his surveyor-general, with the task of surrendering the town. Assisted by a clergyman, the Reverend John Strachan, the two men sought terms that would leave York and its inhabitants' lives untouched. The American negotiators, Colonel George Mitchell and Major William King, were incensed, however, at the deliberate destruction of the magazine and the burning of the warship on the stocks, and were disinclined to offer generous terms. Those eventually agreed were neither generous nor harsh. All weapons and useful stores were to be surrendered to the United States. Any militiamen found in York were given parole on condition that they did not again take up arms. Only the officers would be held captive. And, more importantly for the citizens of York, the sanctity of private property would be respected. The United States government, however, was tardy in ratifying the terms made at York. And, throughout the period of negotiations for the surrender, some of America's soldiers had been showing their darker sides, plundering the houses of the townspeople and carrying off virtually anything that was not fixed down. Towels, teacups, coat stands, bodices, soap, surgical instruments and old shirts and other items of little value found their way on to the lists of plundered items.

Strachan complained to Dearborn. The American, who had been confined to his cabin by a recurrence of his illness, seemed to condone the malpractices of his troops by claiming that a human scalp had been found hanging in Government House and by suggesting that Indians, in British pay, had committed far worse atrocities. The forceful clergyman managed to persuade the general to speed up the process of ratification of the terms of surrender. Forcefulness of personality and a willingness to stand up to the enemy secured what diplomacy and sabre rattling would never have achieved.

While Strachan was elevated to an exalted status, Sheaffe's reputation took a tumble. York's people mouthed oaths of deprecation and audible condemnation of the man who had deserted them. He was far too distant to hear their remarks. Kingston was 190 miles away—and it was towards that town that Sheaffe and the bruised remnants of his army were heading. The rutted road over which the soldiers passed was waterlogged with melting snow. On the way the soldiers encountered hostility, not from the people who had just been let down, but from the rustics of the small towns and villages along the route. Most of these were immigrants from the United States and possessed a weather-vane loyalty which altered with the winds of military victory. '*The majority of the inhabitants of this part of the country evinced great disloyalty as we proceeded, being much gratified with the success of the Americans . . . . In many instances they concealed their horses, waggons etc.in the woods, to avoid accommodating us with them, and told us they had none.*' Patrick Finan, one of the stragglers and only 12 years old at the time, reported. At Kingston, the imperial soldiers found lodgings in the Catholic church and a hardware store. Dispirited, sodden and now apparently leaderless, they were all that stood in the way of America's armed forces.

Yet the United States would be more interested in strengthening her hold on Lake Ontario than attempting any further advance through Upper Canada. The capture of Forts George and Erie on the Niagara would be vital. For this, the troops involved at York would be required as well as additional troops from camps in New York State.

Dearborn, who had played no part in the capture of York, was remarkably quick to take advantage of the success of the invasion. Sensing that he could snatch more of the sunshine of approval, he set about organizing a probe against the first of these forts, which, if successful, would provide America with control of Lake Ontario's shores. Unfavourable winds, however, kept the ships and troops in York's harbour for more than a week, depriving Dearborn of any early chance of taking the fort by stealth. On 8th May, the expedition crossed the water and the blooded soldiers disembarked four miles east of the mouth of the Niagara River. For several days the force remained inactive near the Niagara while Chauncey sailed back to Sackets Harbor to collect Winfield Scott's soldiers and sufficient supplies to sustain the planned attack. '*My intention,*' Dearborn stated simply, '*is to collect the main body of the troops at this place, and, as soon as Commodore Chauncey returns and the forces from Oswego arrive, to commence operations in as spirited and effectual a manner as practicable.*' But the sharp edge of the American fighting knife was being blunted. Ageing Dearborn fell ill again, and the army might conceivably be forced to wait even longer until his replacement arrived.

Brigadier-General John Vincent, the British commander of this central section of the frontier, had watched the American activity and had seen their night time flairs. On his roll, he had 1222 professionals: 392 men of the badly dented 41st Foot, a similar number of the 49th, the 8th regiment of foot and about 200 members of the Glengarry Light Infantry. Prevost had promised to send the 104th Foot from New Brunswick and a company of the Royal Scots, but no date for their arrival had yet been scheduled. In his militiamen, he felt he could place no confidence at all. '*It is with regret that I can neither report favourably of their numbers, nor their willing co-operation. Every exertion has been made, and every expedient used, to bring them forward . . . with but little effect.*'

Seventy pieces of American artillery opened fire on Newark, near Fort George, on the morning of the 25th. Twenty had been placed in a battery near Two Mile Creek, and the rest on the parapets of American held Fort Niagara, just across the river. The British could only field 20 pieces in reply. Caught in the crossfire from both east and west, Fort

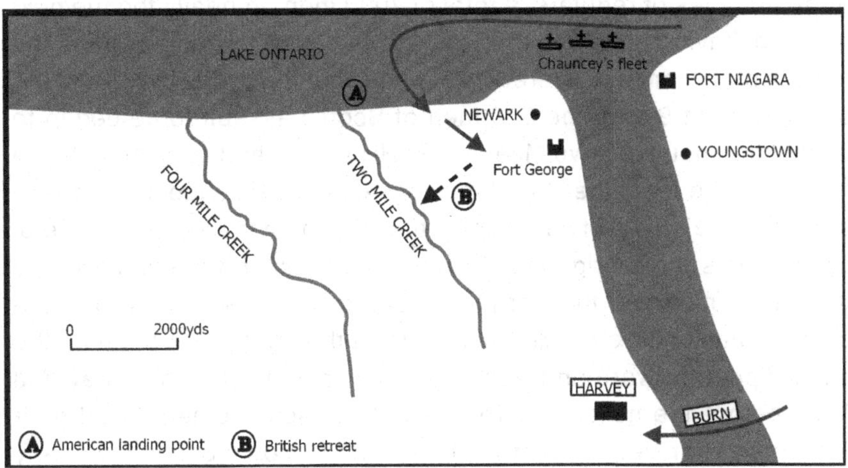

The Attack on Fort George

George's wooden walls were soon consumed in fire—and, by evening, every log-built barrack block had been destroyed. Chauncey returned with his ships during the day, and the navy's guns joined in. With Chauncey were General Winfield Scott and Oliver Hazard Perry, the 27 year old commander of the Lake Erie flotilla, who, having heard that action was imminent, had left his post on the neighbouring lake and travelled eastward to Fort Schlosser in an open boat. From here he had continued his journey by foot or horse to Sackets Harbor, arriving just in time to slip aboard one of Chauncey's departing vessels.

Detachments of 2nd Light Dragoons, Light Artillery Regiment, 1st U.S. Rifle Regiment and 3rd U.S.Artillery Regiment

6th, 14th, 15th, 16th, 20th, 22nd and 23rd U.S.Infantry regiments

U.S.forces in the attack on Fort George

1st, 8th, 41st, 49th, 89th and 104th Foot, 19th Light Dragoons, Glengarry Light Regiment and Royal Newfoundland Regiment

On the 26th the American force began to embark on three of Chauncey's ships, [7]each one of which had barges in tow. Light infantry under the command of capable Winfield Scott led the way, followed by

7 Lady of the Lake, Madison and Oneida

three brigades of regulars, a total of 2000 men. In heavy fog the next morning, having anchored off Crookstown on the Canadian shore, the assault craft went in, covered by the mist and the protective fire of the schooners. At 9 a.m. the 500 men of Scott's assault force began to land at the mouth of Two Mile Creek. His orders had been specific: to reach the shelter of the clay slopes at the landward edge of the beach and await the arrival of the infantry, the 1500 men in Brigadier-General John Boyd's three brigades. Twenty boats reached the shore in the next thirty minutes, their arrival watched by 50 Mohawks from the cover of flanking trees. Men spilled from the vessels as soon as the bows dipped forward and waded clumsily ashore through spray and foam before the next wave reached the beach. Some missed their footing and tumbled, and the accompanying 3 pounder cannon nearly overturned. A uniformed American, one of the first to land, calmly knelt down to pick up something that he saw on the beach. Under fire, he placed the object in his pocket, wiped sand from his clothing and moved on. Another, just as calmly, relieved himself in a bush, wetting the hand of a defender who was trying to remain concealed. Out on the open waters, the ships of the United States Lake Ontario flotilla were firing grape and canister at where they assumed the British would be.

Scott, 6 foot 5 inches tall, and only recently exchanged after his capture at Queenston, was one of the first to come ashore. Inland, positioned in a ravine, stood 1000 men of the Glengarry and Newfoundland regiments, under the command of Lieutenant-Colonel Christopher Myers. When Scott breasted the bank, in apparent disregard of his orders, he was confronted by British steel. Attempting to avoid a redcoat musket point, he missed his footing and slipped clumsily back down the bank into the path of his soldiers. Dearborn, watching the movement of the troops from the deck of the 'Madison', feared the worst.

Boyd's men were now coming ashore, and the American advance began. But Vincent's men were present too, bursting out of the ravine as a disciplined line of steel. Three times the British forced the invaders back down the clay slopes onto the sands of the beach beyond. For a moment, it seemed that the old-fashioned cohesiveness of Britain's fighting forces would excel over muscles and numbers. Three times America re-assembled and climbed up again, served throughout by fire from the warships and the unbreakable nerve of Winfield Scott. The soldiers, if they had paused to think of loved ones and homes, might not have climbed the slopes again. But the past was crowded out by the present; lingering on the beach was not an option, running away was unthinkable, and survival, the immediate future, and fear of being branded as cowards forced them forward.

Two lines of hardening men faced each other at a distance of little more than ten yards. Shooting at each other is a dehumanised business; men would prefer to see their adversary as featureless targets without distinguishing characteristics and no more flesh and blood than a tin duck at a fairground shooting range. But at this short range, opponents wear expressions of fear and emotion—and it becomes harder to shoot. Momentarily, both sides stared at each other in silence, perhaps in respect of each other's right to live. But then muskets were raised, and the soldier took over from the human within.

For fifteen minutes, the two sides fired at point-blank range. Behind the Glengarry men, the British 8th Foot under Major James Ogilvy had formed up, but the defenders were still outnumbered by more than 2 to 1. Myers was one of the first of the officers to fall, shot three times. Command devolved upon Lieutenant-Colonel John Harvey, who brought up the 49th Foot in a desperate attempt to hold the Americans back. Another twenty minutes of nearly static fighting followed—and then the British line, like a punctured dam, suddenly gave way, over whelmed by the numbers of Americans who streamed up from the beach. In the three hours of fighting that had taken place since the first American boot had stepped on Canada's shore, the British had lost 358 men on a battlefield that extended little more than 200 yards inland from the edges of the beach. The United States had lost 40 dead and about 100 wounded, but had not yet planted her colours on the fort.

Poor General Vincent now heard that a detachment of enemy dragoons under Colonel James Burn had crossed the river at Five Mile Meadows to the south and was wrapping around his route of retreat. Part of Boyd's force had moved around the British left flank, further developing a trap in which the British might well become ensnared. Seeing no point in sacrificing any more men, he sadly ordered the evacuation of Fort George and the spiking of the guns. Positioned on the parapets to repel invaders crossing the Niagara River, the weapons had proved to be virtually useless in dealing with an invasion from the direction of the lake. The British general, a realist throughout, ordered the rump of his force to re-assemble near Queenston and sent hurried instructions to Cecil Bisshop, the commander of the small garrisons holding Chippawa and Fort Erie, to abandon the two positions and join him at Beaver Dams, a supply depot twenty miles to the south-west on Twelve Mile Creek. Bisshop promptly obeyed. Blowing up Fort Erie's magazine, he marched out with the men of the 8th Foot on 28th May and joined his superior further west. That same afternoon, Lieutenant-Colonel James Preston, commanding the republic's forces at Black Rock, crossed the Niagara and took quiet possession of the remains of Fort Erie.

Colonel William Claus, the commandant at Fort George, was reputedly the last to leave the fort. When all of his soldiers had departed, he tried to hack down the flagpole with a blunt axe in order to retrieve the Union flag. Giving up the mission, he escaped through a back gate at the very moment that the Americans entered at the front. Scott was reputedly the first to enter the vacated fort. Riding Colonel Myers' horse, he rode through Newark to Fort George and gazed up at the flagpole upon which Britain's intolerable symbol still flew. Picking up the discarded axe, he completed the job begun by Claus and claimed the flag as a personal souvenir.

Vincent, having lost control of the crossings of the Niagara River, retreated through St. Davids, hoping to salvage something from the wreckage of defeat. Three American forces were close on the Britisher's tail. Colonel Burn's dragoons were probably no more than a mile or so behind and were in an excellent position to block the British retreat. Scott was almost as close while Preston, standing in the smoking ruins of Fort Erie, was only about five miles to the south.

But, like a game of chess, either, or all three, would need to make the right moves. A change in the high command at this moment, however, stilled the three forces just when they needed to be mercurial. Dearborn, too ill even to stand without help, had relinquished his field command to Major-General Morgan Lewis, the commander at Fort Niagara and a man senior in rank to Scott. Lewis was to be a most inappropriate choice, more cautious even than Dearborn. He loved the rank, the uniform braid and the pomp and ceremony of a senior soldier's life, but lacked the nerve that the job required. Having instructed Burn to remain where he was, the politician-turned soldier then ordered Scott to pull back to Fort George. The latter, however, chose to disregard the instruction and hoped that Burn would prove to be just as defiant. Morgan Lewis issued the order again and, this time, sent John Boyd to deliver it personally. Both subordinates, Burn and Scott, commissioned officer with respect for rank, felt forced to comply. Burn could see the British columns passing through woodland to his left and must have felt like a cat suddenly deprived of his prey.

Vincent, halting only briefly at Beaver Dams, pulled back to a safer position at Burlington Heights, Lake Ontario's most westerly point, regarding this as a position at which he had the best chance of making his stand. From here he felt that he would be able to protect the British supply route from Kingston to Lake Erie, which had been hurriedly reformed after America's withdrawal from York. Abandoning Burlington Heights, he was fully aware, would jeopardize Britain's chances of holding all of Upper Canada south of Lake Huron. The decision had been made to hold Burlington at all costs.

Morgan Lewis adopted a strategy that was neither aggressive nor defensive. On 29th May, waking himself to his military responsibilities at last, he sent Burn in a token pursuit of the British. Advancing along the lake's shore, the colonel's forces clashed with the British in a nocturnal brawl, but were unable to cast a net wide enough to enmesh the British rearguard. Close to Forty Mile Creek, the Americans were fired upon by a British schooner that lay offshore. Two days later, a British force hit Burns in his overnight camp, capturing 80 men and a large quantity of supplies. Nothing that Morgan Lewis did in the next few days would ever convince the nation that he was the man required for decisive operations on the lakes. '*His own baggage moves in two stately wagons—carrying the various furniture of a Secretary of State's office, a lady's dressing room, an alderman's dining room, and the contents of a grocer's shop,*' one of his many caustic critics had sneered. Like a child bored with a new toy, he lost all interest in campaigning and prepared to settle down to comfortable living in battle-torn Queenston.

His days at the pinnacle of the hierarchy were fortunately numbered. General Dearborn, recovered from his illness, resumed command and began to lay fresh, but vague, plans for dealing with Vincent at Burlington

Heights. But the American interest in Fort George had left Sackets Harbor vulnerable. Sir James Lucas Yeo, the 31 year old commodore, who had arrived at Kingston on 16th May to take over command of the lake flotilla from Robert Barclay, was quick to see that the chance to seize the American base might never occur again. Deprived of Sackets Harbor, the United States fleet would have no place to refit or hide. Prevost held a similar view, and, taking advantage of the dispersal of so much American naval hardware, the two men began to organise an expedition across the water.

On May 27th, the day of the American attack on Fort George, the British duo sailed out of Kingston with the tide of opportunity flowing in their favour. With them were 800 men, detachments of the Royal Scots, the 8th, 100th and 104th Foot, the Voltigeurs and the Glengarry infantry, the units humiliated at York. The wind that day, however, was unfortunately light, and the British ships, whose sails were hanging '*as loosely as a lady's apron,*' were spotted from Sackets Harbor long before the armada arrived. Brigadier-General Jacob Brown, one-time smuggler but now in charge of the town's defences, had ample time to muster his 400 regulars and send messengers inland with requests for assistance. A God-send to America, the officer correctly surmised that the British would land on Horse Island and then advance across the natural causeway that linked this island to the mainland. And, while the sails of the British remained almost motionless on Ontario's frustratingly placid waters, more than 300 volunteers arrived from New York villages, all untrained and few with weapons in their hands. Just before sunset on the 28th, however, the whole operation was called off and the flotilla sailed back towards Kingston.

Two unrelated events then took place to send Britain's ships heading back towards America's shores. The first, the awakening of an onshore breeze, filled the sails '*almost instantly, surprising to us after hours when the wind had refused to blow.*' The second event, human in origin, was even more unexpected. A party of American soldiers in small bateaux approached the fleet under flags of truce and offered to surrender. Their arrival, more than the birth of the wind, persuaded Yeo and Adjutant-General Edward Baynes, commander of the land forces, that the attack had again become a possibility.

Well before dawn on the 29th, Yeo's ships anchored off the American coast. In light rain and under the cover of a moonless sky, the bateaux of the invaders moved towards the shore. The grenadiers of the 100th Foot were the first to land on Horse Island, followed by the Royal Scots. When daylight lit the coastline, the vanguard was already wading ashore along the 400 yard causeway, peppered intermittently by the 500 or so defending militia behind the gravel dunes that adorned this section of the beach. Placing no great reliance upon these men of the plough and workbench, Brown hoped that they would at least remain long enough to fire a few volleys and then fall back as an orderly reserve behind a more reliable line of regulars. In this hope, he was to be disappointed. For, seeing the British menacingly emerge from the surf in gritty determination and with their bayonets already fixed, every one of yesterday's volunteers chose not to stay and argue. The regulars fortunately held, resisting for an hour or more, but gradually gave way to the pressures of British discipline. Their foothold well secured, the redcoats advanced in two columns towards Fort Tompkins.

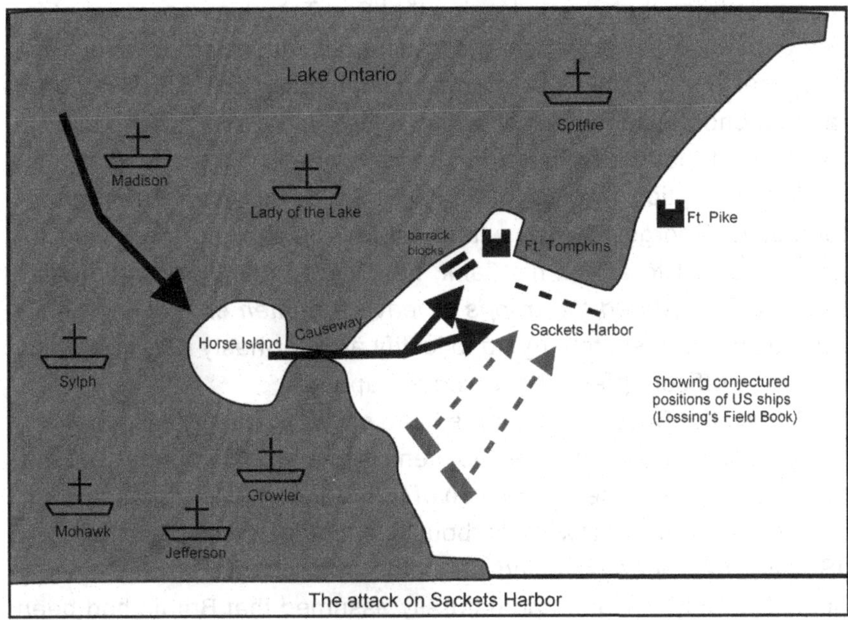

The attack on Sackets Harbor

(for U.S. and British forces involved, see appendices 5 and 6)

This fort, guarding the harbour itself, was manned by America's regulars, and it was here that the only real fighting took place. Blockhouses on the landward perimeter gave added protection to the defenders. The British employed their entire armoury against these wooden structures:

small calibre field pieces, bayonets and the ordnance of the warships on the lake, but nothing would induce the defenders to yield. '*The enemy was so strongly posted and so sheltered by blockhouses and other works that our men could not approach them, weakened as they were by the losses of the morning,'* Lieutenant-Colonel Edward Brenton grumbled. Troops of the 8th, 100th and 104th, phalanx-like on the British left, eventually managed to penetrate as far as the barracks. Taking shelter within the works, they assembled for what they hoped would be a glorious advance. Their colleagues on the right, however, were caught in the open and failed to give any support. Soon this wing was in '*an ordered retreat,'* even Prevost's step quickening after a passing American bullet tore a hole in his coat.

But it had not been just the American regulars who had infused metal into the resistance. Brown, seeing his militia fleeing after the brief battle on the beach, employed the blacker art of subterfuge in an attempt to bring them back. Hoping that Fort Tompkins would resist for long enough, he sent messengers riding out with news of victory and an appeal to the fugitives to return and share the credit. Three hundred had responded and these had begun to assemble south of the town at the moment that the British retreat commenced.

The deception worked admirably, swallowing even the normally perceptive George Prevost within its jaws. Mistaking the militia for regulars about to attack his flank, he ordered complete withdrawal. '*I reluctantly ordered the troops to leave a beaten enemy,'* he pithily reported in his despatch, trying to justify an over-hasty decision which few of the officers present seemed to support.

And so the British re-embarked and sailed away. America lost 160 men that day. Prevost had lost 48 men killed and 211 wounded, but his only gain had been the destruction of the 'General Pike', a warship still on the stocks in the town's harbour. Lieutenant Woolcott Chauncey, US Navy, had been watching the battle from a distance and, seeing the militia body in flight, had naturally assumed that Britain had been victorious. To prevent too much of value falling into the victor's hands, he had set fire to the warship and some of the port's naval stores. About $500,000 worth of government property went up in flames as a result of an overhasty decision. Thick smoke drifted out to sea, engulfing the British ships as they retired. The attackers had left their dead and wounded behind, the latter in the care of Brown's medical staff. In a letter to Governor Daniel Tompkins of New York, the hero of Sackets Harbor's defiance announced that '*America will be distinguished for (its) humanity.*'

Failure at Sackets Harbor hardly helped Prevost's fading reputation. He and Yeo had launched the attack largely to draw enemy attention from the Niagara Peninsula and not, as most Canadian and British strategists would have wished, as the bridgehead for an invasion of United States territory. They consequently failed to assemble a large enough force. Critics were quick to argue that Sir George should have pressed the attack without any regard to the likely risk involved. His detractors might choose to grumble, but he continued to reside at the top of the Canadian military pinnacle and survive all the abuse that was hurled in his direction.

The British setback, however, did not erode Britain's control of the lake. York had been promptly re-occupied—and Prevost boasted that the defences of Kingston were invincible. And, despite the capture of Forts George and Erie, the American victory had not been as decisive as Armstrong and his president would have wished. Vincent's army was still intact and well supplied, and Morgan Lewis's pathetic efforts hardly encouraged Colonel William Winder, given the field command of America's Niagara forces, to make any move of his own. General Dearborn, anxious to muddy any new British initiative, called upon Commodore Chauncey to co-operate in a blocking strategy. Chauncey, however, continued to set his own agenda. No amount of gentle persuasion could induce him to ride in tandem with his colleagues on land. He was determined to achieve naval superiority on Lake Ontario and, for this, he needed to construct as many ships as possible and preserve them from attack. This would mean keeping them in harbour and only venturing into the waters of the lake when the odds were heavily stacked in his favour. America's generals would be forced to develop a strategy of their own and leave Chauncey to wrap up his precious ships in some sort of protective clothing.

Winder, given permission at last to seek out Vincent in Burlington Heights, reached Stoney Creek on 5th June. He had with him 1300 men, a mixed force of dragoons and infantry. Making contact with the enemy's pickets, they bivouacked near the creek, only about seven miles from where Vincent's retreating soldiers were also settling down for the night. It would be the last night on earth for many.

Several individuals took credit for the idea of attacking the Americans during the night. The plan was probably conceived by a local youth, Billy Green, and his brother. They had watched the Americans pass by and, well concealed within brush land that they knew well, had mischievously imitated the calls of Indians and laughed at the panic in the ranks that this had caused. Their high spirits had taken them to the perimeter of the American camp at dusk. Here they had counted numbers, noted positions and even learned the password of the day. Winder remained vigilant that night. His soldiers slept with weapons at their sides and with patrols on full alert. But the sentries failed to spot young Billy, his brother, or young Lieutenant John Harvey, who was also observing the Americans.

Soon after dark, the two brothers reached the British line and asked for a meeting with Vincent. Harvey had just returned and he, too, was present at the candlelight meeting, The trio, regular officer and brothers, accurately pinpointed the positions of the enemy. The American troops, Harvey announced, were scattered, the cannon poorly placed and the dragoons lay far to the rear. Just before twelve, on a conveniently dark night, Vincent and Harvey led 700 men of the 8th and 49th Foot out towards Stoney Creek. Every soldier had obeyed the order to remove flints from their firelocks and observe Harvey's command for total silence.

For three hours they fumbled through the dark, their feet weighed down by thick mud clinging to their boots. Each man was absorbed in thoughts of his own, but each fed on hopes of sweet revenge. They passed a wooden church and saw beyond the flicker of campfires, around which America's soldiers would now presumably be sleeping. Encountering a line of pickets, the British whispered the password, 'Wil-Hen-Har', [8]and, having passed as friends, slaughtered the unsuspecting men where they stood.

But around the flickering fires, not a person was encountered. The entire force had withdrawn after supper to a stronger position on the far side of a little stream. Pickets on the American side of the stream spotted the moving silhouettes outlined in the gold of the campfire glow. The American camp was suddenly awake, men seized their weapons, and the first musket fire of the night was discharged

8 the first two syllables of Harrison's name

as the British splashed through the stream or crossed the narrow wooden bridge.

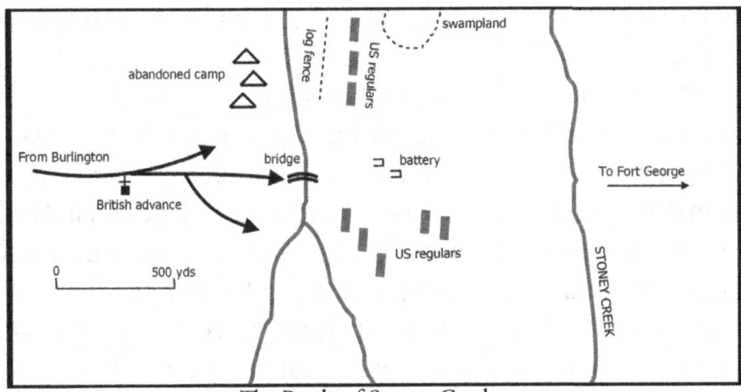

The Battle of Stoney Creek

Muddle, rather than the hoped for massacre, followed. Britons fought Britons, Americans turned on countrymen, mistaking them for British irregulars, and even General Vincent lost his way. Soldiers on the British left managed to cross, but nothing apart from discarded bedding lay at their feet. On the British right, America's regulars had formed a line and hardly any redcoat soldiers approached close enough to use the sharp points of their bayonets.

And now the American cannon were firing blindly into the dark, but somehow finding targets amongst the closely packed British column on the bridge. Vincent must have cursed the eagerness with which he had embraced the brothers' suggestion. A few minutes later, however, the guns were silenced, captured by an enterprising party of volunteers who had crept forward almost undetected.

Disorder was the only universal factor present. The thickness of the night prevented any co-ordination or sense of overall vision. Colonel James Burns's dragoons, camped in the rear, rode in, but they, too, became disorientated and slaughtered some of their comrades in the U.S. 16th Infantry, who happened to be in their way. Winder and Chandler, as confused as everyone else, wandered into the British lines and were taken captive.

Less than an hour before dawn, as a relieving gold-blue touched the eastern sky, the battle faded, each side believing the other to be victorious. The Yankee forces, now under the command of Burns, were already in retreat, fumbling their way along the lake's shore towards Forty Mile Creek. Vincent could not be found, and Harvey called for a withdrawal from this engagement which he had largely engineered. In total, he had lost 214 men, a quarter of his force. The intended victims of the night lost less, 68 dead or wounded, and perhaps 100 taken prisoner. Poor Vincent, dazed and horseless, turned up at his camp in late morning. He had hardly participated in the battle, spending most of the time falling over tree roots and stemming the blood from several gashes. His embarrassment was never mentioned in Harvey's report to Prevost. And, needless to say, Vincent chose not to refer to his experiences in any of the letters that he later wrote. Heroes, too, received no mention; Billy Green went quietly back to his home, carrying the sword that he had been given at the battle's start, but with no other material proof of his involvement.

The British returned to Stoney Creek battlefield that afternoon. Here they found valuable stores and baggage scattered amongst the litter of the American dead. At almost the same moment, the retreating Americans, now at Forty Mile Creek, were fired upon by the 'Beresford' a British schooner that had anchored off shore. The Americans retaliated by building a furnace and firing red hot shot at the 'Beresford', but the missiles had cooled by the time they reached the vessel. An hour or so later, two companies of the 41st and 49th foot landed and drove the last of the Americans towards the east. Often called the Battle of Forty Mile Creek, this was probably the most insignificant action of the war. A detachment of soldiers of the 8th Foot, landing at Forty Mile Creek just after the Americans had passed through, found dinner plates, footwear and discarded supplies to add to the haul found on Stoney Creek's battlefield.

Demoralised America felt, and soon proved, that it could achieve nothing constructive after Stoney Creek. Dearborn at Fort George, unable to grasp the seriousness of the reverse, ordered Lewis to instigate a fresh push towards Burlington Heights. But Lewis, ever the delayer, offered every excuse possible for not obeying and so provoked further rebuke. Lewis, the Congressman Peter Porter sneered, '*could not go sixteen miles to fight the enemy, not because his force was too small, but because he had not wagons to carry tents and camp kettles for his army.*'

In a bout of strangely myopic thinking that followed this period of American success, the decision was made to abandon all the republic's recent gains, apart from Fort George. Fort Erie was abandoned and burned on 9th June, less than a fortnight after its evacuation by the British. On that day, too, the forward detachments of Americans at Chippewa and Queenston pulled back and retired behind newly constructed log palisades and earthworks at Fort George. It was the same old story—a bullish advance, an initial success, a failure of nerve and the abandonment of any gains—and this at the very moment that Prevost was considering the surrender of all of Upper Canada.

Britain's courage fed well on Yankee faintheartedness. Nurtured by his quartermasters in Montréal and the supplies recently captured from the enemy, Vincent returned to the vicinity of Beaver Dams, anxious to destroy the American toe-hold at Fort George, the only part of Upper Canada which Washington's forces still occupied. Here he was joined by the 104th Regiment of Foot, sent to him from Kingston. For a while at least, the redcoated general felt that he would be able to move mountains and, like a man about to play chess, he began to position his pieces with a view to winning the Niagara game.

The Stoney Creek campaign had fostered something other than a resurgence of British spirit. This is perhaps the first occasion in the war when quasi-guerilla bands are particularly noted. Joseph Willcocks, a former member of the Upper Canada House of Assembly, a former Sheriff of York and once one of the most undoubted servants of the Crown, had been curiously relieved by the appearance of Yankee soldiers in his home territory and had eagerly accepted a commission from Dearborn to form a body of 'Canadian volunteers'. Quite why this man changed his colours remains unclear. His sense of ambition, radicalism and hostility to arbitrary power, which caused him to question the province's closed system of administration, might be partly responsible. Wearing a white cockade and green ribbon on their hats, this quickly raised force, numbering 130 men soon after inception, took on policing duties along the Niagara frontier on behalf of the United States Army and successfully flushed out several of their countrymen known to hold anti-American sentiments. Dr. Cyrenius Chapin led the 'Forty Thieves', another group of these rough justice men working on behalf of America. A Buffalo surgeon turned partisan, he, unlike Willcocks, remained loyal to the nation which had fed him since birth.

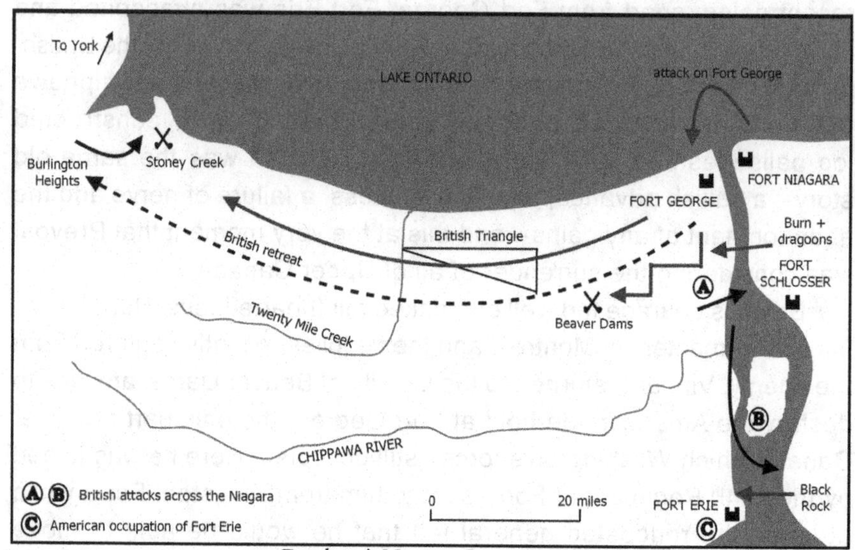

Dearborn's Niagara Campaign

From time to time, these men of the saddle came into conflict with a counterpart unit on the other side, the 'Bloody Boys' led by Lieutenant James FitzGibbon, a regular officer of the 49th Foot. In the aftermath of Stoney Creek, this energetic semi-literate soldier had undertaken to train some 50 or so soldiers of his regiment in the skills of guerilla warfare. Donning grey-green cloaks to hide their uniforms and signaling one another by ringing cowbells, these men resorted to murder and destruction, glorying in the baser forms of warfare. Treating his men '*as a lady would her piano,*' he instilled loyalty and obedience, and his commands were never disputed.

Vincent, confident in the ability of the 'Bloody Boys' to tame a population that did not appear to be strongly inclined to swear total loyalty to the British Crown, now swore that he would retake the fort that bore his sovereign's name. James FitzGibbon had taken up a position at the De Cew House, seventeen miles or so from where the Stars and Stripes flew over Fort George. Built near the banks of the sluggish Twelve Mile Creek, one of the galaxy of streams that tipped their waters into Lake Ontario, the stone built house stood at one tip of a triangle of defence that Vincent had now established near Beaver Dams. The other two angles of this inverted triangle were held by Major Peter De Haren and 3 companies of regulars [9] at their base near the mouth of the Twelve Mile Creek, and by Colonel Bisshop on the Twenty Mile Creek about five miles to the west. Patrolling the intervening countryside eastwards towards Fort George were his more mobile troops—William Merritt's Provincial Dragoons and bands of Indians in British pay. Vincent was, in his own words, trying to *'feel the pulse of the enemy,'* a medical metaphor that Chapin would have found appropriate.

Brigadier-General John Boyd, commanding at Fort George, was sensitive to their proximity. This man had openly expressed criticism of Dearborn's tortoise mentality and, in order to boost his own candidature for high military office, he ordered Colonel Charles Boerstler and the 14th U.S.Infantry to proceed towards the De Cew house and attempt to dislodge FitzGibbon and his irritating force.

Boerstler set out on the night of 23rd June with the 570 men of his regiment, 2 cannon and about 100 additional men—a large enough number, Boyd believed, to deal with the shadowy threat. Along with Boerstler rode Chapin and his 'Forty Thieves'. Chapin claimed to know the area, having recently clashed with FitzGibbon in the brush and marshland of the creek countryside. Boerstler gambled on hitting FitzGibbon when he was asleep—and, to maintain surprise, had taken every precaution to keep the Canadians ignorant of the advance.

This, of course, would be almost impossible; the Americans were observed as soon as they left Queenston. A 38 year old mother of five children emerges from the colourful pages of Canadian folklore at this moment. Recounted many times in later years, the thread of the story is undoubtedly true, but the substance might have been distorted. Claiming to have overheard American officers at Queenston talking about their intentions, Mrs Laura Secord made her way on foot through twenty miles of swampland and warned FitzGibbon of his danger. The officer, in his later reports, fails to name her as the source of information, but did admit that *'a person of slight and delicate frame,'* had visited him at the house.

FitGibbon was therefore prepared for his enemy's arrival. In heavy woodland, just west of St. Davids, he placed a band of Caughnawaga Indians under the command of a soldier fortune, the Frenchman Dominique Ducharme to lie in wait. On the 24th, he prepared an ambush

9 1 co. of the 8th Foot and 2 cos. Of the 104th Foot

for Boerstler's men. Soon after 8 a.m., the 'Forty Thieves' and the head of the American column, already feeling the heat of the morning, entered the woodland. Refreshed by the welcome shade of the trees, they slowed their hectic pre-dawn pace.

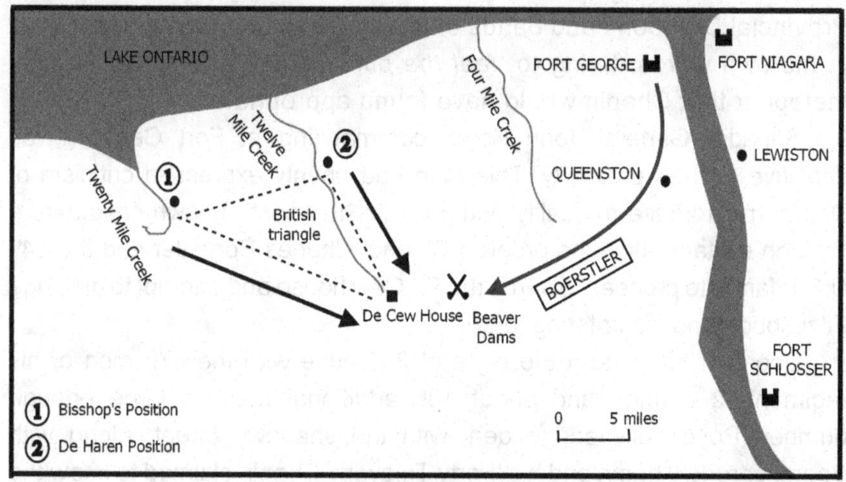

The Battle of Beaver Dams

The resulting fight would reveal all the features of a boy's adventure book ambush. The Indians, concealed behind trees on both sides of the trackway, waited until the entire column had passed and then fell upon the rear. Twenty Americans fell in the first volley. Men scattered, hurrying for the cover of trees, and order was lost. The Lieutenant-Colonel re-organised his men into a single rank and sent them charging with fixed bayonets into the woods on both sides of the track, while his two cannon fired canister and grapeshot at largely invisible targets. Keeping his troops in single line, he fought his way to the top of a hill, which, devoid of trees, allowed him greater mannoevrability and a chance to alter tactics. Here, for two hours, despite exposure to sun and enemy, they held back the Indians in the woodland's fringes and blocked every move that the warriors tried to make.

Amongst the Indians, Boerstler could now make out the faces and uniforms of British regulars and the familiar outfits of militia units. FitzGibbon, hurrying through the night to ensure that Ducharme did not gain all the glory, had arrived in time to witness the first flowing of blood, and it was, in fact, the 'Bloody Boys', now without concealing capes, that Boerstler had just seen. Unsure of the size of the force against which he was fighting, the American looked for a way of obtaining a dignified retreat with minimum casualties.

Young FitzGibbon quickly provided him with the means. Coming forward under a flag of truce, he untruthfully claimed that Major De Haren and more than 2000 men were approaching and that Boerstler consequently stood no chance of survival. The American colonel refused to believe the claim and demanded to see this absent force before surrendering. De Haren, of course, was still far away, and FitzGibbon was forced to think on his feet. Encountering a party of dragoons who happened to be riding close by, he persuaded their commanding officer to impersonate the absent major. The U.S. colonel, duped in his encounter with this officer of dragoons, eventually agreed to surrender, asking only that his officers be permitted to retain their side arms and that the militiamen should be paroled. And, by now, De Haren had at last appeared, just in time to formalize the surrender. 462 men, two guns, and the colonel of the 14th U.S. infantry passed into British hands. Boerstler soon realized that he had been the victim of a brilliant deception, delivered in such a matter-of-fact manner and bare faced way. No additional troops arrived; he had surrendered his entire force to a mere major at the head of a group of men barely half his number!

This colourful little action, soon be known as the Battle of Beaver Dam or, perhaps, more usually, as the Battle of the Beechwoods, would be an episode that America cared not to remember too closely. Boerstler, subjected much later to a Board of Inquiry, was exonerated, and most of the blame fell on Dearborn for sending out such a small force on an errand that could really only be performed by giants.

While America looked for her scapegoats, Britain identified her heroes. The battle had been an Indian victory and few, if any, white men had fired a shot. Ducharme had chosen the point of ambush, but had left the Caughnawagas to secure the victory. FitzGibbon was charmingly honest in his tributes, never claiming to have been responsible for success. '*With respect to the affair with Captain Boerstler, not a shot was fired on our side by any but the Indians . . . . The only share I claim is taking advantage of a favorable moment to offer them* (the American forces) *protection from the tomahawk and scalping knife. The Indian Department did all the rest . . .*' The Caugnawagas received formal thanks but nothing more. Many went home, determined to play no further part in the white man's wars.

Britain's self-esteem fed well on the momentum triggered by their unusual victory at Beaver Dams. Within hours her forces had moved back to the banks of the Niagara River and were staring across the water at the American positions at Black Rock and Fort Schlosser. On 5th July British and Canadian troops crossed the river, the first of several raiding parties that would bait the Americans in the next few days. Lieutenant-Colonel Thomas Clark and a party of the 2nd Lincoln Militia landed near Fort Schlosser and raided the store houses which supplied the fort. They crossed again that evening, carrying back a 6 pounder gun and supplies of salt, tobacco and whiskey. On the 11th FitzGibbon and Bisshop crossed further south, sensing that Black Rock might be an easy target. Soon after midnight, in a thick concealing mist, several boats pushed out from the Chippewa Creek. In them were the 'Bloody Boys' and perhaps 250 regulars. Advancing on the settlement of Black Rock immediately after landing, the raiders set fire to the blockhouses, naval yards and barracks without the loss of a single man. Still unchecked, Bisshop led his men through the town and towards nearby Fort Gibson. Colonel Peter Porter, the war hawk politician now in command of the garrison, was awakened from his sleep and, wearing only his nightshirt, rode off through the night to rouse the men of Buffalo, leaving the British to root out the liquor and any attractive supplies that might be stored within the houses of the town.

By 7a.m.,with the flames of Black Rock's naval yard no longer quite so visible against a lightening northern sky, Porter had assembled 250 men outside Buffalo, amongst them some Seneca Indians. This would be the first time in the war that the Americans had employed Indians as fighting allies. The retaliatory attack came when it was least expected. Half of Bisshop's force had already returned to Canada with boats laden with barrels of whiskey and flour. The remainder, caught like smugglers in the process of dragging their vessels to the water's edge, hurriedly abandoned the task and, reaching for pistols and muskets, turned to face their attackers. Some of the war's most savage fighting took place in those twenty minutes of angry tangle on the Niagara beach—and Bisshop was amongst those that fell, shot in three places. Gathered up by his men, he lived long enough to make his report to De Rottenburg, coughing up blood as he dictated his account.

Nobody, given the revival of British fortunes, now expected Fort George to remain in American hands for very much longer. On 27th July, Peter Porter vented his disquiet at America's failure to resume an offensive. '*The truth is . . . . that we had an army at Fort George for two months past, which at any moment of this period might, by a vigorous and well-directed exertion of three or four days have prostrated the whole of the enemy's force in this division of the country, and yet this army lies panic-struck, shut up and whipped in by a few hundred miserable savages, leaving the whole of this frontier, except the mile in extent which they occupy, exposed to the inroads and depradations of the enemy.*' And, in Washington, the flavours of criticism were even more sour—and scapegoats would need to be found. The Speaker of the House of Representatives, Henry Clay, voiced a demand for Dearborn's dismissal, a demand with which Armstrong and Madison were fully in accord. Dearborn received a letter a few days later. '*I have the President's orders to express to you his decision that you retire from the command . . . .*', Armstrong wrote in a terse, less than diplomatic note to the general. James Wilkinson was confirmed in his place. The latter, receiving the confirmation of his promotion, also received instructions to abandon the Lake Erie and Niagara front and concentrate instead on forcing the issue in the valley of the St. Lawrence.

CHAPTER 7

'I have yet to learn that the color of the skin can affect a man's qualifications or usefulness.'

At Montréal Baron Francis de Rottenburg had been vigilant. The city had long operated as the strategic cockpit for the whole of Canada, controlling the water routes from the Great Lakes through the coveted fishing grounds of the Atlantic coastlands to the wide ocean beyond. Whoever controlled Montréal would soon possess Canada in its entirety, a fact appreciated by every high ranking British official serving in that country.

The city, however, enjoyed few natural defences. The western and southern defence lines were only lightly held and remained vulnerable to an enemy advance from Lake Ontario or northwards from Lake Champlain along the Richelieu River. From the latter direction, where the paths of invasion were masked with the copious growth of lush woodland, the ease with which the Americans could advance against Montréal had been demonstrated during the War of Independence when an American rebel army under Richard Montgomery had briefly taken possession of the city. In order to keep himself informed of enemy movements, Prevost set up an intelligence network that reported every step or glance that might suggest an imminent move towards the city. For this he employed men on both sides of the border, bribing Americans living in New York State with lucrative contracts for the importation of goods into British Canada.

But the Champlain pathway was a source of vulnerability for America as well. Positioned like a knife that had been thrust into the epidermis of the United States, these lowlands would provide a route of entry for the Canadians and offer direct access to the valuable Hudson River system. Yet, for two reasons, Britain, at this point of the war, had no wish to launch an offensive from Montréal. Firstly, it remained in Britain's interests to avoid any disruption to the movement north along the Richelieu River valley of the cattle and provisions purchased from the American contractors in Vermont and New York State. '*I would not have the essential service of the transport of stores to Upper Canada interrupted on any consideration; nor do I think it proper to beget invitation in the mind of the people of the United States by any act that does not bear on the face of it a just retaliation on the military force of that country for wanton and unprovoked injuries,*' he rather laboriously explained in a letter to Lieutenant-Colonel 'Red George' Macdonnel, commander of the Glengarry Light Infantry. Secondly, the sentiments of New Englanders, still solidly opposed to the war and believed to be fairly sympathetic to the British cause, would obviously alter if British soldiers' boots produced a trail of devastation in their wake.

In the United States, memories of that easy advance on Montréal, only 38 years previously, seem to have faded—for her generals made no early attempt to replicate that success. Benjamin Forsyth's autumn raid on Ganagogue was followed by a similar raid on 6th February 1813 on Elizabethtown, apparently in retaliation for a British raid two days previously, when a redcoat detachment crossed from Prescott and set fire to buildings on the fringes of Ogdensburg. Crossing the iced St. Lawrence during the night of the 7th, Forsyth, at the head of 200 men, freed a clutch of American prisoners held in the town's gaol and then took 52 British—and all at the cost of just one man wounded.

'Red George' Macdonnel, however, was intent on stirring up the slumbering hornet's nest. Feeling that Britain should emasculate potential American bases on the opposite side of the river, he ignored Prevost's orders to remain on the defensive and set about organising a campaign of aggression on the St.Lawrence that would test the republic's ability to defend her border. Ogdensburg was again the target. Dividing the 600 men of his Glengarry regiment into two columns, he began to cross the ice from Prescott on 21st February with six light guns, throwing his men at the very centre of the defending force clustered within the small American town. Captain John Jenkins, commanding on the Canadian right, was soon pinned down by heavy enemy fire and his men halted on the ice close to the American shore. Macdonnel, leading the left column, fared better, and his men, passing quickly over ice that cracked and groaned as they moved, reached the American banks and ploughed through snow drifts to engage. Jenkins, inspired by his example, rallied his troops and charged. Forsyth's nervous militia instantly fled, stumbling through the snow, their dark silhouettes providing instantly visible targets for any Canadian who wished to take a shot. Forsyth, with the few regulars in his ranks, retired to Sackets Harbor with tales of his setback.

Macdonnel's victory was more significant than it at first seemed. With him on his return to Prescott were 60 captives, 16 captured cannon, 400 rifles, 800 muskets, 2 tons of ammunition and 1500 barrels of pork. But the less material gains were even more valuable. The merchants of the town, inextricably engaged in the illicit trade across the frontier, were opposed to the war and asked both sides to be left in peace. Prevost, who had expressly forbidden the attack, now changed his tune and congratulated Macdonnel for his action. '*Although you have rather exceeded your orders, I am well pleased with what you have done.*' Forsyth vowed to take revenge. The chance, however, never materialised, for he received orders to take his men to support the garrison of Sackets Harbor. Ogdensburg was degarrisoned and served no further part in the war. Gunfire on the St. Lawrence would not, for a while, be heard.

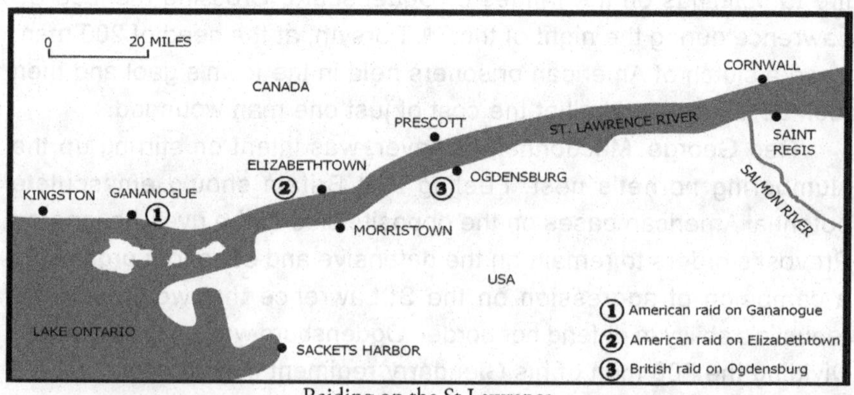

Raiding on the St.Lawrence

Prevost, sensing that America would probably be in no mood to test the St. Lawrence defences for some time, could not so lightly dismiss the possibility of a move from the direction of Lake Champlain. To guard against such a possibility, he established a garrison on Ile aux Noix, close to the point where the Richelieu River tips out of Lake Champlain on its route north. Here Major George Taylor and several companies of the 100th Foot took up post and watched the lake waters to the south.

Congress was anxious to terminate the vibrant cross border trade carried out by American citizens and to punish the entrepreneurs of Vermont and New York, who fed the armies and citizens of the nation's enemy. In an early attempt to stem the flow, two American sloops were positioned at Plattsburgh on Lake Champlain, not far from where Taylor had taken his place of watch. On 3rd June, in the mists of an early summer morning, Taylor encountered the two sloops, the 'Eagle' and 'Growler' at full sail off Rouses Point. A dutiful officer with a keen sense of mission, Major Taylor sent out his three gunboats, each armed with a 6 pounder gun and with supporting soldiers in rowing boats, and tackled the duo in the channel of the Richelieu. Taken completely by surprise, both American boats endeavoured to turn around and tack against the strengthening wind. Slowed, restricted and outmanoeuvred, they were forced to surrender. Taken into British service, they were renamed 'Broke' and'Shannon.'[10]

The action, hardly significant, had reverberations in Montréal and Washington. It triggered thoughts in the former city of a waterborne advance to Plattsburgh, something that contradicted the long-held view that an invasion of the United States from the St. Lawrence would be inadvisable. A division of minds retarded detailed planning, but eventually Major-General Richard Stovin was placed in command of an expedition, with the objective of discouraging the transfer of American troops from this area to the more contentious battle area of the Niagara.

In Washington, the loss of the ships opened up a chasm of concern. An investigation revealed the lamentable shortage of resources in northern New York State and the absence of any cohesive war strategy. Major-general Wade Hampton, army commander in this zone, had only the rawest of recruits, and virtually no experienced officers in his barracks at Burlington.

10 another source suggests that they were renamed 'Chub' and 'Finch'

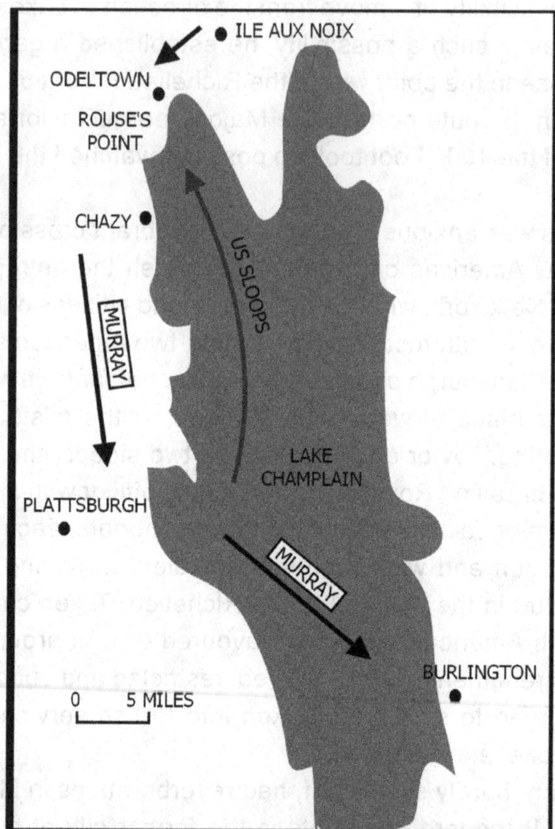

The Champlain Lowlands

But Armstrong, a man who preferred to formulate opinions without ever visiting the fields of war, had long ago convinced himself that Hampton, with the assistance of New York militia forces, was more than adequately equipped to advance in strength against Montréal.

The preparations for this advance, however, developed only in Armstrong's mind, and it was the British who struck first. On 29th July 1813 Commander Thomas Everard, R.N.,and Lieutenant-Colonel John Murray arrived at Ile aux Noix, accompanied by the 13th, 100th and 103rd Regiments of Foot and detachments of Canadian forces, 950 men in all, aiming their sights at Plattsburgh and Burlington. Sailing up the Richelieu in the sloop 'Wasp', Murray landed at Chazy from where he issued a proclamation of re-assurance, telling the inhabitants of the area that private property would not be touched provided that no opposition was encountered. Plattsburgh, held by General Benjamin Moers and a handful of timorous militia, was promptly abandoned and much of its fabric was destroyed during the twelve hours of British occupation. Having tasted the sweetness of an easy victory, Everard crossed the lake, baited the American force at Burlington with his long-range guns and then fell upon American merchantmen hiding in Shelburne Bay. Content with his mischief, the commander, his sloop and the accompanying soldiers recrossed the border, continuing the war-long habit of raiding, looting and withdrawing. Murray's only losses had been a few deserters from the 103rd, who, attracted by the green hills in a land of limitless potential, discarded uniforms and a life of drudgery and harsh discipline for a free but uncertain future. Murray, in pulling out so rapidly, had left America in full control of Lake Champlain's more southerly waters. Protected by a fort on high bluffs overlooking Burlington, three sloops were under construction for the American lake flotilla—and not one of these was even scarred by Murray's Lake Champlain ravages.

With little incentive on either side to further bouts of belligerence in an area of cross-border harmony, this promising channel of invasion fell silent again. America preferred to ignore the lure of Montréal, while Canada, for reasons stated, remained reluctant to launch more than diversionary moves in a region where sympathy with Britain burned so strongly. Whether the participants liked it or not, the issue would be settled in the less complicated landscape of Erie and Niagara, where shorter distances and a higher density of population would make campaigning easier. The dividends to be gained from any victory here would be minor but accumulative. For, unlike the capture of Montréal or Albany, which would end the war at a stroke, the taking of territory on the Great Lakes would serve as bargaining chips in the peace talks that must one day come. This was the pitch, then, on which the generals and naval commanders wished to play—for the immediate future, anyway.

But, despite the unquestionable importance of dominating the waters of Erie and Ontario, gunfire on those waters had remained almost unheard during the spring and early summer. The periodic clashes between the winter-built flotillas had been mainly in support of the land campaigns against York, Fort George and Sackets Harbor. Warships had accompanied the movement of troops, had fired a few rounds at establishments on the land and then pulled back to leave the men on the beaches to fade or shine in glory. Sooner or later, however, the naval men would demand the limelight for themselves and seek to become the heroes of the nation—and a battle on the water of Erie or Ontario, divorced from any campaigning on land, would be sought. The cauldron, slowly warming during the winter while the ships were being constructed, was approaching boiling point and must soon flow over.

Friction between Perry and Chauncey nearly prevented the first sortie of the American fleet. The latter siphoned off the best men recruited from the eastern seaboard and sent to Perry only the dregs and the inexperienced. '*The men that came are a motley set, blacks, soldiers and boys. I cannot think you saw them after they were selected.*' Perry wrote indignantly to Chauncey. The latter disapprovingly responded to his subordinate's near racist remark. '*I regret you are not pleased with them; for, to my knowledge, a part of them are not surpassed by any seaman we have in the fleet; and I have yet to learn that the color of the skin, or the cut and trimmings of the coat, can affect a man's qualifications or usefulness.*'

Almost as debilitating for the American naval effort was the jealousy that had recently gripped Jesse Elliot, the man awarded a sword by Congress for his brilliant capture of the British brig 'Caledonia' the previous summer and a veteran of the recent capture of York. Aged 31, four years older than Perry, he had far more battle experience than his superior and naturally smarted at his subordinate role.

Captain Robert Heriot Barclay, Perry's opposite number, had taken up his station at Amherstburg in early June and felt that the prevention of the union of the vessels constructed at Presque Isle with those built at Black Rock was his most immediate duty. In numbers of ships, the British were slightly inferior, but in broadside power Perry's ships could fire almost twice the weight (896 pounds to 459). All of Britain's available lake launched ships had taken up blockading positions off America's coast by the beginning of June 1813.

The blockaders, however, failed to prevent the amalgamation of the two American squadrons. On the 19th June, the Black Rock vessels left their port in thick fog and successfully combined with the ships of Presque Isle. The timing of this move had been fortuitous. Barclay had been lying off Presque Isle for more than a fortnight, but had withdrawn on the evening before the American sortie. Barclay could only scowl in frustration at the distant masts safely protected by the sand bars off Presque Isle.

This setback provoked his determination to destroy the installations of the port that succoured the enemy ships. He asked Procter to assist him in an amphibious operation. Procter sympathized, but felt that he had insufficient men—and the opportunity for liquidation of the United States base slipped away. *'If means had been afforded me,'* Barclay lamented in a letter to Prevost, *'I could, in all probability, have effected the destruction of the enemy's vessels at Presque Isle, and have secured superiority on this lake.'*

On the very last day of July, Perry noticed that the flotilla blockading Presque Isle had again disappeared, giving him an opportunity at last to sail his ships over the bar into the open waters of the lake. Barclay had been invited to attend a dinner in Dover and, full of his own self-importance, had pulled back all of his ships to port. But another source of information suggests that *'stress of weather and lack of provisions'* might have been the true reason for sailing away. Whatever the reason, Barclay had gone and Perry was free to venture out.

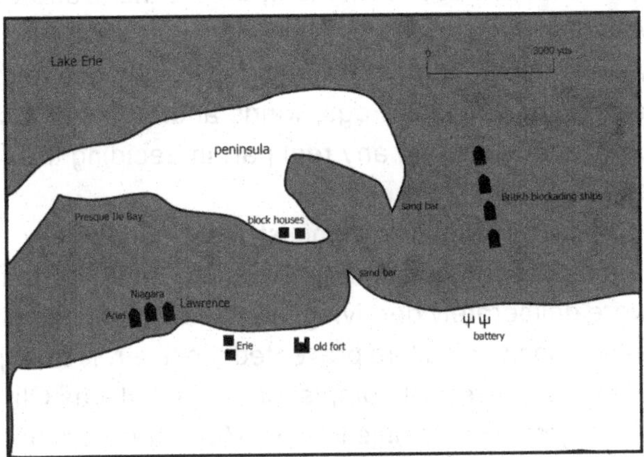

The blockade of Presque Isle

Crossing the protective bar, however, turned out to be far from easy. The wind blew from the east that day, Sunday August 1st, forcing the water against the Canadian shore and reducing the depth of the flow over the bar to just over five feet. Two of the gunboats crossed without impediment and took up defensive positions outside the harbour. The 'Niagara' stood by just inside, her guns ready, while the 'Lawrence', derigged and gunless to lighten her weight, tried to pass over. A number of watertight boxes, referred to as 'camels', were attached to her hull and, with these in place, she was dragged for a mile, a strenuous operation that took more than a day. The 'Niagara' was manhandled in the same manner. Nervous eyes glanced out into the lake during the long hours of suspense and sweated work. Mercifully, the horizon remained clear, the wind remained gracious and Barclay's ships never appeared. By the evening of the 4th, all the ships were over the bar and waiting at the harbour mouth. Luck breathed again on the Americans that night—only hours later, Barclay's flotilla resumed its vigil outside the port. Seeing America's ships in the open water, he naturally assumed that they were primed for battle. Reluctant to fight without the 'Detroit', he cravenly sailed away. In fact, Perry's ships were far from ready for any contest. The 'Lawrence' and 'Niagara' still had no guns.

On the 10th, sinewed by the arrival of Jesse Elliott and some additional seamen, Perry's fleet sailed into the open lake in a quest for mischief. Basing themselves at Put-in-Bay on Gibraltar Island, the Americans approached the British anchorage in the mouth of the Detroit River. An action at thls moment, before the 'Detroit' joined the British fleet, would have comfortably tilted the scales in Perry's favour. Unfortunately he and several of his men fell ill with lake fever, and the fleeting opportunity was lost. Fogs, winds and quirks of luck seemed to be the only factors playing any real part in deciding the fortunes of this campaign.

Discord and an ineffective administration additionally hamstrung the British side. Barclay and Procter, working together, felt that their superiors were deliberately depriving them of men and supplies. A lack of sails, masts, guns and sailors prevented the 'Detroit' from joining the squadron, despite her recent completion. In fact, it was Oliver Perry's navy that was largely responsible for this. More than adequate supplies of all these materials lay at Long point on the far side of the lake, but these had been rendered almost inaccessible by the energies of Perry's nine ships. Prevost, frustrated by Barclay's and Proctor's lack of any assertive move, wrote to the latter in a hectoring and confident manner. '*The experience obtained from Sir James Yeo's conduct toward a fleet infinitely superior will satisfy Captain Barclay that he has only to dare and the enemy will be discomfited.*' In a similar letter a few days later, he was even more forthright in his demands: '*I cannot hesitate in desiring some bold attempt may be made without delay by Captain Barclay to gain the ascendancy and open an outlet for the supplies lying at Long Point for the Right Division of the Army.'*

While Britain was trying to avoid being outclassed on Lake Erie, Perry, despite being laid low by lake fever, which kept him in his bunk, was making detailed preparations. On 31st August he received the welcome support of 100 riflemen from Kentucky, rough and simple men who had never seen a ship before or water wider than a river. Expected to serve as sharpshooters and marines, they were soon climbing masts and rigging as easily as they might have climbed a tree back home. For nine more days, men sweated, trained and drilled, honed to near fighting perfection in the shelter of Gibraltar Island, awaiting the masts of the British, who presumably must one day come. On 9th September, with the 'Niagara' and 'Lawrence' now fully armed, Perry called his officers into conference and outlined his plans for drawing the British into action.

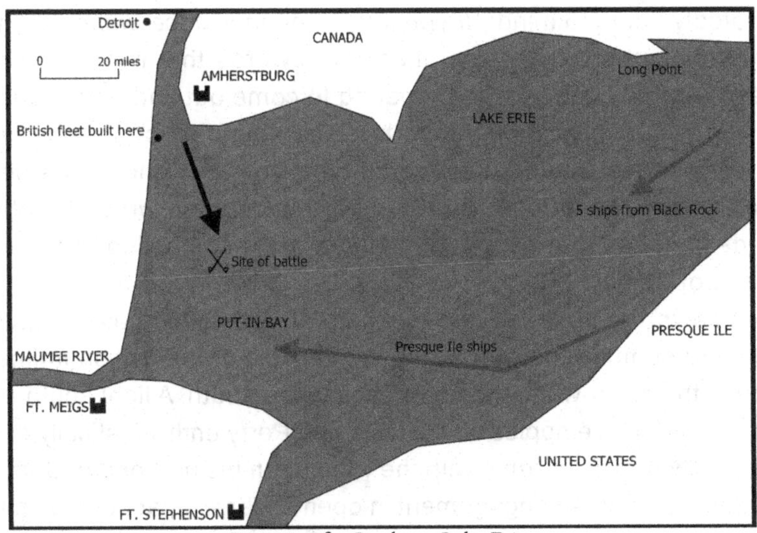

Preparing for Battle on Lake Erie

He chose to match each of his ships with one of the opposing fleet. His own ship, the 'Lawrence', would seek out and engage the 'Detroit', now known to be armed with guns stripped from the fort at Amherstburg. Elliott and the 'Niagara' would take on the 'Queen Charlotte' while the 'Caledonia' was paired off with the 'Hunter'. The 'Somers', 'Porcupine' and 'Tigress' were jointly given the honour of dealing with the 'Lady Prevost' and 'Little Belt', and the commanders of the supporting gunboats 'Ariel' and 'Scorpion' were told to flank the 'Niagara' and use their long guns until the 'Niagara' with her 34 pound carronades could close in on her target. Wary of the long range guns of his enemy, he hoped to approach to within 100 yards of his quarry and batter Barclay's major ships at point-blank range with his carronades. All nine ships were to remain in line, half a cable length apart. A blue pennant flying at the masthead of the 'Laurence', and bearing the inscription: *'Don't Give Up the Ship'* [11] would be the signal to commence action.

Perry had no way of knowing whether his enemy would be at anchor or in sail when he approached, and his orders were general enough to accommodate both possibilities. During the night of the 9th, while a full moon tinselled the dark waters with silver, he rose from his bunk and paced the deck, thinking constantly of Barclay's long-range guns and the damage that could be inflicted on America's ships if they failed to close with the enemy. A maxim of Nelson's repeatedly came to mind: *'If you lay the enemy close alongside, you cannot be out of your place.'* Looking towards the northern shore, he sensed that Barclay was preparing to come out and was probably thinking very similar thoughts to his. The sound of long-range guns and carronades would surely come tomorrow and one of the fleets would emerge victorious. He retired to his cabin to write the letters and despatches that every commander feels compelled to write on the eve of battle.

At dawn the next day, the lookouts of both sides gave the alert, each side spotting the other—the six vessels of the British in line of battle to the north-west, the Americans to the south. A light south-east wind caused gentle ripples on the lake, and Perry enthusiastically drove his line towards the enemy with the wind upon his port beam. Barclay, too, was intent on an engagement in open water and, about nine miles from the mainland, he halted his ships, still facing south-west, and awaited the enemy's arrival. The schooner 'Chippawa' armed with a single long-range 18 pounder on her bow, led the way, followed by the star of the fleet, the three masted 'Detroit', a ship that Perry

---

11 In memory of James Lawrencem whose recent action off Boston had elevated him to hero status (see next chapter)

had never wished to see. Elliott, still chagrined at his subordinate position, had been hoping, even at this late hour, to command the van, but, observing that the 'Queen Charlotte' sailed fourth in the British line, Perry moved the more junior officer and the 'Niagara' even further back, adding even more acid to the mental hurt that festered in Elliot's mind.

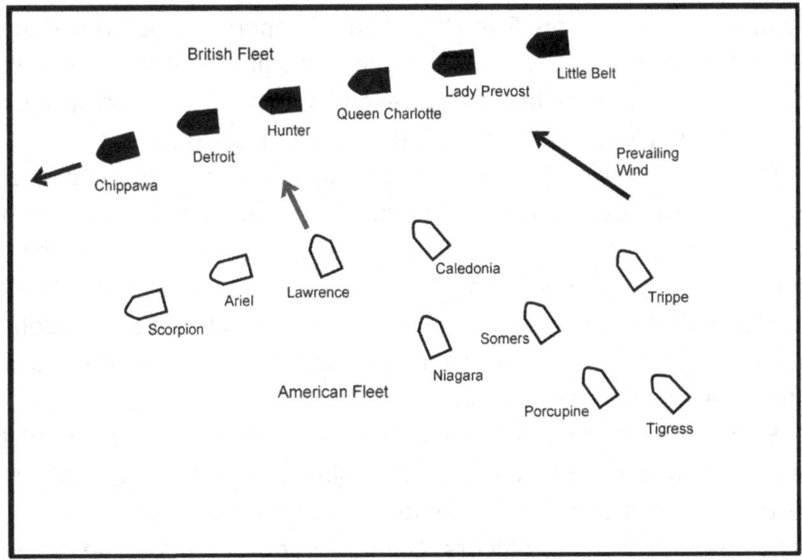

The Battle of Lake Erie - the opening positions

Perry instructed his men to eat an early lunch, reasoning that they would fight better on full stomachs. Then, with the 'Lawrence' in the van, he closed in on the British at a 25 degree angle, a line of approach that would protect his ships from raking fire and enable him to use his broadsides at the earliest opportunity. Then came the characteristic silence, the hush that always prefaces battles as men offer hurried prayers, embrace comrades and think of those at home, followed by the moments of inner preparation, the mental processes, the anxieties and the acceptance of what must soon occur.

Perry was anxious to close the gap as quickly as possible and avoid being caught by the enemy's armament of long-range guns. At 11.45 a.m., according to the logs, the first shot of the battle, a 24 pound ball from the 'Detroit' fell just short of the 'Lawrence'. A second shot killed an American crewman. Below decks, Perry's pet spaniel whimpered. The British had the Americans within range. The little 'Ariel' and 'Scorpion', still faithfully flanking their larger sister, opened with their long-range 32 pounder guns, but their shots caused no harm to the thick frame of the 'Detroit'.

Barclay's strategy quickly became clear. 'Hunter', 'Detroit' and 'Queen Charlotte', together with a combined strength of 34 port broadsides, would concentrate their fire on the 'Lawrence' and batter the vessel into an early submission. Reduction of the supporting ships would then follow. The British vessels remained in static line, half a cable length apart*, standard battle tactics that every British admiral, victorious or otherwise, would probably have imbibed with his mother's milk.

Perry, aware of the peril, led his ships forward, straining every sail to take full advantage of the favourable wind. The 'Niagara' for no obvious reason, failed to obey. The 'Somers', 'Tigress' and 'Porcupine', with less sail area, were unable to keep up, and the two gunboats, 'Ariel' and 'Scorpion', had also fallen well behind. Only the 'Caledonia' sailed faithfully, accompanying the flagship through the murderous fire of the enemy's long-range guns.

By 12.15, according to the logs, the 'Lawrence' was close enough to the 'Detroit' and 'Hunter' to spray both ships with shot—and, of course, the British ships could only employ short-range armament in reply. One of Barclay's senior officers, Captain Robert Finnis of the 'Queen Charlotte' died in the next few minutes, felled by an American shot. Realising that his vessel was too far in the rear to reach the 'Lawrence' with her carronades, he had ordered his crew to draw ahead of the 'Hunter', and was on the deck when the fatal shot was delivered. His first officer died shortly afterwards, and the command devolved upon a young lieutenant. The 'Queen Charlotte' remained in action throughout the battle, and credit must go to the inexperenced youth for his coolness during the two hours of battle. For those two long hours, the British trio concentrated their fire on this single American ship. By 1.45 p.m. 22 of the crew of the 'Lawrence' lay dead and 61 wounded. Masts, rigging and braces had been shot away, and the ship was little more than a hulk. But her guns kept firing, manned by the 20 uninjured crew men, who continued to respond to every one of Perry's commands. Blood seeped though the decking, dripping onto the faces of the injured lying on the surgeon's table just below. Several balls passed through the lower decks, one cutting a midshipman in half. The poor wretch had just had his mangled armed dressed by the surgeon. Another shot upset a pot of peas. A pig greedily ate the peas, despite the fact that both its hind legs had been shot away. Perry, himself, seemed to have been in the care of the angels, for he received not even a minor scratch. His lieutenant, too, seems to have been equally blessed. Standing next to Perry, he was knocked to the deck by a shower of grapeshot. Rising to his feet unhurt, he pulled a handful of grapeshot from his waistcoat pocket! For 200 years, men of the U.S. Navy have talked of Perry's amazing luck.

Further back, the 'Ariel', 'Caledonia' and 'Scorpion' were now engaged, firing their long-range guns with effect. But, on the lips of every sailor on the flagship, the same question remained unasked: where was the 'Niagara'? The guns of the 'Laurence' had fallen silent. The immobilized ship had become a prison for the living and a grave for the dead. But Barclay's ships were suffering as well. 'Hunter', badly fractured but still rigged, moved behind the 'Detroit' and came to the assistance of the 'Chippawa', which had taken on the 'Ariel' and the 'Scorpion'. At the rear, the 'Lady Prevost' had lost her rudder and masts and she was now drifting helplessly. The 'Little Belt', too, was failing and her guns were silent. It was now 2.30 p.m.

And still Jesse Elliott's 'Niagara' remained beyond the zone of action, well behind the 'Caledonia'; not a crewman or piece of timber had even been scarred. The officer's behaviour was unpardonable. Asked later to justify his reluctance to join in, he argued that the wind had been too light and the risk of collision too great!

His subsequent actions did little to earn him any laurels. Believing his superior to be dead, he sent orders to the 'Caledonia' to close in on the enemy while he placed his own ship where he would be screened from the enemy's guns by the dying hulk of the 'Lawrence'. The captain of the 'Caledonia' unhesitatingly moved in front of the 'Lawrence' and, exposing his ship to the full fury of Barclay's vessels, single-handedly took on the 'Hunter', 'Detroit' and 'Queen Charlotte'.

Half a mile of water separated the 'Laurence' from the 'Niagara'. Through that water a small boat was now being rowed. On board was Perry, in full dress uniform, and four sailors. For a while, the boat was spared the punishment of British guns. For, when the 'Lawrence' ceased firing, Barclay had assumed that Perry was about to surrender and held his fire. But, realising that Perry was transferring his flag, he ordered a resumption of fire, this time at the small boat that contained such an attractive target. A cannon ball ripped through the side of the rowboat. Calmly, Perry removed his coat and used it to plug the hole. To Barclay, Perry's intentions suddenly became clear; he was attempting to transfer his flag during battle, something seldom done or even contemplated. The American commodore was about to take over the uninjured ship and, once aboard, return to action. Clambering aboard the 'Niagara', he came face to face with Elliott. *'How goes the day?'* Elliott was fatuously reported as asking. One can only speculate on what Perry might have said in reply!

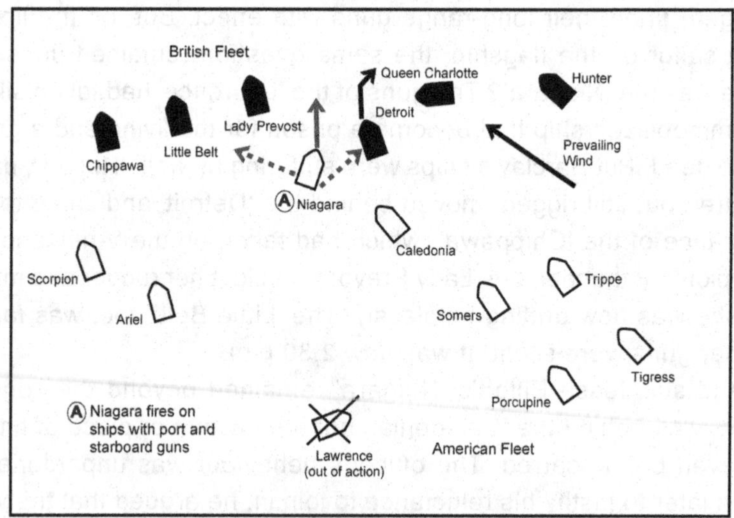

The Battle of Lake Erie - 2:40 pm

Elliott salvaged a little of his reputation in the minutes following. Transferring his own flag to the 'Somers', he was more energetic in his efforts to bring the 'Trippe' and 'Tigress' back into action. Under his command, the three small boats would play a significant part in the closing stages of the battle.

Meanwhile, the 'Lawrence', left in the care of a lieutenant, had surrendered, and Britain sensed victory. But fortune, like the capricious wind, was about to change direction and hand the glories of the day to the other side. Barclay, nursing a wound to the thigh, perceived the change before it happened. Standing on the deck of his ship, he saw the 'Niagara' approach and realised that Perry was planning to break the British line. The south-easterly breeze was threshening and 'Niagara' was bearing down at an oblique angle towards the 'Detroit'. Within minutes, the American would be in a position to rake the Britisher from bowsprit to stern with the full complement of her starboard guns. Hurriedly, Barclay turned to shout new orders, but a charge of grapeshot tore through his shoulder blade and sent him crashing to the deck. His one good arm would now be useless.

Lieutenant George Inglis, assuming command, attempted to turn the 'Detroit' around and bring her unused starboard guns into action, a manoeuvre that any experienced officer would do in the circumstances. But the 'Queen Charlotte' lay close by, and the two British vessels became entangled. Only seven minutes after Perry took command of the 'Niagara', the American was bearing down, firing at the 'Lady Prevost' and 'Chippawa' on his left and the 'Detroit', 'Queen Charlotte' and 'Hunter' on his right. Passing through the shaky British line, he turned about and repeated his performance, supported now by the schooners and gunboats, which attacked the exposed sterns of the two entangled ships. All of Perry's ships, with the exception of the 'Lawrence' were now in action and employing the full complement of their guns.

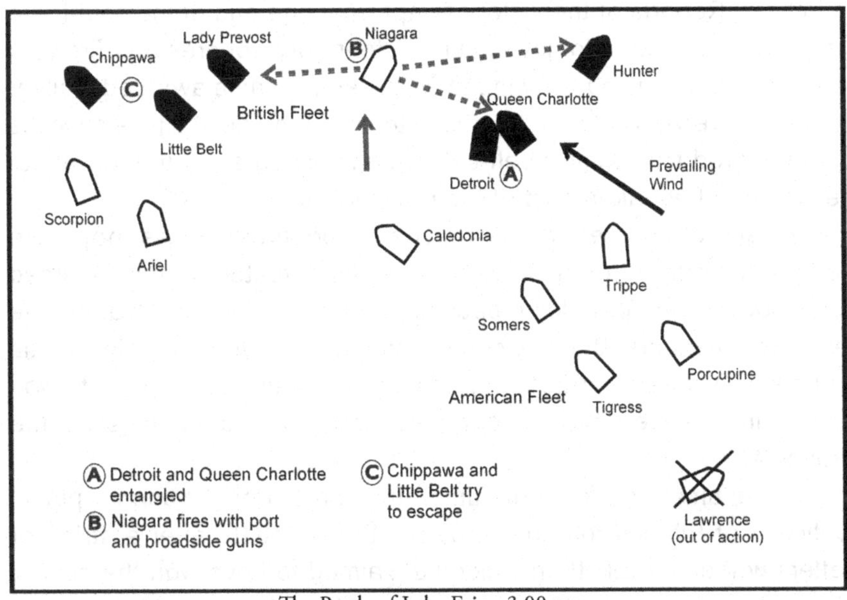

The Battle of Lake Erie - 3:00 pm

The carnage was frightful. Every British captain would be listed amongst the casualties, and all but one now lay moaning in pain below decks. Only Lieutenant Edward Buchan, commanding on the 'Lady Prevost', remained on deck. Shot in the face, he was leaning on the companionway, staring blankly at the 'Niagara' mentally unable to respond to his danger.

Just eight minutes after Perry broke the British line—and about four hours after the first shot had been fired, the 'Detroit' struck her colours and surrendered. The 'Queen Charlotte', her mizzen shot away, the 'Hunter' and 'Lady Prevost' followed her example. The 'Chippewa' and 'Little Belt', however, tried to escape, but were quickly netted. Perry's report of the action to Harrison was pithy and factual. '*We have met the enemy and they are ours—two ships, two brigs, one schooner and a sloop.*' This was to become the most famous despatch of the war. To William Jones, Secretary of the Navy, he was no more expansive: '*. . . . It has pleased the Almighty to give to the arms of the United States a signal victory over their enemies on this lake . . . .* ', he began. Forty-four Englishmen had died that day and 103 lay wounded. America had lost 21 and sustained 63 wounded.

The repercussions of the battle were out of all proportion to these numbers. Reports of the victory swept from one end of the country to the other, the sparks of joy igniting celebratory bonfires and firework displays, and causing the wine to flow. Pennsylvania awarded a silver medal to everyone who had participated in the battle. A single success had restored the nation's self-esteem and wiped away the downbeat feeling that had taken hold of the republic's soul.

Britain, of course, had no reason for bonfires, unless they were to burn the effigies of those who had been defeated. Barclay blamed Commodore Yeo for holding back resources. Yeo, in turn, blamed the army commanders. Barclay, court-martialled a year later for losing his squadron, was exonerated. In England, the press went out of its way to convince readers that the defeated forces had not been part of the Royal Navy!

At the time, and for some time afterwards, Perry made no public criticism of Elliott's role in the battle. But, in 1818, after a string of letters written by Elliott, in which he claimed to have won the action, Perry openly revealed his feelings in a private letter to Elliott: '*Mean and despicable as you have proved yourself to be I shall never cease to criminate myself . . . for screening you from public contempt.'* The reason for Elliott's failure to support his commodore in the heat of battle cannot be hard to find. Resentful at having to take commands from a younger man and denied the chance to lead the van, he had hoped to deny Perry the accolade that would surely follow victory.

Erie's water battle and the delayed completion of the 'General Pike', the ship damaged during Britain's attack on Sackets Harbor, gave America a 4 to 1 superiority in long-range guns. In terms of carronades, however, the British developed an advantage of almost 2 to 1. As a result, both sides would attempt to reverse the tactics that had been employed in the recent battle. Britain now favoured fighting at short distance while the United States would seek to engage at a much longer range.

American land success at Fort George in the early summer had already snapped Britain's water route from Kingston and York to distant Amherstburg. Since that time, provisions and supplies for Procter's garrison in the west had been forced to follow a route along the northern shore of Lake Ontario through Burlington Heights to Turkey Point on Lake Erie's north shore. From here the laden boats would attempt to traverse Lake Erie, relying upon Providence rather than the British fleet to protect them during the journey. On 9th September, the day before the Battle of Lake Erie, five bateaux had successfully run the gauntlet and reached Amherstburg with 171 barrels of flour—and the fort's bakers would be busy for several days. Perry's victory on the following day, however, swept away this gossamer-like lifeline and rendered Amherstburg vulnerable for the battle had handed control of Lake Erie to the United States.

It would consequently be some time before the British fleet dared to expose masts and sails in any action with the Americans. A plan, hurriedly concocted in July to attack Sackets Harbor again, had been dropped when two Newfoundland Canadians deserted and told the Americans of Britain's intentions. Ambitious plans like this would not reappear on British captains' tables for some time. Erie was effectively an American lake.

CHAPTER 8

'May the eternal vengeance of Heaven hurl them to some station where they will terminate their inhuman butcheries'

Sinking America's ships on the ocean's water and suffocating her sea lanes was more likely to purchase British victory than any gunfire on an inland lake. Equally, an ability to resist this slow strangulation and somehow assert her role as one of the world's trading nations should be enough to provide the young nation with sufficient clout to argue for a respectable settlement, or even a little more. By early 1813, with the interior war developing as nothing more than a series of tedious raids, the leading men on both sides had realized that the ocean fringes would be the only theatres where these bargaining chips might be purchased.

Yet, even here, the issue had never been clear cut. A tight blockade of American ports, something of which Britain was highly capable, and a strict denial to America of all trade with the outside world, had not been attempted, despite the Admiralty's orders to Admiral Sir John Borlase Warren to close the Chesapeake and Delaware ports. British double standards had been very largely responsible for this. Consular officials had readily granted licences to American merchants to supply Wellington's army in Spain with flour, grain and other supplies. In consequence, ships had travelled fully loaded to Cadiz and Bilbao, boosting America's exports in value during 1813 by $15,000,000, just over half the total value of her agricultural exports immediately prior to the war.

On 26th December 1812, an official blockade of the Chesapeake and Delaware was proclaimed, and this 'open door' was at last slammed shut, simply because Wellington had now entered France and no longer stood in need of such large quantities of provisions. Britain's forces in Canada, however, were now in need of food—and this the anti-war merchants of New England were still willing to provide. So, when the blockade was reinforced in March 1813, the ports of New England were deliberately excluded. Boston ships sailed to Halifax without much fear of seizure—and often returned filled with the produce of the Canadian maritimes. The lucrative land trade with the enemy was still taking place. Herds of cattle were driven from New England into Canada, destined to be eaten by Canadian forces. '*Two-thirds of the army in Canada are . . . . eating beef provided by American contractors,*' Prevost was approvingly to assert at the end of 1813, looking back on a year when the only successful invasions of Canada seemed to have been those carried out by drovers and farmers.

President Madison would have preferred to see a closed trading border, but was powerless to prevent these independently minded citizens from taking advantage of the opportunities Britain had placed in their path. In a message to Congress in February 1813, he wordily berated Britain for her '*unfortunate progress in undermining those principles of morality and religion which are the best foundations of national happiness,*' and, '*having for its object to dissolve the ties of allegiance, and the sentiments of loyalty in the adversary nation, and to seduce and separate its component parts the one from the other.*'

With her ports left open, New England prospered as a distribution centre for imports and exports. Ladies in Charleston, desiring to dress themselves in the latest European fashions, had only to acquire a contact in Boston. In return, Carolina cotton found its way northward for export to Manchester. Boston's bankers, as well as her merchant classes, grew richer, profiting from a war that should have brought equal frugality and hardship to everyone.

The blockade, for whatever it was worth, was largely designed to keep America's warships sealed in. The 'President', 'Congress' and 'Essex' had long since gone to sea, but it was known that the 'Constellation' lay at Norfolk, while the 'United States' and 'Macedonian', the captured British frigate, were berthed at New London and the 'Adams' was at Alexandria. The 'Chesapeake' and 'Constitution', stationed at Boston, remained at liberty to go where they wished. They had already marked up an impressive list of killings of merchant vessels.

It was at this moment that Britain, having sustained so many humiliations, sought—and found—another tender body part at which to stab. Chesapeake Bay provided something of a soft under belly, and an arterial route inland. A naval expedition in this direction, something more co-ordinated and ambitious than anything attempted in the earlier war, might be the way to injure America terminally. The Admiralty, congratulating itself on finding a vulnerable point, looked for the man needed to lead the expedition.

Their Lordships selected Sir George Cockburn, who had been living before the mast since the age of nine and risen through merit alone to the rank of rear-admiral. On 31st October 1812 he had received an order to abandon his post off Spain and report to Admiral Warren in Bermuda. Here he was given details of his new responsibility and provided with the ships with which to accomplish the task.

Cockburn was almost the stereotype of officer portrayed in novels and films. Hard-working himself, he expected others to match his exacting standards and disciplined those who failed. He applied the lash for even the most minor of irregularities. Stories of his draconian rule and alleged harassment of American citizens would later make him feared throughout the United States. '*May the eternal vengeance of Heaven hurl them to some station that will terminate their inhuman butcheries and savage cruelties—they disgrace human nations,*' an American toastmaster proclaimed, specifically identifying Admiral Warren in his sentiment of hate.

Events and planning, as usual, were to evolve very slowly and out of sequence. On 9th January 1813 Britain belatedly declared its reasons for going to war with America! Among the reasons offered was an argument that the United States had sided with France and was endeavouring to destroy British commerce. And, in this blustering explanation, London denied that it had any intentions of conquering or occupying any of America's expansive territories. Then, in February, the formal blockade of Chesapeake and Delaware Bays was started, followed in March by an announcement of the enlargement of the blockade from the mouth of the Mississippi northward as far as the Hudson.

Britain's first prize was snatched within twenty-four hours of the establishment of the blockade. On 8th February the schooner 'Lottery' was taken in Chesapeake Bay after sailors from the 'Belvidera' and 'Statrira', on duty in the bay, boarded the American ship. Nineteen of the latter's crew were killed or wounded during the brawl on her deck. Britain lost nearly as many. A few day's later, another schooner, the 'Cora', was taken. The capture of the pair was a clear signal that Britain intended to enforce a partial blockade, except, that is, in the favoured area of New England.

Another of America's structural weaknesses was now exposed. There was no unified naval command in Chesapeake Bay. Each of the governors of the adjacent states, Delaware, Maryland and Virginia, was responsible for the defence of his section of the coastline and for the activities of the state's naval forces. Convinced that, sooner or later, the British would attack the city, the jewel of the Chesapeake, Captain Charles Gordon, naval commander in Baltimore, asked the Secretary of the Navy for permission to requisition some of the port's privateers and send them to patrol the Potomac's waters. Major-General Samuel Smith, Gordon's counterpart on land, held the same opinion and so called for militia support from the neighbouring states to shore up the city's defences. By late March the defences were as stout, or even stronger, than those of any other seaport. The British, coming close to Baltimore a few days later, were impressed, and no attack was consequently made.

But Cockburn and Warren were not completely deterred and still felt that the extended fingers of the two major bays provided golden opportunities for a fatal stabbing. Cockburn, days after arriving at the head of the Chesapeake in late March with four 74 gun ships of the line and supporting vessels [12], sent a small flotilla up the York and Rappahannock with instructions to destroy any shipping or facilities found on their banks. Seventeen pinnaces, each manned by 50 marines were despatched up the Rappahanock and destruction of boàting, landing jetties and supplies began. At Windmill Point, four fleeing schooners were discovered. Capt. William Stafford., the commander of the American quartet, was made in the mold of

12 The 3rd rates Dragon, Marlborough, San Domingo and Victorious, the frigates Acasta, Narcissus, Maidstone and Statira and the brigs Fantom and Mohawk

heroes and was determined to fight. Placing his ships in line across the river with their portside guns facing the approaching British, he awaited his fate. Lieutenant James Polkinghorne, commanding the flotilla of British pinnaces, twelve of which had fallen behind, was made of less formidable material and preferred to send forward a single boat armed with a 12 pounder gun to confront the Americans. It was quickly smashed to pieces by the opening salvos of Stafford's four boats, forcing the British lieutenant to rely upon the dexterity and bravery of his marines. He sent all of his boats heading towards the two boats in the centre of the American line, the 'Racer' and the 'Lynx'. Britishers died needlessly in the next few minutes and only five or so attacking craft remained afloat. These were then directed against the 'Arab', the last in line, whose captain, sensing disaster, deliberately ran his vessel aground. The 'Lynx' and 'Racer' were swept up in the British bag in the next few minutes and the 'Dolphin' an hour later. All four were then incorporated into the British squadron and, still bearing American colours, were immediately used to infiltrate and capture a cluster of tiny ships at anchor further up the river. It was not the first or last time that false colours would be flown to effect the capture of enemy ships.

Warren now approached to within twenty-five miles of Washington, but felt that he had too few guns or men to attempt anything spectacular. Cockburn simultaneously scoured the rivers flowing into the bay with the purpose of disrupting the inter-city trade between Philadelphia and Baltimore. It was during his zealous discharge of this task that he began to earn his reputation. Several communities were burned or destroyed in a vicious retribution on a people who had not even sinned. He terrorized the communities on Lynnhaven Bay, plundering farmhouses and stealing livestock. From here he passed to the Elk River and devastated Frenchtown on 29th April, this time sparing the private houses and treating the women and children with courtesy. But every storehouse, wagon and boat was destroyed, regardless of ownership or use.

Havre de Grace, near the mouth of the Susquehannna River, was visited next. For some time, this community's citizens had stood nightly guard, expecting the arrival of Cockburn's harpies. But, on the night in question, May 2nd, the inhabitants had gone to bed, believing that the admiral was raiding elsewhere. That night, guided by negro slaves who knew the area well, he came ashore with 150 men and, at dawn, after firing Congreve rockets [13]and grenades at the fringing houses, he fell savagely upon the town.

After the briefest of fights, the defenders fled. Only Irishman John O'Neill remained. Making his way past the militiamen fleeing in the opposite direction, he loaded one of the abandoned artillery pieces, aimed at Cockburn's ships in the harbour, and fired. But he hurt himself more than he hurt the ships. The rebounding gun knocked him to the ground. Cockburn's marines, advancing very cautiously, were surprised to find just one elderly man defending his nation's honour. He was taken captive, but, admired by Cockburn for his courage, was soon released. Warren, more political, later stated that he would have hanged him had he known the old man was Irish!

Cockburn had become a man unleashed. He now destroyed the foundries at Principio, a base for the manufacture of cannon. From here he descended on Georgetown, comfortably pushing aside a militia group and converting the town to ashes. Fredericktown, Maryland, suffered next, punished for its token resistance.

The man could be merciful as well as merciless. While flames consumed the buildings of Havre de Grace, the wife of Commodore John Rodgers personally appealed to the admiral to spare her house and those of her friends. Falling for her charm, he left several fine houses untouched, but insisted upon searching her property for any papers that the U.S. navy's top officer might have left behind. Finding a mahogany writing desk, the marines slashed at it with their sabres, clumsily searching for concealed compartments. They then ceremoniously took the desk with them; Rodgers later reclaimed it when he captured the ship on which his property had been stored.

Cockburn's desecrations had been cathartic—a release of frustration on those too weak to fight back. In a more composed mood, he sailed to rejoin Warren off the Hampton Roads. Together they commanded the largest British fleet that had ever been assembled since 1782 in

---

13 developed in 1805 by Sir William Congreve to 'fill the gap between the musket and the 12 pound field gun '(Mahon, J.K. 'The War of 1812' p.116

American waters. [14] A major campaign was envisaged. The British War Ministry, distracted for so long by the need to defeat Napoleon, had at last felt that it could promote a heavy strike against the American coast. Accordingly London had sent Colonel Sir John Beckwith and over 4000 troops to Bermuda to act in conjunction with Warren and harass the enemy's coastland in what he considered to be the most appropriate manner. Beckwith's instructions from London were precise: he must avoid general action, attempt no permanent occupation and should not, however tempting it might be, encourage a rising of the slaves.

Warren sailed to Bermuda on 17th May to collect Beckwith's army, leaving Cockburn to conduct the blockade of the Chesapeake. During the hiatus of semi-activity, fifteen troop-filled boats were sent from the 'Constellation', moored off Norfolk, to attack the British ships, the 'Barossa' and 'Junon', which had become separated from the bulk of the blockading fleet and lay enticingly becalmed in the Hampton Roads. The former ship was subjected to heavy fire from guns mounted in the bows of the attacking vessels and seemed likely to be captured or destroyed. But the wind capriciously shifted, preventing the American would-be boarders from approaching, and the stricken vessel was reprieved. This single action more than convinced Cockburn that the capture of Norfolk and its two protecting forts, Nelson and Norfolk, should take priority.

By 20th June Warren had returned with most of Beckwith's troops (2650 men in total)—and the British could now, presumably, do whatever they pleased. In the days following, the port of Norfolk and its approaches were studiously surveyed and plans for an attack laid down. '*We will storm Ft. Nelson and be in Norfolk to supper . . . and for your exertions and bravery, you will have three days plunder and the free use of a number of fine women,*' Cockburn is quoted as saying.

Brigadier-General Robert B. Taylor, Virginia Militia, was in charge of Norfolk's defences. He had correctly divined Warren's intentions and had laboured heavily to shore up the town's defensive points. He had with him less than 300 regulars and was forced consequently to rely upon the citizens and volunteers of the vicinity. He, like his adversary, quickly recognized that Craney Island, separated by knee deep water from the western mainland, would be the key to attack or defence and

14 8 ships of the line and 12 frigates

must therefore be quickly secured. And so Taylor, with a keen eye for any strategic advantage, erected a battery of 18 and 24 pounder guns and installed a garrison of 737 men on the island to guard the shallow waters between the island and the mainland. He placed a supporting battery on Lambert's Point and then connected the two batteries with a line of gunboats and sloops to stretch across the Elizabeth River's mouth. Further back, Fort Nelson's and Fort Norfolk's guns guarded the narrowing river's approaches to the town. The 'Constellation' lay even further behind, a floating fortress forming a final defensive line. The Virginian brigadier, knowing that men will always fight harder to protect homes and loved ones, felt confident that he had a structure of defence strong enough to resist British regulars and the navy's guns.

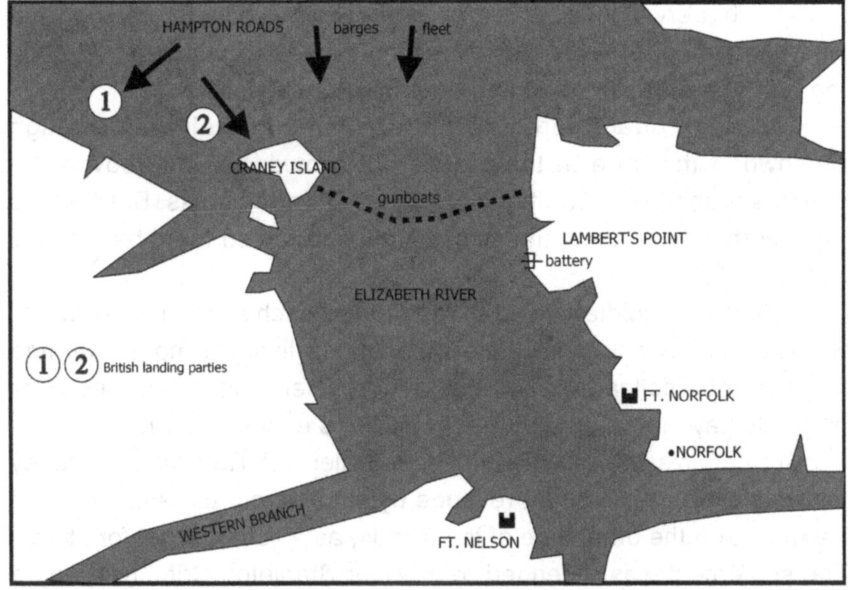

Battle of Craney Island

The British did exactly what Taylor had expected. At dawn on 22nd June, two landing parties were sent ashore. The main force, consisting of 2500 men, half of whom were members of the 102nd Regiment of Foot, landed on the mainland to the west of Craney Island, their task being to wade across the shallow straits and attack the island's garrison from the side. Simultaneously 1500 marines, carried in fifty barges, headed directly for the island, the men confident in their anticipation of a quick and unbloody capture of the battery. Several of the officers took their pet dogs and personal belongings with them, expecting to dine on American food that night.

Timing and precision was essential for Amercan survival. The island's guns remained silent until the barges were within comfortable range and then roared out. The boat carrying Warren was one of the first to be hit, spilling the admiral and other occupants into the water. Two dogs were seen swimming towards the shore. A small carved portmanteau was washed ashore. When forced open by American troops, it was found to contain love poems and sketches. The box stands today in the hall of a private residence in Norfolk. Three more boats were hit soon afterwards. Men, weighed down with equipment, had no chance. Those that were not instantly drowned were killed by the merciless shot from the battery's guns. Warren somehow survived and, seeing what was happening, ordered the remaining barges to pull back. Already the first of the British dead had been washed ashore.

The flank attack fared no better. Working their way through brushwood that tore at their faces but provided a little cover, the marines reached the strait and prepared to wade across. But Taylor's men hit these intruders just as savagely and forced them back to the shelter of the trees.

Few British soldiers lived to reach the beaches of Craney Island. Some of the stronger swimmers—or those living a more charmed life than their colleagues—waded ashore. Here, however, they were promptly bayoneted or captured by Taylor's effervescing men.

But Britain's energies had not been stilled yet. Repulsed at Craney Island, her soldiers sought revenge by singling out the small town of Hampton, on the other side of the Roads, as a softer target for attack. The settlement was defended by a Major Stapleton Critchfield and a detachment of 450 militiamen. On the morning of the 25th Cockburn's warships cockily paraded off the coast while Beckwith landed 2500 men on the shore beyond the town.

Critchfield could not have really expected to hold out for long. Despite the threat to hearth and home, many of his militia deserted in the opening minutes of skirmish and the rest departed when defeat stared out at them from the barrels of British muskets. But they had remained just long enough to deflate the pride of the invader, and more English blood than American was spilled that day. By nightfall Hampton was in British hands. Admiral Cockburn and General Beckwith took up their quarters in the home of a wealthy American lady. They played croquet on her lawns until after 11pm that night. The lawn was dug up the next day and a British officer, killed in the day's proceedings, was interred.

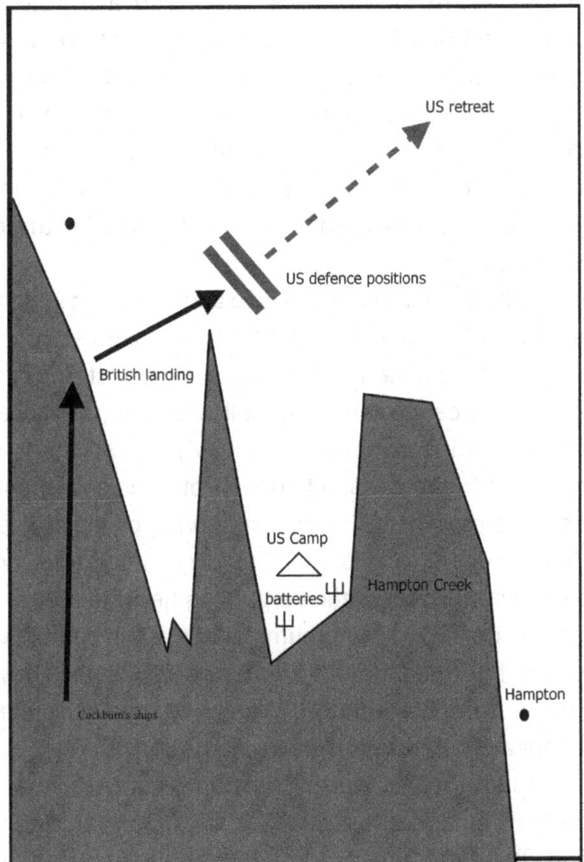

Operations at Hampton (Source: Lossing's Field Book)

The inhabitants of the town were not disturbed that night and consequently assumed that they would be left in peace. What happened next day caused a surge of indignation throughout America and even some pangs of remorse in London. Amongst those who came ashore with the British were a number of French prisoners, who had volunteered to serve His Britannic Majesty rather than face incarceration in Dartmoor

Prison. Uniformed in green and called the Chasseurs Britanniques, the frustrated men indulged in an orgy of looting and raping, tearing away the bodices of the town's women and seeking their pleasure while the women's husbands were forced to look on. General Taylor was the first to lodge a complaint; '*The world will suppose these acts to have been approved, if not executed, by the commanders . . . . It is for the sake of humanity that I enter this protest.*' Beckwith attempted to defend the Frenchmen's actions by claiming that the atrocity was a reprisal for the shooting of defenceless men in the water off Craney Island. He was quick to point out that it had been Frenchmen, not Englishmen, who had committed these crimes, adding that no stain could ever be laid upon the British. The Chasseurs, however, were immediately withdrawn from British service and held in Halifax for the duration of the war with Napoleon.

Cockburn would be far more anxious to avoid causing indignation in the future. Desecration of the Maryland and Virginia coast still continued, but his actions were largely aimed at America's military strength and, where no resistance took place, no retribution followed. Larger, more important, targets were sometimes chosen. On 1st July, seven ships-of-the-line, supported by seven frigates, sailed up the Potomac and anchored within seventy miles of the capital. 600 troops, supported by the frigates, boarded rowing boats on the 14th and pushed up river, intending, no doubt, to strike at the city and turn the nation's pulsing heart to stone. But lack of determination and unfavourable circumstances again combined to disrupt British objectives. Informed that his frigates could not pass beyond Cedar Point, forty miles from Washington, Warren reluctantly pulled back his troops. The capital's heart resumed its earlier pace.

Britain now indulged in purely psychological warfare, hoping to frighten America's citizens by a show of sails, cannon and impressive timber frames. The fleet appeared off Annapolis and Baltimore in July and took possession of Kent Island. But no attack on either city was launched—or probably even contemplated. Perhaps the whole strategy of temporary occupation of small pieces of American territory was under review at that time. Looking back at the British effort over the bridge of two centuries, it is possible to be critical and ask what such strategy was supposed to achieve. Resources were wasted, the British nation's available muscle dissipated and no permanent foothold intended. Parading in splendour in the waters of the Chesapeake caused terror to the local people, but the fear caused was just as ephemeral as Britain's occupation of the American coastlands. The real reason for Cockburn's withdrawal from Baltimore, however, was probably more tangible than any reservations that Britain might have had about the strategy being pursued: the admiral had been informed that 5000 volunteers stood ready to defend Annapolis and 11000 were prepared to die to protect Baltimore. Vastly inaccurate figures perhaps, but enough to puncture Cockburn's balloon of hope.

Still enmeshed in the net of uncertainty, Cockburn and his ships sailed off to menace the Carolinas, leaving Warren to maintain a presence in Chesapeake Bay. On 11th July, Cockburn landed troops on Okracoke Island and captured the insignificant little village of Portsmouth in North Carolina. He hoped, presumably, to encourage the slaves of the area into insurrection—for, otherwise, his raid on an area so marginal to the war was pointless.

The admiral returned to the Chesapeake in early August, and the fruitless pattern of raiding resumed. He selected Sharp's Island, close to the eastern shore of Maryland, as a possible base of operations and a watering place for his crew. Wealthy plantation owner Jacob Gibson, proprietor of the island, sought compensation for the loss of his property and visited Cockburn on his flagship. Here, over a sumptuous dinner, the two men agreed terms, and the satisfied Gibson returned to his mainland home.

His compatriots and neighbours felt that he had sold out to the British. Instead of trying to win them over, he compounded his error by unwisely playing a practical joke. On a particularly hot day in early August, the beats of a drum were heard and a barge appeared, filled with men and with the red ensign flying from its single mast. The militiamen of nearby St. Michael's had been in constant expectation of a British attack and, directed by a General Perry Benson, had prepared fairly formidable defences around their tiny town. Day and night they had been standing guard, watching for the moment that royal masts appeared. Sight of the barge sent St, Michael's folk hurrying home for their muskets, and the battery's guns prepared. But this was no enemy barge. For, when the vessel drew closer, the town's defenders could see Gibson in the stern beating an empty keg. The ensign at the masthead was his red bandana and the crew were his slaves. Gibson made many enemies that day.

A real attack materialized on the 10th. That night the British landed, forcing the defenders to flee. Only Captain William Dodson and one other man remained at the battery for long enough to fire just a single shot. But, behind the town, another battery opened fire and caused casualties on the beach. British naval guns proved to be quite ineffective that night; the town's people had doused their lights and had hung lanterns in trees to attract the warships' fire. Twenty-nine British died or fell injured on the beach, but the only American blood shed was that of a chicken roosting in one of the illuminated trees.

The British appetite for raiding dissipated with the failing summer season. Rebuffs, a failure to ignite a rising of the slaves, poor weather and heavy casualties amongst his men persuaded Warren to close down operations until the Spring. When the first autumn mists hugged the Chesapeake, Admiral Warren took his fleet northward to Halifax and started a paper campaign of excuses and justifications.

In this, he was to be more successful than he had been in any of his naval expeditions. First, he tried to convince Prevost of the success of his summer mission. He assured the man that his activities on the coast had probably prevented an army from marching north to Canada. It had also, he claimed, disrupted the commercial life of the Chesapeake. Those who lived in the blockaded area would certainly have agreed with him that their social lives had been affected. People living on the bay's eastern coast had frequently crossed to visit Baltimore, the scene of society gatherings, soirées and cultural events. British warships in the Chesapeake waters interrupted the movements of packet boats, and only the stouter minded attempted the crossing. Communities became more isolated, nerves frayed, but hostility towards the British became greater, not less. The two admirals' boasts were as hollow as a decaying tree. Continental United States was far too solid a nut to crack. Britain had been tapping at the hard shell, but the kernel was as solid as the land mass itself.

The sea war, however, was clearly going in Britain's favour, despite American success in those earlier single ship actions. But high sea battles between individual ships were like mere swipes at the wind; Britain's enormous fleet, inexhaustible resources and the clear effectiveness of her blockade must eventually grind down American naval grit to nothing. A British ship lost in action could be easily replaced, but America's carpenters and chandlers would have to work for weeks to fill the gap created by the loss of even the smallest of her warships.

The republic, fortunately, continued to be successful in sea duels in the early days of 1813. The 'Hornet', the sloop that had assisted Rodgers in the near capture of the 'Belvidera', had then sailed in company with Bainbridge and the 'Constitution' to South American waters. Here she had been left to blockade the 'Bonne Citoyenne' in Bahia Harbour while Bainbridge set out for the open sea and his later engagement with the 'Java'. The 'Hornet', commanded by James Lawrence, remained on station off Bahia until threatened by the sudden appearance of the British 3rd rate, the 74 gun 'Montagu', on 24th January 1813. Undoubtedly outclassed, Lawrence took shelter in the port and prayed that the 'Montagu's captain would not violate Portugal's neutrality. A stand-off then ensued, the 'Hornet cowering within the port's confines in close proximity to the 'Bonne Citoyenne, and the Englishman waiting at sea with her gun ports open. Eventually slipping out under cover of night, Lawrence escaped a near certain destruction and sailed northwards.

On 24th February he encountered the 18 gun brig 'Peacock' [15] lying off the Demerara River. By 5.30 p.m. both ships were bearing down on each other. The first American shot killed the English captain and, during the resulting confusion on board the 'Peacock', Lawrence managed to wear his ship into a position that allowed him to deliver starboard broadsides at very close quarters. Within minutes, the English brig was filling with water and Captain Peake lay dying on his quarter decks. His first lieutenant hauled down her colours. Ten minutes later, the 'Peacock' had gone, taking with her 13 of her crew and the 3 Americans who had boarded her during the ship's dying moments. Few British ships in the preceding century had been sunk in action.

Lawrence was fêted on his return to land and was rewarded in May with command of the frigate 'Chesapeake', which had recently returned to Boston after a two month Atlantic patrol. Command of the 'Hornet' passed to James Biddle, the First Lieutenant of the 'Wasp' as a reward for his part in the capture of the 'Frolic'. The 'Hornet' would be blockaded in New London for several months, only emerging at the

---

15 she was the sister ship of the 'Frolic', taken the previous October by the Hornet's sister ship, the 'Wasp'!

start of 1815 in time to participate in an attack on British shipping in the Indian Ocean.

News of Lawrence's appointment prompted Captain Sir Philip Bowes Vere Broke, commanding officer of His Majesty's 38 gun frigate 'Shannon', [16] at that time off the coast of Massachusetts, to send Lawrence a written challenge: *'I request you will do me the favour to meet the Shannon with her, ship for ship, to try the fortunes of our respective flags.'*

It is not entirely clear whether Lawrence ever received the invitation to fight. But no summons from an enemy would be needed to send this man to sea. Anxious to see what his new ship could achieve and, having been in command of the 'Chesapeake' for only two weeks, he was preparing to put to sea when he received news that the Englishman was waiting. Both ships threw broadsides totaling over 540 pounds and carried crews of 300 plus, suggesting a contest of close equals. Broke, however, was waiting for him off Boston on June 1st, having sent away his companion frigate 'Tenedos', to cruise in other waters. Bostonians rose early that morning, collecting in their hundreds on the waterfront or on rooftops, hoping to find a vantage point from which to obtain a clear view of the action beyond the harbour. They carried hampers of food: pork, fruit and wine, and settled down for a sporting event that could never be repeated. Some placed bets on the outcome, unpatriotic perhaps, but fully in tune with Boston's commercial instincts. Children, less aware of the significance of the day, lived in their own little worlds of play. Beyond the bazaar-like atmosphere on the waterfront, the 'Chesapeake' remained motionless within the port, sails furled and decks empty. The crowd grew restless and even began to disperse, disappointed by the publicity and handbills which had promised an eventful day.

Then, at noon, the American vessel's sails were set and, carrying a large flag embroidered with the words' *Free Trade and Sailors' Rights,'* she set out to meet her challenger. Those with lenses saw Lawrence and his first officer, Augustus Ludlow, on the deck, and the sense of excitement returned. But few saw the coming action. This, instead of being conveniently staged for the benefit of the city's people, would be a naval action controlled

16 This ship, it might be remembered, had failed to net Isaac Hull and the 'Constitution' the previous year

by wind, tide and seamen's skills. The fight would take place well to the north; the citizens of Salem would obtain a far better view.

Broke, a man whose unauthorised alterations to the mountings of his guns and his unorthodox experiments to improve the gunner's accuracy had exasperated the Admiralty, first saw his opponent's sails at midday. Anxious not to fight too close to land, he stood out to sea for five hours, knowing that the impulsive Lawrence would be bound to follow. As the excitement on the 'Shannon' swelled, Broke called his men aft and instructed them on how he would like this personal battle between two warriors to progress. *'Don't try to dismast her. Fire into her quarters . . . Kill the men and the ship is yours.'* His disdain for flambuoyancy was dispayed a little later. When asked by one of his seamen whether the 'Shannon' should fly three ensigns to match the 'Chesapeake', he was heard to reply: *'No, we have always been an unassuming ship.'*

Rigged with fighting sail, the 'Chesapeake' gradually overhauled her opponent. Both ships sought the weather gauge, running parallel in their efforts to snatch the advantage. The 'Chesapeake', taking the wind, hauled in on the 'Shannon's starboard side and fired her opening shot at 4 p.m. By 5.50 the two vessels were abreast, less than a pistol shot apart, and the first blood flowed. The experienced gunners of the 'Shannon', positioned to leeward of the American, concentrated their fire against the open gun ports of the 'Chesapeake'. Lawrence fell wounded, and the masts and rigging began to collapse in sympathy. When her foresail came down, she clumsily swung into the wind and exposed her stern to the British ship's fury. Soon the protagonists were locked, rigging tangling with rigging. As soon as they touched, the respective commanders yelled for their boarding parties to cross. Muscle and dexterity, not cannon, would now take over. No one heard Lawrence's bugler or saw the moment when Lawrence received his second injury, this time fatal. It was Broke and his party who crossed first, falling on the Americans with all the fury of the legendary Amazons. Above, in the rigging, Englishmen were crossing, too, driving Lawrence's top men towards the deck. The fighting, really a contest between two great nations, had suddenly become entirely personal, governed by the realisation that the only way to survive was to kill the man who stood in your way.

As tenderly as a mother carrying her sleeping baby, Lawrence's men, despite the fighting that took place all around, carried their bleeding commander below. Here, slightly detached from the noise of battle and with his officers kneeling at his side in a scene reminiscent of Nelson's death at Trafalgar, he gave his last command. His words, *'Don't give up the ship,'* have become enshrined in the folklore of his country's navy, passed down to inspire the generations that followed. Perry, it will probably be remembered, had been inspired by Lawrence's stance in his battle with the British on Lake Erie (see previous chapter).

But Broke had already taken the ship. Augustus Ludlow, with just a few of his men, had desperately tried to stem the flow of boarders. He, too, was felled, struck down by a saber. A British officer, attempting to haul down the American colours, was killed by grapeshot fired from his own ship, probably the last casualty in this legendary maritime combat. 146 of the 'Chesapeake's 'crew of 379 had been killed or injured; the toll on the 'Shannon' was about half that number—and Broke, who had insisted on wearing his top hat throughout the fight, was amongst the wounded, clubbed by a musket butt and then struck by a cutlass. Probably no more than eleven minutes had elapsed since the first gunshot of the action had been fired.

H.M.S. Shannon returned to Halifax with her prize in tow. Captain James Lawrence and Lieutenant Augustus Ludlow had been transferred to the British ship, but their life's blood had already been drained, emptying out on the decks of the 'Chesapeake' before the end of the battle, and both men died during the voyage to Canada. Their bodies, at the order of Broke, were draped with American flags and then carried ashore with full military honours. An elaborate ceremony followed, attended by most of Halifax's civic dignitaries, the naval and military officers of the port and the surviving crewmen of both the ships. America, however, claimed the right to bury her fallen heroes. Her request for the return of the two men was honoured, and on 18th August 1813, the bodies, still draped with flags, were landed at Salem. After a slow procession to New York, which took an entire month, Lawrence and his lieutenant found their final resting places in the graveyard of Trinity Church.

The action kindled emotions in both nations. While England celebrated with bonfires and bathed in sudden euphoria, America smothered under a blanket of despondency. Worse still, New England's pulpit barons added a strand of self-righteousness and rebuked the people of Boston for the unhealthy interest they had displayed on the day of the engagement. Josiah Quincy moved a resolution in the legislature of Massachusetts which was both moralistic and political in its tones. '*Resolved . . . . that in a war like the present, waged without justifiable cause, and prosecuted in a manner which indicates that conquest and ambition are its real motives, it is not becoming a moral and religious people to express any approbation of military or naval exploits which are not immediately connected with the defence of our sea coast and soil.'* Despite the cantings of such men, Madison's war would have to continue.

Lieutenant William Henry Allen, commanding the 18 gun sloop 'Argus', briefly carried the war to England's shores. Instructed to convey William Crawford, the new minister to the French court, to Lorient, he set out from New York on 18th June, and headed for the eastern Atlantic, waters which the British usually tried to claim as their own. Offloading his valuable passenger after three weeks at sea, he approached the coast of Cornwall and set about disrupting the commerce of England's western ports. During thirty days of unrestrained movement in July and August, he destroyed twenty merchant ships and $20 million worth of cargo. In so doing, he stirred up the mercantile interests of Bristol and the west, and a hornet's nest at Westminster, where ministers were accused of failing to protect shipping in homeland waters.

Inevitably Allen and the 'Argus' would be confronted by something more powerful than a helpless merchant vessel. She had a number of near encounters during August; on one occasion she glided past a frigate in thick fog. '*We could perceive her hull and ports, but not her masts or rigging,'* a crew member pithily reported. On the 13th, the Americans took possession of a merchantman carrying a cargo of wine, a product far too attractive for men condemned to weeks at sea to ignore. That night, despite Allen's efforts, his crew drank to excess, and the normally tight discipline exerted on a ship at sea drained away almost as quickly as the casks were emptied. The crew was consequently totally unprepared for the appearance of enemy sails and guns in the early hours of the following morning. As the rising sun touched the sea, the American ship met His Majesty's 18 gun sloop 'Pelican', commanded by a man as keen as any officer in the Royal Navy to gain his laurels, and manned by a crew just as eager to win their country's praise.

For Commander John Maples and his men, the surprise and excitement triggered by finding a warship of the United States so close to British shores must have been tremendous. Britons conceived the war as distant, unreal, and, unlike the European war, of no relevance to their daily lives. Many had been aware of Napoleon's invasion plans only eight years previously and the alarm was naturally considerable. Some had even witnessed the vessels assembled in French ports for this purpose. Yet here was a single tiny ship, America's puny threat; and the chance of saving Britain from invasion was presented.

Allen's stupefied men were difficult to rouse, and only the stark reality of an approaching ship sent them stumbling to their stations. Allen ran his ship parallel to the 'Pelican', and, when his target was comfortably within range, fired his first broadside. The normal pattern of the close-quarter fight then followed—broadside meeting broadside, periodic raking of the enemy's decks and crewmen preparing to board. From the start, things went badly for the American crew. The gunners, their expertise still impaired from the night before, aimed badly, and were outclassed by Captain Maples and the gun crews of the 'Pelican'. Allen's leg was blown away and he, too, like gallant James Lawrence of the 'Chesapeake', was carried below to die of his wounds. And, as with that earlier engagement, the second-in-command was also wounded. Parallels with the earlier duel continue. Masts and sails on the 'Argus' were shot away and the ship became unmanageable. Maples, seeing his advantage, took his vessel across the American's stern and raked the Argus for several minutes. At 7 a.m., after 43 minutes of fighting, Argus struck her colours. Captain Allen was transferred to the 'Pelican' and, like Lawrence, died on a British ship. This time, however, his second-in-command, Lieutenant W. Watson, despite his wound, survived to recount his story.

The third notable duel of the year took place a little later off Pemaquid Point on the coast of Maine. The British brig 'Boxer', carrying 14 guns, was accompanying a Swedish ship loaded with English woolens destined for New England merchants. On 1st September (some accounts suggest it was the 5th), she was confronted by the American brig 'Enterprise', with the same number of guns, and the now customary sea duel began to unroll. In an afternoon fight lasting for more than an hour, the usual broadsides occurred, but this time circumstances favoured the American from the start. The captains of both ships fell mortally wounded in the opening minutes of battle, but it was the masts and rigging of the

British ship that fell first. At 3.30., after only ten minutes of fighting, the 'Enterprise' was in complete control, crossing and recrossing the bow of the 'Boxer' and raking her at will. By 4 p.m. the 'Boxer' could fight no more. A British officer signaled a willingness to surrender, but explained that he would be unable to haul down the colours as one of his crew had nailed them to the mast. Captains Samuel Blyth, RN, and William Burrows, US Navy, brief enemies at sea, were landed at Portland and, after a joint funeral, were buried side by side. And, for a while, the British flag flew from Portland's flagpole.

This singular victory at sea, coming so soon after the demoralization of the earlier contests, might have raised American morale, but could do little to alter the trends and the facts. The British blockading net, cast along so much of the North American coast, had caught all but three of America's frigates: the 'Essex', 'President' and 'Congress'. The latter two, taking advantage of particularly foul weather, had eluded the clutches of the 'Shannon', 'Tenedos', 'Curlew' and 'Nympth' that had been responsible for shadowing them, and somehow managed to remain beyond the Royal Navy's reach. The 'Essex', whose captain, David Porter, had been challenged by James Yeo, had not touched a home port since the previous autumn. Now, in the late summer of 1813, she was operating in the Pacific, allegedly searching for whaling vessels that operated off the Peruvian coast.

The search for riches, notoriety and perhaps something more had taken Porter around Cape Horn in January, partly in defiance of his own Admiralty's orders. His story has found a fitting place in the accounts of America's semi-heroes and so only the part that touches on the fortunes of the war will be retold here. Rounding Cape Horn on 15th March 1813, he began his hunt for British whaling ships and Peruvian corsairs. Over the next few months of cruising in the South Pacific, he captured 12 whalers, although his own estimate of $5 million as the value of the trade he destroyed is probably wildly innacurate. Some of the vessels he captured were converted into fighting vessels, and a flotilla mushroomed under his command. One, a merchant vessel called the 'Atlantic', was armed with 18 pounder carronades and rechristened the 'Essex Jnr.'

On 3rd February 1814, beyond the point of the war so far reached, the 'Essex' was sadly taken. Porter, sheltering in the neutral harbour of Valparaiso, found His Majesty's 36 gun frigate 'Phoebe' and the 18 gun sloop 'Cherub' berthed next to him. [17] For hours, the three ships remained at their berths, bound by the port's neutrality to refrain from open shows of belligerence. The crews glared, taunted and hurled insults while the captains negotiated with the port's authorities. Porter slipped out of harbour at 5 pm on March.28th. Damage to his topmast caused during a sudden squall immediately after his departure forced him to linger outside the harbour, giving the predators the moment for which they had been waiting. The 'Phoebe' opened fire with her long-range 18 pounders and, after 45 minutes of ceaseless broadsides from which the 'Essex' had no chance of escaping, and the loss of 58 killed and 65 wounded, Porter struck his colours. He had, apparently, first offered his crew members the chance to jump overboard and swim to shore. The 'Essex', surprisingly undamaged despite the ferocity of the punishing fire, was sailed to Britain and served in His Majesty's navy until being converted to a convict ship in 1823.

A summary of the fates of America's other frigates might be included here. The 'Chesapeake', as already reported, had been captured and now flew Britain's ensign. The 'Constitution' and 'Adams' were under repair, the 'United States' and the 'Macedonian' were confined by the blockade within the waters of the Thames River, Connecticut, while the 'Boston', 'John Adams' and 'New York' had been withdrawn from service. Of the brigs and smaller ships, all but the recently victorious 'Enterprise' had been taken by the British.

The loss of so many ships and the carnage of the sailors who served on board spawned a belief that only the construction of ships-of-the-line, carrying 74 guns or more, would allow the struggling nation to purchase equality at sea. One was already being built at Portsmouth, New Hampshire, and another at Charlestown in Massachusetts. In the continent's interior, on Lake Ontario, the United States had already commenced construction of a 110 gun warship, the 'New Orleans', designed to match anything that Britain might choose to position on the lake. American shipyards on the Atlantic coast also began to buzz in frantic activity; larger vessels than before emerged from drawing board plans and took gradual shape. The 'Adams' and the 'Constitution', too, were being redesigned, their architects hoping to improve the sailing

---

17 They had apparently been sent out by the British Admiralty to disrupt the American fir trade in the Pacific and were probably in port to take on water

qualities of two inferior boats. These activities, coupled with the belief that American carronades were superior, fostered a new hope and expectation. Soon, however, the young nation would be rocked by news that Britain was planning to build larger ships in the expectation that the war would be prolonged. The 112 gun 'St. Lawrence' was already taking place on the shipyard stocks. The frames of two other 3 deckers, the 'Canada' and the 'Wolfe' would emerge a little later. Britain's resources, despite the haemorrhage caused by the long European conflict, seemed to be limitless.

Enjoying so few resources, America turned more and more to the services of privateers, vessels equipped by individuals or companies for war services on the ocean. The risks were great, but the potential profits were even greater, and many commercial concerns, deprived of their normal sources of profit during times of war, turned to privateering in expectation of high reward.

To each vessel President Madison or his deputies issued a 'letter of marque and reprisal', effectively a warrant to prey upon enemy ships. The standard vessel was schooner-like in style, armed with six or more carronades and manned by a crew of about fifty. In the early months of war, privateers were few, owing to the fact that the majority of American merchantmen had left their homeports to escape the presidential embargo. Those selected for conversion to martial functions could not be altered overnight—and very few had come into contact with British commerce during 1812 and the early weeks of 1813. A total of 526 private vessels were commissioned during the war, 364 of which were schooners. Perhaps the most renowned of these early pirate vessels was the 'Rosie' of Baltimore, commanded by the forceful Joshua Barney, a man of daring who deliberately chose the role of quasi-buccaneer in preference to the more regulated life of the uniformed officer. By the end of 1812, after an almost continuous period at sea, he had taken prizes and merchandise to the value of $1.5million.

These vessels, and their strong-willed captains, would become more adventurous as the war progressed, even threatening British trade on the China seas and blockading the mouth of the Thames! *'They go where they please, they chase and come up with everything they see, and run away at pleasure,'* The Niles Weekly Register, a Baltimore area newspaper proudly crowed in 1814, after a particularly successful period of schooner activity.

But this is to anticipate future events, looking forward to a time when America had become desperate. In the mid to late summer of 1813, the war was still largely confined to continental America, its eastern seaboard and its lakes. Here, on the waters of Erie and Ontario, where a naval battle larger than any of those at sea had just been fought, the sparring would continue, fought out by mediocre commanders who somehow believed that they were the giants of their cause.

CHAPTER 9

'Two heads on the same shoulder make a monster'

America, having gained undisputed overlordship of Lake Erie, would probably now attempt to cast the Stars and Stripes over the waters of her sister lake to the east. Here Yeo presided over the British Ontario flotilla, desperate to guard the towns of York and Kingston and the supply routes to Burlington. For a while, he had briefly taken the offensive. On 19th June 1813 his entire fleet had appeared off Oswego, the lakeside town guarding the route between New York and Sackets Harbor, intending to bombard the port installations with long-range guns. Lieutenant Melanchlon Woolsey, one of the most independently minded and resourceful of America's naval officers, had hastily constructed a battery in anticipation of such a visit. When these opened fire, Britain's ships sailed away and resumed their patrols on the lake's open waters. A plan, hurriedly concocted during July, to attack Sackets Harbor again, was dropped when two Newfoundlanders deserted and informed the Americans of Yeo's intentions. Disappointed in these summer endeavours to tip the scales of war in his favour, Yeo began to skulk, keeping his vessels within territorial waters and letting his enemy grow bolder.

Chauncey, for all his faults, prevarications and reservations, fed on this British hesitation. With the 'General Pike' now in full fighting form and with the complete support of Wilkinson, he edged his flotilla into Burlington Bay on 29th July, hoping to soften up the recently built defences. During the night, however, British reinforcements arrived from York, and the newly installed artillery on shore barked back. Chauncey, not one to gamble with the lives of others, turned his attention to York instead, logically assuming that the town's defending force might now be depleted.

In this assumption, he was correct. When Brigadier-General John Boyd, temporarily succeeding to the command when Dearborn again fell ill, landed 250 men on the beaches of York on 31st July, he found no opposition. Every man, civilian or soldier, had been evacuated that morning when the sails of the American fleet were first spotted. Chauncey, meeting with the Reverend Strachan, assured him that private property would be respected, a promise difficult to deliver (or believe) in view of America's earlier desecration of the town. Wealthy merchant William Allan's warehouse, however, was forcibly opened and its contents, mainly flour, removed. The following morning, three boats, packed with soldiers, moved up the Don River in search of supplies reported to be hidden there. Finding nothing, Chauncey's marines burned down the barracks and blockhouses of York and set sail for Sackets Harbor. At the very moment that an occupation of York would have completely severed the British land link between Montréal and Amherstburg, the forces of the United States yet again abandoned Upper Canada's capital and forfeited the psychological advantage that occupation would have provided.

In August, Boyd and Chauncey tried again to bait the spider in his web, this time endeavouring to find the most effective way of flushing Vincent's redcoats from Burlington Heights. The naval officer agreed to convey 1500 men westward in yet another of the limited vision operations that had characterized all of America's offensive activities so far. But, on the night of 7th August 1813, days before the fleet was due to sail, a savage storm struck the anchorage off Niagara and capsized two new schooners, the 'Scourge' and the 'Hamilton', sending crewmen and guns to the bottom of the lake. The following morning, still dazed by the loss, Chauncey was confronted by the British flotilla, waiting for him on the open water. Two days of manoeuvring followed, each side trying to snatch the advantage of the wind and bring his enemy within the range of his guns.

No action took place. On the 10th, Yeo, sailing east with his vessels in battle formation, came across the Americans in two lines. For a while, the two sides sailed parallel to one another, and every man aboard must have felt that action was imminent. But, curiously, neither side fired, and the silent stand-off was uncanny. It was Chauncey who broke away first. Summer dark had combined with his discomfort at losing two new schooners to blow away his normal taste for action, and he gave the order to turn towards the land and away from the enemy line.

His two leading ships, the schooners 'Julia' and 'Growler', either misread the signal or never saw it. Instead of wearing, the pair tacked towards the wind—and their foe. Yeo instantly manoeuvred his ships and cut the two vessels off. It was now deep night, but the moon shone brightly, and a nocturnal battle would have been possible. Silent gunners remained prepared, officers paced decks, inaudible prayers were said and the silent silhouettes of masts passed by, but not a gun was fired.

Chauncey, however, continued to withdraw, leaving the two schooners in the possession of the British. In essence, this was a defeat for America—for four schooners had been lost in the space of seventy-two hours, but not a gun had actually been fired Yeo, in his report to the Admiralty, chose to regard it as signaling the demise of the navy of the United States and as evidence of a loss of American nerve

He was far too optimistic. Chauncey, no longer shackled by the need to work with land forces and commanders with whom he had no real desire to co-operate, was a man re-invigorated and would remain at Sackets Harbor just long enough to re-equip and take on supplies. During this interval of relative inactivity, Prevost, critical of Yeo's failures, ordered the naval officer to combine with De Rottenburg in an attack on Fort George. On 24th August a frontal assault was attempted but, within hours, the troops were recalled. The fort, garrisoned by 5000 men, was felt to be far too strong.

By mid-September, Chauncey's boats were prowling again. On 11th September, at a time when American celebratory bonfires still glowed in the aftermath of the victory on Lake Erie, Chauncey settled his score with Yeo in the waters off the Duck Islands. After half-hearted searches for one other, Sir James Yeo came across the American flotilla largely by chance and, with the wind favouring him, he moved towards the enemy in the hope that he could employ his carronades before the Americans' long-range guns opened fire. The wind, however, savagely turned about, slowing his movement. Chauncey's guns opened up, smashing timber, masts and the limbs of several men. It was Yeo's turn to scramble. Another would-be battle ended, if it had ever begun, with Chauncey in pursuit. But, insisting on towing his schooners, he was far too slow—and Yeo managed to escape.

Wolfe (23), Royal George (20)
Brigs: Earl of Moira (16), Lord Melville (14)
Schooners: Lord Beresford (12), Sir Sidney Smith (12)

British fleet on Lake Ontario Summer 1813

British morale fell faster than the season's leaves that autumn. Moreover, the tilt of the hardware balance again slipped in the republic's favour with the launch on the 18th of the 16 gun schooner 'Sylph', only three weeks after her keel was laid. Definite American superiority on the lake congealed the flow of provisions. More significantly for Britain's native allies, it interfered with the movement of the gifts and pay that had anchored the Indian tribes to the British cause. Tribesmen deserted in droves, and even some of the Canadian volunteer forces set off down the tracks that led back to their homes. Without a naval victory, the army on land, deprived of sustenance would wither like a vine. Prevost, presiding over this collapsing house of cards, blamed everyone but himself, arguing that poor strategy and execution of ideas in the field and water must be largely responsible for the failure to curb the Americans.

Yeo's next meeting with the enemy did nothing to improve his humour. Commodore Chauncey, convinced that Yeo was a fading spark, planned to test this conviction. On 27th September he sailed back to York's inner waters, where all the British ships were now nesting. On the following morning Yeo sailed out to meet him. The two squadrons sailed southward on roughly parallel courses, fuelled by a powerful easterly breeze. The American commodore bore down towards the centre of Yeo's line, perhaps mindful of Nelson's tactics at Trafalgar. But the British, graced with the wind in their favour, tacked away to the north, inducing Chauncey to alter course and steer towards the 'Wolfe'. The manoeuvre, however, failed to save the masts of the 'Wolfe', two of which were brought down when the 'Pike' opened fire. *'In ten minutes from the time I commenced my fire,'* wrote Chauncey's flag captain, Arthur Sinclair, '*he* (the Wolfe) *was a wreck. His main and mizzenmasts . . . were down among his guns.'* The 'Royal George' moved into the gap between the 'Pike' and the 'Wolfe', enabling Yeo and his stricken vessel to sail off to the west, followed by Chauncey. Further fighting followed in this race to safety near Burlington before Chauncey, concerned by the upsurge of a sudden storm for the safety of his own ships, broke off and abandoned the action, hereafter referred to as the 'Burlington Races'.

America was now re-organising on both the land and the lake, and a decision had been made to concentrate her strength at Sackets Harbor. The reasons given for the concentration of America's military strength at Sackets Harbor are not entirely convincing, particularly when the results of such a concentration handed an advantage to the British. The personal whims of General James Wilkinson, Dearborn's eventual successor in command of Military District No.9 [18] were largely responsible for this slightly irrational decison. '*Why should you remain in your land of cypress patriotism and ambition equally invite you to where grows the laurel and where we may renew the sign of Saratoga?,'* Secretary of War Armstrong had written to Wilkinson in New Orleans during March, when Dearborn's illness had finally rendered him unfit to carry on. Armstrong and Wilkinson had never been friends, but had served together during the Revolutionary War, and the latter's subsequent service had been colourful. He had only taken up his post at the lakes in August, after weeks of conferring with Armstrong in Washington.

The concentration at Sackets Harbor was the product of their discussion. Armstrong argued that the venom of any major attack should be directed first against Kingston and then down the St. Lawrence towards Montréal. Wilkinson promptly countered with a suggestion of his own, a campaign in the Niagara area with the object of forcing the British back and taking Fort Malden. Then, with Lake Ontario semi-secured in his rear, an advance against Kingston or Montréal

18 Covering N. New York, Vermont and W. Pennsylvania

could be considered. Secretary Armstrong, beginning to wonder whether his choice of commander had been wise, vetoed such a proposal and curiously gave the officer a choice: Kingston or Montréal as his immediate objective. And so the decision to concentrate at Sackets Harbor, half way between the target towns, was made.

Wilkinson's reasons for opposing the Montréal probe had been personal, not military. A movement in force in the direction of this city would oblige him to work in conjunction with his arch-enemy, the starchy slave owner, Wade Hampton, stationed at Plattsburgh and Burlington in Vermont with 4500 men. In order to buy Wilkinson's consent to the attack on Montréal, Armstrong agreed to subordinate Hampton to Wilkinson's command.

This made the 62 year old Hampton bristle in protest. Commissioned as a major-general at the same time as Wilkinson, he naturally resented to being made junior to a man he despised. He considered himself to be more upstanding and more experienced than Major-General Wilkinson—and probably rightly so. He had served under Marion in the Carolina campaign against the British in 1780, and had believed that Armstrong had granted him a completely independent command. Haughty to the point of being insufferable, he was universally unpopular. Orphaned as a child when his parents were massacred by Cherokee warriors, he seems to have borne a grudge against mankind generally. And now, despite being subordinate to Wilkinson, he was suddenly given responsibility for the northward thrust towards Montréal.

The two men, Hampton and Wilkinson, would find it difficult to inhabit the same planet, let alone move within the same sphere of war. Sparks flew as soon as Wilkinson reached Albany and issued Hampton with an order. The latter refused to obey and wrote to Armstrong with an offer of resignation. The cabinet minister accompanied Wilkinson on his journey from Albany to Sackets Harbor on the 20th August, claming that he wished to attend the new commander's inauguration ceremony. His presence at the lakeside town, however, angered Wilkinson, who now felt that his own freedom of action was threatened. On the 24th he wrote indignantly to Armstrong: '*I trust you will not interfere with my arrangements, or give orders within the district of my command, but to myself, because it would impair my authority and distract the public service. Two heads on the same shoulder make a monster.'*

Secretary John Armstrong then visited Hampton at Plattsburgh and, by re-affirming the independence of his command, managed to dissuade Hampton from resigning. General Hampton, however, refused to consider Armstrong's suggestion that he should move down the Richelieu (or Sorel) River and attack the British on the Isle aux Noix, arguing that the enemy were far too strong. Instead, he positioned his men at Cumberland Head on Lake Champlain, a place from where he could maintain close links with Lt. Thomas Macdonough, commander of America's Champlain fleet. Wilkinson's army nominally consisted of 14,000 men: the 5000 already stationed at Sackets Harbor, a similar number at Fort George, and the theoretically subordinate army of Wade Hampton lying far to the east in heavily wooded Vermont.

Armstrong continued to find himself in disagreement with his truculent new appointee. Wilkinson visited Fort George in order to obtain his own impression of its defensive capabilities. '*This place,'* he dismissively wrote to Armstrong on 20th September,' *neither stops a gap, extends our possession, nor covers or protects a country; it is good for naught but to command the ground it occupies, and therefore I shall . . . . abandon it.'* Armstrong probably concurred with this assessment militarily, but recognized the fort's psychological value. Fort George was the only American possession on the soil of Canada, and its retention warmed the long-term hopes of those who sought the formula for victory. The Secretary agreed to permit the withdrawal of the regulars and replace the garrison with Indiana and locally raised militia. Generally, this is another period of muddled strategy with no clear objectives; every commander in the area having his view about how to proceed and resentful of the interference of others. Stretched along a 250 mile front from the Niagara to Montréal were 8000 British and Canadian troops, centred on Kingston, but sufficiently mobile, if attacked at any one point, to move rapidly to the threatened front. Faced by so many attractive and weakly held enemy points, it is hardly surprising that opinions in America were so varied.

Armstrong continued to muddy the decision making process and his ambivalence during September was infuriating. On 18th September,

Armstrong reminded Wilkinson that, if '*Kingston or the point below (was) seized, all above perishes, because the tree is then girdled',* implying that he favoured an attack on that town. Wilkinson, concurring this time, began to assemble troops on Grenadier Island, half-way between Sackets Harbor and Kingston. For such an objective, a removal of troops from Fort George and a concentration at Sackets Harbor is entirely plausible. It seemed, at last, that both men were riding the same strategic tandem. Two days later, however, Armstrong began to hint that a move down the St. Lawrence towards Montréal would be more sensible. Grenadier Island could still be employed as an assembly point for the troops and Chauncey could be given responsibility for blockading Kingston and preventing the British flotilla from returning to its base. The fears of those who felt that Britain might take advantage of this eastern move by making mischief at the lake's western end were assuaged by a promise that some regulars would be retained at Fort George.

On 5th October Secretary Armstrong, however, issued a further set of orders that were ambivalent and unhelpful, causing the mouths of the commanders to drop open in surprise. '*If the British fleet shall not escape Commodore Chauncey and get into Kingston Harbor',* he said. '*If the garrison of that place be not largely reinforced, and if the weather be such as will allow us to navigate the lake securely, Kingston shall be our first objective, otherwise we shall go directly to Montréal.*

Wilkinson, although sick, gave his own orders on 12th October for a rendezvous of 7000 men on Grenadier Island, where the waters of Ontario tip into the St. Lawrence. Five days later, preceded by eight gunboats and vessels carrying the artillery, the army set off, carried along the St. Lawrence towards Montréal in a chain of 148 scows, bateaux and sailing boats. This was the largest force so far assembled in this war of small skirmishes and semi-achievements. But, even now, Wilkinson was still looking at Kingston and talking of the capture of Upper Canada, and none of his officers that day could be absolutely sure of the intended destination. Commodore Chauncey was protesting vehemently, arguing that only an attack on Kingston made any real sense.

The advance against the undefined target hardly experienced a promising start. Thirty-six hours of gale force conditions ensued, losing the flotilla in a fog of sleet and snow. Fifteen boats went down, supplies were lost and winter announced its intention of arriving early. Yet still Armstrong, and possibly Wilkinson as well, were looking, Janus-like, in two directions at once, unable to really decide which town, Kingston or Montréal, would provide the greatest military harvest.

Meanwhile, General Wade Hampton, on whose support the success of the expedition depended, had not been inactive. Ordered by Armstrong to unite with Wilkinson at St. Régis, he had set out from Cumberland Head in September and headed north through Chazy towards the St. Lawrence. On 20th September he crossed into Lower Canada, throwing aside a small picket at Odeltown on the following morning.

And here he seems to have lost his nerve. Every excuse was now presented in his messages to Armstrong: the illness of his troops, the uncertainty of the terrain, dry river beds and a consequent shortage of drinking water—to mention just a few. From Odeltown to L'Arcadie, the track passed through woodland and swamp, ideal terrain for ambushes by the enemy or for attacks by Britain's Indian allies. Abatis and roadblocks adorned the track, most erected the previous year, but still lightly manned by units of the Frontier Light Infantry under the command of Captain Joseph Saint-Valier Mailloux. Penetrating these unsafe woodlands as far as Lacolle, General Wade Hampton suddenly decided on a retreat, pleading that the problem of thirst had now become insurmountable. Yet only days before, livestock from Vermont had been taken across the frontier past waterways and streams that had been far from empty.

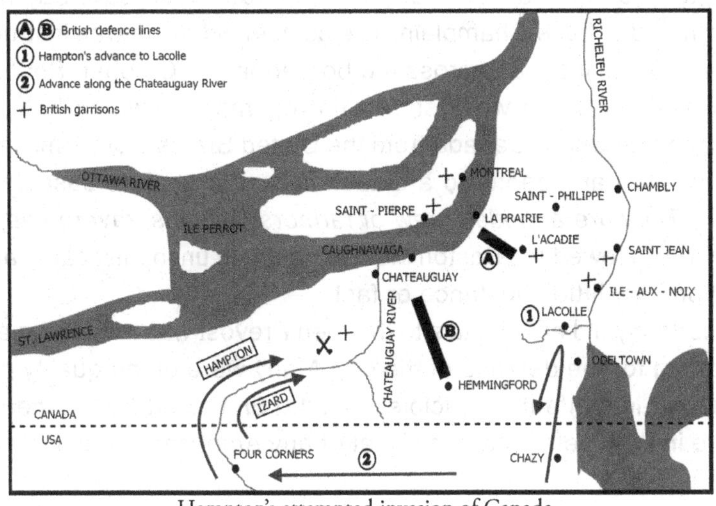

Hampton's attempted invasion of Canada

Armstrong, of course, urged him forward, reminding timorous Wade Hampton that the success of Wilkinson's simultaneous advance down the St. Lawrence would depend upon his efforts. In reluctant compromise, Hampton agreed to try another route forward through territory that appeared to be less hazardous. Returning to Chazy, he swung west along the well-filled Chateauguay River to Four Corners. This route of approach to Montréal lengthened the journey by more than seventy miles, but it would reduce the chances of an attack on his flank by British and Canadian forces stationed at Ile aux Noix. This route, following the river's banks, eventually led to Caughnawaga on the St. Lawrence, the point at which he might cross the great river.

'*Hold it fast till we approach you,*' Armstrong ordered when he heard of the general's arrival at Four Corners. The Secretary, unsure of Wilkinson's progress or destination, could see duel roles for Hampton—as a feint to draw the enemy south while Wilkinson ploughed his way to Montréal, or as a complementary force during the approach to the city.

Wade Hampton's wait at Four Corners would be longer than planned. For, at this moment, more than half of Wilklnson's army had not even assembled at the selected rendezvous point on Grenadier Island. For twenty-six days Hampton and his soldiers were rooted in their camp, training, drilling, improving the road to Plattsburgh and waiting for the order to advance. To divert unseen eyes from observing too much, the general gave instructions to Colonel Isaac Clark, in command at Burlington, to make a demonstration towards Missisiquoi Bay at the northern end of Lake Champlain. The colonel did as he was instructed, sending 200 militia men across the border on 11th October. Snatching the provisions which were stored there, (most of which had been smuggled into Upper Canada from the United States), Clark moved on to Philipsburg and captured a detachment of irregulars based in the village. '*They are a motley crew of farmers, citizens, tavern keepers, traders etc,*' crowed the Boston Messenger in an unsophisticated article based on very little substance or fact.

It certainly did an injustice to the men Prevost was now in the act of positioning for the defence of the city. Many were of the quality of the Glengarry Light Infantry Fencibles and the Embodied Militia, men with real fire in their veins and the equal of any American regular. Several companies of the Glengarrians, with 'Red George' Macdonnell at their head, bolstered the 3000 militia men lined along the Chateauguay River. Nearby, Major-General Richard Stovin and 5000 militia manned Montréal's forward defence line which ran from the Chateauguay to Hemmingford. On the Richelieu River, Saint-Jean was garrisoned and in close contact with the men at Ile aux Noix. As the threat from America swelled, a strong reserve, consisting of both regulars and irregulars, stretched out from La Prairie to Saint-Jean through Saint-Pierre, Saint-Philippe and L'Acadie. Amongst the regulars was a squadron of the 19th Light Dragoons and the Regiment de Meuron, a Swiss unit choosing to serve in Canada. The city itself was held by the Montréal Volunteers and the Montréal militia, organized into one defensive battalion by Colonel James McGill.

Montréal, its people and its civic authorities, were now on battlefield alert. At the sound of church bells, the signal that the Americans had been spotted, every able-bodied man, young and old and from every trade, was required to assemble, bringing with them whatever weapon they might find in their homestead barns. Taverns emptied and the city's life slowed during those days of tense anticipation—few men wished to be far from home. Spies watched the Americans at Four Corners, trying to interpret their likely route of advance. Every parade, patrol and minor movement was studiously surveyed and reported to Prevost. Hampton, after all, could approach the St.Lawrence from any point on the south bank between Saint-Regis and Caughnawaga.

Periodic sighting of the enemy discomforted Hampton, who wrote in his usual wordy fashion to Armstrong on 12th October; *'My solicitude to know your progress . . . . is extreme . . . . The point and moment of my departure from here ought to be indicated . . . . You have said 'Hold Fast', and it might be considered precipitate to advance before I hear at least that the Rubicon is passed above.'* On the 18th, he received the politician's reply, a clear unambiguous command that he was to proceed to the mouth of the Chateauguay without further delay. The letter indicated that Wilkinson was in motion at last, heading down the St.Lawrence towards Ile Perrot, and that no action against Kingston was now being contemplated. Hampton, a far better administrator than a general, prepared his departure from Four Corners with care, sending men with axes to clear the road ahead and hiring in extra wagons to carry his supplies. Far behind, in the nation's capital, expectations of success prevailed; never before had two armies moved simultaneously towards a common goal, the heart of Canada itself. '*The ensuing week settles the fall of Upper Canada forever. The fall of Québec in the ensuing spring will our youth experience to ward against evils of thirty years' neglect of military knowledge . . . Canada once ours we shall have no enemy,*' the National Intelligencer glowed in patriotic warmth, sensing that the wind of victory was more than just a breeze. Unfortunately the weather vane pointed misleadingly, and only fools and the over-optimistic could have believed that the United States of America could expect to be granted the whole of Canada as its prize for winning the war.

Hampton's single-handed invasion of Canada began on 22nd October. He had been correctly informed that only about 350 'Voltigeurs' lay in the immediate vicinity. But the man in charge of the defence of the Chateauguay, Charles Michel d'Irumberry de Salaberry had become a semi-god among mortals, a man admired by his men for qualities of leadership that very few men possess. '*There is no wolf or tiger, who could be so rough,*' they openly claimed. And, with the eyes of the tiger, he had been keenly observing his quarry's hesitant movements and deciding when and where to pounce.

The spot he chose offered strategic advantages, and the positioning of his men would compensate for his lack of numbers. In woodland near Spears Farm on the northern banks of the river, he erected a series of intricate breastworks, each about 500 yards behind the other. His right flank rested on swampland and his left on the river's banks. In front was a gully and cleared land, which provided a clear field of fire for the marksmen that he intended to place in his first row of defences.

Hampton's scouts had performed their job nearly as well, providing the general with accurate details of Salaberry's positions. To counter the lines of abatis sprawled across the roadway, Hampton divided his forces, ordering Colonel Robert Purdy of the 4th U.S. Infantry to take 1500 men across to the south bank of the river and bypass the defenders during the hours of darkness. Recrossing at dawn behind the Canadian lines, he was to fall on de Salaberry from the rear. The larger column, with more than 2000 men, under the command of the highly capable Brigadier-General George Izard would then attack frontally and the two closing pincers would crack the enemy like a nut. Unoriginal, perhaps in its conception, a strategy like this was normally successful.

But this, of course, would depend upon the tiger's eye being closed to the possibility of an attack from behind. De Salaberry, guessing that this would be Hampton's intention, had already taken possession of the upper ford, over which Purdy would need to cross, and had constructed a lunette on the south bank. In the woods beyond, as a double security, he had let his Indians roam, giving these ferocious warriors full licence to deal with any American soldier that they might encounter.

Strategies, pleasing on paper, have a habit of proving impossible to pursue in practice. A suggestion that 1500 men could plunge unnoticed into enemy-strewn woodlands and emerge unscathed was frankly absurd. On the evening of the 25th, Purdy crossed the first ford and entered the woodland of confusion, relying upon guides who had admitted knowing little of what lay ahead. Just two miles in, the party became hopelessly lost. Men stumbled over roots, fell in swamps and became entangled in undergrowth during a night that was particularly dark. More by chance than anything else, the solders, shivering in the dampness of autumn morning, found the higher ford soon after dawn and prepared to cross. They also found the enemy waiting for them. Secure behind the lunette, a contingent of chasseurs under Captain Charles Daly, had their rifles ready when the first Americans stumbled into the open.

Hampton and Izard had planned to attack as soon as they received a signal from Purdy. That, of course, never materialized, and no frontal attack consequently took place that morning. General Wade Hampton had been plunged into a mental woodland of confusion of his own the night before. A fresh message from Armstrong had arrived, instructing him to prepare winter quarters at Four Corners and abandon any forward progress. Interpreted logically, this must mean that the projected attack on Montréal had been called off and that he and Wilkinson were being asked to take root in terrain that was militarily unsafe. Choosing to ignore instructions, he had assembled his men in battle order at dawn and waited for the evidence that a successful attack was being made on the enemy's rear.

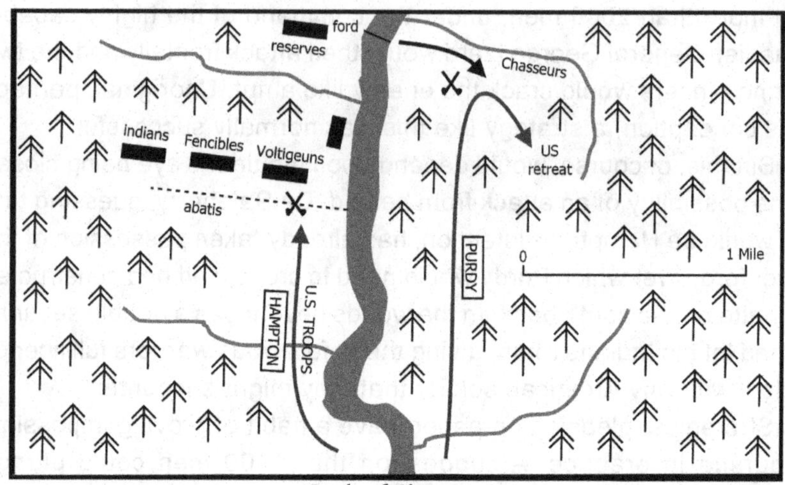

Battle of Chateauguay

At 2 p.m, on the 26th, after four hours of waiting, his patience snapped at last and he ordered Izard forward towards the abatis in his front. De Salaberry, although reinforced the previous day by 'Red George', still had less than 600 men and would need to be cunning if he were to prevent the American body from breaking through. Placing his buglers at considerable distance from one another, he hoped to create the impression that many more lines lay behind the breastworks. Standing on a large tree stump, the Frenchman barked his orders and shouted encouragement. Izard, the professional soldier, sent his lines of blue against the first brushwood defence works, and, for an hour, the Americans fired their volleys according to conventional battlefield format, aiming at any head that protruded above the logs. Hardly a ball found its target.

Izard, confused, as de Salaberry had hoped, by the haphazard sound of bugles, began to doubt his chances, convinced that several more lines of Canadians lay behind. And now a sudden line of red appeared on his left, reinforcing the misconception under which he so sadly laboured. Just as suddenly, the redcoats disappeared, only to be replaced minutes later by men wearing white. A party of Macdonnell's men had paraded in their battle red and then mischievously reversed their jackets, which were lined in white flannel.

Some way to the north, Purdy's men were tied down near the ford, faced initially by just two companies of chasseurs. Salaberry, sensing that the American flanking force were beginning to win the day, lined up his reserve along the north bank of the river and ordered them to fire across the water. The sudden flashes of fire, aimed straight at the hearts and chests of men who had had no sleep the night before, were enough to force Purdy's regulars back. Disorientated, exhausted and wet, they could take no more.

Hampton, the part-time optimist, sensed disaster, not just a setback. Distressed that Izard had failed to storm the abatis and now sadly aware of Purdy's lack of progress further north, he called off the attack, believing that a full 6000 men lay waiting for him behind the works that De Salaberry had so hurriedly constructed. Izard's men had just taken possession of the first enemy defence line.

Hampton, not De Salaberry, had really been the architect of British victory at Chateauguay. The Frenchman's tenacity and cunning, noteworthy qualities that they might have been, would not have been enough, without far greater numbers of men, to have secured a victory. Hampton's failings had been largely responsible. And the battle, despite its marginal character and the loss of only 50 Americans, had been one of the largest battles of the war so far, involving more than 4000 men in total. Canada lost few men, just 2 killed and 16 wounded. De Salaberry, climbing off the stump from which he had directed the fighting for most of the afternoon, was later able to write to his father. '*I have won a victory mounted on a wooden horse.*'

Purdy was unable to extract his men until the following morning. On the 28th, a council of war unanimously voted for a withdrawal of all the American forces across the border to Four Corners, arguing that '*it is necessary for the preservation of this army and the fulfillment of the ostensible views of the Government that we immediately return to such a position . . . . as will secure our communications with the United States, either to retire into winter quarters or be ready to strike below.*'

And meanwhile, Wilkinson's expedition had not even set out! Emerging slowly from the morass caused by Armstrong's vacillation, the general moved from Sackets Harbor on 17th October and headed for his intended assembly point on Grenadier Island. Here powerful storms damaged or sunk several of his boats, destroyed provisions and upturned trees, delaying him for another fortnight or so. On 3rd November Brigadier-General Jacob Brown and his brigade moved from Grenadier

Island to French Creek, the first stage on the nearly 200 mile haul to Montréal. Strung out along the dirt tracks at some distance behind were Wilkinson's other three brigades under the commands of Colonels John Boyd, Leonard Covington and Robert Swartout. Even further behind was Colonel Alexander Macomb and the forces of the reserve, barely ready to move when the call for the advance was given.

Chauncey, ordered to screen the entrance of the St. Lawrence and protect Wilkinson's flotilla from Britain's gunboats, cast a net that was full of holes. Parading his boats in the channel south of Wolfe Island, he allowed Captain William Howe Mulcaster and his gunboats to slip along the river's north channel and torment the troops at French Creek. Chauncey's detractors claim that Chauncey's negligence was deliberate. Prevented from attacking Kingston with his ships, he had sulkily concluded that he and his flotilla had been relegated to the menial role of providing transport for the army. Not wishing to be left in the shadows, so his critics maintained, he was looking for ways of sabotaging the campaign—and leaving access for the British ships to enter the river was almost certain to assist that aim. Whether this is true or not, Mulcaster's pack were now free to follow—all the way to Montréal, if necessary. Off French Creek, as men emerged from tents and packed kit on the 3rd, the British gunboats opened fire. America's march on Montréal was in danger of being brought to a halt by a hundred or so men and a handful of fragile gunboats.

Forced to anchor in open water, however, they were exposed to Brown's artillery and to sharpshooters in the trees. Bows splintered, British crewmen died, guns were knocked off mountings and Mulcaster felt obliged to temporarily withdraw. The 4 brigades of the republican army, nearly 6000 men including the reserve could now safely embark on boats and begin the uncertain voyage downstream, their movement watched from the enemy shore. Consisting of 350 vessels, the procession stretched back for nearly 5 miles, observed at every village, clearing and farmstead by Canadian nationals, who counted, assessed and recorded every detail.

On the 6th, the flotilla reached Morristown, 12 miles up river from Prescott and Fort Wellington, both points known to be bristling with artillery. Fully aware of the likely consequences of attempting to pass such well armed positions, even at night, Wilkinson sensibly decided to unload men, armaments and supplies and prayed that his nearly empty boats could slip past the enemy positions under cover of darkness. That night, the 6th, the lightly manned boats began a hazardous movement past the still silent guns. Simultaneously the troops, accompanied by a train of wagons with wheels muffled in cloth, trudged along the American shore, reminded by their officers that every sound would, no doubt, be heard.

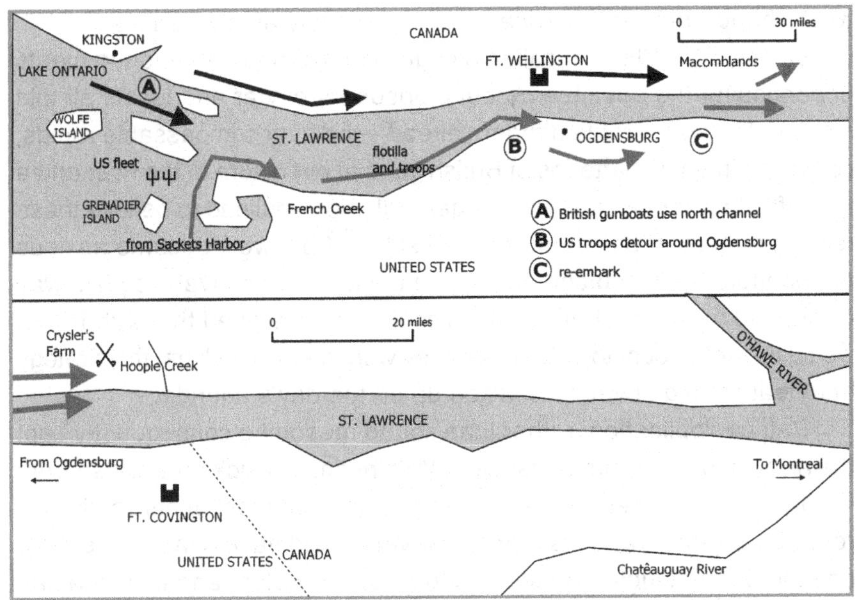

The American Attempt on Montreal

Prescott's guns suddenly opened, hurling 24 pound balls blindly into the darkness. But, moving down the centre of the river, most of the American vessels remained out of range. Running the gauntlet past Prescott cost the life of just one man and the loss of only two barges. On the south bank, where silence was preserved, more out of fear than discipline, the long column of soldiers was undisturbed. The gleam of moonlight on bayonet blades, however, had been seen by the inhabitants of Ogdensburg, many of whom were friendly to the British cause. Other lights now flashed across country, the light of lanterns signaling the news of America's night time movements to British officers on the opposite bank. Wilkinson, suffering hideously with dysentery, had not been inclined to travel with his men and had remained on board, where he would be close to the boat's latrine.

The British were only now coming to terms with the realization that Montréal was America's objective. On the 7th, a force consisting of 600 men of the 49th and 89th Foot, supported by three companies of the Canadian Voltigeurs and a 6 pounder gun, embarked at Kingston, their brief being to follow the Americans and attack the enemy tail if the situation seemed favourable. Commanding this shadowing force was Lieutenant—Colonel Joseph W. Morrison, a reliable soldier who would hang onto the Americans as tenaciously as a leech.

On the 8th, Wilkinson called a council of war and debated the merits of continuing the advance. Scouts, prisoners of war and locals all told stories of immeasurable dangers ahead—the river's impassable rapids, countless Indians, batteries of British guns at every turn of the river and a lack of fodder for the horses. The general, more inclined to believe these reports than most of his officers and still far from well, became anxious to abandon the expedition and return upstream to convalesce. He was dissuaded by stouter hearts on his council, who argued that withdrawal would be tantamount to defeat, and they were determined that the strategy of defeat should never be chalked up on the day's agenda.

Patriotic obligation, rather than sound reasoning consequently kept the army and the boats advancing. Wilkinson, too sick now to rise from his bed, quietly accepted the verdict and ordered most of his soldiers to re-embark. Brown and his men, however, would have a task to perform on land. Increasingly irritated by Morrison's regulars and by Canadian militiamen in his rear, Wilkinson instructed the officer to cross over to the enemy held shore and shield the expedition's advance.

Just ahead lay the Longue Saute (or Sault), 8 miles of white water, probably the most dangerous waters on the river. Negotiating these while under fire from the enemy would be difficult, possibly impossible. Enemy batteries and Mulcaster's ever-present gunboats would first have to be neutralized, tasks that would require the landing of additional troops to co-operate with Brown.

On the 10th, Colonel Alexander Macomb and Winfield Scott with a detachment of troops landed at Crysler's Point at the head of the rapids and set out along the King's Highway towards Cornwall. Near tiny Hoople Creek, they encountered their first opposition, a company of the 49th Foot under Major James Dennis, lying across the trackway leading east. Outflanking them in a move which Dennis should have anticipated, Scott, who had battled with Dennis at the Battle of Queenston, managed to slip past and so force the outsmarted Britisher to withdraw. Later that day John Boyd and his brigade also crossed to the Canadian shore and followed Scott towards the east.

That evening, knowing that it would be impossible for the pilots to navigate the rapids in the dark, Wilkinson moored all his vessels near Crysler Island for the night, planning to traverse the fast waters during daylight the following day. Mulcaster's boats made a token attack soon afterwards, causing damage to Wilkinson's nerves, but probably very little more. On the morning of the 11th, the general received the welcome news that Brown, spearheaded by Scott's troops, had cleared the route all the way to Cornwall. Once the rapids had been passed and the vessels re-united with Brown, now only 5 miles from the village of Cornwall, progress towards Montréal should be fairly rapid.

But Morrison, with Montréal's salvation lying largely on his shoulder, had decided to give battle, despite being heavily outnumbered. Drawing as close to the American camp as possible, he developed a 700 yard line at right angles from the river northward to the edges of an expanse of swamp and woodland on his left. His right, resting on the river, was held by militia and was covered by the gunboats. Indians and Voltigeurs held his left. The centre, standing astride the road to Montréal, was manned by the 89th Foot and a supporting gun. The 49th, which was also in possession of one artillery piece, lay just to their right. In their front lay a log fence and a line of skirmishers. By careful positioning of his troops, Morrison had concealed his shortage of numbers. He was, in fact, outnumbered by nearly 10 to 1.

Yet he enjoyed one potential advantage. Both of the senior American commanders, Wilkinson and Morgan Lewis, were too unwell to command in person. Lewis, dosing himself on blackberry jelly, was an even less effective commander than his superior; only Brown and Scott could be classed as competent military officers—and both men were some distance away—chasing shadowy soldiers who had shown no inclination to fight. Morrison and Harvey, his second in command, by contrast, were both present. Although relatively inexperienced in battle, these two men were parade ground experts and the epitome of the 18th and 19th Century professional British officer.

It was past 10.30 a.m. when Wilkinson first became aware of a British presence less than a mile to the west. Drowning in a sea of panic, he sent orders to Boyd, now following Brown towards Cornwall, to return and take over temporary command. '*It is now that I feel the heavy hand of disease-enfeebled and confined to my bed while the safety of the army entrusted to my command, the honor of our arms and the greatest interest of our country are at hazard,'* he wrote that day.

Brigadier-General John Boyd might not be the man in whom to place that much trust. A soldier of fortune for many years, mainly in the employment of Asian princes, he had returned to the United States and accepted a colonel's commission in the 4th Infantry. Brown, with whom he had been expected to work, detested him for personal reasons. Lewis, hardly a man whose criticism of others could be regarded as valid, described him as a '*combination of ignorance, vanity and petulance.'* But this was the man on whom the republic's fortunes now hung.

The day of battle was snow-infested. Flurries fell for most of the day, blanching the field where men would fight. On the river, American gunboats shielded the flotilla and guarded the approaches along which a few British boats were trying to probe. Boyd took up position on the morning of the 11th, mirroring the enemy positions with his right on the swamp and left on the St. Lawrence. Six pieces of artillery stood near the river, supporting the guns of the American warships anchored on the river.

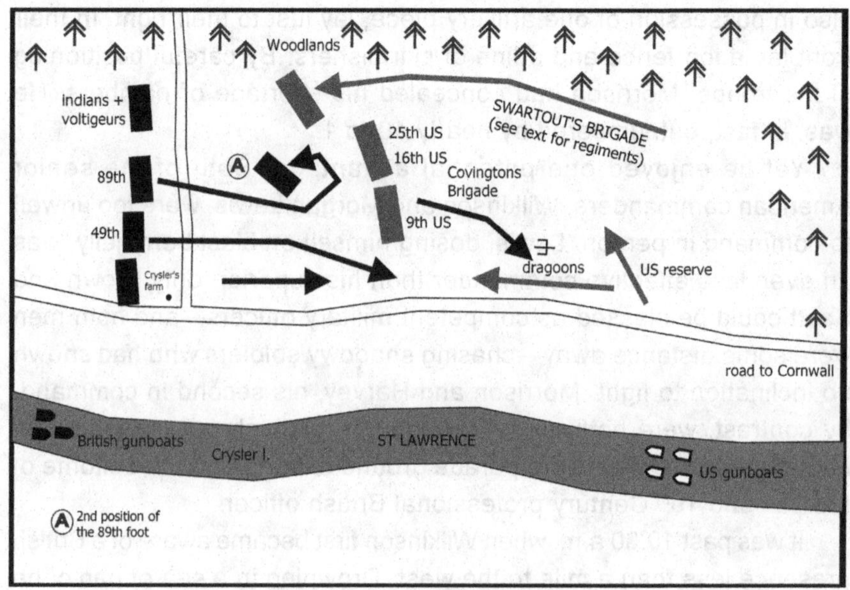

The Battle of Crysler's Farm

1st Brigade: (Brigadier-General Isaac Coles): 12th and 13th U.S.Infantry, a squadron of U.S.2nd Dragoons and a company of the 1st U.S. Rifle Regiment

3rd Brigade (Brigadier-General Leonard Covington): 9th, 16th and 25th U.S. Infantry

4th Brigade (Brigadier-General Robert Swartout): 11th, 14th and 21st U.S. Infantry

U.S.Forces at the Battle of Crysler's Farm

49th and 89th Foot, Glengarry Light Regiment, Canadian Fencible Regiment, Voltigeurs, 1st Stormont Militia, 1st Leeds Militia and 2nd Grenville Militia

British forces at the Battle of Crysler's Farm

America's dragoons opened the battle, advancing against the militia on the British right, but they achieved very little. The attack soon faded, and soon American soldiers were seen retreating and sheltering behind the scattered trees that occupied this section of the muddy field of battle. It was then the turn of America's right to become involved. Lieutenant-Colonel Eleazer Ripley and his regiment, part of Robert Swartout's brigade, now moved forward. Sent by Boyd to worry Morrison's skirmishers in the woodland on the extreme left of the British line, Ripley's men tumbled through bog and undergrowth for almost half a mile. Suddenly a line of Voltigeurs rose en masse from a concealed ditch and fired two disciplined volleys. Private Simon Thorgood's bruised face was caused by running into a tree, not by contact with the enemy. A carpenter from Albany, he had never experienced such an injury in three years as a champion wrestler. The Americans, unawed, were soon firing back, searching for cover as they did so. Fortunes ebbed and flowed, as they normally do in battle, but it was the American ammunition which was exhausted first. Ripley's cursing men retired beyond range; the colonel himself returned with the rest of Swartout's brigade a few minutes later to try to complete the job just started, the task of either driving the British back or penetrating marsh and woodlands in an effort to outflank their positions.

Morrison saw the threat and reacted like the professional that he was, executing a manoeuvre that his men would have practiced many times on parade ground drill. Referred to as a move 'en potence', this involved wheeling the entire regiment, the 89th, from its initial position facing east to a new northward facing front. Emerging from the woods and turning south, Swartout's brigade encountered this solid and ready line of red. Surprise was met by discipline, and despite the larger number of the Americans, they failed to dislodge the 89th regiment of foot.

Boyd, frustrated in what he thought would be a recipe for success, ordered both brigades forward, hoping, by sheer numbers, to shatter British might and pride. Next to the 89th, were men in grey coats, clearly militiamen that should be easy to crack. Advancing across the stubble of a wheat field. Leonard Covington's 3rd Brigade encountered a level of resistance far higher than they expected. The grey coats were already moving into echelon, forming a line of staggered platoons and firing volleys in a manner that irregulars could never manage. Only slowly did Boyd and Covington realise that these were British regulars, the 49th Foot, nicknamed the Green Tigers, their distinctive scarlet uniforms concealed beneath these grey overcoats. The accompanying 6 pounder had opened fire, too—and the cornfield was filling with the casualties of over-confidence.

The action soon lost any order. Smoke obscured lines, mud and swamp slowed movement, and units became less cohesive. This was a challenge, mental and physical for any soldier, things in which Britain's soldier excelled. Certain features were recorded, not necessarily in the correct order. American artillery, hauled from the boats after the battle's start, began to inflict injury on the 49th. Desperate to silence the 6 guns, Morrison ordered a detachment of the 49th forward to tackle the weapons. Pushing across the wheat field and smashing down John Crysler's fences, the British troops were soon within 100 yards of their enemy. But American dragoons, positioned near the river, were in movement as well, trotting along the river road towards the rear of the 49th. Seeing the danger and under a rain of grapeshot, the British infantry turned towards the dragoons, loosed a series of volleys, and emptied several saddles. While the 49th were so engaged, a company of the 89th dashed across the field and took the guns.

Sometime during this meleé in the mud, General Leonard Covington fell mortally wounded, just one of the 102 killed and 237 wounded on the American side. Mounted on a magnificent white horse, he had been too good a target for the British to ignore. More would certainly have fallen had it not been for the cruel cold that numbed fingers and made it difficult for the combatants to load their muskets at the normal speed.

Both brigades were now falling back, starved of ammunition and energy. The supply train, including most of the ammunition, was well on its way to Cornwall and could not be recalled in time. Darkness put an end to the action, about five hours after it had started. Britain had lost 22 killed and 148 wounded, only about half the casualties sustained by the Americans. And, as always in the hours after battle, when men's futures might have been irreparably altered and the survivors become human again, men began to search the field for fallen comrades. Then came the pain and sorrow and the reliving of the day's events during the few hours of interrupted sleep that might follow. Morrison could justifiably claim a victory, boasting that a force of less than 800 had held off more than 2000 for an entire afternoon. The victory, however, was more tactical than decisive—for Wilkinson would still have been in a position to continue his advance against Montréal, if he had chosen to do so.

When battles are lost, the defeated general is often capable of producing masterpieces of falsity or exaggeration in an attempt to justify his failure. Boyd went even further, producing a work of dissembling and a galaxy of excuses without parallel. '*. . . though the results of this action were not so brilliant and decisive as I could have wished, ... yet when it is recollected that the troops had been long exposed to hard privations and fatigues, the inclement storms from which they could have no shelter; this the enemy were superior in numbers, and greatly superior in position and supported by 7 or 8 heavy gunboats; . . . . when all these circumstances are recollected, perhaps this day may be thought to have added some reputation to the American arms,*' he wrote soon afterwards.

British superiority in arms is indisputable and leads to speculation about what Britain might have achieved with more forces and effort. Women and children hiding in the cellar of the Crysler farmhouse during the battle could distinguish between the regular volleys of the British and the sporadic output of the forces of the United States. Only one American regiment, the 25th, impressed the British with their tenacity and fighting skills. Morrison, attributing this to the leadership of Colonel Edmund Pendleton Gaines, wrote to him and expressed the hope that they might become post-war friends.

Boyd and Wilkinson were bombarded by a sustained wind of damning blasts and were criticised for a defective strategy, particularly for the failure to re-unite with Brown prior to the battle. In his report to the Cabinet, Wilkinson, like Boyd, inflated British strength beyond all reason, claiming that 2170 men stood in Morrison's ranks at Crysler's Farm.

General Wade Hampton's own defeat at Chateauguay prevented any chance of a union at St. Régis. Yet it seems that Wilkinson, even after his own battle beside the St.Lawrence, was still unaware of Hampton's failure. On the 12th, he moved down the river to Cornwall, on the Canadian shore immediately opposite St. Regis, to await the arrival of the Plattsburgh contingent. Here he received a letter from Hampton, written on 8th November, in which the writer blamed a shortage of supplies and poor roads as being largely responsible. He chose not to mention a probable shortage of nerve. His army, he explained, would have to fall back on Plattsburgh and wait for sustenance. *'I want language to express my sorrow,'* Wilkinson sadly commented when he had finished reading the dismal news.

Still in bed, he wrote further letters of self-exoneration to those who would sit in judgement. *'I feel compelled to retire by the extraordinary unexampled, and apparently unwarrantable conduct of Major-General Hampton,'* he stated in General Orders to his officers on the 13th. In a subsequent letter to Armstrong, he was even blunter: *'I disclaim the shadow of blame because I have done my duty . . . To General Hampton's outrage of every principle of subordination and discipline may be ascribed the failure of the expedition.'* [2]

The fact remains, however, that the attempt on Montréal had failed, blunted on the rocks of the St. Lawrence's rapids, and sharing the same fate as every previous American attempt at a cross-frontier invasion. Wilkinson took his flotilla 18 miles down river to Salmon Creek and then to French Mills, just inside the United States border, where he erected winter fortifications, naming the makeshift Fort Covington in honour of the fallen officer. The war of recrimination, however, continued, warmed by the breath of vitriol that never seemed to cease. In their winter condemnation of each other, Hampton and Wilkinson showed more passion and energy than they had ever done in the field. The American press was briefly interested, publishing some of the early verbal attacks and even taking sides. But these two men were soon covered in a cloth of disinterest, and the spotlights of the media switched off.

Wade Hampton's sudden request to be allowed to resign from the army might have been triggered by these criticisms. On 23rd November he left Plattsburgh, leaving Brigadier-General George Izard in command, When Wilkinson found out about Hampton's resignation, he maliciously asked Secretary Armstrong to arrest him, oddly implying that a failure in the field was a court-martial offence. The Administration took no regard of such a request, preferring to focus its mind on more important issues.

Wilkinson withdrew from the field as well. But his retirement was only temporary. Anxious to restore his health, he left the ice-crusted camp at French Mills and sought rehabilitation in a hospital in nearby Malone. The winter camp that he left behind was bereft of any joy or homely comfort. Men suffered terribly in temperatures of thirty degrees below, living in hastily constructed huts that provided little protection. The nearest source of sustenance was Albany, 250 miles away, and many of the supplies that reached the camp were appropriated by unscrupulous officers, who sold the food to the soldiers at exorbitant prices. Aware of the collapse of morale in the enemy camp, the British authorities on the other side of the river attempted to entice American troops to defect with the promise of the equivalent of five months pay and a guarantee that they would not be forced to fight against their compatriots. *'All American soldiers, who may wish to quit this unnatural war in which they are at present engaged . . . will receive the arrears due to them by the American Government.'* The message began. General Jacob Brown, left in charge of the camp, did his best to bolster hope and spirit, but few could see the purpose of remaining in a winter-plagued camp—and America's spirit touched its lowest ebb.

Montréal's pulse took quite a while to return to normal. When the news reached the city that Wilkinson's boats had passed Prescott at the start of the expedition, the church bells had rung and the mobilisation of the defence forces had been rapid. The garrisons at L'Acadie, Saint-Pierre and Saint-Philippe were recalled to the city's edges. The 103rd Foot, one of the regiments that had served under John Murray in the summer Lake Champlain campaign, was positioned at Cotéau-de-Lac, in the direct path of the American advance along the St.Lawrence.

Two redoubtable redcoated generals arrived in Canada at this moment. The 44 year old Lieutenant-General Sir Gordon Drummond, who had distinguished himself in Egypt in 1801 and was now junior only to Sir George Prevost, was immediately given responsibility for all the troops on the southern shore from his headquarters at Chateaugay. The other, the Irishman Sir Phineas Riall, who had commanded a regiment at the capture of Martinique in 1809, took charge of the forces on the north shore between Cornwall and Les Cedres, operating from his base at Lachine. Described by a fellow officer as *'very brave, near sighted, rather short but stout,'* he would lose an arm and his liberty during this war of freely flowing blood.

Then, as men waited for the first signs of the American tornado to sweep towards them, the wind of anticipation abated. On 14th November news reached the town that the Americans had turned back. Dispersal of the city's defence units followed almost immediately in an air of presumptive euphoria. And, in an attempt to disrupt the comatosed American camp at Fort Covington, Captain Mulcaster in early December sent a canoe load of men to set fire to the gunboats ice-bound near the camp at French Mills. Although the attempt failed, the alarm caused Wilkinson, who had just returned to assume command of the camp, to reconsider the wisdom of remaining there. On 20th January 1814 Secretary Armstrong directed Wilkinson to abandon camp and divide his forces, sending half his men to Sackets Harbor, under the command of Jacob Brown, now a major-general, and the rest to Plattsburgh with George Izard at their head.

Almost immediately Britain's forces pounced. In mid-February, Colonel Hercules Scott, with companies of the 89th and 103rd Foot, supported by the Fencibles and 5th Embodied Militia, crossed the St. Lawrence and savaged the American rearguard as it was leaving Fort Covington. From here the raiding force moved on to visit Malone, Madrid and Hopkinton, seizing provisions and burning public buildings in an act of revenge that bore few of the decencies of civilised war waging. Some patrols went even further, reaching Four Corners and even the outskirts of Plattsburg. Men still seemed to believe that the strategy of the Hun or Vandal would achieve more than masculine-type combat in a field of battle.

And the legacy for those weeks of used energy? Broken fences, lives, emptied barns and mental scars that would take even longer to repair.

CHAPTER 10

'It is really a novel thing that raw militia stuck upon horses . . . should be able to pierce British lines'

Brigadier-General Henry Procter felt troubled by the weight of responsibility that now rested on his shoulders. Even before America' victory on Lake Erie, he had become aware that Amherstburg was untenable. On 9th September, the day before the battle, 5 bateaux, carrying 171 barrels of flour, had managed to reach the fort from the east—and the fort's bakers could have been busy for several days. Perry's victory on the morrow, however, swept away this gossamer—like lifeline, making it highly unlikely that any more supplies could successfully cross the lake.

Procter consequently believed that he could easily justify his opinion to his superiors. On the 12th he informed De Rothenburg of his intention to withdraw, citing enemy activity and the number of mouths that he was expected to feed as just two good reasons for his retreat.

One of the reasons was quite convincing. Although his fighting strength consisted of only 1000 regulars, mainly the 41st Foot, (none of which had been paid since early summer) and about 500 of Tecumseh's warriors, the wives and children of the Indians swelled the number of dependents to over 13,000, a number logistically impossible for the commissariat to sustain. He probably felt that he could justify himself on personal grounds, too—for clearly Provost, Yeo and De Rothenburg felt little sympathy for his predicament and were not prepared to provide him with additional manpower—apart from the 100 or so extra members of the 41st, which arrived during late summer. Lake Erie and Upper Canada were apparently expendable. The struggle, the trio surmised, would be won, not on the western margins of Canadian civilization, but on the fields and shorelines of Ontario. Left to make a decision that none of his superiors wished to face, he began the unilateral process of withdrawal from the two forts, Malden and Detroit, that so much life blood had been shed to hold. On the 13th he gave orders for the destruction of the forts and the removal of stores and artillery to a temporary depot at the mouth of the River Thames. Curiously, he failed to inform his second-in-command, Lieutenant-Colonel Augustus Warburton of his intentions. The poor man remained in the dark for 48 hours until he was informed by one of the garrison's junior officers.

He also took some time to inform Tecumseh. The chief, of course, was not at all happy with the decision when he was told on the 18th, a week after the battle on Lake Erie. His loyalty to the British crown was not yet in doubt, but his ability to hold together the disgruntled tribesmen for much longer would now be sorely tested. The British general had tried to prevent the Indian chief from discovering the truth about Barclay's defeat on Lake Erie. Martial law was proclaimed and the movements of the Indians severely restricted. Tecumseh had paddled his canoe into the middle of the lake in the hope of observing the battle, but had failed to approach close enough to form an opinion of how the fighting had developed. *'Our fleet has gone out, we know they have fought, we have heard the great gun, but know nothing of what has happened to our Father.'*

And now, Tecumseh urged him to stand firm. '*We must compare our Father's conduct to that of a Fat animal that carries its tail upon its back, but when affrighted, it drops it between its legs and runs off,'* he disparagingly said in condemnation of the British non-strategy. He then spoke of a British abandonment of promises and of Indian tribesmen who had served the redcoats so well. In vain, Procter tried to reason, pointing out the vulnerability of his position, of a fort stripped of its guns to arm the 'Detroit' and of the closing of the route to the east. These practical considerations, however, were of no concern to the men of the plains, whose way of life depended upon self-sufficiency and the frequent need to kill.

Major-General William Harrison was preparing for the invasion which Procter feared so much. He had, at his side, two brigades of regulars, about 2500 men in total, under the command of Brigadier-Generals Lewis Cass and Duncan McArthur. In order to add weight to his intended blow, he appealed to the 63 year old Governor Isaac Shelby of Kentucky to provide him with State militia forces, and even suggested that the veteran politician and Revolutionaary War soldier should take joint command. *'I have such confidence in your wisdom that you, in fact, should be the guiding Head and I the hand . . . . Scipio, the conqueror of Carthage, did not disdain to act as the lieutenant of his younger and less experienced brother Lucius.'*

Shelby, affectionately known as 'Old King's Mountain' for the part that he had played in that battle, keenly accepted the summons and, within days, had assembled 4000 Kentucky men, mostly mounted, more than Harrison had ever considered possible. Included in this horde was a 1000 strong contingent of expert riflemen and Indian fighters, trained to precision by Colonel R.M. Johnson. They were, in the opinion of a British soldier who encountered them in battle, '*wretches . . . . capable of the greatest villainies. They are served out with blanket clothing . . . . with a long scalloping knife and other barbarous articles and with red paint with which they daub themselves all over and in summer nearly went naked*'. A force on horseback, however, would serve no purpose in Canada, and Harrison felt obliged to find a place of safety where Kentucky's horse could be corralled until their owners returned. He fenced off a narrow peninsula in the lake, a mile or so wide, leaving the contented animals on rich pastureland with a minimal force of guards. Only Johnson's riflemen were permitted to ride their mounts across the border. By early September the combined force of militia and regulars, collectively forming the Army of the North-West, was camped on the shores of Lake Erie between Sandusky Bay and Port Clinton. With this 6000 strong force were a number of Indians, serving the Republic for monetary payment and an unchallenged right to scalp.

In dealing with Governor Return Jonathan Meigs of Ohio, Harrison was far less diplomatic. This politician had been just as active as his Kentucky counterpart, raising 10,000 volunteers for the defence of the northern frontier. But, with so many Kentuckians in his lakeside camp, he felt no need for the Ohio men's service. Meigs was obliged to send the volunteers home, but the bitterness of rejection caused many to vow that they would never again turn out for their country's defence . . .

On 23rd September 1813, the force of invasion left Sandusky and moved up to Put-in-Bay. Leaving McArthur's 700 man brigade to protect the American shoreline and instructing Johnson's horsemen to proceed by land into Canada, Harrison began embarking the rest of his army on Perry's boats at Put-in-Bay. Army and navy were reported to have worked in finely tuned harmony, and the whole operation consequently only took four days to complete.

British troops were also on the move. On the 27th, while Harrison's embarkation of troops was in progress, Major Adam Muir destroyed the last of the public buildings at Detroit, hauled down the Union flag, and crossed the river to Sandwich in Canada. Territory, purchased with a little British blood in 1812, was being returned to its former owners, but without a price being asked. Simultaneously, Procter at Fort Malden, waiting only for the column of soldiers, Indians and camp followers to leave, set fire to the fort's service buildings and began his retreat to the east.

America, therefore, found no opposition. Landing the army on Bar Point, Middle Sister and Bois Blanc Islands, Harrison and Perry sailed towards the Canadian mainland in the schooner 'Ariel', scouting the coast for the signs of an enemy presence. At 4 p.m. on the 27th, the first of the invasion boats touched Hartley's Point, and the troops waded ashore; not a single enemy soldier had remained to observe their arrival. Here he divided his army into two columns, detailing three brigades of militia to concentrate on clearing the Indians believed to be operating in the woodlands on the British right, while the column on the American right followed directly in the path of Procter's retreat.

Amherstburg and Malden were occupied that same night. Procter, receiving the unwelcome news within an hour, promptly abandoned Sandwich and retreated east towards the Thames River, which flowed from Lake St. Clair parallel to the northern shore of Erie. McArthur, sent by Harrison to occupy Sandwich, encountered brief opposition from a British rearguard unit which was in the act of setting fire to a bridge over the Aux Canard River. On the 29th his troops entered Sandwich, finding the tents, clothing and provisions left by the British in their haste to be gone.

Colonel Richard Mentor Johnson's and his 1200 mounted riflemen, entered Detroit that night. They had ridden through Frenchtown, site of the long remembered and still not forgotten massacre, and had found the unburied bones of their countrymen strewn across the apple orchard . . . '*The bones . . . cry aloud for revenge. The chimneys of the houses where the Indians burnt our wounded prisoners . . . yet lie open to the call for vindictive justice,'* Captain Robert McAfee wrote in his diary. Stopping just long enough to inter the remains, the party arrived at Detroit with the fires of revenge burning uncontrollably in their veins and with the words, '*Rembember the Raisin*' imprinted on their lips. They were greeted by several Americans who had remained in the town after Hull's surrender. In an act of great ceremony, which lasted for most of the night, the Stars and Stripes were raised again, and the Kentucky horsemen, hailed as liberators, were carried shoulder-high by their compatriots.

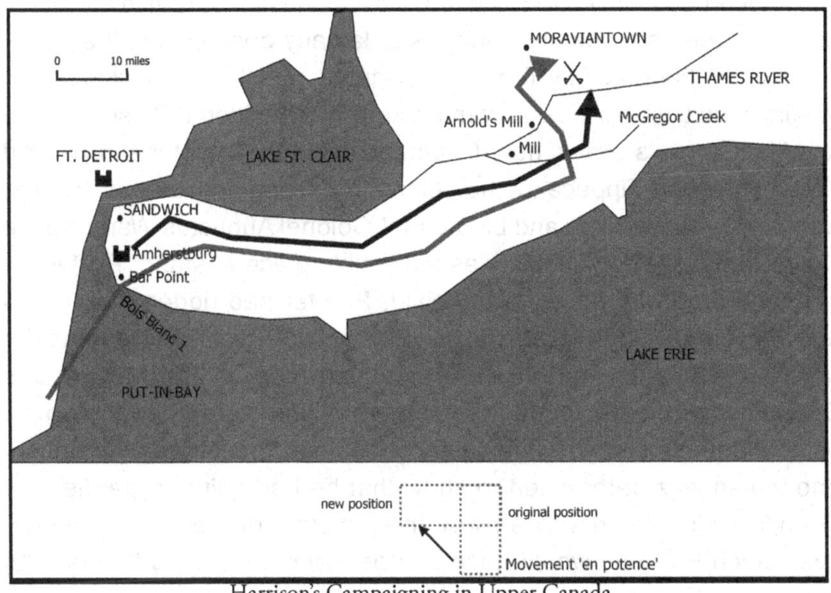

Harrison's Campaigning in Upper Canada

Detroit's liberators crossed the river the following day to join the rest of the advancing army at Sandwich. Leaving about 1000 men to take possession of their two conquests, Harrison set out again on 2nd October in pursuit of Procter, pushing through dense stands of walnut trees to the point where the river's waters join Lake St. Clair. An air of restrained optimism had developed—for here was an American army marching through enemy territory and meeting no opposition. The stoop of men who had known only inactivity or the shame of defeat was replaced by a more energetic spring—and the bites of Autumn's flies were hardly noticed.

The gap between the two sides was lessening. Procter, fifty miles further on, was slowed by his baggage train and the families of his Indian warriors and barely travelled five miles a day. Harrison, by contrast, was moving at more than nine miles daily. Johnson's horsemen, if they had been allowed, would have progressed even faster.

The Thames River, flowing into the corner of Lake St. Clair, was navigable for most of its course, and this enabled Procter to place his burdensome baggage and womenfolk on board boats, while the troops continued by foot along the river's bank. But the Americans, now only two days behind, also took full advantage of the waterway, and, less encumbered, continued to close the gap. Curiously, the British officer did not order the destruction of bridges or lay any obstacles in the path.

Procter, badgered by Tecumseh's taunts, reluctantly concluded that the time had come to make a stand. Briefly he considered Dolsen's Farm and MacGregor's Creek, near Chatham, the latter a spot that reminded Tecumseh of his Tippecanoe homeland. Rejecting both places, he sent Captain Matthew Dixon and Lieutenant-Colonel Augustus Warburton to Dover to assess its suitability as a possible place to stand. Preferring to spend time with his wife and child, Procter had ridden ahead and had, it seems, left Warburton to take on all the arrangements for retreat. Tecumseh and his 400 remaining men, still at McGregor's Creek, consequently found themselves making a stand on their own, an abandonment for which he later condemned Procter and the British. The Indian was determined to show that he had spine, regardless of the odds. His warriors tore away the planking of the narrow bridge, over which Harrison would have to cross, and concealed themselves in the woods beyond.

There would be no heroism or real spilling of blood at MacGregor's Creek. For, when the Indians opened fire on an American scouting force, Major Eleazer Wood, the defender of Fort Meigs, coolly positioned two 6 pounder guns and scattered the Indians as effectively as mosquitoes before a spray. In less than two hours, the bridge was repaired and the army's boots were clattering across. There would be no fighting at Dover either. The baggage train had been hurriedly packed at Amherstburg, and the entrenching tools could not be found. More in relief than disappointment, Warburton continued his retreat, remembering that every step towards the east brought them closer to Vincent at Burlington Heights.

On 4th October the British crossed the river at the Arnold's mill to the north bank, still searching for the site at which to make a stand and, presumably, for the tools which they would need to make their stand effective. Christopher Arnold, the mill's owner, was standing outside the building when Tecumseh, in buckskin and headdress, approached. Minutes later, the loyal Canadian was agreeing to watch out for the American vanguard, signaling their arrival by throwing up a shovelful of earth.

Procter went to ground at last at Moraviantown, a mission station of the Christian Munsee Indians, pacific folk who had nothing whatsoever to do with this conflict of the whites. The redcoat had been forced to realize that escape was nigh impossible. Two of his gunboats had just been captured, both carrying large supplies of ammunition. Butchered meat was plentiful, but bread was in short supply. Moving too quickly to cook, the soldiers ate the meat raw while marching. The time had come, Procter surmised, to find out whether salvation was more likely to be obtained from the barrels of his muskets in a determined stand, rather than from constant flight. away. Three miles past the mission on the evening of the 4th, he began to make his dispositions. Marshland gave adequate protection on his right, a smaller patch offered protection to his centre, while, to his left, lay the blessings of a river. It was the stereotypical site for battles in this war; a river, marshland and scattered trees.

His available men were about to be positioned in the standard battle format, too. Tecumseh's Indians formed on the edge of the bigger swamp, positioned there to outflank the attackers. By dawn the 41st Foot, about 500 strong, [19] and the 290 men of the Royal Newfoundland Regiment had formed a single line. Their left rested on the Thames River and, from here, the line stretched north for five hundred yards, past the small swamp in the centre, to the extensive swamp on the far right, which no wise man should ever attempt to cross. On the road, Procter placed his solitary gun, loading it with canister. The Britisher,

19 About 200 had been captured in earlier skirmishes

by choosing a position that would restrict the front over which the Americans would have to advance, felt that he had chosen well.

The haphazard assembly of his troops, however, was far from conventional. British rigidity and discipline of stance had been replaced by a casual indifference, the result, no doubt, of endless marching and lack of food. Moreover, the men of the 41st were too few to form shoulder to shoulder in continuous line and so formed clusters behind scattered trees. In the absence of the tools, entrenching was impossible. Britain would need to rely upon a sudden swell of military self-discipline to halt Harrison's host.

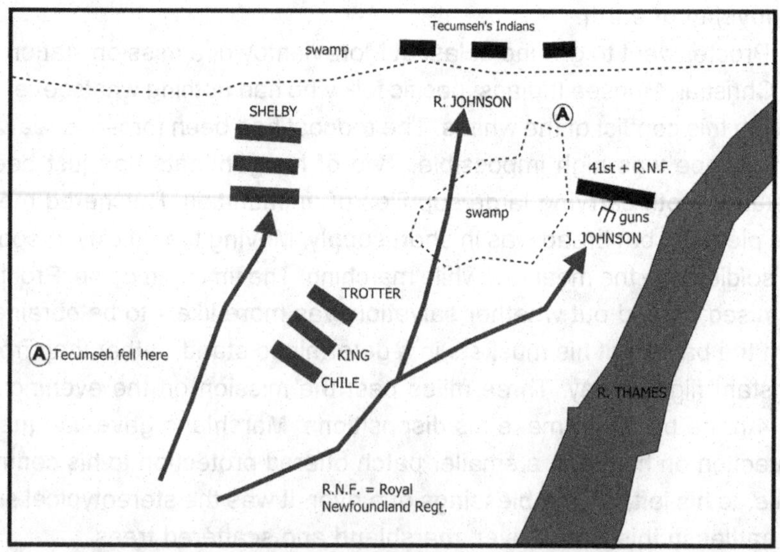

The Battle of Moraviatown (The Thames)

Here they stood in semi-readiness for more than two hours. The once bright uniforms were faded and torn, and the faces of the men were pale and unshaven. Seldom had British troops appeared like this and rarely would they do so again. The only supplies of ammunition available were the musket balls that each man carried in his pouch—and a rumour had spread amongst these scattered souls that Harrison had more than 10,000 men in his ranks. Tensely they searched the trees to the west, anxious to see the locust like force before it arrived.

Harrison was already aware that the British had halted. Perry, the seaman, and Colonel Johnson were at Harrison's side when he surveyed the British line, their redcoats visible amongst the green-brown of autumnal trees. Johnson immediately requested that his horsemen, who carried tomahawks and scalping knives in addition to their rifles, should be allowed to strike at the regulars on the enemy left. At this very moment, however, Tecumseh was prevailing upon Procter to form a second line, one hundred yards behind—and the scattered front line grew even thinner. The redcoat soldiers, still watching, would have been unable to distinguish the sombre uniforms of the Americans from the foliage of the trees. Few would have been aware of the proximity of the enemy.

Harrison's troops, consisting of 140 regulars and Shelby's 2000 men of Kentucky, formed up behind Johnson in three successive lines. The men on the left of the American line were to be 'refused' at an angle to the front in order to counter any British or Indian outflanking moves. And, in a yet more resourceful attempt to embarrass the British, a small detachment was positioned on the river banks with the task of slipping past Procter's left if any opportunity should arise.

Harrison, in accepting Johnson's suggestion, abandoned orthodoxy in favour of a plan that was bold, daring and potentially flawless. The American mounted unit, honed to a plane of perfection far beyond the level normally achieved by volunteer soldiers, could be relied upon to carry the weight of the attack. The infantry, under the field command of 34 year old Brigadier-General George Trotter, would now be assigned a supporting role if and when the need arose. Shelby's Kentucky infantry's role would be even more minor—to stabilise the left flank, watch the Indians and only attack if the warriors attempted to outflank the American positions.

Johnson, in his saddle, now saw yet another chance to create even greater mischief. Informed by one of his officers that the small swamp was penetrable and sensing that the front between the river and this swamp was too narrow to deploy all his men, the colonel split his force, sending his brother, James, with half the men towards the 41st, while he took on the perilous task of crossing the smaller swamp and dealing with Tecumseh's men. '*You have a family, I have none,*' he explained.

James Johnson, on the right, led his soldiers in a gallop against the British left. Only briefly wavering in the face of the first ragged volley of British fire, his men formed again. *'Damn that gun!,'* Procter, looking at his still silent fieldpiece, was heard to say. *'Why doesn't it fire?'* Then came the second charge, more determined than the first. *'Superb, magnificent,'* a British officer who had fought at Talavera, exclaimed in disbelief. A second British volley, this time from the second line, and the 41st had dissolved. The force of the American charge had taken the horsemen through both redcoat lines in an engagement that had lasted little more than ten minutes. Wheeling to the left, Johnson's men dismounted and opened casual fire from the rear. Ensnared by musket fire from American infantry at their front and Johnson's men in their rear, the men of the 41st surrendered. *'It is really a novel thing that raw militia stuck upon horses, with muskets in their hands instead of sabers, should be able to pierce British lines with such complete effect,'* Eleazer Wood mused. Cavalry charges had been almost non-existent in American wars so far. And this, far from being the conventional charge by saber-wielding professionals, had been a movement of mounted amateurs, who preferred to rely upon their rifles rather than a blade of steel.

Colonel Richard Johnson met with a little less success on his brother's left. Swamp, trees and broken ground made a charge on horseback less effective, and the Indians, knowing how to take full advantage of the cover of trees, were more like faceless spectres than men. Men sunk in the soft ground as far as the saddle girths of their horses, and the Indians' fire was merciless. Dismounting, the horsemen crawled for cover, reached the trees and, once there, fought on more equal terms. Pistols discharged, tomahawks came down, and the first of many scalps was taken. Johnson, brought to the ground, fired at point blank range, dispatching his would-be killer with a single ball through the head. Grey, faceless shadows emerged, went, and re-appeared again. Shelby, seeing Johnson's predicament, now brought his brigade around the edge of the swamp to the woodland's edge and prepared to get involved.

For a while, Shelby's volunteers were confused, unable to distinguish friend from foe in the smoke and hell-like noise that marked the scene of battle. An American, finding himself without ammunition, threw nuts at the enemy. Another, losing his weapon, killed an Indian witth a tomahawk he had found on the ground. Somewhere, within, Tecumseh's shrill voice could be heard above the din—and this, more than anything else, goaded them into action. For years, men had dreamed of the day when they might encounter this living legend. No white man there that day, apart from Harrison, had ever seen Tecumseh. Invisible, formless, he might have been the product of men's imaginations. Here was the chance to discover if the man had blood—and Shelby's men went in.

Their involvement, however, was hardly necessary. The tenor and mood on the field had suddenly changed. The legend had fallen mortally wounded, and the fighting spirit of his warriors drained away with his blood. Within minutes, they had gone, leaping over their fallen colleagues in their anxiety to be gone. It is said that the 44 year old Tecumseh had a premonition that this would be the day of his death. If so, he had accepted it stoically and done nothing to prevent it. Many have claimed the credit for killing Tecumseh; Richard Johnson's election to the post of office of Vice-President of the United States in 1836 was attributed partly to his own contention that he had shot the chief.

The warrior's body was never found amongst the fallen. His faithful followers bore him away, determined that no white man would ever view or mutilate his body. He would remain as invisible and intangible in death as he had been in life. Vengeful soldiers tore strips of skin as souvenirs from a body that Johnson and others believed to be that of Tecumseh; some of the strips were later fashioned into razor strops.

Tecumseh unfortunately has never been granted his rightful place alongside the early super heroes of America. For William Henry Harrison, the fall of 'Tippecanoe Tecumseh' was particularly poignant. The government of the Unites States of America had indirectly spent $5 million in combating this great warrior. How many of his men fell with him has never been estimated. The British lost 12 killed, 22 wounded and perhaps 600 captured. America's fatalities were less than ten in total and two dozen or so wounded.

Procter attempted to position the blame elsewhere. The conduct of his troops was not what '*I have on every other occasion witnessed with pride and satisfaction . . . nor did I receive that cordial aid I sought.*' He particularly singled out his artillery team for their failure to bring the 6 pounder into action, deliberately ignoring the fact that the weapon had become entangled in trees at the start of the battle when the horses had reared in fright. He also chose to gloss over the fact that the gun had been starved of ammunition. But there was one thing that he never mentioned or explained: he had left the field before the rout in order to avoid capture. Lieutenant Richard Bullock, commenting on Procter's deployment of men during the battle, was critical of the soldiers as well, claiming that '*they were ready and willing to fight for their knapsacks; wished to meet the enemy, but did not like to be knocked about in that manner, doing neither one thing nor the other'.* At the war's end, when censorship and opinions could be more freely exercised, Procter was court-martialled and accused of failure, negligence and faulty judgement. Influential sources, however, worked in his favour, and his only punishment was a reprimand from the Prince Regent. In the interval between battle and reprimand, he remained in command in the west, attempting to hide his shame with fresh efforts to consolidate and hold an untenable position.

The men of Kentucky received the laurels that Ohio men felt that they had been denied. *'The militia of Ohio have been made pack horses, and merely served as convenience for others to receive the honor and glory',* John Gano, commander of the Ohio State militia, bitterly complained. But the victors did not remain for long on conquered soil. America seemed entirely satisfied with this simple tactical victory. On 15th October, the republicans departed, pulling back around Lake Erie almost as quickly as they had come. Stopping at the lake's peninsula to collect their horses, the Kentuckians then rode home to loved ones and a hero's welcome.

William Henry Harrison's involvement in this war was rapidly coming to an end as well. He had outmarched his supply routes, making any advance against Burlington Heights an act of national folly. Returning to Detroit on 9th October, he dismissed his volunteers and then set about making an armistice with the tribes of the area. Thirty-seven chiefs representing six tribes turned up at Detroit, quietly signed an agreement and departed again, leaving their wives and children as hostages. On the 17th, Harrison handed over the civil administration of the region to Lewis Cass and set out for Sackets Harbor, hoping to be applauded as a saviour on his arrival at the town. Here, however, he found little applause, nor much for him to do. Continuing on his journey to New York, he encountered mixed receptions. The inhabitants of Albany had no idea who he was. Further south, the welcome was generally warmer, but never rapturous, and he was forced to accept that he had become no hero in the eyes of the American people. The Secretary of War turned out to be even colder, virtually ignoring the general when he finally reached Washington. General Harrrison's lack of skills had been exposed. He had few of the qualities of greatness and could never have extended himself beyond his obvious limitations. Run-of-the-mill leaders, America had in plenty, but extraordinary qualities continued to be lacking. And so another opportunity slipped past, unmourned by most and, at the time, regretted by none. Disgusted, Harrison returned to his home in Cincinnati, where he was given a minor command. Jolted politically, he resigned his post in May 1814. Despite this, he would eventually be catapulted to the presidency of the nation.

The nation's victory at the Thames ended any Indian involvement in the war in this sector. It also completely extinguished the British presence in Upper Canada, apart from a small detachment which remained on isolated Mackinac Island on Lake Huron's northern shores, and Vincent's light hold on Burlington Heights. That general, on receiving news of the disaster, pulled back his advance post at Twenty Mile Creek and destroyed quantities of supplies and ammunition that would have proved too time-consuming to move. Of the 1100 men on his roll, 800 were sick. American forces, without exaggeration, would now be free to sweep along the northern shores of Lakes Erie and Ontario to York, Kingston and even to Montréal beyond. The capture of the lonely outpost on Lake Huron was briefly considered in the heady weeks following the victory at The Thames. But Canada's snows were not appealing, and Harrison and Perry expressed no real interest. Several days later, Perry requested to be relieved of his command on the Lake. On 25th October Jesse Elliot took over the naval reins on Erie, and Perry set out over land to Rhode Island to seek command of a sea-going frigate. Harrison shifted his gaze towards the Niagara, leaving the administrators of Michigan and Ohio to sustain the garrisons of Detroit and the frontier posts.

And meanwhile the border was under constant vigilance.2000 men watched from lonely blockhouses for any signs that Britain might attempt to resurface in the region. These were to be the war's forgotten warriors, the pioneers of the wilderness who had left loved ones and farms to protect their nation's border. Of fighting they did very little, but the challenges imposed were considerable. Chauncey and Elliott were unwilling to provide naval support for any move against Vincent at Burlington. Without their input, fighting on the lakes frontier would stagnate. Neither Chauncey, nor Elliot was impressed by the requests of politician-turned militia brigadier-generals Peter Porter and George McClure, the latter commanding at Fort George, for a late offensive on the eastern end of the Ontario peninsula.

Canada's reigning trio was constructed of no better material than any of the Americans against whom they had been pitted. Prevost immediately ordered the abandonment of Upper Canada, an instruction that was fully endorsed by De Rottenburg and Procter. Vincent, however, pointed out the errors of their thinking. The roads to Kingston, little better than mires at this time of year, were nearly impassable. Lake Ontario was studded with Chauncey's warships. Withdrawal eastwards to Kingston, with wagons laden with the sick and the baggage of his army, would be more than merely hazardous. He argued that a withdrawal from the Niagara Peninsula should be sufficient and proposed instead a concentration of men and resources at Burlington Heights. And so he remained, entrenched at Burlington Heights. He would now be pitted against Brigadier-General George McClure and an army of 1600 irregulars based at Forts George and Niagara. Supporting McClure was the turnncoat Joseph Willcocks and his Canadian Volunteers.

McClure had long been aware that his force of unreliables could be the prey, rather than the predator, in Vincent's intended game of cat and mouse. Moreover, the period of enlistment of many of his men would expire in mid-November. About one-third of his force, 500 or more men, would be able to return to their homes. Enjoying the ability to write in florid words, he issued a number of appeals to patriotic Americans, urging them to ignore the '*false, absurd and ridiculous scruples of the injunctions of the constitution,*' which had always inhibited military service across the international frontier. But only men of courage, not the '*faint-hearted effeminate poltroons,*' should put themselves forward. In an appeal appearing in the 'Buffalo Gazette,' he invited '*the Old and Young*' to join '*my Brigade in defence of their Country and Rights,*' concluding with his belief that '*no other consideration need be urged, than a love of country, to excite the patriotism of the hardy Yeomanry of the Western District.*' But not even a bounty, nor a label of shame, could induce his enlisted men to stay or others to join his ranks.

Desperation prompted him to indulge in the sort of methods that did him and America no credit. Resorting to farm burning and intimidation on the border lands, he permitted Willcocks to hound out personal enemies and arrest anyone who was believed to have a Hanoverian heart. To counter this Hunnish war strategy and protect the Niagara Canadians, Vincent instructed Colonel John Murray to take 378 regulars of the 8th Foot and establish himself at Forty Mile Creek, nearly 20 miles east of Burlington Heights. By the end of November, McClure, too, had moved a little way forward, positioning his advance posts at Shipman's Corner (St. Catharines) on Twelve Mile Creek. Falsely informed (by Willcocks, it would appear) that Murray had 3000 troops under his command, McClure felt only strong enough to watch Murray's fragile movements and avoid sustained contact with the enemy.

His move to Twelve Mile Creek had left Fort George almost defenceless, manned by only 70 regulars. Murray, at Forty Mile Creek, was only 30 miles away. Britain's repossession of the fort would endanger America's hold on the Niagara River and make Buffalo liable to attack. Armstrong, in one of his rare moment of vision, had recognized that undefended Newark, in British hands, would provide billets and cover for the redcoats during an assault on Fort George. Writing to McClure in October, he had ordered the town's destruction. '*Understanding that the defense of the post committed to your charge may render it proper to destroy the town of Newark, you are hereby directed to apprise its inhabitants of this circumstance, and invite them to remove themselves and their effects to some place of greater safety.*'

The atrocity which followed was committed by a man who had lost his head and had drunk too deeply from the bitter chalice of war. Hastening back from Shipman's corner on 10th December, he ordered the burning of every house in Newark and the destruction of Fort George. The inhabitants were left with no shelter in the depths of a North American winter. '*In the village, at least 130 buildings were consumed*', the Ontario Repository reported, ... '*the miserable tenants . . . . to the number of nearly four hundred, consisting mostly of women and children, were exposed to all the severities of deep snow and a frosty sky, almost in a state of nakedness.*' One lady, seriously ill at the time, was taken from her bed and left in the snow to watch the burning of her husband's valuable collection of books. Some beautifully carved toys belonging to twins were snatched from the children's hands and thrown on the fire. A cat was also roasted, apparently because the animal's owner had been slow in answering the door. Another lady saved only the mantelpiece from her previously comfortable home. Perversely, Fort George escaped the fate intended for it. Discovering that the British were closer than they had expected, the American firing party only just had time to spike the cannon and force them from their mountings before fleeing. The intact fort passed unceremoniously back into British hands.

General Sir George Drummond, now in command in place of De Rottenburg, who was about to sail home, angrily demanded whether the burning of the village had been authorised by the American government. McClure retorted by stating that he was under no obligation to explain his action to anyone except his political superiors in Washington. Later, however, he replied to critics that he had merely been obeying orders and wanted to deny shelter to the enemy. And in a blast of self-defence, he cited as precedent the British destruction of Havre de Grace and other settlements on the Chesapeake.

A British counter-move followed in the track of the flames. On the 18th, Murray, acting on orders just received from Drummond, reviewed his troops at St. Davids and began the crossing of the Niagara. Assembling on the cold plains near this little village were several companies of the 41st, the 1st (Royal Scots) and the 100th Regiment of Foot, about 600 men in total. The preparations for this intended attack on Fort Niagara had been going on for a week, ever since McClure had evacuated Fort George. Boats had been dragged overland from Burlington Heights and concealed in woodland near the river's edge. '*It should be impressed on the mind of every man that the bayonet is the weapon on which the success of the attack must depend.*' Drummond had stressed in his instructions to Murray. The grenadiers of the 100th Foot were given the task of storming the fort's main gates, the Royal Scots had responsibility for attacking the salient in the south, and the remaining regulars, supported by militia, would throw their weight against the eastern bastion. In a further elaboration of detail, Drummond had insisted that a party of axe men were on hand to break down fences and doors.

At about 10 p.m. that night the invading party crossed and set foot on American soil, about three miles below Fort Niagara. Tales of what happened next have been embroidered over the decades since, but the thread of the night's events remain simple enough. Silently moving soldiers first surrounded a tavern at Youngstown, where about 20 members of the outer picket were playing cards. Obliging them first to divulge the current password, the British sent the unfortunate revelers to Heaven. The second picket line, hearing the correct pass word uttered, allowed the British to approach too close—and these Americans, too, joined their careless colleagues in another world. Not a sound or hint of the intruders' approach had reached the sleeping fort.

Fort Niagara, in theory and in practice, should not have been an easy fort to subdue. Captain Nathaniel Leonard had 27 pieces of artillery and 430 men with which to defend the place

But, despite being warned that the British were likely to attack, Leonard was absent, and his remaining officers, after a night of revelling, were snoring noisily in their quarters. Ice cracking under soldiers' boots was fortunately borne away by a north-east wind. At about 2.45 a.m., the British reached the fort and found the drawbridge down. By chance, they had arrived at the very moment when the sentries were being changed. A solitary British sergeant calmly crossed the bridge, gave the pass word and strangled the guard. Minutes later the soldiers of the 100th Foot were rushing through the open gateway.

The Royal Scots had no real need to storm the southern front, for, within minutes, the fort was in undisputed British hands. Only 20 Americans escaped to carry the news to Buffalo that the British and Canadians had set an uninvited foot on American soil. 65 of the defenders lay dead and 16 wounded, all despatched by bayonets during a night when hardly a shot was fired. 344 prisoners were taken: 27 guns, 7000 muskets, supplies of clothing and several thousand pairs of shoes were included in the haul. Britain had paid a low price—6 dead and 5 wounded. Every one of the nearly 600 redcoat soldiers received two pounds sterling as a reward for his work. Yet the greatest reward of all was the feeling that they had avenged the humiliation of Moraviatown. Moreover, Murray and Drummond planned this time to hold on to this valuable piece of Republican soil.

The invasion of America would not end here. At 5 a.m. on the morning of the 19th, a cannon shot from Fort Niagara informed the Irishman Major-General Phineas Riall, who had replaced Vincent as commander at Burlington Heights, that the way was now clear for his own invasion of the United States. He landed soon after the signal, putting ashore the Royal Scots and the 41st Foot, about 1000 men, and 500 Indians at Five Mile Meadows, just north of Lewiston. No Americans were present to contest their landing. The citizens of the riverside town, too, had decamped; men, women and children were tumbling down the road to Buffalo, convinced that the British would follow. Atrocities followed instead—children scalped, houses pillaged and cattle decapitated, crimes for which Riall's unrestrained Indians were largely responsible. The British had never tried to cork the genie that they had first unleashed in 1812, continuing to justify their decision to retain the services of Indians on the ground that America's white men had recently proved themselves to be equally as savage.

Sixty of Willcock's volunteers briefly stood on the road south of Lewiston. Pushing these aside with ease, the British moved south, destroying Fort Schlosser and Manchester, and laying waste farmsteads, storehouses and homes as they went. At Tonawanda Creek, just 10 miles from Buffalo, Willcocks had hacked down the bridge in a pathetic attempt to stay the speed of Britain's boots. But Britain's soldiers failed to appear at Buffalo that night. Sensing that he might have too few men for an assault on this major American town, Riall withdrew to Lewiston on the 22nd and recrossed to home soils.

The respite, however, would be brief, for Drummond promptly overruled this craven decision and sent him forward again, explicitly ordering him to destroy both Black Rock and Buffalo. On the 30th, Riall re-invaded, bringing with him the 8th, 41st and 89th Foot and the supporting Indians, crossing the Niagara without opposition about two miles below Black Rock.

Northern New York's folk were gripped with panic. Many in this border area had not, so far, been touched by this war between neighbours. Some had joined the state's militia forces and participated in frontier campaigns, but for those who had been able to avoid enlistment, life in Buffalo township had continued much as normal, except for the occasional glimpse of an itinerant brigadier-general and his entourage, a sweating horse messenger from Albany or wagons loaded with supplies from the front. Few of those engrossed with the daily chores of life would look for long at these passing signs of war; for most the farm and workbench were their only concerns. Canada, after all, was a long way to the north, and Canadians, despite their anger, would surely never feel the need to come so far south.

1st, 8th, 41st, 89th and 100th Foot, William Merritt's Provincial Dragoons, 2nd and 3rd Lincoln Militia

British troops involved in attack on Black Rock

McClure, at bay in Buffalo, was now a stained man, ethically beyond salvage and held responsible for the crimes committed at Newark. *'I have to represent that the men of my brigade are unwilling to come under the command of General McClure . . . . His conduct . . . . has disgusted the greater part of the men under his command . . . .'* Brigadier-General Timothy Hopkins, the town's commander reported on the 20th in a letter to the Governor of New York. Armstrong's instructions to Governor Tompkins were terse and to the point. *'Relieve the man,'* the order began. Major-General Amos Hall, a spirited man with a keen sense of urgency, took McClure's place. Making his headquarters at Batavia, east of Buffalo, he tried to build a human wall. By 27th December he had about 2000 newly-raised men positioned between Buffalo and Black Rock.

News of the thresh threat only reached Buffalo's homes minutes before the sound of cannon fire at Black Rock. For a while the residents invested their hopes in Hall's defences and the panic was contained. But this was to become a contest of psychological and military inequality. Hall's untrained woodmen, farmers and urban artisans saw the polished professionalism of Britain's regulars and an armoury of weapons that was designed to impress. The first wave of the invaders, consisting of some companies of the 89th and militia under the command of Lieutenant-Colonel James Ogilvie secured a bridge over the Scajaquada Creek and formed up just beyond the bridge while the rest of the army disembarked. Fiery Lieutenant-Colonel John Gordon brought the Royal Scots ashore at daylight, landing under fire on the shoreline above Black Rock in an operation that cost more than a dozen British lives. The 8th and 89th reached the edges of Buffalo and there found General Hall standing in their way. Most of his citizen soldiers fired off a few rounds before melting away. A few, *'with the shady coolness of veterans,'* continued to volley from a distance, but these too were soon gone. The population of both towns was now in flight. Some tarried long enough to fill carts and barrows with their personal possessions; one man had a monkey in a tiny cage, another had to abandon a harpsichord on a rutted trackway. A farmer, returning from market wih a wagon full of cheese, generously dumped his cargo and loaded it with refugees. Buffalo, it seemed possible, might become just one point on the line of smouldering ruins that some feared might eventually extend as far as New York.

Such a scenario, however, would be unlikely. Those who expected the trail of ruin had failed to remember that all previous invasions in this war had only pierced the skin of enemy territory and had never penetrated beyond. Stopping long enough to burn down both towns, and also to set fire to the 'Chippewa', 'Ariel'. 'Trippe' and 'Little Belt' that had been resting at anchor in Black Rock's harbour since their involvement in the Battle of Lake Erie, the British began a withdrawal. In Buffalo, only 3 buildings were left standing: one tiny cottage, the jail and the blacksmith's forge! Riall had lost just 112 men killed, wounded or missing in the entire time of his invasion. A Squadron of the 19th Light Dragoons and supporting infantry was then sent up river to garrison Fort Niagara and '*destroy the remaining cover of the enemy upon his frontier.'* Completely satisfied with this desecration of the American frontier, and believing that he had emasculated the enemy's ability to take revenge, Riall and his men retired to winter quarters, pleased that the year had ended on a more harmonious note.

CHAPTER 11

'Despise fawning smiles or snarling frown'

The 1812 War, painted so far as flat and two-dimensional, had its offshoots in the south along the coast from the Mississippi to Florida. Initially involving different enemies, the contrasts with the war on the Canadian border are more obvious than the similarities. The Spanish sat as hostile neighbours of the young republic's lands in Mississippi territory. Their animosity had been fed by America's invasion in 1810, and Madrid was now perceived as being in debt to the British for liberating the homeland from Napoleon's rule. An invasion of the United States could conceivably come from this direction—or from the waters of the Gulf itself.

Since the war's start, a small fleet of undermanned craft under the command of Captain John Shaw had been patrolling the Gulf of Mexico's waters, ostensibly to challenge pirates operating in the region, but more covertly to watch for the appearance of the British. Several of the war's republican generals began their military service here. Wade Hampton, the man who scored so little in the Lake Champlain campaign in the autumn of 1813, briefly served as army commander of the territory of Mississippi. Wilkinson had taken over in May 1812 and immediately flooded Washington with an impossible list of resources that he felt were needed to defend a coastline six hundred miles long—40 gunboats and 10,000 regulars would be the minimum force. A few days after his appointment, his sphere of command was enlarged to incorporate Louisiana and Tennessee—and his list of demands increased proportionately.

Within days of his arrival in July, just as war was declared, he was clashing with Shaw, who refused to accept orders from an officer of the army. Over-eloquently, the naval man informed the Secretary of the Navy of his reasons. ' . . . . *however eminently skilled a military officer may be in the profession of arms, if he be arrayed in the amphibious garb of a naval-military commander, he will, in acting under it, be much less likely to acquire laurels than to bring disgrace on himself and the services . . . In a word the military knows nothing of naval affairs.'*

Washington remained unclear who its enemy in the south really was—Spain or Britain. Governor William Claiborne of Louisiana, however, had no such doubts and was enthusiastic for a contest with the Spanish. '*Cuba is the real mouth of the Mississippi, and the nation possessing it can at any time command the trade of the westerns states. Give us Cuba and the American Union is placed beyond reach.'* To back his view that Spain ought to be dispossessed of the island and its mainland territories, he provisioned Forts Stoddert and Mins, both on the Mobile River, sending the supply vessels through the fringes of Spanish territory and ignoring the loud protests of Spanish officials.

All these outpourings of thought took place at a time when the repercussions of America's 1810 invasion of the Floridas were still being felt. Georgia troops under Colonel Thomas Smith retained a presence on Spanish soil between the St. Mary's River and St. Augustine. In March 1812 Georgian settlers seized Fernandina in Florida and declared it a free port open to the vessels of all nations. Days later, the Americans made their first attempt to seize St. Augustine. By late June 1812, arguing that he had been provoked, Smith aggressively laid siege to St. Augustine. Worse still perhaps, Members of Congress were discussing proposals to annex all of Spanish Florida. Faced by the imminence of war with Britain, the Senate and Administration sensibly stepped back from formal annexation. In a letter to Governor David Mitchell of Georgia, Monroe even seemed to recommend a complete withdrawal of all American troops from Florida's soils. Mitchell, however, clearly read between the lines and, sensing an ambivalence in policy, left the troops in place. '*I have carefully avoided making any proposition for withdrawing the troops, under the fullest conviction that such a step was not intended,'* he wrote in his reply to the Secretary.

By now there had been several other, seemingly uncoordinated incursions into Spanish territory. Although Smith had given up the siege of St. Augustine, Colonel Daniel Newman had taken a militia force in September 1812 from Georgia towards Picolata, promising to award his adherents with parcels of land in the area. But, instead of staking out farmland, they found only hunger and Indian bands, and were forced to eat their horses and the St. John's River's abundant alligators. Political events in Washington, London or Canadian York had now become irrelevant. The leaders of Louisiana and Georgia seemed hell-bent on an invasion of Florida, whether the Federal government consented or not.

For much of November 1812, the Washington administration, anxious not to enflame Spain any further, worked on a policy of appeasement. But so many irritating incursions into Florida had provoked Spain's New World officials beyond endurance, and, almost overnight, politicians cleared the path to annexation. On 25th November, the President ordered Thomas Pinckney, the new military commander of the 6th Military District, a region covering Georgia and the Carolinas, to concentrate troops at Point Peter in Georgia and take by force all of Madrid's possessions on mainland America.

Tennessee's Andrew Jackson makes his entry at this point. Circumstances, events and his own ambitions undoubtedly combined to make him the war's most famous general—and future president. He had served in Tennessee's militia for ten years, but had never experienced military action. As a verbal critic of Jefferson's and Madison's administrations, he never expected to secure high military office or to be given a command of regular forces.

On 21st October 1812 the state's governor, Willie Blount, received a request that he should assemble a force for the defence of New Orleans. Since the near quarrels in summer between Captain Shaw and Wilkinson, the town had seemed increasingly likely to become the target of an enemy attack. The hurricane season had now passed, but the storm that year had destroyed several gunboats and locally built brigs. The British frigate 'Southampton' was nearly always present outside the town's harbour, watching and reporting on America's flimsy efforts to construct a solid defence.

Blount commissioned Jackson to lead the expedition to New Orleans. More discerning than the governor and determined to give his mission a more offensive hue, he hoped that the real targets were Mobile and Pensacola. '*I am now at the head of 2070 volunteers*', he wrote,' . . . *and, if the government orders, will rejoice at the opportunity of placing the American eagle on the ramparts of Mobile, Pensacola and St. Augustine.'*

On 10th December, in particularly cold weather, the raw general assembled his force at Nashville. He had formed two regiments under the commands of William Hall and Thomas Hart Benton, and a powerful regiment of cavalry, nearly 700 strong, under Colonel John Coffee. On 7th January 1813 Governor Blount watched the infantry board flatboats and set off down the Cumberland River on the thousand mile journey to Natchez on the Mississippi. Coffee's cavalry, setting off at the same time, were to proceed by land. On 15th February the three components of Jackson's force reunited at Natchez and set about preparing for the next leg of their journey to New Orleans.

A message from General Wilkinson was awaiting Andrew Jackson's arrival. The letter instructed the Tennessee men to wait at Natchez and proceed no further, arguing that he had insufficient resources in the city to sustain a company of 2000 men. But Jackson's shrewd political mind quickly deciphered the real reason for Wilkinson's reluctance to allow the men of Tennessee to participate in the defence of New Orleans. He, Wilkinson, considered that Jackson was a rival, military and political, and was likely to disobey the orders of a man for whom Jackson had no respect. For three whole weeks the men remained in their makeshift camp. The letter which eventually arrived from John Armstrong in Washington was as galling as the orders from Wilkinson. '*The causes of embodying and marching to New Orleans, having ceased to exist, you will, on receipt of this letter, consider it* (the corps) *as dismissed from public service* . . . . It elaborated not at all on what the reasons might be.

Some, in Washington, knew what the reasons were.: Washington had once more had a change of heart over its attitude towards Spain's American colonies. By a close vote of 19 to 16 the Senate had just reversed the earlier resolution to invade East Florida and advocated instead that only marginal West Florida be annexed. Whatever the reasons, Jackson regarded the cancellation of his expedition as a personal insult, and his subsequent actions and remarks did nothing to reduce the rift between Jackson and the Administration. Letters passed in one direction only—from Jackson to the President. Few were factual and none complimentary about any of those who worked in Washington. He and his men had marched 800 miles, having left homes and family, and would now have to find their way back to Tennessee.

The return began in late March, the troops travelling at about 18 miles a day. On 18th May 1813 the dispirited band reached Nashville. Here, without any ceremony, Jackson dismissed his men. In recognition of their effort, the government allowed each man to keep the musket with which he had been provided—a scant reward for their sacrifices. Jackson, for his untiring efforts to keep his men supplied and safe, was nicknamed 'Old Hickory' by the men, and it is by this sobriquet that he has ever after been known.

The republic, or her agents in the south, was now about to become embroiled in conflict with the Creek Confederation, adding another edge to this multi-dimensional war. Occupying the north-east corner of modern day Alabama, this nation, numbering, at most, 18,000, had been living fairly contentedly under the flag of the United States and had settled down as farmers in a land that had few white settlers. War against Britain, the successful involvement of Indian warriors on the side of the British, and the influence of Tecumseh, however, had persuaded a small band of malcontents, perhaps 4000 in number and referred to as the Red Sticks, to abandon the plough and pick up their bows and muskets. Led by a half-breed who had adopted the name Peter McQueen, they were influenced by suggestions that England would support them in an insurrection against the United States. But it was to the Spanish in Pensacola that the Red Sticks first appealed for help. The governor, responding to a visiting deputation, provided powder, musket balls and more than just a verbal hint of support.

When the American settlers in Alabama heard of the visit to Pensacola, they became anxious to blunt McQueen's fighting edge. An ambush of the party on their return would involve only a minimal loss of white man's blood. 180 mounted men under Colonel James Caller advanced along the Tombigbee River from St. Stephens and scored an initial success by surprising the Creeks in their camp on 27th July 1813. McQueen, however, organised his men and got the better of the Alabama men later in the day in a skirmish which later historians chose to call the Battle of Burnt Corn (or Cork) Creek.

This symbolic Indian victory caused an epidemic of fear. The statesmen of Georgia, anticipating a Creek invasion, began to construct a string of forts along the frontier. Ten miles apart from one other, the forts were each manned by a couple of dozen men and supported by mounted troops. Georgia, for this reason, regarded herself as safe. The western frontier of the Creek territory, however, remained less well defined. Brigadier-General Ferdinand Claiborne, recognising the weakness, advocated striking hard at the Red Sticks before their numbers swelled in strength. Major-General Thomas Flournoy, commanding the Seventh Military District, however, refused any pre-emptive action and reminded the officer that Washington still demanded a purely defensive stance.

In pursuance of this policy of containment, America continued to build. By late summer 1813, Fort Mims, between the Alabama River and the Tombigbee, had become impressive. Here, within its stockade, over 500 settlers had taken refuge out of fear of an imminent attack. Claiborne gave Major Daniel Beasley responsibility for their welfare and the supervision of the defences. Totally unsuited for such a challenging role, he dissipated his strength by sending out detachments of troops to the neighbouring forts, but simultaneously assured Claiborne that Mims was virtually invincible.

The storm clouds of insurrection, however, were getting closer. On 29th August two negro slaves, flushed with terror, breathlessly reported that they had seen Indians in war paint. Beasley sent out a scouting party, but when this returned without having sighted any Indians, the major had the duo lashed for lying. Men were still hoping to find a silver lining within a greying storm cloud.

The following day found the community of Fort Mims totally unprepared. The wooden stockade was more a psychological reassurance than a physical shield. The gate remained open, men dozed in the sunshine, women washed clothes or cooked and children played in the open gateway. Not a single guard patrolled the walkway or watched the distant bushes. Dinner was about to be served.

The prepared food would later be consumed by those for whom it had never been intended. Led by William Weatherford (or Weathersford), a half-breed with a Scottish father, 100 or so Creeks suddenly rushed through the open gateway and fell upon the queue of diners. Cooking pots were turned over and the slaughtering commenced: men, women and children, many still with spoons in their hands. Major Beasley ran to try to close the gate, but he was clubbed to death during his pathetic attempt to push away the sand that had accumulated in the doorway. Two companies of soldiers, the only fighting regulars present, attempted to resist. Commanded by Captain Dixon Bailey, a half-breed like Weathersford, they hurried the surviving women and children into a building near the northern perimeter fence, and maintained a musket fire for more than three hours. Women fought alongside the men or reloaded guns and held back the advance of several hundred screaming warriors. Few showed any outward signs of fear. Bailey was everywhere, often stooping to calm sobbing children and wipe away their tears.

But the Indians were now discharging arrows tipped with fire. By late afternoon, the guns fell silent and the war cries ceased. 400 or more of Mim's community lay disembowled, scalped or roasted alive, their blooded bodies periodically concealed by the drifting smoke. Exaggerated accounts of what happened in the final moments were broadcast. The tales of atrocities grew more terrifying through repetition. The British, it was said, had offered the creeks $5 for every American scalp they took. Weathersford apparently tried to stop the massacre, but he was powerless to harness the monster that he had unleashed. The flames had died down by morning. The rays of the rising sun cruelly illuminated the hideous dismembered shapes of men, women and children, rigid in hideous postures which no-one would ever want to witness.

Weathersford unleashed a second monster that day: an insatiable mood in America for vengeance that tore at the souls of everyone capable of human emotion. Fear had no part; anger was all consuming like a disease that turned men's hearts to iron. It sent them in their hundreds to join the ranks of the militia. In every settlement in Georgia and Alabama, they drilled in groups and waited only to be told when and where to assemble.

The skills of organization needed, however, were sadly lacking. Georgia, Alabama and the Carolinas had few real leaders capable of forging the weapons of anger into a weapon of glistening steel.

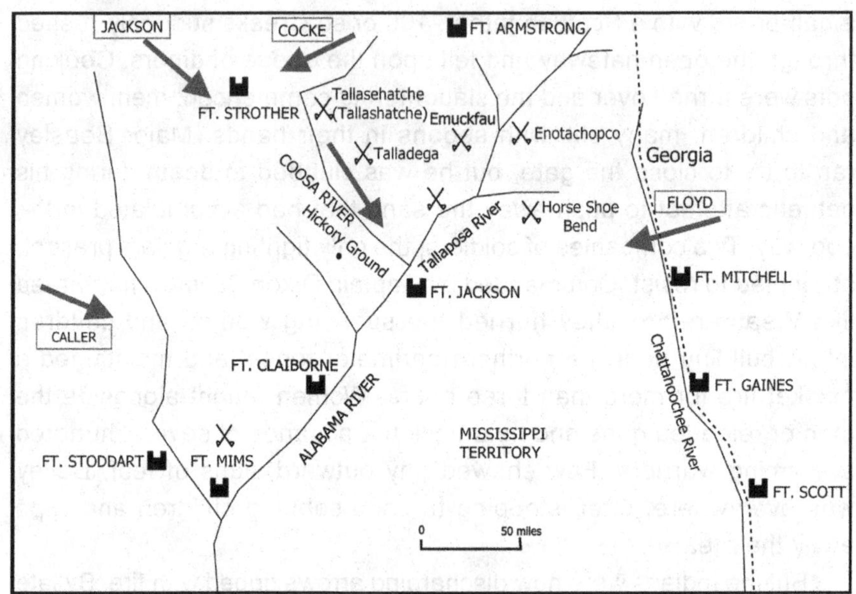

The Creek War

But, beyond the Tennessee River, Andrew Jackson, although recently wounded in a street brawl and with a bullet still lodged close to his heart, had left his bed and put on his sword. The troops which he would command were quickly assembled by Governor Blount within days of the broadcast of the massacre. Jackson joined them at Fayetteville on 7th October, and promptly set out at the head of 2000 men, destined to become his nation's hero in dealing with the Creeks. His close friend, John Coffee, with 1300 mounted men, had already crossed the border and was waiting for him near Huntsville. A contingent of East Tennessee men under John Cooke had mustered in Knoxville, but, from the start, showed itself determined to act independently. This was to be the start of the campaign, which would turn Jackson into a legend and propel him on his way to the eventual presidency of the nation. Establishing a base of operations at Fort Deposit, he cut a road south to the junction of the Coosa river and Canoe Creek. Here he began to construct Fort Strother, the base from which he could launch his campaign.

The logistics involved in supplying this force were tremendous. To feed his horses, Jackson estimated that he would need at least 1000 bushels of fodder weekly. His whiskey drinking men would require a gallon each per week to keep them in the manner to which they had been accustomed. Twenty tons of meat weekly would also be needed—and this during a time when the waters of the Tennessee River were too low for the transportation of supplies. Men such as Jackson, however, are not deterred by surmountable obstacles such as a shortage of food, and he soon found ways of solving the problem. Foraging parties burned down two Indian villages and confiscated the supplies of corn stored there. And the road that he built south from Fayetteville would surely serve as a fast supply route for provisions shipped out from Nashville.

'Old Hickory' saw his chance of meeting another objective, too. This new road would, not only enable him to thrust into Creek territory, but, if extended, would also provide a route to Pensacola and the heart of Spanish Florida. For this dual campaign, he intended to rely upon no-one but his Tennessee troops. Ten miles east of Fort Strother lay Tallashatche, a settlement at which the Creeks were known to be assembling. Time, planning and opportunity all seem to have favoured this determined man from Tennessee.

The tactics employed at his first engagement with the Red Stick Creeks were flawless. At dawn on 3rd November 1813 he approached Tallashatche, forming a line of men with the flanks stretched far beyond the village. At a given signal, the two wings moved forward to encircle the settlement and trap the quarry. 186 Creek warriors were killed in the fight at a cost of just 5 American dead and 41 wounded. Further advances towards the Tallaposa River, near where the Creeks were concentrating, would leave Fort Strother vulnerable to attack during his absence, and, for a moment, he hesitated. Hearing that Major-General John Cocke's East Tennessee troops were near, he sent a request to Cocke to hurry his step and assume responsibility for the fort's defence. This would enable Jackson to move to Talladega, a village occupied by loyal Creeks. Informed that the inhabitants were being threatened by hostile warriors, Jackson felt obliged to deliver the friendly tribesmen from evil. Cocke, unfortunately, was an independent-minded soul searching for laurels of his own. As a man of Eastern Tennessee, he also felt ill-disposed to co-operate with the men from the west. He consequently ignored the request, and Fort Strother was left in the hands of the sick and the lame. Jackson, in sortying out to deal with the belligerents threatening Talladega, was taking a calculated risk.

The strategy that he employed on the 9th was similar to that used on the 3rd at Tallashatche. But this time the men of the Tennessee militia were not quite so spirited. Some fled when the Creeks fought back, and the widely cast net of entrapment was holed. Over 700 of the Creeks escaped and only 290 were slaughtered, a disappointing tally for a man whose tactics so far had been almost perfect. The cost to America was 17 killed and 83 wounded out of a force of 1000 or so engaged.

'Old Hickory' Jackson was relieved to find that the undefended fort had not been molested during his two day absence. Cocke, clearly intending to remain unsupportive, was busily constructing his own fort, Fort Armstrong, one hundred miles to the north-east, and had created his own agenda for dealing with the Creeks. Jackson, in negotiation with the defeated party after Talladega, had treated only with the Hillabee, part of the Creek alliance, and accepted their request for peace. Cocke, however, was unaware of this agreement and, on 17th November, burned one of their settlements to the ground and slew 60 of their men folk. Of course, the Hillabees construed this as evidence of the treacherous nature of the white man. But the error forced Cocke to be contrite. On 12th December he finally rode with his men to Fort Strother and from then on he rode in tandem with Jackson.

The union of eastern and western Tennessee in a common purpose hardly compensated for the homeward flow of men that General Jackson now began to experience. The men in his command had been enlisted a year previously for the aborted expedition to New Orleans. They now felt a yearning for a return to the relative comforts of Tennessee domestic life. In vain Jackson argued that they had spent most of the year of enlistment at home. Determined to be gone, they packed their bags and set out northward.

Single-handedly the general stopped the outflow. Somewhere along the route, the travellers found Jackson barring their path. Mounted on a horse with his musket levelled across the horse's neck, he threatened the first man who moved. This produced a stand-off exciting enough to be featured in a Hollywood movie. An earnest man on a horse facing down a sullen, silent and potentially mutinous mob. The thoughts flitting through the minds of those men can be guessed at; a sudden rush would have felled the lone man, and the Jackson legend would never have enriched the folklore of the United States. Their chance was soon gone. John Coffee and several loyal troopers appeared. Standing at Jackson's side, they placed their muskets in the same threatening manner. That night the discontented men ate their suppers within the confines of Fort Strother, the place they had been so anxious to leave.

They tried again a few days later. Jackson faced them as before, this time with two cannon laden with grapeshot and with regular soldiers at his side. On 10th December their year of enlistment officially ended, and legally 'Old Hickory' could not hold them any longer by the reins. They left en masse, nearly 2000 of them, and the army which he had led south from Tennessee had virtually ceased to exist. Sadly for him, the fighting force of the Red Stick Creeks remained virtually intact.

Governor Blount was remonstrating too. Realising that Jackson's fighting edge had been eroded by the defections, he wrote to the general and suggested temporary withdrawal. Jackson countered with a withering blast: '*Arouse from yr. Lethargy—despise fawning smiles or snarling frowns . . . . the campaign must rapidly progress . . . . Save Mobile . . . save the Territory-save your frontier from becoming drenched in blood . . . . What, retrograde under these circumstances? I will perish first.*' He concluded with a refusal to withdraw and he remained, with his skeleton force, at Fort Strother.

He was not, however, the only military presence in the area of the war-waging Creeks. Brigadier-General John Floyd, heading a contingent of 950 Georgians and supporting Indians, crossed the Chattahoochee River and attacked the Creek village of Auttose on 29th November. Congratulating himself on killing 200 Indians for the loss of only 11 of his own men, he put down temporary roots at Fort Mitchell. Simultaneously Claiborne advanced into Creek territory from the south with the 3rd U.S. infantry regiment and searched for Weathersford. He set upon the inhabitants of Econochaca, the half-breed's home village, and, in a dramatic pursuit after the fight, almost succeeded in capturing the warrior chief. Surrounded by U.S. infantry, Weathersford rode his horse over a bluff and plunged into the water below and made his escape. Amongst the items that Claiborne's soldiers found in the ruins of the village was a note from the Spanish governor congratulating Weathersford (or Red Eagle) for the massacre at Fort Mims. Claiborne, finding himself with only 60 men, after his short-term enlistments went home, men, retired south to Fort St. Stephen.

The year ended in disappointment for the people of the southern United States. More than 7000 soldiers and militiamen had entered Creek territory since the summer, participating in a series of uncoordinated and piecemeal attacks on the Creeks. 800 or more warriors had been killed—about one-fifth of the Red Sticks' fighting power—but the heart of the resistance had not been pierced. Only Jackson and the residue of his army, about 150 men, now remained within Creek territory. And, it was here, within the stockade of Fort Strother, that he began to plan his next campaign, choosing to rely upon no-one but himself to impose a settlement on the renegades.

On 14th January 1814, 900 Tennessee recruits, enlisted for 60 days service, arrived at Fort Strother, giving him the instant means to effect his scheme. He immediately set out in the direction of the Tallapoosa River. With him and the new recruits was faithful John Coffee, a few volunteer horsemen and 200 Indians, Cherokee and Creeks, the latter just as anxious as Jackson to deal with the renegades of their tribe.

The hostile Creeks attacked first. Just after daylight on the 22nd, they struck Jackson's column near Emucfau, but were defeated by superior tactics and a well-timed bayonet charge. But, with 75 wounded and with too few supplies, Jackson felt obliged to return to Fort Strother and wait for the additional men that Nashville's politicians had been promising. The enemy hit his rear on the 24th, as his men were in the act of crossing the Enotachopco Creek. While artillery men struggled to extract the guns from the stream, the Tennessee general called back his advanced guard, which had already crossed, and confronted the assaulting force on the south bank.

His tactical mind immediately saw the possibilities of an encirclement of the foe, and he ordered the two flanks to spread out. At the crucial moment, however, his raw men in the centre, with their backs to the stream, broke and fled. His strategy seemed in danger of becoming unstitched. However, John Caroll, one of his officers, stood in the stream and, with just 25 men, stabilised the line. Gradually order was restored, and the Creeks, suffering most, pulled back. In the two skirmishes at Emuckfau and Enotachapco, the green men of Tennessee lost 20 killed and 75 wounded while the Creeks are estimated to have lost nearly 200. Jackson's men, however, had served their term and again the general felt the need to withdraw to the sanctuary of Fort Strother.

Meanwhile Floyd was advancing from the east in yet another of the Creek war's uncoordinated attacks. Advancing from a forward base at Fort Mitchell on the Chattahoochee River with 1200 volunteers and

400 Indians, he met the Creeks on the banks of the Calebec on 26th January. Employing weight rather than the tactics of encirclement, he charged the warriors frontally and forced them to retire, losing almost as many men as the Creeks in the process.

He, too, retired after the battle, hamstrung by the same short-term enlistments that prevented Jackson from remaining in the field. Georgia undertook no further involvement in the war against the Creeks. Floyd was an effective strategist and skilled in the arts of soldier management. But he, like the legislators and military administrators in the state of Georgia, failed to appreciate that campaigns must be pre-planned, armies supplied and potential weaknesses foreseen. Jackson, of course, was aware of such realities and so commenced another bout of road building, supply collecting and harassing of state officials. And the result? The arrival on 6th February at Fort Strowther of 600 regulars of the 39th U.S. Infantry, recruited entirely in Tennessee, and 3000 fresh and untested volunteers.

These turned out to be veined with the same strands of discontent and dissatisfaction. For apparently inciting the men, he blamed General Cocke and sent him back to Tennessee to face court-martial. Having dealt with a near mutiny, Jackson turned to the more persistent problem of insubordination and made an example of a young man, John Wood, who had refused to obey an order. Court-martialled, the eighteen year old was taken out and shot. He was the first militiaman since the Revolutionary War to be executed. Discipline in Jackson's army was, hereafter, never to be a problem.

Materially and spiritually strengthened, Jackson now felt that he could finally settle the issue with the Red Stick insurgents. He was soon informed that the residue, about 900 warriors, and their families had built a defensive position within a pronounced meander of the Tallapoosa River. Probably with Spanish assistance, the Creeks had constructed earthworks across the open end of this bend, the Tohopeka or Horseshoe bend, and enclosed an area of about 300 acres. Jackson immediately saw that this position was more a self-made pen of slaughter than a place of strength. Here was a golden opportunity of destroying the entire community while it was imprisoned within the river's bend.

He first checked that he had the resources necessary for an atttack. Using the navigable Coosa river as an artery for the transport of supplies from Fort Strother, he built a military trackway through the woods and a small fort at the midway point. Confident that his supply route was firm, he secured the assistance of the local Cherokees and prepared his attack.

On the morning of 27th March, the Cherokees crossed the river above the bend and positioned themselves in the rear of the Red Stick camp. When this appeared to have been satisfactorily effected, he positioned his infantry within less than 100 yards of the log earthworks and placed two guns on a hill dominating the bend and the Creek's camp. While this movement was in progress and the Creeks were being distracted by the sudden sight of the artillery, several Cherokees swam across the bend and stole the canoes that lay unattended on the beach. 200 of Coffee's men then used them to cross the meander and positioned themselves for an attack. At 10 a.m. Jackson's 6 pounders opened fire on the log works, and for two hours or so, Jackson was content to bombard the Creeks at fairly long range from both front and rear. The Creeks fought manfully and desperately, but the death toll began to mount.

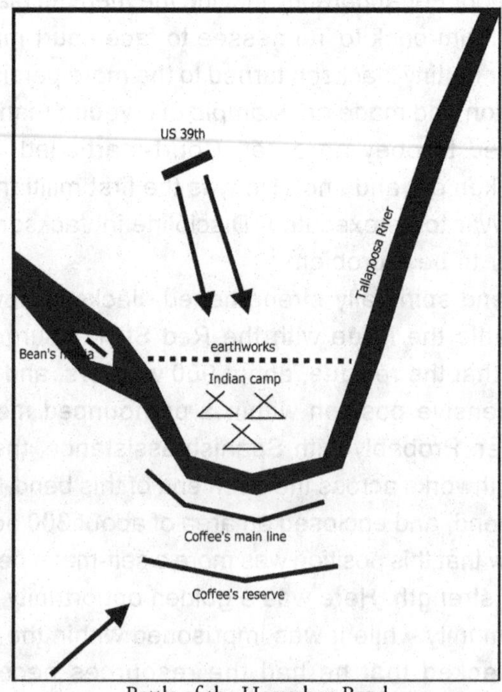

Battle of the Horseshoe Bend

At noon, or soon after, Jackson ordered the U.S. 39th to charge the earthworks and sent in a brigade of East Tennessee militia in support. The outcome, of course, was well beyond any doubt. Major L. Montgomery, commanding the 39th, was apparently the first to reach the works. At his moment of glory, he fell dead. Others behind him fared better, and soon the log works, constructed by the warriors to keep intruders out, swarmed with American troops. Snatching the command at this moment of obvious victory was a young ensign, the Virginian Sam Houston, later to collect much fame in the Texan War of Independence.

1st Regiment of Volunteer Mounted Gunmen (Col. Robert Dyer)
2nd Regiment of Volunteer Mounted Gunmen (Col. John Coffee)

Col. John Coffee's Brigade at the battle of Horsehoe Bend

Slaughter followed. The unhappy defenders, fleeing for their lives, were cut down in their hundreds. Some tried to swim the river, but sharpshooters on the opposite bank found easy targets. By sunset, 550 bodies were counted on the peninsula alone, and perhaps 200 more floated in the river. America lost 32 killed and 99 wounded. The Cherokees, allied to the whites, lost 18 dead and twice that number bled.

'Red Eagle' Weathersford, left without a following, later walked into Jackson's camp on the Hickory Ground and surrendered, asking for nothing but help and sympathy for the starving women and children of his band. Moved by Weathersford's humanity and manly courage, Jackson permitted him to go free. William Weathersford eventually settled down as a planter in Alabama and lived as a contented subject of the United States.

The victorious nation, despite Jackson's commendable compassion, was determined to secure its pound of flesh. For several months, a mere 3500 renegade creeks had defied and held down no less than 15,000 American regulars and militia—and at a financial cost which is beyond calculation. The cry for retribution was consequently pronounced, and the settlement imposed was favourable only to the whites. On 9th August 1814, in the Treaty of Fort Jackson, the United

States, represented by 'Old Hickory' from Tennessee, took possession of 20 million acres of Creek tribal land. Several thousand Creeks had either fought on the side of the United States or had remained largely neutral. They might have expected some recognition of their loyalty. But, with no rebellious Creeks left to fear, the Americans terms were imposed without distinction on friend and foe alike. 'Manifest Destiny' had already taken hold of America's psyche.

CHAPTER 12

'He seems to be destitute of military fire and vigour of decision'

Thoughtful heads in London and Washington, reflecting on the course of the war so far, would, if they were completely honest, accept that no progress had been made at all. Men had died needlessly, reputations had been both made and tarnished, and fencing and farming destroyed. Up to this moment, the doves still had audiences on both sides of the Atlantic, speaking in tones that touched on reason, logic and common sense. By mid-1813, however, the freshening gale of belligerence that swept through both nations, even when Britain still faced the challenge of Napoleon in Europe, had rendered these sweet voices almost inaudible. The hawks held sway.

Now, in early 1814, the gale had begun to subside and the pacifists in England insisted on being heard. Britain and America were blood brothers from the same stock and shared a common enemy. '*Great Britain . . . . is exerting her utmost strength against the common enemy of independent nations, we have to contend against a country whose real interests . . . . must be the same as ours,*' a report from the House of Commons claimed. Only stubborn pride and a wish to avoid the level of humiliation that had occurred in 1783 impeded the advance of those who advocated inviting America to the negotiating table.

London's administrators, by now, had very little faith in those responsible for the execution of the war in America. The Duke of Wellington had little respect for General Prevost's capabilities, but generously recognised that a lack of manpower was partly to blame.

Admirals Warren and Cockburn, for all their posturings in favour of more thrusts at the American coastline, had been largely discredited. In November 1813, Warren was ordered home. '*I am extremely surprised in being recalled at this moment, after having undertaken the command (and) . . . having zealously and faithfully served my sovereign and country under so many disadvantages.*' He announced in a tempestuous letter to someone he supposed was a supporter.

Prevost survived the reorganisations in the High Command, but many of those on whom he relied to effect his orders were recalled. Major-General de Rottenburg, a man on whom no credit for success can be placed, had already sailed home. Drummond, a far more energetic and resourceful man, had found himself restrained by Prevost, who was a cautious man by nature. '*In the present state of the war I would have you refrain from unnecessary hostility calculated to weaken our force and widen the breach existing between the two countries and unproductive of real advantage.*' Procter also survived, perhaps because he remained cautious and unassertive like his master Prevost and the war ministers in London. Riall, the man who had succeeded Vincent at Burlington, had fortunately shown promise in his recent successes at Buffalo and Black Rock.

Commodore Yeo remained solidly in place, despite his inability to prevent American lake-born successes. Prevost, not necessarily one for finding faults in others, was mildly critical of the naval officer's shortcomings. '*My only complaint*', he wrote, overlooking his own limitations, '*is that you do not view as I would wish you to do the consequences of leaving in critical positions our troops exposed to the joint operations of the American fleet and army.*'

America was seldom disposed to talk of peace, except in the states comprising New England, where the sense of waging war had always been questioned. Connecticut had provided 6000 men in arms, but had stipulated that they were only to be used in defence of the state. Independent-minded Massachusetts, the cradle of the revolution, had ironically so far provided no men for federal service and preferred, through its Committee for the Defense of the Sea Coast, to manage its own defences. Rhode Island and New Hampshire, more distant from the theatres of war, but with a coast as vulnerable as anywhere else, remained aloof and offered the Federal government virtually nothing, apart from the right to station small garrisons in its ports. Vermont, of course, was more affected. Adjoining New York, the state militia felt obliged to assist their neighbours in the protection of the Champlain lowlands. And, even in those states that contributed in strength to the forces of the United States of America, there were always men who tried to avoid the call-up to the militia. Some claimed to be physically disabled and even employed physicians to press their case.

Both sides used propaganda to discredit the other. America, in particular, condemned Britain for employing Indians, mistreating prisoners, violating flags of truce and continuing to impress American sailors to serve in Royal Navy ships. But both nations were equally guilty of these charges: the United States used Indians on the Canadian border more than once to flush out British loyalists from their homesteads. On 3rd March 1813 Congress, trying to be pious, passed a measure to exclude any British-born mariners from being forced to serve on American ships.

Individuals were vilified and portrayed by the newspapers as semi-human. The attacks on Cockburn and Warren have already been mentioned. It was even rumoured that a bounty had been placed on their heads. The entire British nation was characterised as '*degenerate, ferocious disgraces to civilisation'*. That same source asserted that the British used Irishmen's fingers as spoons. Such allegations, true or false, played well on a receptive public opinion and were used to support suggestions that America had the right to resort to less ethical behaviour and methods of conducting war.

Yet, in spite of a hardening of attitudes in America, hopes for peace were never completely extinguished. Late in 1812 it was rumoured that the Czar of Russia had expressed a willingness to mediate between the two belligerents. Madison, probably with a genuine desire to resolve differences with Britain, sent Albert Gallatin, Secretary of the Treasury, and James Bayard to St. Petersburg to start the process. The conditions for peace which the two men were asked to convey to Britain were extremely generous and must surely be accepted by any nation anxious to secure peace. Only three main demands were made by Washington—the ending of all British impressment, a promise not to interfere with the movement of goods between American ports, and the removal of all British warships from the Great Lakes. Beyond these three conditions, there was flexibility in the American terms. The two envoys reached St. Petersburg on 21st July 1813 and, it was assumed that talks would soon begin. Campaigning on the Great Lakes in the summer and autumn of 1813 was undertaken against a small hope that the negotiations would succeed.

But on 1st November 1813 reports reached America that the British had turned down the Czar's mediating services. Galled by this, Washington turned to closing the trading loopholes that had allowed American exporters to make vast profits by supplying grain to Wellington's army in Spain. Britain's blockading ships had continued to allow vessels laden with grain to pass freely through the wooden cordon. The legislation passed in the summer of 1813 threatened confiscation of boats and heavy fines for any American merchants caught in the act, but, of course, such laws could not touch the dozens of neutral vessels involved. Amongst these were several British vessels, flying the flags of non-belligerents—and the flow of grain was never staunched. In a mood of desperation, Madison extracted an embargo measure from Congress in December 1813, which prohibited food and a number of other goods from even being loaded into ships. But the illicit cross border movement of cattle from the United State to Prescott, Montréal and Kingston was still not stemmed. British stomachs continued to feed on American beef, and Drummond's troops, according to his Commissary-General, were supplied by the Yankees*' with all the necessities of life in great abundance.'* New Englanders, of course, were mainly involved. Their commercial lifeblood depended upon trade with the enemy, and every possible way of circumventing the embargo was explored. And all of this occurred at a time when John Armstrong was putting forward proposals for national conscription.

Drummond, the 42 year old administrator and commander of His Majesty's forces in Upper Canada, expected America's avenging move across the frontier to begin as soon as the ice thawed. To contest their crossing, he strengthened the garrisons of Fort George, Erie and Niagara, and placed men in a newly constructed stone fort on Missisauga Point. And, in a speech to the Legislature on 15th February 1814, he called for an improvement to road surfaces in the province, a compulsory enlistment for one year for at least one-third of the men in each regiment of militia, and for the continuation of a ban on the distillation of grain in order to ensure adequate supplies of cereal and fodder. The tight-curled man, resplendent in full uniform in a dark chamber, impressed the legislators, and some believed that he might be Brock reincarnated. Others had their doubts: '*He seems to be destitute of that military fire and vigour of decision which the principal commander of this country must possess in order to preserve it*', the Reverend John Strachan pronounced. Drummond demanded more—the right to declare martial law, the removal of habeas corpus in certain situations and the power to confiscate the property of convicted traitors. Men questioned the wisdom of conferring so much military and political power in one man and denied him all his requests. But the times required an iron man, and Drummond became armed with sufficient powers to provide him with that ferrous strength.

He would also need to become a man of other talents—financier, economist and magician. A lack of coinage made small transactions almost impossible, and the absence of army bills in denominations of less than twenty-five pounds complicated the settlement of even the simplest payments. A man owed £15 by the Government received nothing; a creditor owed £30 would receive just £25 and an I.O.U. for the balance. The pot of financial torment was stirred even more by Canadian creditors' doubts about the validity of the paper money that they were asked to accept. Most consequently demanded payment in gold, a commodity that was in short supply. Debts incurred by the army since the war's start frequently remained unpaid—and the Canadian merchants were now refusing to supply the army with the essential items of clothing and food. But traders across the international border seemed to have been paid promptly, financed from loans acquired from the wealthy merchants of York

General Drummond hoped that he might at last have found the means of securing victory or, at least, a way of nullifying the psychological effects of the American success at Moraviantown. Recovery of Detroit was practical, sound and achievable. The garrison in the town was remote, linked by a fragile supply line to Ohio. No more than 400 Americans held the fort, with perhaps another 200 responsible for the defence of Sandwich and Fort Malden, the strongpoints over which Drummond felt the Union flag ought to be flying again. Illness and discontent over a lack of pay, however, dictated the speed at which Drummond could implement his plans. Colonel Robert Young, commanding at Fort Niagara, had recently reported that several members of the 8th Foot, the regiment garrisoning the fort, had deserted, and dysentery made others unfit for sentry duty.

The campaign year began with two damp fuses that failed to light. General Wilkinson's last act as commander was a sudden and unexpected movement along the Richelieu River on 30th March 1814. It came at a time of passivity when the forces of both sides were struggling to keep warm. On the 17th he personally led forward 4000 troops from Plattsburgh to Chazy. From there he ordered Colonel Alexander Macomb and a brigade of infantry to scout the area around Missiquoi Bay. Days later the whole force crossed the Canadian frontier and occupied Odeltown, where he expected to be confronted by the troops of the Crown. Surprisingly, he found the place unprotected. In a mood of increasing confidence, Wilkinson pushed on down the Richelieu River, hoping that his path would continue to remain free of the tangles of opposition. But in the sturdy mill beside the Lacolle (or La Cole) Creek, scene of the earlier muddled fighting, he found 200 regulars of the 13th Foot and militia under the command of Major Richard Handcock waiting for his approach.

Dislodging a force from a building constructed of stone, however, would be far less easy than ejecting a force of several times that size from a strongpoint made of wood. Wilkinson's two 12 pounder guns opened fire and so began a mini—siege, first closing Handcock's line of retreat, and then commencing a two hour bombardment with a battery of light guns that proved to be quite useless against such well-built walls. An 18 pounder gun, brought up in support, sunk up to its axles in mud and had to be abandoned. Handcock hit back, sending a company of his regular regiment to attack the gunners and firing a quantity of Congreve rockets. America's riflemen crept closer to the blockhouse, but, in so doing, almost exposed their positions to the defending marksmen. The battle between invisible rivals took on new dimensions when a company of Voltigeurs, hearing the firing, hurried up from Ile aux Noix to assist the blockhouse garrison. Wading through the ice cold waters of a nearby creek, they took up positions behind the Americans and turned their muskets on the enemy's artillerymen. Driven off, they joined their colleagues in the mill and brought the number of defenders to nearly 500. Two gunboats under the command of Commander David Pring also moved up from Britain's Ile aux Noix position and hurled shells into the American lines. Wilkinson's half-hearted attack on an insignificant building was taking on the dimensions of a small battle. The setting sun's weak beams fell upon a building still virtually intact. Both sides were critically short of ammunition, and Wilkinson could probably have taken the place by storm. His nerve, however, failed before the last of his ammunition had been spent and he began to retreat instead. 500 men had held off eight times that number.

In retreating, he stepped firmly onto a path of military disgrace. His campaigns on the border, seldom illuminated with success, had ended in the darkness of yet another failure. Even before news of the fiasco at Lacolle Creek reached Armstrong, the Secretary had written a letter relieving the general of command of Military District Number Nine. In the letter, Armstrong accused the officer of neglect of duty, poor judgement and military ineffectiveness, sufficient 'crimes', it seems, for a court-martial. This met a year later, but acquitted him with honour. Wilkinson later published his memoirs and, in so doing, aroused controversy in some of the claims he made. But, as far as the story of this war goes, he had now marched out of any further involvement or blame.

Britain's late winter effort was no more spectacular. Drummond, with his hands still full of administrative complexities, was in danger of underestimating exactly how difficult reduction of Detroit might actually be. Yet the precision of his planning at such a time does credit to this man of many parts. As finalised in February 1814, the plans involved the employment of all his regular battalions: the 1st, 41st, 89th and 100th Foot with supporting militia and Indians, and their convergence on Sandwich from three directions. One column would move from Talbot, another would pass through Woodstock, while the Indians, advancing in their characteristic manner, would creep forward from Pointe aux Pins. Even more precise planning covered the movement of the supply train. Carried in 300 sleighs, the stores would be dragged along the course of the frozen Thames and the road on its southern bank. When the Detroit River was reached, the train would divide; one section would cross the solid ice from Sandwich and the other would cross at Bar point to the south. As icing to his delicious plan, Drummond proposed that a party of seamen should cross Lake Erie by foot from Put-in-Bay and torch any American warship they found. Only Prevost's support for this ambitious aggression had now to be obtained, something that might be harder to achieve than the capture of the fort itself.

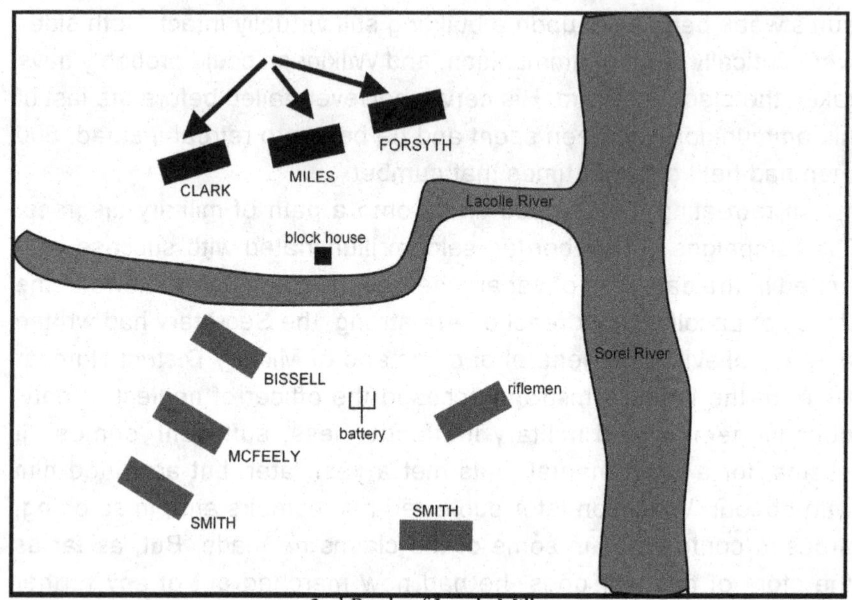

2nd Battle of Lacole Mill

But it was a bout of unseasonal warmth that thawed the ice, not Prevost's lukewarm support, that scuppered the launch of the expedition. By 3rd February 1814, while he was awaiting Prevost's reply, the first cracks were appearing in the ice, and the project was erased. Upper Canada, for the rest of the war, would hardly feature as a theatre of military activity.

One engagement, however, might just merit the description of a battle. American raiding parties had remained active throughout the winter, many led by charismatic men fighting a microcosmic war without the instructions of senior commanders. In a wish to terminate such unlicensed acts, Drummond ordered Riall to send some companies of the 1st and 89th and supporting militia to take up positions in the region of Oxford and Delaware and, as he put it, '*circumscribe the bounds of the enemy*'. General Drummond, wishing personally to view the area's defensive possibilities, came out from Burlington Heights to define in detail the points at which British advance posts should be placed. Oxford, Charlotteville, Delaware and Port Dover, all serviceable from a supply base at Long Point, were eventually chosen. De Rottenburg's earlier decision to abandon Upper Canada had been reversed by his successor.

On 5th March 240 men of the 1st and 89th Foot encountered an American foraging party entrenched behind breastworks at Longwood. Captain Andrew Holmes, commander of the American force, had sparred with Canadian ranger forces and tasted the ferociousness of their unsophisticated bite. Taking no further chances, he had secured a strong position behind which to rest. A deep ravine lay along one side and this was extended by lines of abatis which his men had taken care to build.

The brief Battle of Longwood was an insignificant American victory. With so few men on either side and with no obvious consequences, the skirmish is just another event in a sequence of trivial border incidents. Captain James Basden, the British commander, had launched a three pronged attack on the makeshift fort, sending his militia on a flanking movement on the right, his Indians towards the left and the regulars through the ravine against the centre. Straight volleys at point-blank range shattered all his hopes—for not a man managed to get within ten paces of the American logworks. Fourteen British were killed and 52 wounded, including the commander. The Americans lost 7 dead and wounded.

More world orientated Canadians and Americans found things of far greater interest in their newspapers in March 1814 than accounts of brushwood skirmishes in a landscape of little importance. For this was the month when the armies of the nations opposed to Napoleon entered Paris. This distant event, several thousand miles to the east, was likely to have enormous repercussions in America. The ending of the French and British blockades and the likely termination of any British impressments of sailors removed some of the grounds on which the United States had gone to war. The assumed defeat of France, however, would release many redcoat regiments for service in America—and Wellington, it was conjectured, might even be sent over to lead them! Ships, supplies and equipment would be plentiful also—and Britain, whose troops in America had been too poorly equipped to undertake major offences, would now be able to fight with a far sharper sword. Finding a commander of the same calibre as Wellesley to lead the Americans to victory before the first of these regiments arrived was consequently a priority. Harrison, despite his victory at the Thames, had resigned. Jackson, promising material but unpopular with the politicians in Washington, was still involved in dealing with the Creeks. Secretary Armstrong's finger therefore pointed at the Quaker, General Jacob Brown. Despite his limited military experience, he had impressed his superior in his defence of Sackets Harbor. More recently, he had more than fulfilled his obligations in the Montréal campaign. He was regarded with affection by his fellow officers and held in respect by the soldiers.

Whatever was expected of him, he now had the resources to move mountains. His army consisted of two solid brigades of regulars under the commands of Brigadier-Generals Winfield Scott and Eleazer Ripley, stationed at Buffalo and Black Rock respectively. An additional 600 soldiers of the militia commanded by Brigadier-General Peter Porter and a handful of Seneca Indians brought his army up to a strength of 3500 men.

Everything consequently pointed to 1814 being the year of decision in America—and the Niagara would probably be the ground on which the decision was made. The British under Phineas Riall were well ensconced in Forts George, Erie and Niagara, about 2700 men in total, with another 600 or so stationed at Chippawa and Queenston. The newly arrived Riall, an Irishman of no proven ability, is said to have purchased his rank, having won the favour of the Prince Regent. Another 1700 men were distributed between Long Point, York and Burlington, giving the two sides rough comparability in numbers. But, whereas it would be in Britain's interests to stall any offensive until those new regiments arrived, it served America to stamp noisily and aggressively as soon as she could.

As in 1813, so now, with new men commanding in the field, confusing orders still came from the top. On 21st February 1814 Armstrong ordered Brown to invest Fort Niagara, only to contradict the instruction later that day and order an attack on Kingston instead. Brown chose to interpret the order in his own way. On 24th March he set out with his two brigades for Fort Niagara, planning to haul Forts Erie and George into his net on the way. Armstrong, observing what appeared to be a streak of stubborn independence in his officer, was hardly forceful or clear in a subsequent letter to Brown and seemed to concede his right to make his own decisions. '*You have mistaken my meaning . . . If you hazard anything by this mistake, correct it promptly by returning to your post. If on the other hand you left the Harbor* (Sackets) *with a competent force for its defence, go on and prosper . . .'* Nerves, lack of supplies and perhaps further cloudy instructions from the Secretary, however, induced Brown to pull back to Buffalo and await events.

Jacob Brown, despite this early hesitation, was a considerable improvement on all those who had preceded him: Van Rennselaer, Dearborn and McClure. Together, Brown, the military adventurer, and Winfield Scott, the military technician, would begin to forge a sharper offensive weapon—an army of discipline and fighting precision, honed to sharpness by drilling for 10 hours each day and regular bayonet practice. Scott emphasized the importance of hygiene, personal and communal, and insisted on respect for officers. Americans, in so doing, were encompassing one of the qualities that they had most hated in the British military establishment—draconian and unsympathetic discipline and a slavish over respect for superior ranks. An 'esprit de corps' consequently began to develop, and even the militia began to think of themselves as professionals with a definite sense of mission.

Drummond, of course, was in charge of an army whose officers had imbibed these skills and qualities in their mothers' milk. The general was still marking time, developing strategies that would enable him to hold the frontier until those vital regiments arrived from Europe. In early March the 103rd Foot was sent down from Lower Canada. Anxious to maintain garrisons at York, Kingston and at his newly acquired strong points on the Niagara, he wrote to Riall to point out that Burlington Heights, threatened from the rear by the Americans at Detroit and by the build-up of enemy forces at Buffalo, might no longer be tenable. Rather than shredding unnecessary blood through a stubborn resistance, Riall should be prepared to retire fighting and allow the garrisons of Forts Niagara, George and Erie to draw away some of the sting of any American advance west into the peninsula of Upper Canada. Some aggression, however, seemed necessary. Informed by an American deserter, Constant Bacon, of the size of the enemy concentration at Buffalo, Drummond felt that a raid on the huge depot at Oswego would provide the British with much needed provisions and, at the same time, impede the American invasion plans. Weeks were spent in preparation for Britain's first tentative step of the year into America's territory.

On 4th May Yeo's ships sailed out of Kingston, carrying the Glengarry Light Infantry, one of the two volunteer Swiss regiments serving the

British cause, and a number of marines and gunners, the latter armed with Congreve rockets. By 3 p.m. the next day the boats lay at anchor off Oswego's soft waterline, so far unmolested by any opposition.

The town, once the site of the French Fort Chouaguen, had attracted little interest until now. Placed on the main supply line from the Hudson River, its defences had been neglected and could never have withstood purposeful bombardment from the water. Lieutenant-Colonel George Mitchell had only taken command of the garrison of 300 a week previously, and he found nothing better than wooden defences on which he could rely.

Drummond was the sort of man who might have been expected to launch an instant assault on a point so weakly held. Yeo, a man so cautious that he appeared ineffective, would not, however, risk his boats until he had located the exact position of America's batteries. Having discovered this, he and Drummond planned to come ashore at 8 p.m. that night, the landing preceded by only a short bombardment of the defences.

But that evening an unwanted squall developed and grey clouds suddenly threatened. Yeo, fearing wreckage in the shallow off-shore waters, ordered his vessels to retire to the depths of the lake and wait for the tempest to pass. The next morning, in far kinder conditions, he tried again. The shallowness of the waters, however, prevented him from bringing his heavier ships too close. The 'Montréal' and 'Niagara, his two lightest vessels, took on the job of bombardment on their own. Red-hot hot was sent back from the defenders' positions. The 'Montréal' was severely burnt, and the fort was fragmented, but neither side showed any intention of yielding.

Landing of the troops took place a few hours later. The Swiss beached first, followed by boatloads of the Glengarry men. Facing into the offshore breeze, the row boats were slowed and the troops on board exposed to the hellish fire of Oswego's guns. Survivors of many battles, these men still realised that no life could be guaranteed, and no-one recklessly exposed themselves as they came ashore. Musket fire might be dangerous, but cannon shot could decapitate or remove limbs. Every man lay low in the boasts for as long as possible, huddled behind planking, spars and decking—or the bodies of their colleagues.

Once through the surf, however, the men sprang up and moved as quickly over the beach as limbs would allow. Within minutes, the assailants were storming Oswego's fragile defences, wishing only to finish the task that they had set out to do. The marines were pouring ashore now, many armed with pikes, and were soon swarming like cockroaches over the rough fort of Oswego. The Battle for Oswego was a short, one-sided affair, probably lasting for less than 30 minutes from start to finish. Outnumbered by 3 to 1, Mitchell's men withdrew in reasonable order, seeking the road to Sackets Harbor and the sanctuary that this town would provide. The conquerors moved into Oswego that evening and took possession of 1000 barrels of much needed flour, quantities of salt and pork and valuable supplies of rope and tar. A schooner recently scuttled by the Americans was laboriously raised and taken to Kingston—and all of this was gained for the loss of 18 dead and 73 wounded. If they had chosen to push forward to the Oswego Falls, the British would have taken an almost priceless haul: the armoury and equipment intended for the new ships that Chauncey was constructing at Sackets Harbor. The consequences of losing this valuable naval equipment would have been more devastating for America than the loss of Oswego. But, following precedent, the British abandoned Oswego a few days later and returned with their booty to Kingston.

Stung by the realisation that he had failed to snatch this glittering prize that had been well within his reach, Yeo took his squadron towards Sackets Harbor on 19th May, with the expressed intention of blockading the harbour and preventing the Oswego Falls armaments from reaching the American naval base. Chauncey, who had never before experienced such resolute action from his over-cautious opponent, was quick to pen his frustration: '*Five sail were now anchored betweenPoint Peninsula and Stoney Island . . . . and two brigs between Stoney Island and Stoney Point, completely blocking both passes . . . . This is the first time I have ever experienced the mortification of being blockaded on the lakes*'. Held fast in these chains of frustration, Chauncey desperately searched for the means of breaking the blockade and finding a route to move the equipment that did not take him past Yeo's watching guns. On the 30th he instructed reliable Master Commandant Melanethon Woolsey to load the naval guns and equipment stored at Oswego Falls on board bateaux and, hugging the southern shoreline of the lake for as long as possible, run the gauntlet to Stoney Creek under cover of the night.

The British gunboats, however, spotted the flat-bottomed craft in Sandy Creek and moved in to intercept. Landing on reed-concealed shores in an operation that was as discrete as the American movement down the creek, 200 British sailors crawled through the reeds to find positions from which they could fire on the American vessels as they passed. The results of such a battle should have been predictable. Exposed on the open decks of the passing vessels, Woolsey's marines and supporting Indians must have been at an initial disadvantage. Superior numbers, coolness under fire and a level of marksman which the British failed to match, however, counted in America's favour—and 18 British sailors would never rise again from the muddy banks of the Sandy Creek. A further 70 were wounded, their positions in the reeds revealed to the American marksmen by sudden movements or the smoke discharged by muskets. Not one British sailor escaped; those not killed or maimed were captured, and Woolsey's name shone in blessedness. The guns and equipment reached Sackets Harbor and were united with the new warships for which they had been intended.

The British blockade, however, remained in place. But America would never need to run the gauntlet again. A road was constructed from inland Rome north to Sackets Harbor, and the water route across the lake could therefore be avoided. The heavy cables for the ships, so nearly lost in the Battle of the Sandy Creek, were said to have been carried on the broad shoulders of 200 volunteer farmers. Whether true or not, this story has become deliciously embedded in the folklore of the United States.

Superiority in numbers of ships and guns on the lakes swung periodically in both directions. During the winter the two warring factions had been continuously building. In terms of the numbers constructed, they remained roughly equal, but the launching of the 42 gun 'Princess Charlotte' and the 58 gun 'Prince Regent' in April gave the British a clear superiority in gun power. On 1st May 1814, however, America launched the 64 gun 'Superior' on the lake of that name—the most heavily armed American ship to date—and the republic's supremacy on that lake was beyond question. Finding manpower for these new ships taxed the resources of both sides. America and Britain were forced to raid their saltwater fleets for crewmen with experience. The United States, with so many of her Atlantic fighting vessels forced to inactivity in inland creeks by the British blockade, found this task comparatively easy. Britain, however, could only man her lake fleets by reducing the number of ships on Atlantic blockade duty.

Throughout the early summer of 1814, both sides engaged in raids of dubious military value. Many of the expeditions were clearly launched out of a motive for revenge and were frequently led by men with low ethical standards. The American colonel John Campbell's expedition to Port Dover could never be described as militarily justifiable. On 14th May he loaded 800 men into boats at Put-in-Bay and landed them near the tiny settlement on Lake Erie's northern shore, where many of the militiamen who had burned down Buffalo were believed to live. '*In a short time the houses, mills and barns were all consumed, and a beautiful village, which the sun shone on in splendour that morning, was before two o'clock a heap of smoking ruins,*' wrote a witness. Probably without any danger of being accused of exaggeration, the writer continued: '*A party of sailors appointed to man the artillery killed the hogs in the streets, and severing them in the middle carried off the hind parts, while the head and shoulders were left in the street.*' Washington, feeling slight unease at what had happened at Port Dover, set up a court of inquiry, but this did no more than criticise Campbell and claim that the officer had committed a slight error of judgement! Andrew Westbrook's raid on Port Talbot on 30th May was just as vindictive and aimed at livelihoods and home life, not military hardware. Mills, houses, barns and homes were destroyed, together with the tools of sustenance, during a day that even medieval society might have described as barbaric.

Justice, however, was sometimes meted out, particularly for those British Canadians who served an alien cause. A series of trials began at Ancaster on 23rd May 1814. Writs for high treason were brought against 19 men held in custody and for another 50 still at large. Verdicts were reached in June. Eight of those tried were hanged in July. And, in a return to medieval practice, their bodies were decapitated and their heads exhibited in public.

These executions took place at a time when British Canada was gripped by the panic of another American invasion. Throughout the Spring and early Summer, Armstrong, in his usual muddled fashion, failed to identify any fresh plans or strategies for winning the war. Scott and Brown continued to drill their men and wonder and wait, hoping that the dull Secretary would somehow emerge from his lethargy and show sudden skills of leaderhip. When a communication arrived on 6th June, it contained suggestions, not orders. Moreover, Armstrong's reasons for focusing on an attack on Fort Erie, like all of the summer's expeditions, had no strategic foundation and seemed largely concerned with a wish to amuse the troops. '*To give . . . . immediate occupation to your troops, and to prevent their blood from stagnating, why not take Fort Erie?*' The Secretary wrote, as nonchalantly and unwarlike as if he were merely organizing a Sunday School outing for children.

Scott and Brown had long ago prepared for this day and together had finalized the details of their plans for invasion. Disagreeing only over the timing, they hoped first to seize Fort Erie and then advance along the Niagara against the enemy garrison at Fort George. For this, they would need to snatch possession of the bridge over the Chippawa River. Scott's brigade would attack Fort Erie from the north while Eleazer Ripley, the other brigade commander, was to cross from Black Rock and support his colleagues in an attack from the south. Dissension, caused largely by personal jealousy, rocked the two men's well laid plans on the eve of invasion. Ripley, an over-cautious man by nature and perpetually at odds with his colleagues, felt that the force involved would be too small for the task and threatened to resign. Brown, who had just been forced to discipline two senior officers for gambling, was in no mood for dissension or discussion. Tearing up the letter, he refused the man's resignation and curtly told him to obey his orders.

During the very early hours of the morning of 3rd July, Scott's brigade began to cross the river in driving rain and squalls. Phineas Riall, with his army stretched thinly along the 30 mile frontier of the Niagara, could offer no opposition, and Scott's men landed without loss. The brigadier himself, wishing, yet again, to be the first man ashore, jumped too soon from the bows of his boat and disappeared in deep water. The embarrassed man was hooked out of the water by his sailors.

Riall received the unwelcome news of the American's unwanted presence in Canada at about 8 o'clock the next morning. He could do nothing to prevent the advance on Fort Erie, which, garrisoned by only 137 men under the command of Major Thomas Buck and virtually indefensible on the landward side, had no chance of resisting. Ripley's brigade landed at daybreak. Peter Porter's brigade, the third unit of the invasion force, followed soon afterwards. By noon on the 3rd, 3500 American soldiers were ashore. By 5 p.m. Major Buck, after firing a few shots in token resistance, had surrendered; America was free to press northwards, and Riall was heard to express his disappointment at Buck's over hasty surrender.

July 4th, Independence Day, was a day of activity as well as one of national pride. It was also a day of cloudless skies, and the corn rich fields over which the Americans marched shone in golden sunshine. Riall was as active as his enemy, galloping across country in an attempt to organize his force of defence and place his men across the enemy's path. In his rear, however, American militia from Buffalo had advanced along the American side of the river and taken post at Lewiston, Queenston's American twin. Riall fortunately turned out to be the sort of man upon which Britain could rely in a crisis. He had soon assembled 1500 men on the north bank of the Chippawa, including the 1st (Royal Scots), the 8th (King's) regiment and the 100th Foot. A man with a superior eye for assessing terrain, he placed these men in favourably advantageous positions.

Throughout that heat-strewn day, the Americans pushed forward, making some contact with British light infantry under Colonel Thomas Pearson. By dusk, the last of the British rearguard units were withdrawing across the Chippawa Bridge, having removed the planks of every one of the bridges crossing the creeks that flowed into the Niagara between Fort Erie and the Chippawa. Now, as the sun at last began to set, two 24 pounder guns, almost the only British units left on the south side of the Chippawa, opened up on Scott's vanguard, compelling the Americans to halt just short of the coveted bridge. Events, not pre-intention, had decided that Chippawa (or Chippewa) would be the site of a major battle. Brigadier-General Winfield Scott, having discovered that he had outpaced his two supporting brigades, could do no other than encamp for the night behind Street's Creek, a mile or so south of the Chippawa river. Ripley joined him soon after midnight, and the welcome news reached him that Porter was only four or five hours away. Soon after

2 a.m. the two opposing armies, separated only by the Chippawa and a mile of resting countryside, settled down for sleep. The coming field of battle once again became the domain of nocturnal birds and animals and the haunt of the occasional shadow.

Brown rose earlier than his soldiers and breakfasted in a farmhouse belonging to Mr. Samuel Street, after whom the tiny creek had been named. Here he was almost captured by Indians in British pay who, possibly informed by Mrs. Street of the general's presence in her house, arrived just after his departure. By 7 a.m. Brown was reviewing his position. The plain between Street's Creek and the Chippawa was edged on the east by the parent river, the Niagara, and on the west by forest, the sort of ground which every conventionally minded general would wish to choose as the venue for his battle.

Little happened in the hours before noon—just the periodic rattle of musket fire, mainly from keen British pickets on the far side of the Chippawa or in the forest to the west. Increasingly annoyed by their presence, Brown ordered Porter and his newly arrived militia brigade to deal with this irritant. The brigadier, the man who had been forced to flee in his night shirt from his home at Black Rock, was reluctant to send out his 300 Pennsylvanians and 400 Seneca on an expedition against uncounted numbers. One of the most belligerent hawks in the American military establishment, he felt a strong desire for a moment of true glory that would elevate him in his critics' eyes. Skirmishing with regulars in unchartered woods would hardly provide such a chance, and he nearly refused to obey Brown's first battlefield order and argue for a more favourable role in the coming battle.

Soon after 2 p.m., Porter, assured by Scott's assertion that no British regulars were in the vicinity and by his promise of immediate support on his right if the need arose, reluctantly led his mixed force into the woods on the left. At almost the same moment, Riall was ordering an all-out attack across the Chippawa River on the fluid American positions. In preparing to attack, the redcoat was probably well aware that he was outnumbered by almost 2 to 1. But Sir Gordon Drummond had recently assured him that American regulars lacked training, discipline and courage, the qualities that rendered disparity in numbers largely irrelevant. Perhaps it was for this reason that he failed to call upon the manpower of the 103rd Foot located at Burlington Heights or the units of militia that also lay within his call.

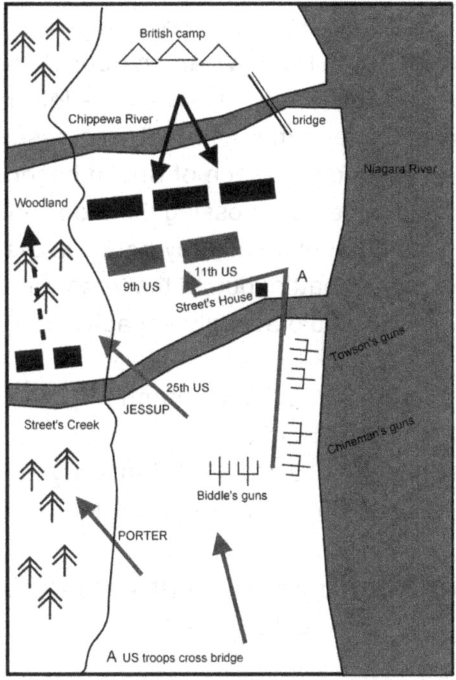

The Battle of Chippawa (or Chippewa)

Scott had seen the British movements and read the signs clearly. Porter and he were about to be confronted by Britain's most well-trained forces. Surprisingly, however, Riall had chosen to advance his men in three columns, the movement favoured by the French, curiously abandoning the more orthodox movement in line that had been the standard practice of British generals since the time of the great Marlborough.

It would be Porter who would meet those British regulars first. He had moved into the woods in a column, assured by Scott that he would find only Indians and militiamen across his path. But, a few hundred yards to his right on the rim of the clearing, scarlet coats had halted. Now, caught between the militia and the regulars, Porter found himself involved in the very situation which he had hoped to avoid. Reports of what happened conflict: most talk of an instant American withdrawal and of the savage work done by Indian and British muskets. One account, however, suggests a more glorious outcome, claiming that the Pennsylvanians actually drove the redcoats back towards the Chippawa. '*We drove them till their main body let loose their artillery on us when we were obliged to retreat a short Distance till General Scott came to our assistance with the regulars which soon compelled the enemy to retreat . . . .'* A Pennsylvanian trooper crowed. Whatever the truth might be, an American retreat on the left now undoubtedly took place and all of Porter's men hurriedly recrossed Street's Creek in an effort to keep beyond the reach of British bayonets. At that very moment, Scott's main force was crossing the creek and was deploying in line formation on the flat plain that lay between the two creeks. He had committed his men to battle, but, at that moment, he probably still wondered whether Riall would actually engage.

1st Brigade: (Scott) 9th/22nd U.S.Infantry, 11th U.S.Infantry, one company of the 21st, 25th U.S. Infantry

2nd Brigade: (Ripley) 21st and 23rd U.S.Infantry

3rd Brigade: (Porter) 5th Pennsylvania Militia and supporting Indians

American Infantry regiments at the Battle of Chippewa

The Irishman feared little when he saw the grey uniforms wading across Street's Creek. American regulars conventionally wore blue, and he and the Marquess of Tweeddale, the commander of the 100th Foot, assumed that the men in drab grey were members of the militia. Both men felt confident that the 1500 regulars of the three British regiments now in place would prove to be more than a match for the 3000 or so poor quality troops lining up on the northern bank of the winding creek. Britain's three battalions of regulars were now fully deployed for battle, drawn up on the plain in front of the Americans and partly hidden by a screen of bushes. At the front of the 100th Foot was the imposing figure of Tweeddale, a giant of a man. Famed in England for his skill as a swordsman, a horseman and his unceasing luck at the gambling table, he might easily have stepped out of a work of fiction. Wounded three times during the Peninsular campaign, he was reputed to have swum a river under fire to rescue the wife of a German hussar officer. Included in his baggage train during his time with Wellington were his gaming table, a number of saddles and several cases of claret and champagne, which he would generously serve in his mess to captive officers. It was now just after 4 p.m.

There would be no long drawn out semi-silent prelude to battle, those tense moments when both sides try to assess the determination of the enemy and look for visible signs of weakness. Grape and cannon shot from the 9 guns placed in front of the British lines passed harmlessly over the heads of the American, and very little interrupted the final deployment of the US 9th and 11th regiments, the two units of Scott's brigade that had formed up to confront the British. To protect his left flank, he ordered Major Thomas Jessup and the US 25th, the third of his regiments, to occupy the adjacent woods. Then, watching the counter movements of the British, he positioned Captain Nathan Towson and his battery of 12 pounders at an oblique angle near the bridge, where the guns could most effectively play on the British centre and left. General Riall, watching the grey American line unfolding, was heard to exclaim in sudden shock: '*Those are regulars, by God!*' The British, with their backs to the Chippawa, were probably not in the most enviable of positions.

The Battle of Chippawa would be fought in the 18th Century manner. Artillery fire first, an advance of infantry in line or column, a round of musketry, reloading and another discharge of muskets. The British advanced first, half-stumbling over the long grass of the meadows, in an attack that they felt would undoubtedly prove successful. Scott, holding back his centre, pushed forward both wings, a tactic that enfiladed the British flanks and left them dangerously exposed. In those opening minutes, the commanders of both British regiments, Colonel John Gordon of the Royal Scots, and the Marquess of Tweeddale, were wounded, the former in the mouth and the latter by a musket ball in the leg. Several more junior officers of the 100th were killed in the next few minutes, most by Towson's canister fire, which was now heavy and accurate enough to bring the British column to a gradual halt

Scott took the opportunity that Providence, or his men's fighting skills, had just given him. '*The enemy says the Americans are good at long shot but cannot stand the cold iron. I call upon you instantly to give the lie to the slander,*' he was heard to shout above the din of intense excitement. Advancing to within 80 paces or so of the British, the two regiments set off on a bayonet charge that equalled in quality and ruthlessness anything that the British had ever achieved. There, within a mile of the great falls of the Niagara, the sound of which could still be heard despite the noise of battle, the two sides locked in close combat in the finale of one of the war's few really conventional battles.

It was all over within just a few minutes. The red line, shredded by the intensity of the artillery fire and musket volleys, was suddenly overwhelmed. Riall, fighting at the head of his troops, seemed deliberately to court death in those closing moments. Spurring his horse straight at the Americans and accompanied only by his aide, he only halted when his companion fell wounded. The British general might be considered guilty of impetuosity and poor judgement, but he can never be accused of cowardice. But now, facing indisputable defeat, he rode from the scene of battle, calling upon the King's Regiment, which had been held as a reserve, to cover the retreat and rip up the planks of the Chippawa bridge.

America chose to pursue as far as the shattered bridge, but no further. Jessup, on the American left, joined in the rout; his regiment, like the 9th and 11th, continued in pursuit until artillery at the bridge dissuaded them from following any further Ripley, true to his reputation, had remained south of the creek, and his men never participated. The United States had, consequently, fought at Chippawa with slightly fewer men than the British; the victory is therefore all the more remarkable.

The following hours were as dramatic as the battle itself. A thunderstorm of Valhalla proportions drenched the field and stilled the movements of both victors and vanquished. The Americans, stunned by the near miracle they had achieved, remained where they had fought content to let the rain wash battle wounds clean and refresh exhausted limbs. But both sides had lost heavily; Brown had lost 61 dead and 255 wounded: the British 236 killed and 320 wounded, nearly one-third of the force engaged. By late evening, both sides had withdrawn to their morning positions, and the field was quiet and deserted. There was little to indicate that a battle had taken place.

Drummond was chivalrous, but defiant in his report and in his subsequent movements. Praising the conduct of the British troops, he also spoke highly of the Americans and the steadiness of Scott's brigade. But he was still unprepared to concede a metre of Canadian territory to an enemy who had no right to be there. He ordered the 89th Foot, the victors at Crysler's Field, and the Battalion of Incorporated Militia to move from the St. Lawrence to Forts George and Mississauga, and sent the 6th and 82nd Foot to assist the 104th in the defence of Kingston. Riall's position on the Chippawa, however, he knew to be untenable, and he no longer entertained any notion of defending this point.

Brown was anxious to exploit the redcoat general's embarrassment. On the 6th, Ripley's fresh troops began the construction of a bridge over the Chippawa and a road north to Lyons' Creek. America's exploitive advance began soon afterwards. Riall withdrew immediately and never stopped until he had reached Twenty Mile Creek, near Fort George. Beyond the plain where the fort stood were the waters of Lake Ontario, the haunt of Chauncey's fleet and the route of communications with Sackets Harbor. Generals of the army of the United States might be forgiven for believing that no obstacles now lay across their path of invasion.

But this path could only be kept clear of enemy impedimenta if Commodore Chauncey and his naval guns assisted. The horizon of Lake Ontario, however, remained empty, with no sign of American sails. An assault on Burlington Heights, Fort George and Mississauga would consequently be inadvisable.

On the 13th, Brown, after resting for three days at Queenston, composed a terse letter to Chauncey. *For God's sake, let me see you . . . at all events have the politeness to let me know what aid I am to expect from the fleet on Lake Ontario.'* Twice, during his three day wait at Queenston, Brown tested the defences of Fort George, hoping to provoke the garrison of 600 to come out and fight. General Jacob Brown, revealing all the human weaknesses and frustrations of a man who has overreached himself, had become a victim of a timetable over which he had absolutely no control. Chauncey had his reasons for his failure to respond. He had been laid low in bed with a fever and was rendered completely incapable of commanding a naval expedition. Yet, feeling that he was the personal guardian of America's fine ships, he refused to allow anybody else to take over the command or permit the vessels' employment as troop transports for the army.

Brown's arrival at Queenston had fermented the borderlands into a brew of national panic, and every day of delay was likely to stiffen Canadian resistance. Guerilla bands re-organised, farmers left tools unattended and, leaving hay uncut, went to join the new units of militia that assembled at Burlington Heights and Twenty Mile Creek. Militia inflows continued to increase the size of Riall's force. The Glengarrians came in from York, the 89th and 103rd, with two companies of the 104th moved up to Twelve Mile Creek from Burlington Heights, providing Gneral Riall with an army of nearly 4000 men, some even taking up station on the American side of the river. Brown, by sad contrast, could rely upon little more than 2500. And, worse still, Drummond was planning to move down from York to take personal command of Britain's expanding force.

In such moments of heightened emotion, atrocities were again committed. American Colonel Isaac Stone's militia unit burned down St. Davids on 19th July, an action which the officer, who was not present, had apparently never sanctioned. The affair says something about the lack of discipline existing within America's armed forces and even more about the passions that governed behaviour. Stone, rightly held accountable, despite his absence, was dismissed from military service. Harsh though this might seem, the punishment of the officer gives some indication of the decency under which Brown chose to operate.

Riall was under strict orders to avoid acting precipiately, despite his advantage of numbers. '*You are to concentrate the whole of the regular force at that place,* (St. Davids), *throwing the militia and the Indians into the woods towards the enemy's position and the lake.'* Drummond had written to him. He hoped to retain this defensive posture until the build-up of forces was completed and Drummond felt confident that he could win.

Brown, informed of the British movement along the Niagara's eastern bank towards Fort Schlosser, America's forward supply base, recognized the sudden swing of fortunes in Britain's direction. On 24th July the American commander decided that a retreat from Queenston was his only option. '*You know how greatly I am disappointed, and therefore I will not dwell on that painful subject . . . ,'* he wrote to Armstrong on the following day, blaming Chauncey as well as himself for the failure of arms. When he wrote these words, he could have had no idea that he was on the eve of the bloodiest battle of the war. By that evening the entire American army was on a slow withdrawal to Chippawa. From here, Brown hoped that it might later be possible, if circumstances improved, to move directly against the main British position at Burlington Heights or back towards Fort George.

Circumstances obviously alter the fortunes of war. So, too, do rumours. Suggestions that Yeo's gunboats had recently entered the Niagara River remained unsubstantiated, but added to Brown's discomfort. Moreover, reports had reached him that Drummond himself had just arrived at Fort George. But national pride, rather than rumours and facts, catapulted America northward again towards Queenston, creating a bizarre situation of two invasions taking place simultaneously, each side with an army on the territory of the other.

It was probably Scott, not Brown, who authored the new advance to Queenston. He clearly hoped that Britain, anxious to defend the town, would feel compelled to withdraw its forces from American soil. Brown's dominating weakness, perhaps the only discernible one, was a tram like mentality that made it difficult to come up with an alternative strategy when his original one had been revealed as faulty. Persuasive and strong-minded, Winfield Scott could do no wrong in Brown's view. Consequently, Brown had accepted Scott's recommendations, almost as if he were the more junior commander of the two. Both men, however, were still working under the shadows of mistaken perception. They had been misinformed about the size of the force threatening Lewiston and Schlosser. Drummond's detachment was only 500 strong, and he had already abandoned any real thoughts of challenging the fort. And, as Brown had hoped, this tiny force promptly recrossed the river when reports of the enemy's return to Queenston had reached Drummond's ears.

Riall's British were now in bullish mood. '*You are . . . . by means of the Glengarry Light Infantry and Incorporated Militia, to endeavour to check his light troops until you reach an open space in which, keeping your guns in the centre and your force concentrated, your flank secured by light troops., militia and Indians, you must depend upon the superior discipline of the troops under your command.*' Drummond had ordered as soon as he had divined the American's new intentions. During those two days of American prevarication, more than 3000 regulars and militia had begun a journey south, intent on claiming back as much Canadian territory as possible.

Winfield Scott encountered the British on the 25th in line of battle along Lundy's Lane, a trackway running at right angles to the Niagara River, only a mile or two from the mighty falls. Riall had occupied a high knoll over which the trackway passed. Near the top of the hill, just south of the road, stood a tiny church and graveyard, the products of peacetime, but now to be at the very centre of a battlefield. A more cautious, less precipitate man than Scott might have hesitated before preparing to engage. But Winfield Scott had a reputation to uphold, and the counting of enemy heads became irrelevant to him. Riall, on the other hand, believed that he was faced by the entire American army and was on the point of withdrawing when Drummond arrived to bolster his strength and his nerve. Scott had just 1070 men on the field when the battle started. The British, with Drummond present, would have 1800 men. Six miles further back, another British force of 1200 men under the command of Colonel Hercules Scott was hurrying forward. Lieutenant-Colonel J. Tucker with units of the 41st had just left Fort Niagara and would arrive soon afterwards.

Riall had chosen a position that complied with Drummond's instructions. His centre, manned by the 1st and 89th Foot, with a company of the 41st, nestled on the top of the hill. Here, too, was positioned the British artillery, commanding a clear view of the terrain over which the Americans would be obliged to advance. The Glengarrians extended the line to the right, placed almost at right angles to the centre. The Incorporated Militia and one company of the 8th lay to the left of the hill, covering the road.

Scott deployed his men in a similar manner: the 9th taking up their responsibilities on the extreme left, the 11th and 22nd formed the centre, while the 25th Regiment extended the line to the right. It appeared that both sides were planning a battle with a largely conventional format. The American keenly searched the field for any advantages that it might offer, and his eyes focused on the woodland that lay near the Niagara's edge. He immediately ordered Major Thomas Jesup and the 25th regiment to try to outflank the enemy left, while the other three regiments concentrated their entire punch on the British centre and right.

All four American units began an early evening advance towards the hill. The 9th, acting independently, soon found itself in danger of being enveloped by the unemployed Glengarrians on Riall's right. But, despite this emerging danger, early events were to favour the Americans.

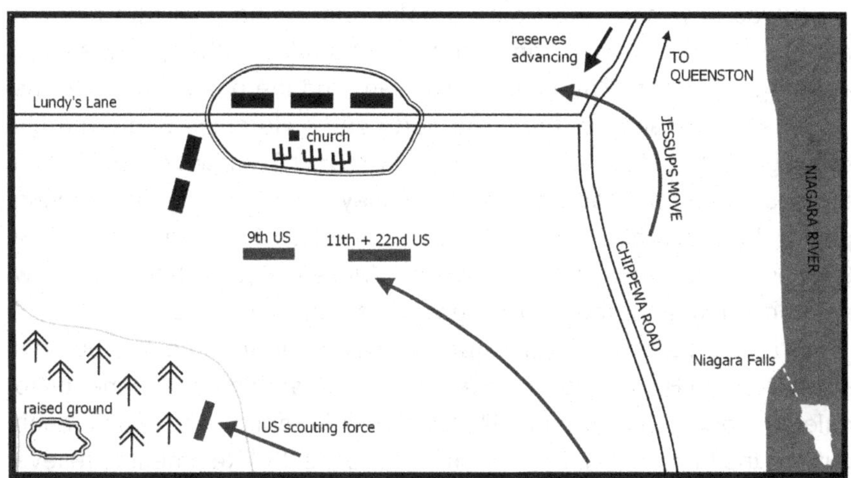

The Battle of the Niagara Falls (Lundy's Lane)

Jesup's men, creeping through the darkening undergrowth, were not observed and quickly caused havoc in the British rear. Outflanking the Incorporated Militia, the unit drove back two troops of dragoons and prepared to swing down and attack the battery on the knoll from the rear. Realising just in time that British troops were travelling south down the Queenston Road, Jesup changed his mind and ordered his men to wait for the unsuspecting British to arrive. In the next few moments, during a time of fading daylight that produced no favours for either side, General Riall, bleeding from a wound that would cause him to lose his arm, was taken captive. Riall and his staff had no inkling of an American presence so close to the heart of the British defence, and Jesup and his men, as surprised as their victim, would hardly be expected to recognise the uniforms and insignia of high rank. '*I am General Riall,* a voice in the shadows called out. '*And I, Sir, am Captain Ketcham of the United States Army.'*

The general's capture did little to improve the situation which Scott and his four regiments now faced. The British gunners on the knoll had torn the American ranks to pieces, breaking up every charge launched by the 11th and 22nd. The regiments of the British centre, particularly the 1st and 89th, held firmly, repelling in hand-to-hand combat, any American that managed to reach the British line.

It was now close to 9 p.m. Smoke and fading light had made it hard for Drummond to distinguish friend from foe. Other players were entering the stage, British and American, and the battle's dimensions would soon be altered. From the north came Hercules Scott and his two regiments of foot, the 103rd and 104th (New Brunswick) Foot. From the south came Porter's militia and Ripley's unused brigade, arriving just at the moment when the U.S. 11th and 22nd began to break. The 9th, despite its precarious position on Winfield Scott's left, somehow held on, clinging to the British right like a limpet to a rock.

Britain's battery of guns had not been silent since the battle's start. General Brown, now on the field, was searching for the means to quieten those guns. Ordering Ripley's 1st U.S.Foot, fresh from garrison duty on the Mississippi, Porter's militia and the 23rd Regiment to relieve Scott's torn-up ranks, he instructed Colonel James Miller and the 21st Regiment to attack the guns.

'I'll try, sir.' Miller's immortal words have become part of America's military folklore, and what occurred next has thrilled generations of schoolchildren. The 300 men of the regiment crept forward in the night's fresh darkness, taking advantage of every shadow, tree and bush. No training manuals had prepared them for this. Veterans of the Revolutionary War's battles had never been required to perform such a feat. At the base of the hill on which Britain's gunners swore, sweated and reloaded their weapons with well-trained precison, Miller's men, semi-rigid with tension, waited and watched. Periodically, in the brief moments when the artillery pieces were silent, they could hear the conversations of the British gunners. Every man present felt the uniqueness of the moment and the consequences of failure. At a given signal, they sprung into action, firing their first volley as they rose at point blank range. The redcoats had no chance; they fell, every one of them in a matter of minutes. Seizing the moment, the men of the 21st rushed at the guns and engaged a cluster of infantry that had been positioned behind the hill to protect the guns. It was now past 10 p.m. The moon, silvering the battlefield for the past hour, was setting. Fighting for ownership of the guns continued for some time. Muskets discharged at distances of twenty yards, men engaged silhouettes, and shadows faded with the dying moon. *'Desperation bordering on madness,'* was how one of Miller's officers described those long minutes on the hillside. The battery that had so savagely mauled Scott's brigade was in American hands.

Elsewhere the fighting had re-ignited. Ripley's 23rd Infantry was vigorous in its attack, but the fighting soon became uncoordinated. Men fired at the flashes emanating from the muzzles of opposing muskets. Everyone present, packaged within their own little fear-filled world by the darkness, fought a personal battle, unaware of what others might be doing. Every regiment, including the newly arrived, was committed now, adding to the confusion and the numbers stumbling across the battlefield. The Royal Scots, after holding off the Americans since 8 p.m., mistakenly turned their fire on the Glengarrians, the British 103rd thought that the advancing U.S. 23rd were friends, and Jacob Brown, suddenly finding himself on the Queenston Road, well to the rear of Lundy Lane, was very nearly captured. Winfield Scott almost fell into his enemy's hands as well. Returning to the action in support of Ripley, he formed up the remnants of his brigade behind the American right and led them on another attempted move around the British left flank. Here he encountered some companies of the 89th, kneeling in the cover of an unharvested hayfield. Scott's men were soon in retreat, pressed back by the bayonets of the 89th.

The Royal Scots came closer than any of the American regiments to feeling the sharp points of British steel. In the darkness, the 89th lost both their quarry and their sense of direction. Swinging too far to the right, they took their neighbouring redcoat battalion for the American fugitives. Scott, taking full advantage of this muddle and unexpected reprieve, hurried his men down a path that be believed led to safety, but then found himself in front of Hercules Scott's two fresh regiments. Blooded, tired and resigned, the Americans stoically awaited their fates; Britain's units lay across all possible lines of escape. No Americans, however, would fall. *'It's the 89th',* an Englishman called out, just as the muskets of both British regiments were about to fire. Muskets remained silent and the battlefield's confusion went on. But Scott's thorny route of retreat was not clear yet and the danger was no less. Swinging too far west in his attempts to find his own lines, his men blundered into the rear ranks of the 41st, who were now well forward of their supporting battalions.

This brought on some of the most energetic fighting of the night. With four British regiments close by and with little chance this time of just tripping away like thieves in the night, Scott and his men swung and jabbed, each man desperate to slip through the closing net and find sanctuary in the darkness beyond. The Glengarrians, now facing very little opposition, joined in, but, affected by the epidemic of confusion that had swept through every British unit, they turned their firepower on the British regulars to their left. Through the providentially holed net, Scott's men escaped at last. Their losses, during the last hour, had been few.

British Forces:

Riall's Division	Scott's Division	Drummond's Division
Light Brigade (Col.Thomas Pearson) Glengarry Infantry 2nd York, 1st, 2nd, 4th and 5th Lincoln militia (detachments)	103rd Foot 1st batt. 8th Foot 104th Foot 1st and 2nd Norfolk, 1st Essex, 1st Middlesex, 2nd York, 4 and 5th Lincon militia (detachments)	2nd batt. 89th Foot 1st batt. 1st Foot 41st Foot (light co.)
Merrill's Provincial dragoons 19th Light Dragoons (1 troop)		
Royal Artillery 2 x 6 pdr guns 1 x 5.5 inch howitzer	Royal Artillery 3 x 6 pdr guns	Royal Artillery 2 x 24 pdr guns Royal Marine Artillery 2 Congreve rocket launchers

American forces

Scott's 1st brigade	Ripley's 2nd brigade	Porter's 3rd militia brigade
9th U.S. Regt. 11th U.S.Regt. 22nd U.S.Regt. 25th U.S.Regt.	21st U.S.Regt. 23rd U.S.Regt. 1st U.S.Regt (part of) 17th U.S.Regt. (part of) 19th U.S.Regt. (part of)	5th Pennsylvania Militia Canadian Volunteers N.Y. Militia Volunteers
Towson's Artillery 2 x 6 pdr 1 x 5.5 inch howitzer		Hindman's Artillery -Ritchie's co. 2 x 6 pdr 1 x 5.5 inch howitzer -Biddle's Co 3 x 12 pdr det. Of U.S. dragoons N.Y. Volunteer dragoons

The opposing forces at the Battle of the Niagara Falls

Ironically, Scott was to receive a shattering wound in the moments of comparative safety following the escape. Passing around to the right of the American line to seek out Jesup, he was felled by a musket ball in his shoulder, and was forced to leave the field. Brown received a wound at about the same minute. Winded and bleeding profusely, he handed over command to the unreliable Ripley. Drummond, too, had just been wounded in the neck.

Fighting stopped at about 11 p.m. His reasoning possibly affected by his injury, Brown gave Ripley an order to withdraw from a battle, which, to many present, did not yet appear to have been lost. Yet, unlike Chippawa, there were no unused regiments that could still be committed to action, and the casualty rate was mounting. Henry Leavenworth, now commanding Scott's brigade, had less than 200 men, and countless numbers of Ripley's brigade lay face down on the night shrouded hill. America had exhausted her strength and had no other sinew to involve. Their own reasoning impaired by the din and trauma of battle, those who felt that fighting could continue were failing to face reality.

Attempts to remove the captured, guns, however, brought on a final burst of activity. Drummond, reminded that a small American detachment remained on the knoll to guard the captured guns, sent troops to flush them way. When the American officer Jacob Hindman, who had been given the responsibility for the task of dragging off the guns, returned with horses, he found that the knoll, guns and the detachment of United States troops were in British hands.

British claims to victory became uncontestable during the course of the next morning. The exhausted redcoats had thrown themselves down to sleep amongst the dead and wounded. When the sun rose on the 26th, the full extent of the previous night's carnage became apparent. *'The morning light ushered to our view a shocking spectacle,'* wrote one participant of the battle. *'Men and horses lying promiscuously together, Americans and English, laid one upon another . . . . It was found impossible to bury the whole, so we collected a number of old trees together and burned them—which, although it may appear inhuman, was absolutely necessary.'* When Ripley and his brigade headed back towards the battlefield soon after 9 a.m. in the vain hope that they might yet force the British to retreat, he found his enemy in buoyant and immovable mood. The American force was soon in full retreat towards Fort Erie, their only remaining toehold on foreign soil. The casualty rate at Niagara Falls had been fearful, the largest of the war so far. The official tally listed the British dead at 84, with 559 wounded. America suffered even more: 171 killed and 572 with wounds, amongst them Brown, Scott and Jessup.

As with all retreats, recriminations followed. Brown, glossing over Ripley's recent energetic posture at Lundy's Lane, remembered only his earlier tardiness at Chippawa and his failure on the 26th to re-engage the British. Scott was equally contemptuous of Brown as a commander and for the general's failure to give him much credit for what he and his men had attempted in the recent battle. Wilkinson, analysing the results from a distance, felt that Brown had incurred needless slaughter, while Scott had *'ranged the field in quest of blood, regardless from what side it had flowed.'* Porter, playing minor roles in both battles, complained that Brown had used his men in both battles as *'the tools and drudges of the regular troops.'* He would later argue coherently and convincingly that Brown should never have ordered Ripley to withdraw.

While Brown might have underplayed Scott's role, the nation would soon be guilty of magnifying Scott into an Achilles-style hero. His promotion to a major-generalship was well justified, but the minting of coins in his honour, the forging of commemorative swords and the plethora of banquets at which his praise was sung seem out of place.

If Drummond had moved speedily against Fort Erie, he might have taken the place with ease. Ripley's measures to fortify the place in the days after Lundy's Lane would sweep away many of the criticisms of his earlier inadequacies. Anxious to maintain this fragile hold on the Canadian side of the river, Ripley ordered the construction of stone bastions and earthworks as additions to the fort's existing defences. When Drummond finally moved against Fort Erie one week after the battle, he found the place's defences impressive and the garrison's mood almost as solid as the bastions themselves.

His first move, however, was intended to bring further misery to shattered Buffalo. On 4th August 600 men of the 41st and 104th Foot, under the command of Lieutenant-Colonel J. Tucker landed downstream from Black Rock. The move fortunately had been anticipated. Three hundred republican riflemen under Major Lodowick Morgan had dismantled the bridge at Conjocheta Creek and lay in wait behind a breastwork constructed from the bridge's timbers. Outnumbered by 2 to 1, they knew that they could never expect to prevent the enemy's move on Buffalo, but hoped that they might delay the advance and so buy the town's defence a few precious hours to prepare. The two sides clashed on the 13th in an explosion of close range musket fire that rocked both sides wiitth its suddenness.

Tucker's men were sadly infected by what he later described as an '*unpardonable degree of unsteadiness, without possessing one solitary excuse.*' Veterans of the long war with Napoleon, fired upon by irregulars, prostrated themselves, took cover and failed to fire back. Three hours of almost one-sided gunfire ended in Britain's shameful retreat—and Buffalo's sad and broken buildings were spared further punishment. *It is . . . . the duty of all officers to punish with death on the spot any man under their command who may be found guilty of misbehaviour in front of the enemy . . . . Crouching, ducking, or laying down when advancing under fire are bad habits and must be corrected,* 'Drummond asserted in his admonishment of Tucker, raising the interesting question of whether a commander should be expected to single-handedly shoot his entire command at the very moment when the enemy were attempting to do the same thing!

Drummond's own force were fortunately less spineless and he had little difficulty in commencing his investment of Fort Erie—on the very day that Tucker faced embarrassment on the river's American shore. A safer pair of hands now ruled at Fort Erie. On the day after the first earthworks of the besiegers was established about two miles north of the fort, Brigadier-General Edmund Pendleton Gaines, Ripley's replacement, slipped into the fort to take command of the defences.

General Drummond knew that he would first have to deal with a trio of schooners that protected the fort. 75 men were selected for the task. Having cut a trail for eight miles through the flanking woods, the party lifted five light vessels on their shoulders and carried the boats all the way to Lake Erie's waters. They then rowed out to the American ships and, when challenged, claimed that they had been sent out to supply the ships with food. The resulting fight did not go quite as planned. The 'Ohio' and 'Somers' fell into British hands, but the 'Porcupine' slipped her moorings and sailed out of harm's way. The looming American threat from the lake had been largely removed, and Drummond could now position his men without too much fear of a bombardment from that direction.

Fort Erie was a star-shaped works, which had been extended southward by an abatis and entrenchment stretching for 750 yards to Snake Hill, a thirty foot high mound of sand on which Towson had placed his battery of guns. In the 100 yard gap between the fort and the lake's shores, David Douglass had positioned an artillery battery at the point where the British were expected to attack. 2125 men stood within those lines of defence. Beyond the screen of trees to the north, Drummond had nearly 3000. America, with its strong abatis and works, could be judged to have the advantage.

On 7th August the British, having taken four days to construct a four gun battery near the lake, opened long-range fire from their works to the north. For an entire week the bombardment continued, but only very superficial damage was done to the defence works—and this was repaired during the frequent lulls in fire. '*I very much doubt if one shot in ten reached the rampart at all, and the fortunate exceptions that struck the stone building . . . . rebounded from its sides as innocuous as tennis balls.*' Dr. William 'Tiger' Dunlop, a medical officer in the besiegers' lines observed. On the night of the 18th, the cannonade was more intense, indicating that a British assault was probably imminent. That night Gaines posted a stronger guard, giving them instructions to be particularly vigilant for any signs of an attack.

At midnight the following day, the British camp was ominously silent, far too quiet for an army intending to continue with a siege. Sir Gordon Drummond had fixed the following day for his assault and had already briefed his officers. Lieutenant-Colonel Victor Fischer, with 1300 men from Watteville's Regiment, the 8th Foot and the light companies of the 89th and 100th Foot, received their orders to attack the unmeasured defences of Snake Hill. A smaller group, about 360 men under the command of Colonel William Drummond of Keltie (or Keltie), the general's nephew, were instructed to try the strength of the seven foot high earth wall that stretched from the hill to the fort. Lieutenant-Colonel Hercules Scott, with nearly 700 men of the 103rd New South Wales 'Fencibles', whose ranks had been filled before sailing from Australia with released convicts, was assigned the task of tackling the short line of works between Fort Erie and the river's shore. Scott, who despised Drummond for personal reasons, was convinced that an assault would never succeed, but, out of a sense of duty, said nothing.

He rested under a piece of canvas that evening and wrote his will; his premonition of his death the next day was well founded.

At 2 a.m on the 20th, Drummond, having first ordered the bulk of his troops to remove the flints from their muskets, sent out Fischer on a long detour through woodland to the west. The remaining two columns were instructed to advance as soon as gunfire confirmed that Fischer's men had engaged. Men stood in lines for two more hours; the unattended campfires behind them were allowed to burn and catering staff clattered pans in an effort to convince the American observers that the dreary camp life of the besiegers had not altered in any way.

Gaines sensed their coming, and he and his men were undoubtedly ready. '*At half-past two o'clock, the right column of the enemy approached, and though enveloped in darkness, black as his designs and principles, was distinctly heard . . . . and promptly marked by our musketry and artillery,'* a participant recorded. From that darkness, full of rain, men came running, some carrying axes, others with scaling ladders, all sent out on a task for which few felt adequately trained. Three hundred yards from Snake Hill, they stumbled across an American picket line—and all chance of surprise was lost. In front, the abatis was formidable.

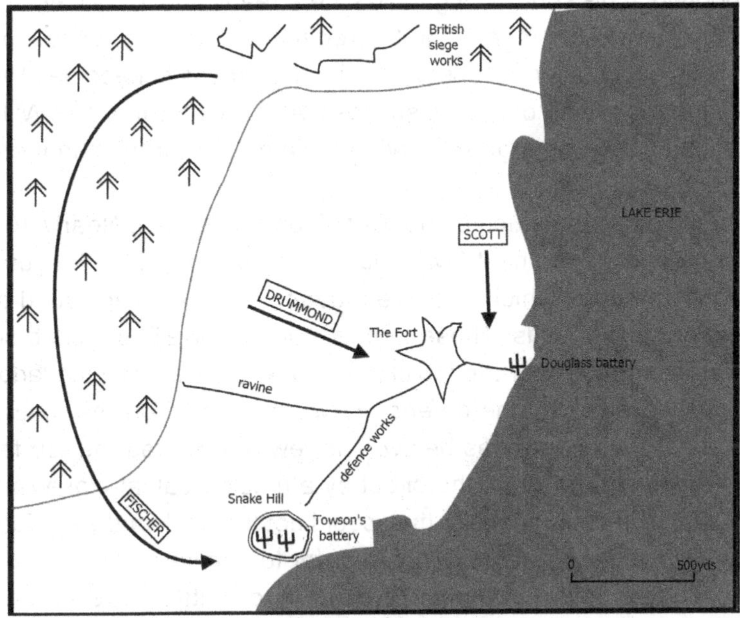

The Siege of Fort Erie

Whole trunks lay in the way, some with boughs sharpened and virtually impossible to penetrate. A few of Fischer's diehards tried to find the end of this tangle and drowned in the waters of Lake Erie. Others tackled the boughs and trunks, but were soon faced by the dreadful fire of the defenders' musketry. Some of the more highly seasoned regulars kept their nerves, negotiated the abatis and reached the walls, only to find that many of their ladders were too short to scale the parapets.

Gaines, peering out of the darkness, barked his orders just as the first of the ladders was raised against the walls. Towson's gunners, supported by 250 men of the U.S. 21st regiment, were firing continuously, often at redcoated chests barely a yard in front. The attackers, without flints in their muskets, could not reply—and most became yet another of the statistics of wartime casualties. Few irregulars ever appeared on the stockade's walls. Many of de Watteville's regiment, immobilised by the abatis and the enemy fire, had already deserted or were skulking in the woods. Within half an hour or so, the attack had faded and Fischer had clearly failed. Drummond could only hope that his other two columns would be more successful.

The American Douglass had seen the flares and flames and heard the shooting to his south. His gunners were ready and their matches lit. Around him were the men of the 9th Regiment of infantry. They looked out in solid expectation, almost willing the blackness to become alive to relieve the monotony of night's stillness. At 3 a.m. Scott's and William Drummond's men emerged, hurrying towards the fort with ladders in their hands.

The attacks cost much blood, British and American. Nearly 100 of Scott's men fell in the next few minutes, brought down by the guns of Douglass's battery, which had been loaded with canister, round shot or bags of musket balls. Those that reached the walls perished soon afterwards, shot as they tried to climb. Some, falling when the ladders were pushed away by the defenders, were impaled on the upturned bayonets of their comrades below. The few that scaled the top fared no better, pierced through the chest by a musket ball at close range. Without flints in their muskets, they could not fire back and were forced to rely upon muscle and dexterity in order to survive.

On Scott's right, Drummond's men were a little more fortunate. Sensing that the north bastion of the old fort was less well defended, some of his men took advantage of the smoke and noise to creep towards this point, scale the walls and cross with little opposition into Fort Erie's upper works. Here, in the confined space of the breach, men fought hand to hand for almost two hours. In the dark, uniforms and insignia were indistinguishable, and the fighting was formless and individual. Men swung or fired at any approaching body, hardly caring whether it was friend or foe. Colonel Drummond was amongst the victims, shot through the heart and then bayoneted. If the British break-through had been properly supported and reinforced, the Union flag would have flown over Fort Erie by evening.

An hour later, all those that had survived this pre-dawn fighting were killed or injured in an explosion that rocked the fort. Just as the sun crept over the distant horizon, a powder magazine blew up, claiming the life of Hercules Scott and many of the men in his command. Douglass, more than 100 yards away at the time, felt the ground shake violently and saw severed limbs and bits of timber rain down. '*War is not glorious at times such as these,*' a survivor wrote. By 6 a.m. the attack was over. In the five hours of fighting, Britain had lost 221 killed and over 140 wounded. Another 500 were classified as missing. Some were prisoners, but most, probably, had deserted. America had lost only 17 dead and 56 wounded in the action. Miraculously, less than a dozen defenders had been maimed in the deadly explosion.

Another hero had been made. Gold medals were struck in Gaines's honour and resolutions of praise given in parties of thanksgiving throughout America. Drummond, for his part, would not indulge in self-reproach for the disaster and hoped that others would be kind or forgiving in their judgements of his failure. Hercules Scott, his sternest critic, was dead, but others would prove to be acidic. The general had acted precipitately, some claimed, and had not even reconnoitred the defences of Snake Hill, or seen the tangled roots and branches over which Fischer's men would need to pass. And, perhaps more significantly, he had refused to bombard the American lines immediately prior to the assault. Confident that he outnumbered and outclassed his adversary, he assumed that he could conquer by surprise alone. In the days after the fiasco, while still grieving for his nephew, he wrote to Prevost, passing the responsibility for what had happened to those in his ranks: '*It signifies not to the public to whom the culpability of failure in military matters is attachable; the Commander, at all times, falls under censure . . . . The agony of mind I suffer, from the present disgraceful and unfortunate conduct of the troops committed to my superintendance, wounds me to the soul.'* De Watteville's regiment he particularly blamed for Britain's humiliation at Fort Erie, and never once in his later letters would he accept that his own lack of insight might have been at fault. Since the Battle of Chippawa, the British and Canadian forces had lost 2300 men—but, for this, Drummond declined to accept full blame.

Yet he would hold tenaciously to the quarry, like a dog to a rat. The siege continued, and the cannonade began anew. He tried not to be demoralised by reports that fresh militia units were forming on the other side of the river. But he could not ignore the rain, the mud and the poor humour of his troops, who sat and slept in makeshift huts and succumbed to the typhoid which swept through the camp. Provisions were again in short supply, and men questioned afresh the sanity of continuing a war which had no purpose and which was proving to be far from glorious. Soon, only his personal bombast and wish to salvage a deteriorating reputation kept him and his men in front of the well-built fort.

Gaines, the American hero of the hour, would, nevertheless, not remain at his post for very much longer. On 29th August a British shell dropped through the roof of the fort, demolished the desk at which he sat and wounded him so badly that he had to be evacuated to Buffalo. A few days later the tried and tested Jacob Brown, largely recovered from his wounds, returned to Fort Erie and assumed the mantle of responsibility for Fort Erie's preservation. Morale was falling faster than the season's leaves, and most of the senior officers were now advocating evacuation of the fort. What, they argued, was the purpose of maintaining just 15 acres of enemy soil? Beyond, in woods less than half a mile away, Drummond's army lingered, threatened and was, for all they knew, becoming stronger by the day.

Drummond's army, in fact, was now far weaker. The 6th and 82nd Foot were brought in to replace the battle shattered 41st and 103rd, but his requests for the services of the 9th Foot, stationed at Kingston, seemed to be falling on deaf ears. Yeo eventually consented to ferry the regiment in his brand new ship, the 'St. Lawrence', but, afraid of overloading the vessel, he took only a small number of men on board—the rest were forced to follow a land route that took them through mud, streams and the still heavy summer rains.

America snatched the initiative during Britain's period of hesitation. Two thousand freshly raised militia under Porter's command joined Brown in Fort Erie in the first week of September, a force large enough to enable the general to confidently suggest an attack on the British lines. The plan he outlined was daring, but was dependent on harmony of minds and complete co-operation. Ripley, of course, objected. But his was to be a voice in the wind—for the majority of the council now supported Brown's proposals. Porter was appointed to lead a column of 1200 men from Snake Hill around the right flank of the British and fall on the three batteries situated at that point. Simultaneously, Miller, now commanding the 1st brigade in place of the still incapacitated Scott, was to move through a ravine near the shoreline and attack the same enemy batteries.

The attack, executed in heavy rain on the afternoon of 17th September, was a success beyond the most optimistic of Brown's dreams. Porter and Miller, operating in tandem, worked their way through woodland to a position close to the batteries. Crashing through the skin of pickets, the Americans spiked two of the batteries, blew up the ammunition magazines and only narrowly failed to neutralise the third set of guns. Drummond's men, however, rallied and were soon fighting back in a battle that was no less intense than any of the earlier fighting within the fort. The Americans were forced to draw back, losing 511 men on the way, more than they had lost during the defence of the fort. Drummond lost 565 men, an enormous casualty rate for an action which had started as a sortie and could hardly merit the description of a battle.

But, in its consequences, the day's event was more momentous than either Chippewa or Lundy's Lane. A failure to contain the Americans, let alone take the fort, persuaded Drummond that any further demonstrations against Fort Erie would be pointless. On 21st September, despite the arrival of the 97th Foot, Drummond began his withdrawal to Chippawa Creek. '*The sickness of the troops has increased to such an alarming degree, and their situation has really become one of such extreme wretchedness from the torrents of the rain . . . . that I feel it to be my duty no longer to persevere in a vain attempt to maintain a blockade of so vastly a superior and increasing force of the enemy,*' he wrote to Prevost, making no attempt to conceal his despondency from the man who would be sitting in judgement. Neither he, nor Brown, would be prepared to admit publicly that the war on this frontier had reached a stalemate. Both forces were like equally matched wrestlers, who, having sparred in the ring through several rounds, had reached the point of mutual exhaustion. Porter, who had been allowed to do so little in the earlier battles on this frontier, could now feel that he and his militia forces had at last been permitted to show their true abilities.

The war on this front, left in the hands of jaded men who saw no prospect of victory, might now have stagnated and crumbled into dust. A new man, however, stepped into the Niagara arena, and, for a while at least, he seemed likely to stir up these dusts of despair. Appointed as commander of the Northern Army in Brown's place, Major-General George Izard arrived at Batavia, New York, on 28th September with 4000 fresh troops, anxious to prove that some fires of generalship still burned in the belly of one of America's most senior generals. Responsible for the defence of Lake Champlain since April, he had been hastily instructed to involve himself in the war effort on the Niagara, an area where Armstrong still felt the war would most likely be won.

For two or three weeks, boots began tramping again on Canada's by ways. Determined to win the sort of acclaim that none of his predecessors had ever achieved, he crossed the river on 10th October at Black Rock and set out to confront the British on any battlefield that Drummond might care to choose. The British general, still despondent and numerically far inferior, pleaded again to Prevost and Yeo to assist him in this fresh locking of horns. Neither man, however, seems to have responded. Prevost had the whole frontier to consider. Yeo, still anxious to protect the sails and planks of his newest warship, remained inactive at Kingston. Izard, America's new broom, could undoubtedly have swept a path through Canada towards York or Kingston if he had felt inclined.

Britain and America clashed again briefly on 19th October. General Izard, sensing a sudden opportunity to seize the Chippewa crossings and deprive the British of essential resources, sent 1200 men under Brigadier-General Daniel Bissell to seize the supply depot at Cook's Mills on Lyon's Creek. Drummond, informed of the threat, despatched Lieutenant-Colonel Christopher Myers, his most reliable officer, to shadow the American force and engage it if conditions seemed to be favourable. A miniature battle unfolded when Myers and his men almost stumbled over the enemy picket established in woodland just to the east of the mill. Withering under the fire of an almost invisible enemy using the trees for cover and then outflanked by American soldiers on his right, Myers, probably sensibly, withdrew. The mill and its contents, mainly grain, was destroyed. Izard claimed later that he had won a significant victory.

One company of the 1st U.S. Rifle Regiment plus 5th, 14th, 15th and 16th U.S. Infantry regiments

Bissell's Brigade at the Battle of Cook's Mill

But, by early November, Izard, the enthusiast, had become Izard, the downhearted. He had naively counted on the support of Chauncey, the man who had failed to assist his army predecessors. '*This defeats all the objects of the operations by land in this quarter,*' he destructively wrote to Armstrong. '. . . . . *if he (*the enemy*) falls back on Fort George or Burlington Heights, every step I take in pursuit exposes me to be cut off by the large reinforcements it is in the power of the enemy to throw in twenty-four hours upon my flank or rear.*' Perceptions, not weapons, had defeated both sides equally.

So, too, had the autumn weather. The rain had not stopped and the sun had seldom shone.

The roads, over which men, wagons and provisions were expected to move, had disappeared. Dysentery had brought men down still lower, removing the last strands of stamina and hope, and even Drummond was now pleading to be sent home.

The last act in this horrible drama was played on 5th November 1814. Izard, having done little after destroying the wheat stored at Cook's Mill, had fallen back to Fort Erie, and here voiced an opinion with which every American officer probably concurred. '*It commands nothing, not even the entrance of the strait.*' On that day, the garrison blew up the fort and abandoned it. American lives had been sacrificed in the effort to hold the fort, almost as if America's national identity and the lives of future generations depended upon it. Now it had become evident that dying in the defence of Fort Erie had served no purpose at all.

CHAPTER 13

'It is unfortunate to scar a landscape and consign it to hell,'

'A*ny invasion of the metropolis should be met with vigor and successfully repelled,'* a resolution put before Congress on 15th July 1813 had maintained. The alarmism that had generated the summer debate had been realistic. Cockburn's British fleet still found Chesapeake Bay attractive, largely because it enabled His Majesty's ships to penetrate deep into the United States, something that the King's armies had been completely unable to do. Strategists and diplomats in Washington, trying to interpret British reasoning, considered that it would be only a matter of time before Britain tried to take Washington and reduce this shiny new capital to ashes.

Hence the long, interminable debates that took place during one of the hottest summers of the century. Resolution after resolution tumbled from the members in session, all of them aimed at making the city safer from invasion. '*Resolved: That in the opinion of the House, a distribution of such arms as are in the possession of the government within the District of Columbia should be immediately made to be placed in the hands of all able-bodied men within the district willing to be embodied to perform military duty . . .,'* one of the typical defensive measures read. The Committee of Military Affairs, however, saw few causes for real concern. '*The Committee . . . . are satisfied that the preparations are, in every respect, adequate to the emergency, and that no measures are necessary on the part of the House to make it more complete,'* a report declared. They chose to place their confidence in one man. When the British fleet explored the Potomac in the summer of 1813, Captain

Joshua Barney had just put on a commodore's uniform and had taken on responsibility for supervising the building of a new defensive flotilla of brigs, sloops and gunboats.

Barney devoted himself to the task with passion. By April 1814 he was in command of 26 gunboats and was soon playing a game with the British. However, in every engagement, he was outclassed and soon his little flotilla was bottled up in Leonard's Creek. A forceful action on 26th June managed to liberate the boats, but, even then, the strong British presence in the Potomac and Chesapeake made it impossible for Barney's ships to venture outside the Patuxent.

America's Congressmen had been entirely correct in their assessments of Britain's intentions. The British had long viewed the city of Washington as a glittering target. But, until the fall of Paris in March 1814, the nation had too few resources to effect such an aim. Revenge partly motivated the decision to launch an attack. Prevost and the Canadians felt that the damage done to York, Queenston and St. David's by the American invading force would justify a retaliatory destruction of their enemy's administrative capital.

Another general now landed on America's shores. Major-General Robert Ross, an Irishman who had dome so much to distinguish himself under Wellington in the Peninsular War, was given command of a new force of veteran regiments, about 3000 men, that sailed from Europe on 27th June. His task was officially to create a diversion and relieve pressure on the Canadian frontier. The Ministers in London reminded him that his force was neither an army of permanent occupation, nor an invading army stabbing at America's heart. In fact, the exact target was to be determined by Admiral Alexander Cochrane, the man still in charge of Britain's American fleet. The army was to be subordinated to the navy and was to be used purely to assist the fleet.

President Madison, getting wind of the departure of this force from France, called a Cabinet meeting on 1st July to discuss the threat. Armstrong, brusque and ill-tempered as usual, remained convinced that the British had no designs on Washington. For that reason, he had not stationed a single regular anywhere in the city. The President, fortunately, felt quite differently and began the task of requisitioning the 15,000 troops that it was estimated would be needed for the defence of the nation's capital. The following day the Tenth Military District was created and Brigadier-General William Winder of Maryland was given the command. He had been taken captive by the British at Beaver Dams, but had been released in order to negotiate an exchange of prisoners. The task now was to find him soldiers to command, and, for this, the President took personal responsibility. Each neighbouring state was ordered to provide a quota. State jealousies and constitutional obstacles, however, made it unlikely that all the required 15,000 would be obtained. A sense of nationhood had still not fully emerged.

Robert Ross and his troopships anchored off Bermuda on 24th July. Here the major-general organised his army into three brigades led by Colonels William Thornton, Arthur Brooke and Charles Malcolm. He then conferred with Admiral Cochrane. On 18th August the troopships and fleet of invasion were spotted approaching the Patuxent River, and the news rocked the nerves of everyone in the District of Columbia.

The capital's mechanism of defence had not yet been constructed, despite Winder's strenuous efforts. He had selected Bladensburg, north of Washington, as the assembly point for the militia units requisitioned from the adjacent states. Less than 6000 had assembled by the end of July, but almost no supplies had been collected. '*It will be necessary that arms, ammuntion, accoutrements, tents and camp equipage be deposited . . . I have no knowledge where these articles are in store . . . nor under whose charge they are,*' he wrote in frustration to Armstrong.

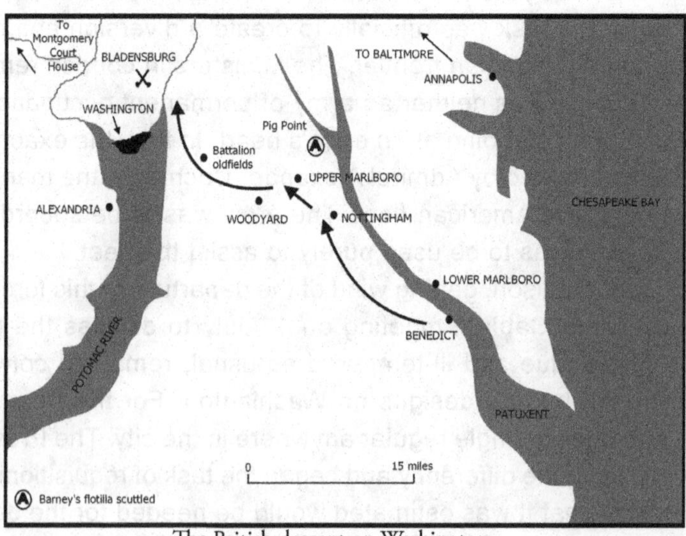

The British descent on Washington

No defence works were evident by that date—nor a single tree had been felled, nor a breastwork raised—and, for this, Armstrong was again responsible. Even when English sails were being counted in the Patuxent, the Secretary was repeating his long-held view that Washington was not the target. *'Baltimore is the place, Sir; that is of so much more consequence,'* he told the President and the senior officers of the District of Columbia militia.

Cockburn and Ross had been a lot more decisive and energetic than their enemy. They had settled on little Benedict on the shores of the Patuxent, only 45 miles from Washington, as the point at which they would come ashore. The area could furnish all that was needed: a quiet anchorage, food and horses.

The landing operation, which started on Friday, 19th August, was performed without difficulty. By Saturday afternoon, more than 4000 men, each supplied with 3 pounds of pork and 7 1/2 of bread—enough to last for three days, had splashed ashore and formed into line of battle. Beyond, Benedict and the neighbouring settlements had all been deserted, the inhabitants scuttling to find refuge in Washington. They left behind a peaceful scene: whitewashed farmsteads with neat fences, crop-filled fields and orchards where apples were beginning to swell. It was almost idyllic; one officer remarked, *'it is unfortunate to scar a landscape and consign it to hell.'* But horses there were none—and all but the most senior officers would have to proceed by foot.

At dawn on the 21st the advance on Washington began with textbook precision. A flotilla of small boats followed up river, giving protection to the right flank. Ahead, beside and behind were advance guards, flanker units and a rearguard, and every unit remained in visible contact. Two men, armed with muskets, were captured. They denied being American soldiers and claimed to be hunting rabbits, but had considerable difficulty in explaining why they had bayonets fixed to their guns. The army billeted that night at Nottingham. The officers occupied the empty houses of the village and drank on the verandahs until late at night. The lower ranks slept in fields, gardens and orchards, enjoying the touch of the cool night after the intense heat of the previous day. The following morning, which was even hotter, the army advanced through Upper Marlboro. The sun was merciless, more so than the enemy could ever be. The soldiers, attired in woolen uniforms and weighed down by knapsacks, weapons and blankets, found the march worse than anything that they had experienced on their way through Spain.

That night the troops were awakened from their light sleep by the sound of distant explosions. Commodore Barney was blowing up his boats, anxious to prevent them falling into the hands of the invaders. The expeditionary force, without firing a shot or making contact with the enemy, had achieved its first objective: the destruction of the defenders' boats.

Every movement, pause and hesitation made by the British was now being watched and monitored from a distance. 300 American regulars and a large accompanying force of militia and volunteers, probably nearly 2000 men in total, had assembled at a place called the Wood Yard, just to the east of the Potomac. Here, on the 21st, General Winder had taken formal command and from here he made fresh appeals to the citizens of Baltimore and Pennsylvania to join him in the defence of the Federal capital. Although Britain's activities were being meticulously observed, the number of troops following Ross was never accurately counted and was estimated at more than 10,000. Moreover, these sweating men in red were known to be the veterans of the pitched battles of the war in Spain, drilled to perfection by the great duke and used to the hardships of prolonged campaigns.

Winder was having difficulty in divining British intentions. He, like the forever confused Secretary of War, still considered that Annapolis or Baltimore was the object at which Britain gazed. A concentration of troops to the north of the city, however, would expose Fort Washington, on the east bank of the Anacostia, to attack. Unable to anticipate the enemy's likely route of advance, he felt that he might be obliged at some point to divide his forces.

When Ross reached Upper Marlboro, Winder fell back from the Wood Yard to Battalion Old Fields, where the road to Bladensburg and the route to the Anacostia River met. Diminutive President Madison, wearing a cockade hat, which made him look slightly taller, came out from Washington to review the troops. Commodore Barney arrived as well. With him were the guns rescued from the scuttled flotilla. His sailors had dragged the weapons all the way from the ships' resting place on the Patuxent and were the first of the men present that day to be commended by the President. A little while later, just after Madison had returned to Washington, General Winder received a particularly alarming report that Ross had left Upper Marlboro and was advancing towards the American position at Old Fields by way of the Wood Yard, the American rendezvous of only two days previously. He personally watched the British that afternoon, the 23rd, in a column just a mile to the east. Fearful of the consequences of a premature battle, he turned his back on the enemy and retreated across the Anacostia.

It was Winder's turn to visit the President. That evening he consulted James Madison and openly admitted that he had no strategy for dealing with the British. Convinced at last that Ross was intending to force the Anacostia bridges and attack Washington from the east, Winder set out to the river to personally make arrangements for the destruction of the river's two bridges On the way back to his command post, he fell into a deep muddy ditch and injured his arm. At 8 a.m. the nest morning, the 24th, an American navy detachment blew up the bridges and so denied the British army a direct approach from the east.

The enemy commanders, Ross and Cockburn, had also been active that night. At 2 a.m. on the 24th, a messenger arrived at Ross's overnight residence with instructions from Admiral Cochrane to abandon the advance and return to the ships. The two men, who had ridden side by side throughout the advance from Benedict, conferred alone in the garden of the house. Staff, looking through the windows, could see the pair, outlined by pre-dawn light, pacing and probably arguing. Then, at 6 a.m., the two announced their joint decision to ignore the craven orders of their superior and proceed as planned. The army set out soon afterwards. In the early afternoon, when the redcoats reached the Old Fields Crossroads, Ross and Cockburn turned north-west into the road that led to Bladensburg. They had decided to approach Washington from the north instead of the direct approach from the east. America's hasty destruction of the bridges had been unnecessary.

The American general was informed of Ross's change of direction almost immediately. Fortunately, two strong Baltimore militia regiments, under the command of a Brigadier-General Tobias Stansbury, had set up camp at Lowndes Hill, east of Bladensburg, and should be in a position to challenge the British advance. Stansbury, however, was reluctant to risk his 2000 men in a conflict with a numerically superior and battle-hardened enemy and he began to withdraw towards Washington. Orders from Winder and the President fortunately stopped his movement and he returned to Bladensburg and prepared to receive the invaders at this,

his chosen point of defence. Here he was to be joined by Winder's men and other locally recruited units.

The village of Bladensburg lay on the east bank of the Anacostia, close to the bridge over which the Baltimore to Washington highway crossed. America's positions had been randomly chosen. Within a fork formed by this road were stationed two companies of artillery from Baltimore and 6 pounder guns within a barbette of no great strength. Positioned as they were within the angle of the roadway, the guns would only be able to shoot obliquely across the bridge instead of being able to command its length. About 160 riflemen were stationed to the left of the cannon. Behind, in an orchard, stood the militia regiments of Lieutenant-Colonels Ragan and Schutz. These had been joined the previous afternoon by the Fifth Maryland volunteers under the command of Colonel Joseph Sterrett. The unit, nearly 1000 strong, had been recruited from amongst the higher levels of Baltimore society, and the men were now present, dressed in blue jackets, white trousers and helmets with red and black plumes. Even further back, forming a second line, were Colonel Beall's Marylanders and Barney's sailors, next to the guns that they had so strenuously dragged across land. A deep ravine lay between the two defending lines, giving some protection to the right of Winder's line. In total, America had more than 6000 men in position; at least half the men had arrived in the last few hours.

The politician James Monroe, eager to be involved, had also just arrived. Feeling that he had the qualities of a general, he rearranged the troops, moving Ragan, Schutz and the Fifth Maryland back for nearly quarter of a mile and away from the cover of the orchard. Five hundred yards from the bridge, these men would now be far too distant to give any support to the companies of riflemen stationed near the bridge. Just as the British dust clouds became visible in the east, the Washington District Militia led by General Walter Smith arrived and took up position next to Barney and his marines. The United States had effectively formed three lines, but none was in a position to support the others. In fact, the men at the bridge were unaware that there were any units lying behind them in support.

President Madison had ridden in behind the last of the reinforcements. Armed with dueling pistols [20] and still wearing his cockaded hat, he

20 During the battle, his pistols were stolen

was trying to adopt, like Monroe, an air of martial superiority at a time when America's reputation lay in the hands of military men.

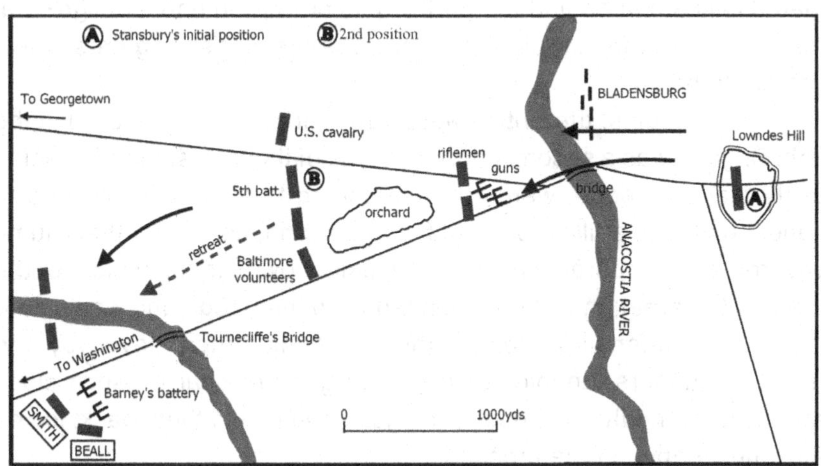

The Battle of Bladensburg

Personal anecdotes decorate the accounts of the day. One of the dandies of the Fifth Maryland, John Pendleton Kennedy, had brought his cook and a wagon of food with him, intending to have a banquet al fresco before the fighting started. That night, in the orchard at Bladensburg, he and his friends dined on ham, chicken and vegetables and drank imported wine. He had also packed a pair of dancing shoes, strangely supposing that military campaigns are always followed by celebratory balls. Aroused before daylight by reports that the British were coming and unable to find his boots in the confusion, he slipped on his patent leather pumps and fought the next day in his dance floor footwear. Another of the Marylanders, leaving his camp to steal eggs from a farm, was trapped in a hole for two days and so missed the coming battle.

At noon on that eventful day, Colonel William Thornton's British brigade advanced on Bladensburg Bridge. The raw, untrained watchers on the far side observed the regular step of redcoats in column, heard the resonating drums and saw the occasional flash of bayonet steel and the impact was unnerving. They, the British, came on six abreast, the Light Brigade leading in the approach to the bridge. America reacted quickly. Her 6 pounders suddenly opened and tore down the leading redcoats. Another round of fire from the artillery forced the brigade to halt and then fall back. The British took refuge in the village and within a thick growth of willows that grew along the banks. The shabby coated militiamen behind the earthworks crowed in naïve delight. But they were unaware of just how tenacious the British regulars would turn out to be.

Within minutes, the British were advancing once more. Behind the Light Brigade was a second brigade. Some of these, instead of heading for the narrow bridge, went north, intending to force the stream at a higher point. The artillery opened fire again, and, as before, the column wavered and temporarily halted. This time, however, the weight of the tide was too great; men were soon crossing the bridge and wading the stream. The defending riflemen, their left flank turned, gave way and fled. The gunners, unable to bring their guns to bear on such close targets, unhurriedly disengaged the guns and pulled them back, losing only one weapon in the process.

The redcoated flood moved in, sweeping around the left flank of the second American line, formed of the 5th Maryland and the regiments of Stansbury's command At almost the same instant as the British breakthrough began, Ross laid down a barrage of Congreve rockets. Possessing a range of about two miles and accompanied by a roar, these missiles caused fear, mayhem and destruction to the commands of Schutz, Ragan and Sterett exposed in the open after Monroe's injudicious repositioning. The regiments of the first two men gave way quickly, diseased by the noise and sight of the missiles, and unnerved by the proximity of the British to their left. Winder sent an order to Sherett and his dandies to hold at all costs. For a while, the human peacocks did as they were instructed, standing as firmly as regulars and firing just as solidly. But, injected by the fear that had now become fashionable, they, too, speedily left the field.

4th, (King's Own), 21st, (Royal North British Fusiliers) 44th, (Essex),85th, (Bucks Volunteers)

Regular regiments involved at Bladensburg and the advance on Washington

All now would depend upon the fighting tenacity of Barney's sailors and the Washington District Militia of America's third line. Unruffled, the commodore ordered his sea guns to open fire—and the British, at last, were forced to take cover. Spirited by this, the militia on Barney's flanks joined in, pouring down the only effective musket fire of the day. For a brief moment, hopes were rekindled—and the victory dance which young Kennedy expected might still take place. Winder, however, poisoned these hopes. For no explicable reason, he ordered these exuberant militia units to retire, despite the fact that they were holding so manfully. Barney's sailors and gunners, however, either did not hear his order or chose to ignore it. Veterans of several sea fights and consequently accustomed to the horrific noise of battle, they felt no wish to disperse.

And so the fight continued: 500 sailors confronted by 3000 regulars who, steeled by their battle experience in fighting against the armies of the French, were now pressing on again and moving towards Barney's flanks and rear. The commodore fell badly wounded in the moments following, his fall heralding the end of resistance. Winder, seeing the evaporation of his third and final line, ordered his tiny cavalry unit to charge. The inexperience horsemen blinked in disbelief and terror: they were being asked to sacrifice themselves in a charge against arguably the world's best soldiers—and not one remained on the field to obey.

By 4 p.m., another battlefield lay silent. The casualty rate had not been high, and the British, with 64 dead and 185 wounded, suffered more than the defenders, whose total casualties only just topped 70. Oliver Creed, a soldier of the 44th Foot, was one of the wounded. He lay unattended on the field and only remembered shadows moving around him in the darkness. He was awakened in the morning by sunlight on his face and discovered that he was sharing a bedroom with a girl. Her parents, who could never be accused of loyalty to King George, had carried him from the field. Oliver married the pretty 18 year old when the war ended.

The battle later earned the apt description of 'Bladensburg Races' and won immortality in hackneyed verse because of the speed at which American forces fled the field. Aspiring or failed generals re-fought the battle several times after the day and most concluded that America might have fared a little better if Winder had kept his three lines in closer contact and if Monroe had not interfered. A British subaltern, used to the ordered battlefield precision of the French, had dismissed the disordered and non-uniformed groups of opponents as '*country people, who would have been much more appropriately employed in attending to their agricultural occupations than in standing with muskets in their hands on the brow of a bare green hill.'* Yet not all had fought like pitchfork yokels, and some of the British confessed to being impressed. The wounded Barney was regarded as being particularly worthy. Captured with most of his men, he was courteously treated by Ross and provided with the services of a British surgeon.

Yet the route to Washington, despite his efforts, lay open. Winder managed to maintain some order amongst his fleeing troops and still hoped to make another stand. Stansbury's regiments, however, had been driven from the field in the direction of Georgetown, not Washington, and the two halves of the defending army had been forced apart. Winder, Monroe and Armstrong hurriedly met. Accepting that it would be impossible to protect Washington, the two politicians permitted Winder to withdraw his forces and reassemble at Montgomery Court House.

Two hours after the battle's conclusion, the British began the 7 mile march to the capital. News of defeat, of course, preceded them, giving time for politicians and administrators to leave. The inhabitants had listened to the sound of the distant guns, trying to interpret the significance of every pause. Then the first of Winder's distressed soldiers had arrived, and the awful truth was broadcast. Papers, documents and valuables were hurriedly packed. Dolly Madison, the nation's first lady, was one of the few eminent persons who did not leave the city immediately. Anxious to prevent valuable family possessions and Gilbert Stuart's full-length portrait of George Washington from falling into the hands of the British, she calmly packed the valued items in trunks, assisted by just one servant, the faithful John Siousa, who refused to leave her side. Together they cut the canvas from its frame, while the horses of her carriage stamped impatiently on the drive outside. Just as the first British soldier set foot in the city, Dolly climbed into her carriage and set out to find temporary refuge in the green hills of Virginia. Ross and Cockburn, on white horses, rode with the vanguard into the town and searched vainly for anyone in authority with whom they might treat for the surrender of the town. In those early minutes in Washington, with the sun low on the horizon, a shot rang out. General Ross's horse dropped dead with a bullet through its side.

Perhaps it was this single action that prompted Ross to wreak vengeance on the town. Cockburn is reputed to have entered the Capitol at the head of troops. Standing on the House Speaker's chair, he asked, '*Shall this harbor of Yankee democracy be burned?'* All of the public buildings were set on fire: arsenal, Capitol, Treasury and War Office. The mahogany furniture and pine paneling of the House of Representatives burned particularly well, creating a heat so intense that the glass of the dome above began to melt. Outlined by the dark, the flames were as hideous as hell itself. The British soldiers, feeding the flames, seemed like the Devil's servants and their faces appeared hideous in the flickering light. A Treasury report survived the flames. An inscription on the flyleaf states that Cockburn gave it to his brother. It was returned to the Library of Congress in 1940. The White House followed next. But not before the victors had eaten the meal prepared for the President and 40 guests. Cockburn, sitting in the President's chair, raised his glass and drank a toast to 'Jemmy', the name which he had given to Madison. Commodore Thomas Tingey, commandant of the Navy Yard, expecting the same fate to be meted out to his charge, ignited the place himself, destroying warehouses, provision sheds and a new ship of the line that rode at anchor there. To complete the scene of destruction, the bridge over the Potomac between the city and the Virginian shoreline was now burning. The British, afraid that American forces would approach from that direction, set fire to the Washington end, while the Americans, in an attempt to halt the British, set it alight at the opposite end!

Washington in flames! Reports of the conflagration set fire to American public opinion. The media in Baltimore, Charleston and New York denounced the act as bestial, sub-human and something that even Napoleon would never have considered. It was also suggested that a dinner given in Vienna by the Duke of Wellington should be boycotted by the Foreign Ministers of the victorious allies in protest at the action. And even in Britain newspapers excoriated the action as '*more suitable to the times of barbarism.'* The same newspaper, the 'Annual Register', continued to denounce what had happened: *'If there is such as thing as humanized war, its principle must consist in inflicting no other evils upon the enemy than are necessary to promote the success of warlike operations.'* The London Statesman, in similar vein, pointed out that, *'The Cossack spared Paris, but we spared not the capital of America.'* There is no record of Ross or Cockburn ever offering an apology to the American people.

American born critics blamed Winder, his Bladenburg soldiers and even the President for the flames and the humiliation! But very few of the defending troops had stayed to test the sharpness of British bayonets. Madison, on horseback for most of that day, had ridden for sanctuary into Virginia. At a wayside inn on the night of the 25th, he was re-united with his wife. Not all were as pleased to see him as she was. On the way, people had cursed and sworn at him, holding him personally responsible for the black disaster that had befallen the American people. The British regarded the 25th as a day of celebration. While Washington's buildings burned, Cockburn rode around the town on his white mare with the mare's young foal trotting at her side. The depredations committed by his troops on that day of unbridled licence are not recorded, but the shame inflicted on the British nation can never be expunged by the passing of time.

A violent thunderstorm extinguished the city's fires on the afternoon of the 25th, blew down the tents of the British and killed 30 of the king's soldiers. Washington's citizens were curfewed in the evening, and therefore failed to see the disappearance of the enemy's forces. When the timid inhabitants looked out next morning, they found the invaders had gone. Cockburn and Ross, in deference to their orders from London, had packed their bags and carts and taken their soldiers away. On the night of the 26th, the entire force bivouacked at Upper Marlboro and then re-embarked on their vessels on the 30th at Benedict. During the four days taken to withdraw, no-one living in the area caught even a glimpse of a departing redcoat! Madison returned to his capital on the evening of the 27th, but the tangible structures of the Republic had ceased to exist. Prevost, in distant Canada, receiving the news a few days earlier, called the destruction of Washington *'a just retribution, the proud capital at Washington has experienced a similar fate to that inflicted by an American force on the seat of government in Upper Canada.'*

And even now Britain was still involved in acts of destruction. While the troops burned Washington, her navy's ships were wreaking havoc in the Potomac. A flotilla, consisting of two frigates, a schooner and four supporting ships, had warped [21] its way as far as Maryland Point, 40 miles below the city by the 24th, and, from here, the sailors watched the golden flames in the sky to the north. The violent thunderstorm on the next day damaged rigging and spars, and it was not until the 27th

21 Hauled by a rope attached to an object on shore

that Captain James Gordon, in command of the flotilla, felt ready to deal with Fort Washington, the main target for his expedition.

The fort's commander, with only 80 men to hold its walls, had witnessed the destruction of the city and consequently saw little point in resisting. He quietly evacuated the place in the evening. Either the Americans or the British then blew it up. Reports violently disagree on who might have been responsible. Gordon, regarding himself as Britain's hero of the moment, threatened Alexandria the next day. In return for 16,000 barrels of flour and large quantities of wine, cotton, tobacco and navy stores, he agreed to spare the town.

Gordon's return downstream was a little more hazardous than his journey up river. A hastily erected naval battery of 13 guns set up at White House, near Mount Vernon, and at Indian Head on the Maryland shore opened fire on the King's vessels. The ships, laden with the spoils of war, were too low in the water to shoot back, and some time was spent in shifting the ballast to raise the gundecks high enough to respond. The Americans, their guns now in danger, moved the battery away from the shoreline and poured out grapeshot. Gordon, unable to reach the teasing guns, sent a party of marines ashore to seek out and destroy them. Militia and marines engaged in an hour's combat, and the guns were eventually taken. Three fire ships, sent into the flotilla later during the journey downstream, did no damage at all, and on the 6th September the warships reached Chesapeake Bay and rejoined the fleet.

Other naval detachments were simultaneously causing mischief elsewhere. One of His Majesty's ships sailed to the very head of Chesapeake Bay to spy on the defences of Annapolis and Baltimore. British marines landed near Chestertown and, on 30th August, found themselves confronted by local militiamen. In this battle by moonlight, grandly referred to as the Battle of Caulk's Field, the British suffered most—and only 60 or so of the 124 men who had gone ashore returned to the ship.

Only one political head fell in the days following the sack of Washington. Secretary Armstrong, in the aftermath of Bladensburg, had openly blamed the militia. '*. . . . the determining cause of the failure is to be found in that love of life which . . . . predominated over love of country and of honor,*' he is quoted as saying. But his poor handling of the preparations for the defence of Washington and his ostrich mentality had caused the execution axes to be sharpened. Days later, he resigned, and was succeeded by James Monroe, who combined the two departments of State and War.

Britain's desire for blood and punishment had not been satisfied by destruction of the capital. The day after the army embarked at Benedict, Ross spoke of his wish to advance against unsubdued Baltimore. Ever since the fleet had started to prowl Chesapeake's waters a year earlier, the city had awaited attack. $26,000 had been voted for the reconstruction of fortifications and the militia had been drilled almost daily. On the day of the Battle of Bladensburg, a Committee of Vigilance and Safety had been set up. This decreed that every white male between the ages of sixteen and fifty should be drafted to defend the city. The command was given to Samuel Smith, a senior officer of Maryland's militia, member of the Senate and a critic of Madison's administration. From 27th August, when the British hound was known to be on the loose again, Baltimore's citizens dug furiously and ate rarely, constructing earthworks along the water approaches to the town. General Winder, one of the architects of failure at Washington, joined the defenders of Baltimore on 10th September, having managed to collect together a few of the braver members of his broken force at Montgomery Court House, now the tiny town of Rockville. He reluctantly agreed to serve under Smith and so avoided the sort of rivalry that had so often caused friction in the command in the crucial hours prior to a battle.

Baltimore, even then, sprawled along the banks of the Patapsco River, creating an extensive and vulnerable waterfront. Within the fork dividing this waterfront stood Fort McHenry. This was one of the nation's more formidable strongholds, sporting 32 pounders and ramparts of masonry. 1000 men, many regulars, lived within, all under the command of Lieutenant-Colonel George Armistead. Not wishing to rely entirely upon this fortress, the defending officers had arranged for a cable to be stretched from McHenry to Lazaretto Point, where an additional battery had been placed. Behind, in the northern arms, gunboats lay in readiness, providing the city four miles west with a feeling of some security. Other defence points also crowned the city's approaches: Fort Covington and the City Battery at Fort Babcock were manned by sailors, the latter by some of Barney's battle-battered seamen. Baltimore's limited land defences comprised a mile long earthwork on Hampstead

Hill (or Loudenslager's Hill). Several batteries and bastions lay along this line. Perhaps 10,000 defenders now stood ready.

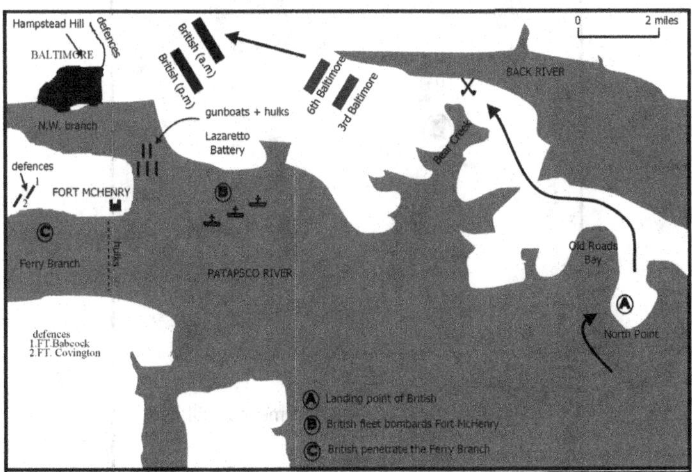

The defence of Baltimore

Britain would not disappoint them. On the evening of the 11th, the fleet was seen anchored at the end of the Patapsco. Church bells and dispatch riders carried the news back to the city's dignitaries and officers. Volunteers for the defence took leave of their sweethearts and proceeded to their sectors. Those less inclined to fight sought refuge to the west. The inns and taverns on the road out of the city were full that night with Baltimore's more affluent refugees. In the stables slept the family servants, responsible for guarding horses and coaches. The rich and poor of Baltimore were, for the first time, united in common concern. His Majesty's fleet provided an impressive but unwelcome sight. Looking at a distance like a flock of water birds with wings still outstretched, 50 ships had assembled, carrying 6000 soldiers, marines and an array of heavy guns. Baco Dredge, 74 years old and a veteran of the fighting at Guilford Court House, was waiting outside his house that night with his musket loaded. Clearly suffering from senile dementia, he later claimed that he was looking for the soldier who had killed his brother. Simon Parsons, another veteran of the earlier war, was holding a weapon reputed to have been used by his ancestor during the Thirty Years War, over 180 years previously.

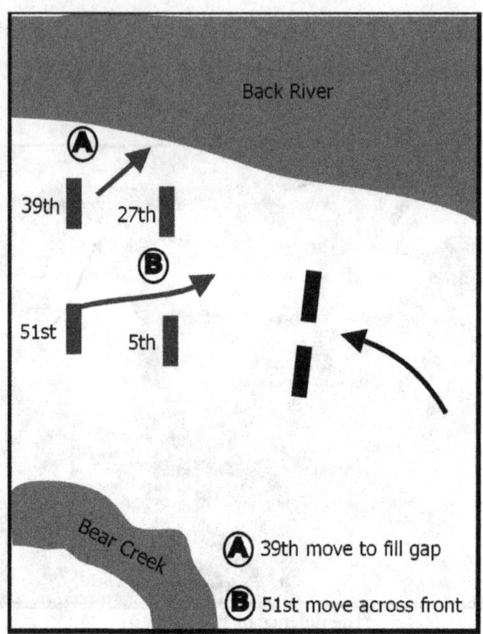

The Battle of Baltimore

That evening the ships anchored off North Point, Cochrane's chosen spot for disembarkation. Just 14 miles from Baltimore's streets, North Point was believed to afford an ideal site which would allow the fleet to protect the army's flank as it marched towards the city. Without their sails, the skeletal masts now looked more like the vessels of the dead than those of the living. Their presence inspired a sense of '. . . . *dread, an unreasonable fear that subsumed even the most doughty. I mean, who can believe that the sight of damp wood and creaking timbers could weigh down the soul, even the souls of the veterans of the revolution?'* Few of those who remained in Baltimore that night could have had much sleep. Dreams, pleasant or otherwise, were the privilege of the few.

Those who chose to watch might have noticed sudden activity in the early hours of the following morning. At 2 a.m. that day, the 12th, the first boats were lowered. At 3 a.m. these touched the beach at North Point. The numbers landing were impossible to count; American scouts, searching into the darkness, estimated these to be more than 7000. This was the figure they gave to General Samuel Smith, who had probably had no sleep for the last three days.

Despite his lack of rest, he responded with the alertness of a stag who had sensed the approach of hounds. He immediately ordered Brigadier-General John Stricker to advance with the Baltimore City Brigade, 3185 men, and take up a position on the narrow one mile wide peninsula between Bear Creek and the Back River, just 5 miles from Baltimore's outer defence lines on Hampstead Hill. His flanks consequently rested on the two streams. To protect his front, he hurriedly erected pilings and placed six 4 pounder guns astride the North Point road. The 5th Regiment of Baltimore Militia, with its right on Bear Creek, and the 27th, with its left touching a swamp beside the Back River, formed his front line. About 300 yards further back, the 39th and 51st Militia regiments were placed, the 51st on the right and the 39th immediately behind the 27th. The 6th, his only other regiment, was held back in reserve. Smith, in a final positioning of troops, then sent 150 riflemen well forward of the line in an effort to locate the enemy. Sensing a sudden presence on Long Log Lane, this 'Forlorn Hope' quickly retired with their ammunition unused and joined the 5th behind the pilings.

Britain was now advancing in ceremonial style in a column of three brigades from the beachhead at North Point. At about midday the redcoats halted at Gorsuch's farm, about half-way between the beach and the city, and stretched out on the grass for a rest. Stricker, awarded with a brief and golden opportunity, immediately sent a detachment down the road with the intention of spoiling the calm. The British, abandoning their meals and their rest, snatched up their weapons and engaged the 200 or so Americans in a skirmish that lasted for only a few minutes. Indecisive though it turned out to be, the fighting claimed the life of General Ross. When he heard the firing, the Irishman rode off to a small hill to assess the enemy's strength. Concealed in a hollow near his feet were two young lads, Daniel Wells and Henry McComas, both from Baltimore. Hardly believing their luck, they took careful aim and one of them lodged a bullet in the general's chest. The officer, mortally wounded, lay unnoticed until one of his infantrymen eventually found the almost lifeless body. He died minutes later in the arms of one of his aides.

Far more intense fighting soon followed. Colonel Arthur Brooke, taking over the command from Ross, did not wish to be labeled as a general who failed. He immediately sent his columns forward against the main American lines. Reports differ about the timing of the main engagement, but it is clear that, by 3 p.m., the two armies were facing each other across the narrow strip of land between the two streams. The engagement started with an intense artillery bombardment and a barrage of Congreve rockets fired from the British positions. The guns of the United States opened in response, and soon the field was smothered in the battle's preliminary smoke. Until this cleared, the commanders of both sides were blind to the battlefield's opportunities and advantages.

Stricker was relieved to discover that both his forward regiments were still in place when the smoke dispersed. Brooke, surveying the field at the same crucial moment, noticed that the line of the American 27th regiment did not extend all the way to the swampland on their left. A British unit moving through the gap, he surmised, could comfortably turn the regiment's left flank, and Brooke needed only to find men to accomplish this task. Stricker, a man with a similar strategic vision, fortunately saw the danger and immediately moved up the 39th to fill the gap. To strengthen the position still further, he instructed the 51st to advance across the front and take up a position at right angles to the 39th.

The completely inexperienced regiment began the complex manoeuvre. Brooke was watching their clumsy move. He promptly ordered an intense bombardment of the area through which the Americans would have to pass. Exposed to unbearable rocket and artillery fire and terrified by the noise as much as by the missiles, the men of the 51st, their nerves torn to shreds, broke and fled. Their fear was infectious and spread to the 39th, many of whom dropped their arms and followed the 51st from the field. The American left flank had been fragmented beyond repair, making it impossible for Stricker's remaining units to remain. The 5th and the 27th retired in some order and briefly took up a position 300 yards further back.

But this position was just as untenable. Soon all four regiments, or what remained of them, had taken refuge behind Baltimore's defences. The entire battle had lasted only 55 minutes, and it was barely 4 p.m. Very few muskets had been fired; the killing and the injection of fear had been almost entirely the result of artillery and rocket fire. The Americans had lost 35 killed and perhaps 115 wounded or missing. The British had, rather surprisingly, lost about twice that number.

Brooke, by nature a more cautious man than his predecessor, felt unwilling to test the Baltimore works that day. His army bivouacked on the field of battle and so lost the opportunity to profit from the fluidity of America's confusion. His caution, perhaps, was justified; unlike the situation outside Washington, where no defensive works had existed, Baltimore had its lines of defence. Moreover, its protective force, although demoralized, had not been broken. Further fighting would be inevitable.

Breaking Baltimore's will to resist would require destruction of Fort McHenry. This was clearly a task for Admiral Cochrane and his gunners. But the waters near the fort were far too shallow for his heavier vessels to approach and, consequently, it was felt that the task of silencing the fort should be given to the five shallow bomb vessels. At dawn on the 13th, the five took up positions about two miles from the fort and delivered their bombardment at long range. Major George Armistead responded with every one of the guns mounted in the fort and the nearby Lazaretto battery. But none of his guns had a range which could reach the British and every shot fell harmlessly in Patapsco's waters. The major sensibly discontinued firing, and the bombardment became purely one-sided.

And so it continued for most of the morning and early afternoon. Men of the garrison, unsure of the wisdom of resisting such firepower, crouched in anticipation of death, injury or the consequences of defeat. Britain's bombs, however, did comparatively little damage to limbs or fabric and spirits grew bolder, At about 2 p.m. a chance shot unfortunately smashed one of the fort's 24 pounders, killing or wounding most of those in the vicinity. Morale again evaporated, dissipating with the smoke of the explosion. Under the impression that all the guns had been dislocated, the commander of one of the bomb ships moved within range. Immediately Armistead's gunners took careful aim and competed to put the over-adventurous ship out of action. A little of the vaporous morale probably returned.

Cochrane now searched for another way of subduing the fort. The channel to the north was blocked by sunken vessels and protected by the batteries on the north shore, making an approach from that direction extremely hazardous. The southern channel offered a greater avenue to success and the admiral, more in a mood of frustration than in any expectation of success, decided to run the gauntlet through the Patapsco's main channel and land troops on the beach beneath the fort. 1200 men consequently embarked in the barges some time after midnight on the 14th and rowed as quietly as they could past the darkened fort. With them in the barges were the scaling ladders with which the attackers hoped to ascend McHenry's walls.

The blackness of the night was to offer a mixed blessing. For, although it allowed the boats to pass by undetected, it prevented the men from finding a suitable landing point on the peninsula's south shore. Unwisely the sailors sent up rockets to illuminate the shoreline near the fort—and the fort's defenders were alerted and the attackers' barges located. Fort Covington's guns joined the senior fort in a punishment of the poor men in the boats. Surprisingly, only one boat was sunk and its crew drowned. In the others, men rowed for their lives—and the attempt to subdue Fort McHenry had failed.

Britain's armoury continued to fire for several more hours. During those hours of bombardment, the nation's anthem emerged, its words inspired by the sight of the starred flag still flying unsubdued over Fort McHenry. Days before Britain's ships had dropped their anchors in the Patapsco, a young lawyer, Francis Scott Key and a friend, Colonel John Skinner, had gone on board one of His Majesty's ships, the frigate 'Surprise', to negotiate the release of Dr. William Beanes, a civilian seized by the British at Washington. Admiral Cochrane had agreed to release the prisoner, but, sensing that the two amabassadors had discovered too much about British intentions and dispositions, he decided to detain his visitors until the fighting was over. And so it was that Key witnessed the fort's distress: the fireballs, flames, thick smoke and opaque orange glow that hovered over McHenry for much of the day. And throughout that hell-like ordeal, the 42 foot long national flag, with its fifteen stars, continued to fly, a symbol of defiance that inspired the amateur poet to write on the back of an envelope the immortal words that instill pride in every American.

'*O, say can you see by the dawn's early light*
What so proudly we hail'd at the twilight's last gleaming?
Whose broad stripes and bright stars through the perilous fight,
O'er the ramparts we watched were so gallantly streaming?
And the rockets' red glare,
The bomb bursting in air,

Gave proof through the night that our flag was still there.
O, say does that star spangled banner yet wave
O'er the land of the free and the home of the brave?'

While British naval power was trying to wear down the garrison's spirit, Colonel Arthur Brooke was threatening Baltimore City from the land. Marching from the battlefield on the morning of the 13th, he had approached the fortifications and made careful observation of the lines. Convinced within minutes that these could not be taken by a frontal attack, he edged his men to the north as if he intended to turn the left flank. Here he met a mobile force under Winder and was driven back. Estimates reached him that 100 guns and 15,000 men stood behind the parapets. That afternoon, the 14th, he conferred with Admiral Cochrane, and the decision was made to abandon any further attempt to subdue Baltimore and its forts. Britain's navy and army, working in conjunction, had failed to take town or fort.

At 3 a.m.on the 15th, the withdrawal began, with no laurels at all being placed on Englishmen's brows. By the 19th, Baltimore's waters were completely free of British ships. General Smith, perhaps, could justifiably claim these laurels for himself. Soon afterwards, the pens began to flow—for those who had lived through the ordeal had a story to tell. '*Awful was the period from Sunday (11th) till Wednesday evening,'* wrote one of Baltimore's residents at the start of her account. The newpapers, of course, could be less than factual and deliciously plain spoken. The city's 'Register' spoke of Britain as a '*new race of Goths, outraging the ordinances of God and the laws of humanity'*. The same paper highlighted acts of pure vandalism committed by the British, no doubt exaggerating a little in its efforts to shock the readers. The editor then went on to propose that a monument be raised to Britain's fallen general, the Irishman Robert Ross . . . . '*near this Spot was Slain . . . . the Leader of a Host of Barbarians who destroyed the Capitol of the United States . . . . and* subjected *the Populous City of Baltimore to rape, robbery and conflagration.'* And, of course, British personnel present in the campaign claimed that American forces had poisoned wells, crops and the fruit on trees, and had tortured British prisoners.

Amongst the ethical dimensions that crept into focus were attitudes to slavery. Britain, having officially abolished the institution in 1807, adopted a sanctimonious opposition. Nevertheless, when Lord Bathurst first issued his orders to Ross, he forbade him to encourage a negro insurrection, but simultaneously indicated that it would be perfectly acceptable to enlist runaways into British service. The British approach to slavery would remain ambivalent with no clear policy emanating from London and with the generals on the spot reacting to the needs of the moment. Cochrane, in rough harmony with Bathurst's directions, ordered that the runaways were either to be recruited into the navy or dispatched as free individuals to British colonies. But, in variance with London's orders, he induced desertion by sending ex-slaves to inform those still in bondage of Britain's commitment to break their chains and manacles. Substantial numbers followed Cockburn when the fleet returned to Halifax on 19th September. It was impossible to accommodate such numbers on British vessels, but about 1000 were shipped from the Nova Scotia port and transported to Bermuda and elsewhere. 300 or so with more martial qualities were recruited into a newly raised battalion, the Royal Colonial Marines.

Britain still had a sting left in its receding tail. As late as 1st December, when most of Chesapeake's folk were reassembling their livelihoods in expectation that British raiding was a thing of the past, a landing party emerged from the mists of nowhere and captured the village of Tappahannock, forty or so miles from the mouth of the Rappahannock, and then, just as quickly, disappeared. The British presence, so substantial and destructive throughout 1813 and 1814, at last, like the Cheshire cat, faded away, but left behind no remnants of a grin.

CHAPTER 14

'He that wavereth is like a wave of the sea'

Warfare of this sort, even if it lasted for one hundred tears or more, would never secure a victory. Bold invasion, permanent occupation and political determination are the pre-requisites for success at the negotiating table. The non-coperative Chauncey, criticised by Brown and just about every other American general, eventually replied, pointing out, yet again, that he had too few resources to aid the Niagara operations, contain the British in Kingston and defend Sackets Harbor. Responding to Brown's September appeal, he acidly dismissed the general's recent suggestion that the fleet could assist the army by carrying provisions. ' . . . *We are intended to seek and to fight the enemy's fleet . . . . I shall not be diverted . . . . by any sinister attempt to render us subordinate to, or an appendage of the Army.'* Yet, in a token of sympathy for Brown's position, he left the 'Oneida', 'Sylph' and 'Jefferson' in the waters of the Niagara River, a hollow gesture that was to be of little practical use to the American army in a war that was clearly stagnating.

Idiocy now took the place of confusion at the tables of the American High Command. Never quite sure of exactly what he hoped to achieve in the Lake Ontario area, but presumably still believing that this would be the avenue to unquestioned victory, Armstrong turned his back on the Champlain and St. Lawrence and effectively closed the war on that front. Major-General George Izard, still serving as commander on the Lake Champlain front until his appointment to command of the Ontario-Niagara front, was quick to point out the vulnerability of the Champlain corridor. *'I will make the movement you direct . . . but I shall do it with the apprehension of risking the force under my command, and with the certainty that everything in this vicinity . . . . in less than three days after my departure, be in the possession of the enemy. He is in force superior to mine in my front; he daily threatens an attack on my position at Champlain; we are in hourly expectation of a serious conflict.'* Unable to impress his political master with the reality of the situation, he dutifully headed west on 29th August 1814 with 4000 men, reaching the Lake Ontario town on 17th September. He left behind General Alexander Macomb with just 1500 men to hold the works at Plattsburgh.

Izard was undoubtedly right. In ordering Izard north, Armstrong overlooked the fact that, for most of the war, Champlain had been regarded as the natural gateway by which America might advance against Montréal, despite Wilkinson's failure a year earlier to reach the Canadian city. But the lake served equally effectively as the doorway into United States territory and the fault line along which the republic could be cleft in two, severing anti-war New England from the more belligerent states lying on the other side of the Hudson. Burgoyne had attempted to use this route and now, in the closing season of this later war, it was obvious that Prevost, with his reinforcements from Britain, would use this route again.

General Izard, since taking up his appointment at Plattsburgh in April, had been energetically assisted by Lieutenant Thomas Macdonough, commander of the Lake Champlain flotilla. This capable officer had based his ships at Vergennnes on Otter Creek, Vermont., close to Lake Champlain's southern shores. Fearless and supremely agile, Macdonough had served his naval probation in the Mediterranean and fought the Tripoli pirates. Involved in a hand-to-hand combat with a giant of a man, the lieutenant's cutlass had broken. Grabbing a pistol, he shot the pirate dead. He then survived an epidemic of yellow fever that killed all but three of his shipmates. His capabilities and resilience had been tested on 14th May when a British squadron based at Isle aux Noix had appeared off Otter Creek and attempted to engage. Macdonough had had the presence of mind to erect a battery at the creek's mouth and eventually forced the British to withdraw.

The general had been well supported by Macomb and by Thomas Smith, his other brigade commander. Together, the three men had supervised the construction of a battery on Cumberland Head and a number of strong points just south of Plattsburgh town. But now Izard had gone with the bulk of the army, and Macomb had been left to weather the probable storm. The new commander's first moves were to call in all his scattered detachments to Plattsburgh and make an appeal to Governor Martin Chillenden of Vermont. Within days, 2500 Vermont men had joined Macomb at Plattsburg and another 800 men from New York volunteered for service in the front line under their general Benjamin Moeers. By 10th September, at the very moment when Baltimore came under threat, all of these men were behind the Plattsburgh works.

Events were now to prove the error of Armstrong's thinking. Prevost meant to capitalise on America's recent mistake and fully exploit the weakness of the Champlain's valley. Heartened by the arrival of the 3rd, 5th, 16th, 27th, 39th, 58th and 59th Foot from the Spanish Peninsula in August, he organised these reinforcements into a powerful division which he placed, perhaps unwisely, under the command of the aged de Rottenburg. With these new arrivals were a clutch of young bloods, three proteges of the Duke of Wellington: Thomas Brisbane, Manley Power and Frederick Robinson, all now sporting the rank of major-general and placed in command of the three brigades of de Rottenburg's division. In addition to these three brigades, Prevost assembled a reserve brigade under Major-General James Kempt and stationed this at Montréal, and a force of 300 light dragoons. The British in arms now numbered at least 10,500, possibly more, a force larger than anything that had so far been put together in this war of miniature armies.

Macomb would not have long to plan his final positions. Plattsburgh stands on elevated ground above the lake. A pronounced peninsula south of the town lies between the lake and the Saranac river. Within this naturally defended feature lay the core of the American defences. Water protected the north and east, but the southern land front would be vulnerable to an attack. Here, Izard and James Totten, both accomplished peacetime engineers, had constructed three impressive redoubts. Fort Moreau, the largest, was under the wardship of Colonel Melancton Smith and was manned by the 6th and 29th Regiments. Fort Brown, under the command of Lieutenant-Colonel Storrs, was defended by detachments of the 30th and 31st foot regiments. Fort Scott, nearest the lake, held for America by the 33rd and 34th regiments, was the responsibility of a Major Vinson. In addition, United States units had taken up positions in an old mill with stone walls and from here they could observe the approach of the British army towards one of the two bridges that crossed the Saranac. America's Champlain fleet had become part of the formula for defence. Macdonough's four vessels rested at anchor within Plattsburgh Bay, a sheltered inlet protected on the far side by the peninsula of Cumberland Head. An additional shield was provided in the south, where the bay opened into the lake, by Crab Island. Here a battery had recently been erected.

4 companies of 1st U.S.Rifle Regiment and the 4th, 6th, 13th, 29th,30th, 31st, 33rd and 34th U.S. Infantry Regiments

American forces at the Battle of Plattsburgh

Britain began its move south in the week after Izard's departure. On the eve of invasion, Captain George Downie took over command of the flotilla based at Chazy, replacing Peter Fisher, a man no longer felt to be reliable. On 5th September, Prevost's invasion force was reported to be at Sampson's, just five miles north of Plattsburgh. Macomb, reacting in the way that an experienced and unruffled officer should do and reading the signs clearly, sent two weak detachments north to watch on the two roads down which the British would be obliged to advance. First contact with the enemy occurred at Culver's Hill, when Major John Wool, the man who had distinguished himself so well at Queenston, and 250 men joined with Mooer's militia in a brief delaying action on the Beekmanstown road, down which the brigades of Power and Robinson were advancing. A matching force under a Lieutenant-Colonel Appling, had performed a similar function on the Dead Creek Bridge road nearest the lake. It, too, withdrew when the nose of Brisbane's column approached.

Further sprightly actions followed later that day. At Halsey's Corner, on the Beekmanstown road, Wool's command, with the support of two artillery pieces and the help of Mooer's militia, took up a position behind a stone wall. The guns were placed at right angles to the road, positioned to pour flank fire on the redcoated column. Wool was to show the same qualities of courage and tenacity that he had revealed at the Niagara front battle. Aided by the fact that the British insisted on remaining in column throughout the engagement, he managed to slow the enemy and fell 30 of Power's exposed men. A bayonet charge, however, eventually scattered the American units—and the road to Plattsburgh lay fully open.

A simultaneous action was taking place on the Dead Creek Bridge road. Here Captain John Sproull, with 2 large guns and 200 men, and assisted by a couple of gunboats in the bay, was not quite as leech like. Forced to retire more quickly than Wool, he fell back across the lowest of the Saranac's two bridges, but removed the structure's planking as he left. Mooer and Wool, crossing at the upper bridge a little later, similarly deactivated that bridge and rendered the structure impassable.

Sir George Prevost must have been impressed by what he now saw. A river without usable bridges lay in front of formidable fortifications, behind which nearly 5000 defenders stood. The quality of those men would, no doubt, be sharpened by the realisation that they were fighting to protect Vermont and New York, the beloved homelands in which they had been born and raised. Every one of the grim-faced watchers would be determined to yield not an inch of their precious homelands to the redcoated men who had no right to be there.

The British made some efforts to cross that day, the 6th, but every attempt was repulsed. The day's fighting cost the Americans 45 dead and wounded, but Britain lost more than 200. Any further attacks would cost yet more lives, and Prevost decided to attempt nothing more until the British fleet had arrived. For five days the two sides faced each other across the waters of the Saranac. The British occupied Plattsburgh's river front houses and periodically fired from the upper storeys. America employed her artillery in a bid to flush the snipers out. And, on his left flank, Prevost was being harassed by the guns of the American ships in the bay. Failure to anticipate the nature of the American defence and his apparent poor planning came in for considerable criticism both at the time and later. Robinson, writing some years later, contended that '*the army moved against Plattsburgh without any regularly digested plan . . . . There was neither guides, spies or plans . . . . A strange infatuation seems to have seized upon the mind of Sir George Prevost.*'

Sir George busied himself erecting batteries on the higher ground behind the town. In those days of frustrated waiting, he sent fresh appeals to Downie and his ships to hurry to the army's assistance. Downie, however, was awaiting the completion of the 31 gun 'Confiance', the jewel of his fleet. On 8th September, he informed Prevost that he intended to remain at anchor at Chazy until this addition to his fleet was ready. Exchanges of opinion followed—mostly acrimonious. Prevost could not command Downie, but he could apply the sort of pressure that men of prestige and social standing can so easily generate. The very next day, Downie ordered the semi-ready 'Confiance' to join the fleet and sent a message to Prevost that he and the flotilla were now on their way. That night the general was embarrassed by the capture of some of his guns. A Scotsman in Macomb's army, Captain George McGlassin, led 50 men across the river and seized an almost unguarded battery. Spiking the guns, the Americans retired without the loss of a single man. Insignificant in so many ways, the action mortified Prevost, who liked to think that his arrangements and dispositions were impeccable.

Macdonough, aware of the imminent arrival of his waterborne adversary, was a keen disciple of Horatio Nelson and was about to apply the sort of tactics that this great man might have used. He placed the 'Preble', 'Ticonderoga', 'Saratoga' and 'Eagle', all with their bows facing northward. Gunboats filled the intervals between the anchored warships. Britain's approaching ships would find their freedom of movement restricted and would be forced to form into a line and fight within the range of America's short-range carronades.

On the 11th, a clear day refreshed by a gentle north-westerly wind, Downie rounded Cumberland Head and sailed his ships over the lip of Plattsburgh Bay. Observing the stationary line of waiting ships, he showed the resourcefulness needed to deal with the situation. He instructed the commanders of the 'Chubb', 'Linnet' and 'Confiance' to group together to neutralise the 'Eagle'. When this was accomplished, the trio should then turn their venom on the 'Saratoga' The commanders of his twelve gunboats were ordered to assist the 'Finch' in a chastisement of the 'Preble' and 'Ticonderoga.'

Macdonough, a devout man, ordered his men to kneel in prayer. '*He that wavereth is like a wave of the sea driven with the wind,*' he was heard to pronounce. The chaplain then offered a short blessing. Every crewman, reminded by the commodore that their own survival might depend upon the benevolence of the Almighty, stood with head bowed and hands clasped.

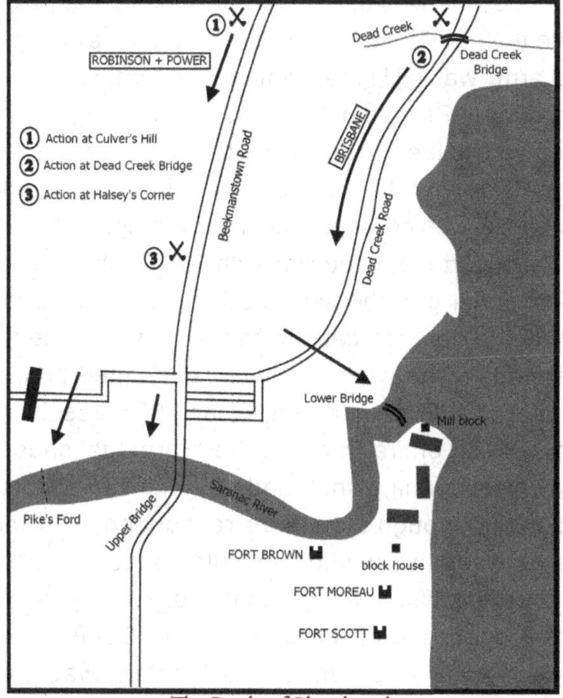

The Battle of Plattsburgh

The British, far more in need of Divine forgiveness, had meanwhile sailed closer. Perhaps, in those pre-battle moments, they, too, remembered to ask God for victory.

Britain was at an immediate disadvantage. Downie's vessels, tacking north-west with the wind, would be initially unable to employ all of their broadside guns. The Americans, by happy contrast, anchored in line facing north, could bring every one of their starboard guns into instant activity.

The 'Eagle', according to some reports, fired the first shots of the battle soon after 8.30 a.m., aiming her four long-range 18 pounders at either the 'Chubb' or 'Linnet'. The latter vessel, now abreast the 'Saratoga', opened with her guns but her shots did almost no damage to the 'Saratoga', and merely unhoused a cockerel from a coop kept on the deck. The bird landed on one of the guns and crowed; it was regarded as a favourable omen.

Poor communications or misunderstanding affected British progress from the start. Downie was under the impression that Prevost's forces would engage the American army as soon as the navy opened fire. But Britain's land army was still breakfasting, and Robinson, whose brigade had assembled near Pike's Ford, a possible crossing place to the west of Plattsburgh where the Saranac's waters were known to be shallow, had categorically been told not to attack before 10 o'clock.

The 'Confiance' was now opposite the 'Saratoga'—and Macdonough did not miss the opportunity of dueling with the British flagship. Personally aiming a 24 pounder gun, he sent a ball hurtling towards the vessel. Unpeturbed by the damage caused to his ship, Downie tried to close with the 'Saratoga'. The wind, however, prevented him, and he was forced to anchor at a distance of more than 300 yards and conduct the duel from there. The entire frame of the 'Saratoga' shudded with the impact of Downie's opening shot, and 40 American sailors were killed or wounded. Macdonough's gunners responded, and the winner of the dialogue between the two boats would be the one whose gunners showed the greatest skill. Fifteen minutes or so later, a shell from the 'Saratoga' dislodged one of the guns of the 'Confiance' and sent it hurtling across the deck. Downie, unfortunately, was standing in its path, and the undiluted weight of the weapon crushed the officer and killed him instantly.

The other ships were dueling too. For thirty minutes or so, the 'Chubb' and 'Linnet' clung to the 'Eagle' like leeches and poured in shot. At last a broadside from the American crippled the 'Chubb' and she began to drift helplessly through the American line. Another shot from the 'Saratoga' removed her last fighting breath and she struck her colours in an act of surrender. Only 6 men were left on deck.

The 'Eagle' now cut her cable and turned south to seek out the 'Confiance'. Finding a position between the 'Saratoga' and the 'Ticonderoga', she brought her port guns into battle and put several holes through the Englishman's decking. The 'Finch', however, was performing well in her dialogue with the 'Ticonderoga', and four British gunboats closed in on the American's stern—only luck, pure skill and gallantry kept the 'Ticonderoga' in action.

Observers on shore might have concluded at this point that the United States was losing. The 'Preble', hounded by gunboats since the battle's start and periodically fired upon by the 'Finch', had been disabled and was drifting towards the Plattsburgh shore. The shift in position southward of the 'Eagle' had exposed the bows of the 'Saratoga' to raking fire from the 'Linnet'. Every starboard gun on the 'Saratoga' was now out of action. Macdonough himself seemed to be protected by Providence's shield. He had been knocked down several times during the engagement, but, each time, emerged virtually unscathed. On one occasion, he was bowled over by a rapidly moving object, which turned out to be the severed head of one of his midshipmen. Picking himself up from the reddening deck, he wound his ship round on the hauser to allow his port gunners to take a more active part in the battle. Lieutenant James Robertson, stepping into the command of 'Confiance' and the fleet after Downie's fall, tried to perform the same action, but with limited success. Exposing her stern to the 'Saratoga', the 'Confiance' was punished cruelly for her clumsiness, and soon the pride of England's Champlain fleet struck her colours. In the next few minutes, the 'Finch' pounded by the artillery on Crab Island, also struck, leaving only the 'Linnet' and gunboats in action. Fifteen minutes later, the brig, Britain's last hope, abandoned the struggle, pulverised by the guns of the 'Eagle' and 'Saratoga. The gunboats, observing her surrender, took the opportunity to escape. By 10.30 a.m. the battle on the lake had ended. It had lasted for just 140 minutes. Macdonough, greeting the defeated officers on the splintered deck of his flagship, generously complimented them for their gallantry and refused to accept their swords.

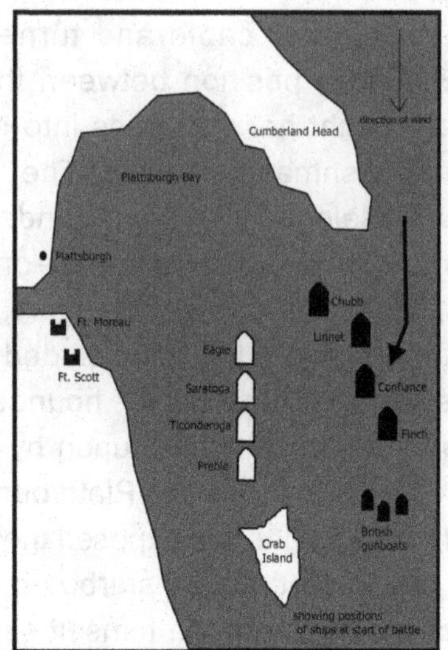

The Battle on Lake Chaplain (Plattsburgh)

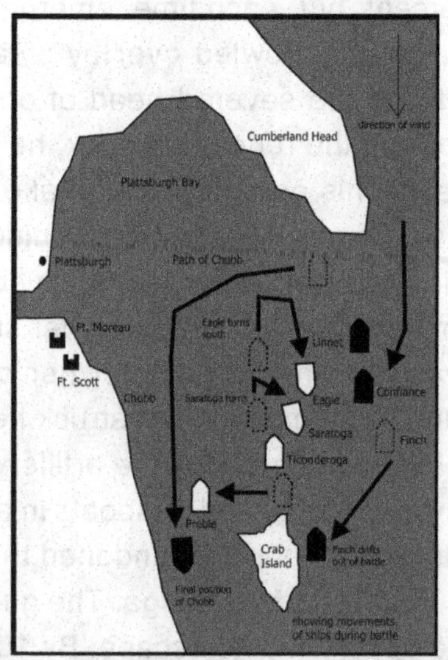

The Battle of Lake Champlain (Plattsburgh) –the final movements

British fleet	American Fleet
Confiance (38)	Saratoga (26)
Linnet (16)	Ticonderoga (17)
Finch (11)	Eagle (26)
Chubb (11)	Preble (7)
12 gunboats	10 gunboats
4 with 1 gun, 8 with 2 guns	4 with 1 gun, 6 with 2 guns

The opposing fleets at the Battle on Lake Champlain (naval battle of Plattsburgh)

'The Almighty has been pleased to grant us a . . . . victory on Lake Champlain in the capture of one frigate, one brig and two sloops of war of the enemy,' his pithy message to the Secretary of the Navy reported. The shortness of his message understated the enormity of his victory, which America had managed to purchase for the death of only 47 men. Britain had suffered more, losing 54 dead and 116 wounded.

Prevost was denied a victory on land, too. Robinson, in charge of the attack on the ford, claimed that he only received his instructions at 10 a.m, by which time the water battle was almost over. His brigade, ordered to cross at Pike's Ford, tried to find its way along cart tracks west of Plattsburgh, but lost itself amongst the tangled trees and roots of woodland and so reached the ford at about 11 a.m. On the far side, 400 of Mooer's riflemen prepared to prevent the crossing, every weapon pointing at the sandy banks at which the British column would emerge.

Far to the east came the sound of cheering, an indication, so Robinson felt, that the British had won a victory on the lake. Sensing that he could now be the architect of victory on land, he sent his men splashing into the river's water. The New Yorkers promptly began to retreat, enabling Robinson's brigade to form in perfect order on the south side of the river. The general, who had achieved so much at the side of Wellesley in Spain, considered that his task would now be easy.

At that very moment, however, his aide rode up with a message. *'I am directed to inform you that the 'Confiance' and the brig, having struck their colors in consequence of the frigate having grounded, it will no longer be prudent to persevere in the service committed to your charge, and it is therefore the orders of the Commander of the Forces that you will immediately return with the troops under your command.'*

During this attempt on the ford, Brisbane's column at the bridges had been held by tremendous firepower and had failed to cross. Brisbane, like Robinson, later protested, claiming that he would have been able to force the crossings if given sufficient time.

The retreat began almost immediately, ordered, sullen and forever controversial. Prevost and his disgruntled commanders had reached Chazy, 8 miles distant, before Macomb was even aware of the Englishmen's departure. Prevost defended himself with bombast and dignity, even against Robinson's unceasing vitriolic blasts. '*Your Lordship must have been aware from my previous despatches that no offensive operations could be carried out within the Enemy's Territory for the destruction of his Naval Establishment without Naval Support . . . . The disastrous and unlooked for result of the Naval Contest by depriving me of the only means by which I could avail myself of any advantage I might gain, rendered a perseverance in the attack of the Enemy's position highly imprudent as well as hazardous*', he long-windedly wrote in his explanation to Lord Bathurst.

Perhaps he was correct in his assessment; a modern historian is kinder than the critics at the time, concluding that Prevost was '*a good administrator in the defence of Canada . . . He is essentially a diplomat, circumspection is his hallmark*', but he was a man who '*prefers to slide around a problem rather than meet it head on . . .*' Whatever angle one chooses to take in an approach to this complex character, the hasty retreat ended the last offensive from Canada and accelerated the peace negotiations that had already begun. '*Precipitate and disgraceful*', Robinson called the retreat, '*This country can never again afford such an opportunity, nothing but a defensive war can or ought to be attempted here, and you will find that the expectations of His Majesty's ministers and the people of England will be utterly destroyed in this quarter.*'

Comparisons are sometimes made with another British offensive launched at this time. It is often suggested that the September 1814 invasion of Maine was intended as the more important of the two. Plattsburgh, in this interpretation of events, was designed purely to draw troops away from the Atlantic and so increase the chances of success in an invasion of lukewarm New England. The governments of Maine, Connecticut and Massachusetts, by this stage of the war, had come to recognise the dangers of 'sleeping with the enemy', and the anti-war fervour of the earlier years had recently become diluted. A charm offensive by the British would no longer appear likely to seduce the three states—only a military drive into Maine, Connecticut and Massachusetts would achieve that objective. The stick, rather than the carrot, seemed to be the most appropriate way, and from the Spring of 1814, provoking New England became fashionable.

The first move was political rather than military. In March the New Brunswick legislature advanced an argument that the international boundary between Maine and New Brunswick established in 1783 should be adjusted in the latter's favour. Hardly provocative in itself, the declaration was followed by a far more belligerent utterance that the Passamaquoddy islands, which America had 'annexed' in 1791, should be recovered by force. Further proclamations followed, culminating in Lord Bathurst's summer instruction to Sir John Sherbrooke, commander in the Maritime Provinces, to take possession of that part of Maine '*which intercepts the communication between Halifax and Québec.*'

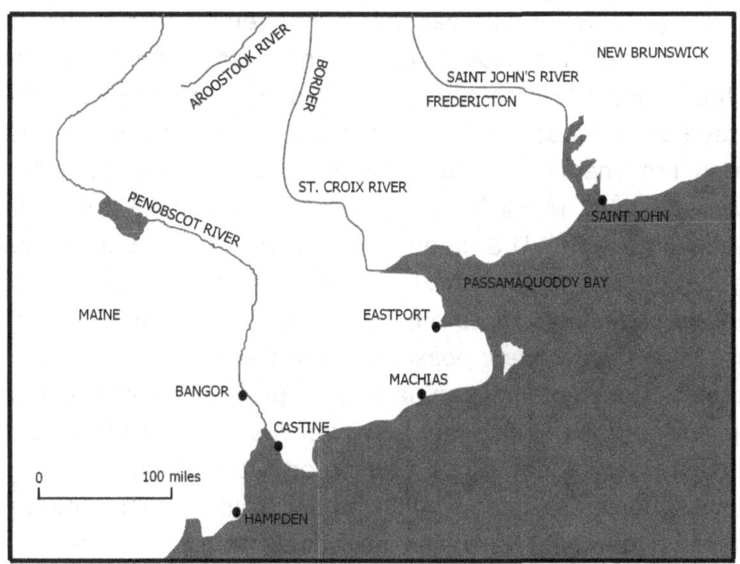

New England and the disputed frontier

Undoubtedly the enthusiasm for an invasion of Maine was fueled by encouraging events south of the border, which seemed to indicate a sudden swing again in New England's sentiments. During the early weeks of 1814, the Massachusetts legislature had received petitions from more than 50 towns, stressing the '*suffering condition of the people*' and dissatisfaction with the measures of the national government in dealing with these grievances and in the conduct of the war. Then, in the Spring, gubernatorial elections in Massachusetts had catapulted Caleb Strong, a man openly critical of 'Mr. Madison's War', into the highest State office. The 'Boston Gazette' frequently carried articles from the more articulate of the discontented. Some, written by a man who called himself 'An Old Farmer', highlighted the damages caused by the war to New England's interests. '*I can see no benefits in the war; I can see no justice in it,*' one of these anonymous articles began.

New England's will to resist would need to be tested. And so a series of raids were launched, most with questionable objectives. On the night of 7th April 1814 two hundred men on barges rowed up the Connecticut River to attack shipping resting 6 miles above the river's mouth. By 10 a.m. the next day they had destroyed 27 ships, some clearly designed to carry guns, and property valued at more than $100,000. In June a similar raid on Wareham in Massachusetts wrecked $40,000 of shipping, an act of pure vandalism that served only to strengthen, rather than weaken, republican opinion in Massachusetts. On July 11th Sir Thomas Hardy with a squadron, headed by the 74 gun 'Ramillies' entered Passamquoddy Bay on the disputed border and anchored off Eastport. From here he sent an ultimatum to the governor of Fort Sullivan on Moose Island. Major Perely Putnam, commanding a detachment of 87 men of the 40th U.S. Infantry, at first refused, but, impressed by the appearance of a number of landing vessels laden with troops, he agreed to capitulate. Three days later, Hardy declared Eastport and Moose Island '*permanent possessions of the King,*' and insisted that the area's inhabitants take an oath of allegiance. Two-thirds promptly complied—and the British flag flew over the customs house. And on 9th August Hardy appeared off Stonington, Connecticut, claiming that the townspeople had been stockpiling or manufacturing torpedoes for use against the Royal Navy. The inhabitants dragged out some pieces of artillery and fired at the aggressor's ships. Hardy threw back a few shells and rockets in reply before sailing away.

Diplomacy, not fire power, however, achieved the next success. Informed that the people of Nantucket and Cape Cod were starving, Admiral Hotham told the inhabitants that he would permit free importation of food in exchange for a clear renunciation of American sovereignty. The desperate people complied, and on 23rd August, Cape Cod's townships declared their neutrality in this war between Britain and her estranged colonies.

By now, Sherbrooke had prepared for an attack on Penobscot Bay. The 29th, 60th, 62nd and 98th Regiments of Foot, recently arrived from Gibraltar, gave him a force of 4000 men with which to annex the territory of northern Maine. On 18th August he wrote to Bathurst that he planned '*to occupy Penobscot with a respectable force, and to take that river . . . as our boundary, running a line from its source in a more westerly direction than that which at present divides us from the Americans.*' Border shifting and permanent annexation of territory seems, at last, to have been adopted as the official British war policy.

Initially Sherbrooke centred his gaze on Machias, a haven of anti-British sentiment. But, receiving a report that the damaged American frigate, the 'John Adams', had taken refuge in Penobscot Bay, he decided to bypass Machias and make straight for this island studded bay. On the morning of 1st September, 10 warships under the command of Rear-Admiral Edward Griffith approached Castine, the site of the bay's main defence works. Fort George, built by Britain during the Revolutionary war, had fallen into disuse, but a small redoubt and half-moon battery sported four 4 pounder guns and a garrison of 140 men. The American commander fired just one volley before fleeing across the narrow isthmus that connected Castine to the mainland.

The 'John Adams', however, was still at liberty and might yet prove able to oppose British penetration of the River Penobscot. Sherbrooke therefore sent Major-General Gerard Gosselin and the 29th Foot across the bay to Belfast. Supported by the frigate 'Bacchante', the 600 troops of the regiment took quiet possession of this tiny settlement, which commanded the routeway north from Massachusetts. British forces could then feel free to sweep up river in search of the frigate and the fluid American forces operating in the area. A combined naval and army force headed by H.M.S. 'Dragon', a 74 gun ship-of-the-line, and comprising all four regiments of foot, about 700 men, set out on the evening of the 1st, and, moving up river in barges, came ashore at Frankfort the following afternoon.

From here, the British moved towards Hampden, where the hunted frigate and Maine's militiamen were now known to be. The damaged vessel, seeking the shelter of the Penobscot River's banks, was protected by heavy artillery mounted nearby. Riflemen of the 18th and

60th clashed with militiamen just beyond Frankfort and, dispersing these irregulars as though they were merely irritating cobwebs, passed on to Bald Head Cove.

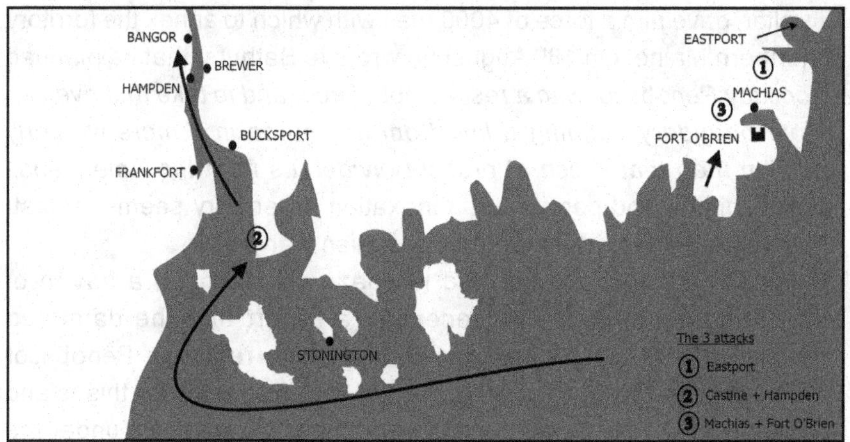

The Penobscot Bay Campaign

America had prepared her positions. Major-General John Blake, the area's militia commander, had ordered out the 10th Massachusetts Militia regiment and, by nightfall on the 2nd, 600 irregular troops were waiting near the tiny town. Charles Morris, captain of the 'John Adams', had removed his heaviest guns from the vessel. He had mounted some of these on a ridge beside the river; the residue he placed at Crosby's Wharf further upstream. None of these waiting militiamen had ever fought before—and none had any real idea of what to expect.

Dawn on the 3rd was shrouded in fog. The men of Maine and Massachusetts stood in disordered line, their left anchored on the river and their right protected by a battery positioned on the Bangor-Belfast road. They listened for sounds from the south, heard none, and relaxed. Nothing but thick, swirling fog lay at their front.

But only until about 3 p.m. Britain's soldiers began to emerge from the fog, faceless shadows perhaps, but in almost perfect battle order. The Americans, sensing rather than seeing their enemy, fired wildly into the fog, hoping that the shadows would possess substance, hearts and blood that flowed. They caused few casualties and the vague lines continued to move forward. The British began to fire rockets, several at a time, towards the heart of the American positions. Terror took the place of impatience. When the British prepared to charge with bayonets raised, there could be only one possible outcome.

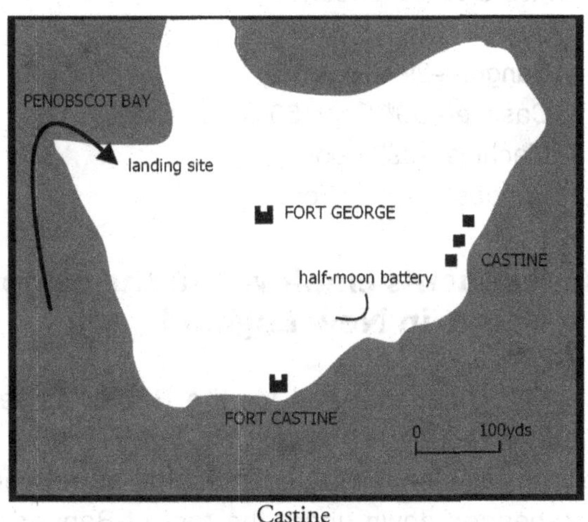

Castine

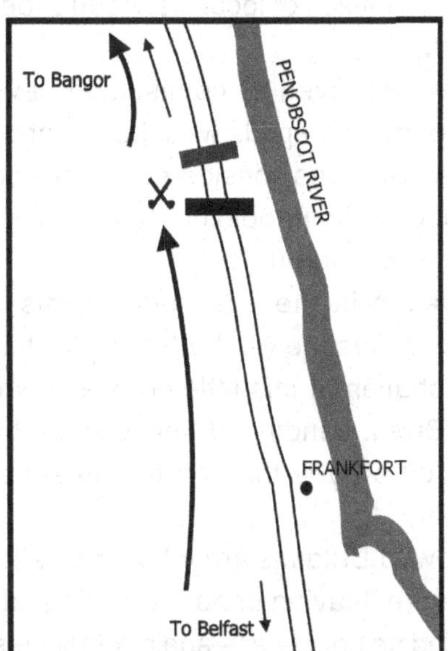

The Battle of Hampden

The rout was total. Every single defender fled, despite the supporting fire of the American artillery and the guns from the frigate. Soldiers of the British 29th regiment of Foot charged the battery and overran the guns. Pushing forward, they found the frigate in flames; her crew had no other choice but to burn their precious ship. The battle had lasted an hour: Britain had lost 10 men killed or wounded. America had lost 94, 81 of whom were taken prisoner.

Bangor—29th Foot
Castine—29th Foot, 60th Foot and 62nd Foot
Machias—29th Foot
Penobscot—60th Foot

British regiments employed in the campaigns in New England

Grim-faced Americans waited for the British at Bangor with a flag of truce and a request for terms. No arguments or discussions followed—only an insistence on unconditional surrender. That night British soldiers bedded down under the roof of Bangor's courthouse and consumed vast quantities of local ale. Asurrender without ceremony took place next day.

The conquerors destroyed or confiscated several vessels in the days following. Amongst the spoils was the privateer 'Decatur'. Blake, the defeated general, who was considered to have done too little to stop the British, was vilfied by the people he was supposed to be defending, and his effigy was burned in public.

Machias was taken in the aftermath of this unqualified British success. Returning to Castine on the 9th, the victors sent out another combined force to challenge this little coastal town and its protecting garrison in Fort O' Brien. Landing 10 miles south of Machias, Colonel Andrew Pilkington led a party through the darkness and approached the fort from the rear.

No fighting followed Britain's arrival at the walls. The garrison had left only minutes before, leaving uneaten meals and personal property. Machias was occupied an hour later—again without resistance. In contrast with the ostentatious and numerically superior invasions of American territory that had taken place simultaneously, this minor incursion in the twilight weeks of war had probably achieved more than had really been intended. While the Washington and Plattsburgh campaigns had ended in failure and withdrawal, the almost unnoticed advance from New Brunswick resulted in the hoisting of Britain's flag from flagpoles within American territory. For, in the aftermath of victory at Castine and Machias, Sherbrooke announced the annexation of nearly 100 miles of Maine's coastline and its absorption *'for ever'* within the province of New Brunswick. Few accounts of this war report in detail on this successful campaign on the fringes; most are only interested in the daily movements of British troops along the Patuxent river from Benedict and the fiery destruction of Washington's public buildings.

Sherbrooke, of course, enjoyed an advantage which neither Cockburn nor Prevost had possessed. Many in Maine's community were touched by something more than sympathy for King George's cause and regarded rule from New Brunswick or Halifax as preferable to the dictates from Washington and the statesmen from the south. Sherbrooke neatly summarised New England's sentiments in a letter to Lord Bathurst: *'New England may be conquered easily by kindness—permit it to be thought that she cannot be so easily by arms, and why should the people of New England, who have long viewed the English nation and government to be less hostile to them than the southern states, be less worthy of the generosity of the British nation than those of France?'*

'The Times' of London was just as forthright. Stamping on the moral high ground, the paper declared: *'It would seem that we were merely taking possession of our own, for the Americans have only such a footing there as they had attained since the peace of 1783 by encroachment on their part and inattention on ours.'*

On the 18th, a week after Plattsburgh, Sherbrooke returned to Halifax. He left behind a force of about 1800 men under the command of Major-General Gosselin to ensure that Britain's flag was not hauled down. All males over 16 years of age were required to take an oath of allegiance—and the majority complied.

Federal United States made little effort to drive the invaders out. Massachusetts, angry at Washington's proposals to nationalise the state's militia, felt disinclined to supply funds and any more troops to satisfy the President's wishes. Madison, a little more circumspect than previously, realised that the movement of regular troops northwards through Massachusetts, might be regarded by Caleb Strong as a violation of state sovereignty. The Union flag fluttered undisturbed in territory that the United States regarded as hers.

Massachusetts was again moving in a dangerous direction. On 14th July New England Federalists had met for a dinner at Butler's Hotel in

Hartford, Connecticut, and voiced strong anti-Union sentiment. Talk of a rebirth of the two hundred year old Confederation of New England States became fashionable, fed largely by frustration at Republican control of Congress and the increase in anti-New England rhetoric emanating largely from Georgia and the Carolinas.

Relationships with the Federal capital plunged to new depths in the aftermath of Britain's destruction of Washington. New England's political masters, convinced that Britain had won the war, saw little point in shoring up Boston's defences. But some needless destruction of American property at Alexandria reminded Bostonians just in time of the true nature of the British conqueror, and Governor Strong now called upon Washington for funds and support. The Administration agreed to assist, but only if the militia forces of Massachusetts were placed under Federal control.

Strong and his counterparts in the neighbouring states chose to refuse. On 5th October, at a meeting of the Massachusetts General Court, a resolution was passed which called upon delegates from all New England states to consider '*the best means of preserving our resources and the defense against the enemy, and to devise and suggest . . . such measures as they may deem expedient; and also to take measures . . . . for procuring a convention of Delegates from all the United States, in order to revise the Constitution . . . . and more effectively to secure the support and attachments of all the people, by placing all upon a fair representation . . .*'

The resolution came at the moment that Washington chose to ignore state sensitivities by proposing measures to introduce compulsory conscription of the nation's young men. Twenty-six delegates from 3 of the 5 states [22] met at Hartford on 15th December. The 'Boston Sentinel' published the demands made by this '*unconstitutional and treasonable assembly.*' (John Quincey Adams) '*We demand deliverance, New England is unanimous. And we announce our irrevocable decree that the tyrannical oppression of those who at present usurp the power of the Constitution is beyond endurance.*'

Talk of civil war was heard in smoke-filled salons and in city streets. Monroe sent orders to Colonel Thomas Jesup, commander of the military district which included Connecticut, to keep a vigilant watch. The officer soon reported back that the utterances of the Hartford Convention were

22 Vermont and New Hampshire declined to send representatives

no cause for alarm and that the spirit of rebellion was entirely lacking amongst the common people. But, despite an obvious lack of popular support, the delegates continued to sit and pass resolutions. The politics of this assembly, however, are of little relevance in the story of the war with Britain. For peace negotiations had now begun at Ghent in Belgium. At this table of peace, New England would be permitted no separate representation or right to decide her future.

CHAPTER 15

'The day that witnesses our departure from the Mississippi forever loses us the country'

An overlooked war had been taking place since the spring in the 'Fur country' of the North-west, the huge expanse of Michigan territory and its bordering lakes. Guarding British interests on the northern shores of Lake Huron was Michilimackinac Island, the isolated strongpoint which had been in the hands of the British since July 1812. Harrison's victory at the Thames in October 1813, the Battle of Lake Erie in September and America's subsequent construction of Fort Gratiot at the southern end of Lake Huron had robbed Britain of her water communications between York and Michilimackinac and placed the fort within possible reach of America's stretched out hand. Only the onset of winter had prevented the Americans from sending an expedition against this outpost in the snow. Those on guard in distant Michilimackinac expected American boats and soldiers to be carried north on the warming spring waters.

America's first action of the 1814 campaigning year, however, was an attempt to seduce the Indians of the Upper Mississippi and Wisconsin from their earlier support of the British. This, it was felt, could only be achieved by a show of military might. Accordingly, Governor William Clark of the Territory of Missouri moved up the Mississippi from St. Louis in May 1814 at the head of 60 regulars of the 7th U.S. Regiment and 240 militiamen towards Prairie du Chien, where the British had positioned a token force under Captain Francis Dease. At Rock Island Rapids the governor swept aside feeble resistance from a band of Saux Indians in British pay. Dease, under no illusions about his ability to resist, sensibly withdrew. Clark immediately constructed a fort at Prairie du Chien and named it Fort Shelby.

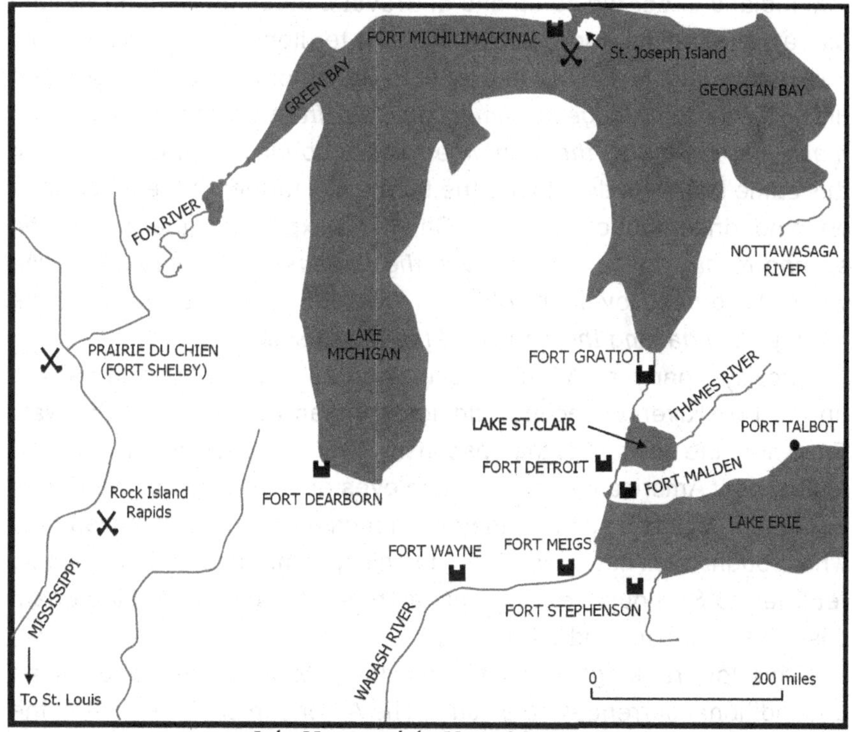

Lake Huron and the Upper Mississippi

The politician-turned general was less successful in winning over the allegiance of the local Indian tribes. Rumours that Clark had ordered the killing of eight Winebago Indians, who had taken refuge at the new fort spread, like grassland flames, across the territory. Four other unfortunates, according to the same apocryphal report, were locked up in an outhouse and then shot. One of the victims, apparently, was the wife of Wabasha, Chief of the Sioux.

Amongst those who listened with interest to these stories was Lieutenant-Colonel Robert McDouall, an officer of the 8th Foot and now commander of the garrison at Fort Michilimackinac. And, it was to him that the tribesmen appealed for revenge. Choosing to neglect the danger to his fort, the adventurous officer enthusiastically prepared an expedition against Clark at Fort Shelby, confident that this would satisfy the Indians' cry for retribution and also meet Prevost's demand for some activity on the Upper Mississippi.

He consequently assembled a force of 75 Michigan Fencibles and 136 Indians under the command of Brevet Lieutenant Colonel William McKay, a retired fur trader familiar with the territory over which he would have to operate. McDouall, in a letter to Drummond, acknowledged that his task was '*to dislodge the American Genl. from his new conquest and make him relinquish the immense tract of country he had seized.*' In this same letter, he developed the theme still further. If the Americans were not driven out of Prairie du Chien, he explained, '*there would be an end to our connexion (sic)with the Indians . . . . Tribe after tribe would be gained over or subdued. Nothing could then prevent the enemy from gaining the source of the Mississippi.*'

McKay's party left Michilimackinac on 28th June 1814 and passed up the Fox River, collecting additional Indian tribesmen on the way. From here the descent of the Wisconsin River was easy and uneventful, almost as if America had no scouting eyes or awareness of the British approach. Mckay's scouts, however, functioned well, and it was they who brought back news that Clark, the alleged murderer of Indians, had returned to St. Louis, leaving only a small garrison under Lieutenant Joseph Perkins to fend off attack.

This low ranking officer turned down McKay's demand for an unconditional surrender on 9th July. The American could rely upon the support of the 'Governor Clark', a 14 gun warship moored beside the fort, and two lateral blockhouses, each equipped with artillery. McKay, by contrast, seems to have had a single brass 3 pounder, and, moreover, would have to fight in the open where his men would present easy targets. Several hours later, the fort surrendered, overwhelmed by the numbers of the assailants. The 'Governor Clark', leaking badly had cut her cable and slipped away in the early stages of the duel, leaving the garrison of just 66 men in an untenable position. 28 barrels of pork and 46 barrels of flour were amongst the items captured by Britain after a fight in which only 3 people, all Indians, were wounded.

The fight for domination of the Wisconsin region, however, was not yet over. McKay sent a detachment of Indians in canoes down the Mississippi in pursuit of the crippled warship. At Rock Island Rapids, they encountered the slowly moving ship and a party of American troops advancing up river from St. Louis to relieve the garrison of Fort Shelby.

This battle at the rapids was almost unique, quite unlike any other 'battle' in this war of great variety. Indian women accompanying the party apparently joined their men folk, swarming over the decks of the vessel and tearing away the planking in an attempt to sink her. Somehow the ship survived, but the American relief party was forced to retreat, and Britain's allies could proudly boast of an unusual victory. This engagement, described by McKay as '*one of the most brilliant actions fought by Indians . . . . since the commencement of the war,*' was one of the very few engagements in which no white man was present on the British side. Britain gained an unquestioned supremacy in the Wisconsin area and upper Mississippi for the few remaining months of the war. Unlike other areas snatched from the enemy, no force of occupation would be required.

A week after the Battle at the Rock Island Rapids, the British garrison on Michilimackinac Island would wake to find America virtually knocking at their gate. Projected and planned in April, the expedition to take the fort had been delayed by American procrastination and nerves in the American high command. On 3rd July Colonel George Croghan, who had successfully defended Fort Stephenson earlier in the war, sailed from Detroit with 700 men. Supporting this small force were the brigs 'Lawrence' and 'Niagara', the schooners 'Scorpion' and 'Tigress' and two gunboats. Their initial destination was to be Macadesh Bay on Lake Huron's south-eastern coast. Thick fog, however, hid the bay from sight and, having searched in vain, the force moved north to St. Joseph's Island, the site of Michilimackinac's long deserted sister fortification.

On 26th July Croghan anchored off Michilimackinac Island, watched by McDouall and his 140 soldiers in the fort on the hill above the Indian village. Croghan, who would have been incapable of leading a large force or conducting standard battle strategies, had made little allowance for the terrain or made any estimate of the number of Indians who might be in British pay. His initial optimism rapidly evaporated when he found that his naval guns could not be elevated sufficiently to reach the fort's defences. Exposed to a heavy fire from the British guns and the sniping of the Indians, Croghan moved his ships out of range and considered his narrow range of options.

At first he tried to construct an artillery platform on the island, but his working party was harassed by Indians. One unfortunate individual, who had stopped to pick raspberries, was bundled into a canoe. Abandoning all plans to batter the fort into submission, Croghan decided on a frontal assault. But McDouall had built breastworks in the woodland south of the fort, making an approach from this direction hazardous. Seeing his options diminish even further, the American had to be content with a fresh landing on the island's north-west corner.

Immediately behind the beach, however, lay a labyrinth of trees and knotted undergrowth, the sort of landscape in which Indians prefer to fight. The fort itself lay 3 miles away at the opposite end of the island. Croghan, limited by his own abilities as much as by the terrain, realised that he would have to fight for every inch of ground—and at a considerable disadvantage.

On 4th August, his 700 troops landed, supported by gunfire from the schooners. Musket fire greeted them from the woods, and thirty or more Americans fell in just a few minutes. Some of those who survived later told of their first sight of the defending Indians in the shadows of the trees, faces hideously painted and every one of them with a look of unspeakable hostility in their eyes. It would be an almost impossible battle to win. On high ground, behind abatis and tangled branches, McDouall had placed 2 guns and almost all his regulars, leaving the Indians to man the flanks. Nature, ingenuity and Indian support seemed to be about to hand him an inexpensive victory. But the Britisher was thrown into sudden confusion by a report, false as it turned out, that America's two brigs were landing men in his rear. Afraid of entrapment, he withdrew his soldiers to the fort, leaving his Indian allies on his flanks to force the intruders back.

A brief but enticing glimpse of possible victory encouraged Croghan to an act of semi-folly. Anxious to outflank the retreating British, he ordered Major Andrew Holmes, resplendant in a conspicuous uniform of blue and gold, to lead his men along the lakeshore. Within seconds, five bullets tore into the major's body and another sliced off some of his silver braid. Several other officers were also mortally wounded in the firefight that resulted from Groghan's impetuosity. McDouall brought his men forward again, but it was to be his Indian warriors who were to be the real architects of victory. They, the tribesmen McDouall had earlier described as being '*fickle as the wind,*' forced the Americans back towards the beach. All of the twenty or so dead that Croghan left in the forest were scalped and stripped—and the same fate would have befallen the four dozen wounded if McDouall had not personally intervened to ensure their safety.

George Croghan, the hero of Fort Stephenson, had failed at this northern island. Rather than return immediately to Detroit and join the list of the military tarnished, he remained with the 'Niagara', 'Tigress' and 'Scorpion' in an effort to blockade the fort, starve the defenders into surrender and finish the job that he had so keenly started. For this, he would first need to snap the supply lifeline to Michilimackinac from York than ran across land from the city to Lake Simcoe. From here it passed through the Nottawasaga River and Georgian Bay to the now invested fort. Serving this route was the little sloop 'Nancy', her task being to take on supplies at the mouth of the Nottawasaga River and transport them past Mantoulin Island to the little fort where Britain's flag still flew.

On 14th August Croghan and his schooners sailed into Georgian Bay in search of the solitary sloop. Warned of their approach, Lieutenant Miller Worsley and his crew concealed their craft three miles up the winding Nottawasaga behind jutting rocks and overhanging boughs, falsely confident that no American ship or soldier would dare to venture so far along such a tortuous river and through unfamiliar terrain.

Unfortunately, Croghan and Captain Arthur Sinclair, his flotilla commander, had spotted the tips of the fugitive's masts from the lake. On the 14th, two howitzers and 300 troops were landed at the river's mouth and sent scrambling over rocks, ledges and ridges with instructions to blow up the boat. Worsley's forty or so men would, of course, be badly outnumbered and, despite the support of a 24 pounder gun and a hastily built blockhouse, could hardly expect to protect the 'Nancy' for long. Soon after noon, a shell from one of the howitzers hit the blockhouse magazine and destroyed the flimsy defensive shield behind which the brig had been hidden. Reluctantly, Worsley and his crew blew up their beloved vessel. Aboard were clothes, candles, flour and pork loaded only days previously for the sustenance of the defenders of Fort Michilimackinac. Confident that the 'Tigress' and 'Scorpion' would together be able to maintain the blockade, Croghan and Sinclair sailed south to the St. Clair River and a possibly less than favourable reception at Detroit.

McDouall, soon informed that the two remaining schooners were prowling in Georgian Bay, one off the Nottawasaga and the other off French Creek where the Ottawa River supply route tumbled into the bay, was determined to bring an end to their naval careers. In this, he would be assisted by the irrepressible Worsley and another of the brig's defenders, a truly remarkable man named Robert Livingston. After consigning the 'Nancy' to her death, the two men, accompanied by a handful of sailors, set out on the 18th in open canoes for Fort Michilimackinac, paddling through waters patrolled by the two American ships.

Six days later, eight miles from St. Joseph's Island, they spotted the two schooners and, under cover of darkness, stole quietly past, probably less than 100 yards from the ships, On the 31st, after 12 days in canoes, the party reached the fort and found the garrison on half rations. Despite cramp and sores, the duo set out again two days later with 50 Newfoundland men and 200 Indians in four crowded bateaux, intending to settle scores with the two harpie vessels that had reduced McDouall's men to near starvation. They found the 'Tigress' on her own near Drummond Island. Boarding the vessel that night, they overcame the sleepy crew and claimed the vessel as their own.

Three nights later, they took possession of the 'Scorpion' in an even more colourful and storybook manner. Keeping the American pennant at the masthead, Worsley sailed the 'Tigress' in search of her companion. Dressing his officers in American uniforms and ordering his men to lie concealed beneath greatcoats spread out on the deck, he hailed the 'Scorpion' and cautiously approached. Then, just as the two ships were about to touch, grappling irons flew out, the hidden men sprang out with cutlasses waving, and, five minutes later, the ship was in the hands of a British crew. Britain now had a fleet of her own on Lake Huron and undisputed control of the lake's waters. Supplies to the men of Fort Michilimackinac flowed again, carried from Nottawasaga Bay by the ships that had previously tried to prevent these movements.

The United States felt that the capture of Fort Shelby at Prairie du Chien, now renamed Fort McKay in honour of that officer, might be some compensation for this humiliation on Huron's remote northern shoreline. At the request of General Benjamin Howard, commander of the 8th Military District since Harrison's resignation, Major Zachary

Taylor set out from St. Louis with 8 gunboats and 350 men at the end of August, hoping to place himself in front of Fort McKay before Captain Thomas Anderson, commanding at the fort, had wind of his approach.

Local Indians, however, tracked every American step and, in receipt of British wages [23], reported Taylor's movements to their paymaster at the fort. Anderson promptly sent 30 men under the leadership of Duncan Graham to the Rock Island Rapids, hoping that this eloquent subordinate would be able to mobilise the Sauks and Winnebagos of the area into an effective fighting force. In this he was remarkably successful and, on 5th September 1814, assisted by 1200 Saux and Fox Indians under the charismatic Black Hawk, he intercepted Taylor's party travelling unsuspectingly up the Mississipi in their gunboats. Near Taylor's Island, Graham's artillery, two swivel guns and a 3 pounder cannon, opened on the dangerously exposed gunboats. Taylor's men, caught unprepared, could do little more than take cover behind splintering woodwork and fire back through specially prepared slits in the sides of the boats.

This was another of the war's one-sided, but varied skirmishes with the victory likely to pass to whichever side enjoyed the initial advantage. More injuries were inflicted on Taylor's men from flying splinters than from enemy shots. A practical man not given to fanciful notions, the American major turned his boats around and headed downstream. At the mouth of the Des Moines River, he paused to construct Fort Johnson, but this was soon abandoned. America was forced to accept the loss of its north-western territories and pray that the negotiators at Ghent would somehow win back what her feeble military effort had given away.

Perhaps in anticipation that this area would soon be returned to the United States, McDouall was anxious to impress on the peacemakers Britain's strategic need to retain the Mississippi's headwaters. On 29th October he commissioned Andrew Bulger, a man who had assisted Worsley in the capture of the two American ships, to be the new commander at Fort Mckay. To him he stressed the importance of holding the fort, pointing out that its loss would '*be a measure in every point of view pregnant with the most eminent danger, and not only*

23 50-70 cents per man per day

occasion the loss of this island (Michilimackinac), but ultimately place the Canadas themselves in jeopardy. For of this be assured, that the day that witnesses our departure from the Mississippi forever loses us the country . . . .' These words, alarmist but hardly prophetic, were intended for politicians' ears as much as for those of the military. But his success in keeping Britain's flag flying over the territory of Wisconsin, and British fur traders' renewed activity failed to purchase bargaining stakes at the Ghent peace talks—the entire fur country was returned to the United States. McKay's and McDouall's efforts would prove to be unenduring.

It was perhaps inevitable that some of the last heavings of the war would take place on the Lakes Peninsula, the heartland of Upper Canada on the northern shore of Lake Erie and its eastern and western fringes, the Niagara and Detroit Rivers. Here, in the course of more than two years, more than three-quarters of the war's battles and skirmishes had taken place: Queenston, Moravian Town (The Thames), Chippewa, Lundy's Lane and the sieges of the bordering forts. Surprisingly, Fort Detroit, despite being held by a garrison of only 68 men since August, when most of its defenders had been sent east in the build up of forces at Sackets Harbor, was hardly touched in this period prior to peace.

Few of the autumn's actions had any real military objectives; most were merely raids of destruction, punishment or revenge and reflected poorly on those who led them. Andrew Westbrook, a Canadian who had defected to the republican cause in 1812, took a particularly malicious swipe at his former homeland on 9th September. Leading a party to Port Talbot, he burned down mills and homes, maimed or killed cattle and destroyed huge quantities of recently harvested grain. Just as reprehensible, although with clear military goals, was the spectacular campaign conducted by Brigadier-general Duncan McArthur. Taking 800 men, he marched them north from an assembly point at Detroit along the American side of Lake St.Clair and up the Thames. On 4th November the raiders reached Oxford Mills, their arrival there triggering fears that their intended target was Burlington Heights, where 103rd Foot, Drummond's right flank, was stationed. Lieutenant-Colonel Henry Bostwick, commander of the militia based at Burford, felt unable to offer any resistance and so slipped away to Malcolm's Mills on the road between Port Dover and Burlington Heights in order to conserve his strength. Guarding the crossing of the Grand River was Major Adam Muir and 50 men of the 41st Foot. Muir, aware that his tiny force offered no real opposition, attempted to mobilize the local Iroquois into active support and called upon Colonel John Norton and the 103rd Foot, stationed closer to Burlington Heights, to join him on the Grand River's banks.

McArthur reached the river on the night of the 5th, having ransacked Oxford and its flour mills on the previous day. The Grand River was in an angry and swollen mood that week, fed by heavy autumn rains and so impossible to cross. Moreover, a redcoat presence on the far side dissuaded him from rashness. After exchanging a few shots across the river, he camped for the night, intending a grander effort on the following day. That night, however, he heard that America had abandoned Fort Erie and their last foothold in Canada. A move towards Burlington in these circumstances made no sense at all, and so he swung south to tease Bostwick at Malcolm's Mills.

The iron-souled Henry Bostwick, despite having only the 400 men of the 1st Regiment, Oxford Militia, grittily determined to hold his ground. He had selected a strong position on high ground overlooking a ravine and with his front protected by a completely unfordable stream. A mill pond lay on his left, leaving only his right exposed to possible attack.

McArthur, however, was far too experienced a soldier to be tempted into a frontal assault across such impressive physical obstacles. Leaving a small force of Kentucky men to keep Bostwick engaged, he took the bulk of his command to search for a possible crossing further along the stream. Indian scouts, however, observed his furtive movements and sent warnings back to Bostwick, who immediately recognised that his position was now untenable. He pulled back, leaving McArthur to enjoy another bout of unrestricted mill destruction.

Duncan McArthur's tidal wave of destruction swept south to Port Dover, followed by mounted militiamen and by stories of the atrocities he apparently committed. Before leaving Malcolm's Mills, the Americans had, according to apocryphal accounts, '*killed and mutilated* (a sergeant of the 41st Regiment) . . . . *in the most horrible manner.'* The man was '*butchered (no symptoms of having been shot) both scalped and cut shockingly.'* The rapacious raider then swung west and continued to scythe down mills, barns and cattle yards on his way. In mid-November, McArthur re-crossed the Niagara at Sandwich and received, no doubt, a hero's welcome at Detroit.

The man had carried out one of the most despicable and controversial raids of the war, but also one which achieved unquestionable military dividends. By destroying so much of the agricultural infrastructure of the peninsula, he had undoubtedly prevented Drummond from launching a winter offensive against Detroit and had certainly restricted the ability of the British to maintain troops or shipyards on the northern shores of Lake Erie. At the same time, however, he had stoked up an anti-American sentiment amongst the folk of the peninsula and an unquenchable hatred towards the Canadians who had travelled at MacArthur's side.

Izard, since leaving his Plattsburgh post to take up command at Sackets Harbor, had found himself with little to do. He had spent much of the time in conference with Brown, at that time conducting the defence of Fort Erie, and the two men, for a while at least, juggled with a number of fairly ambitious projects. Izard eventually formulated a plan for an attack on Fort Niagara, and, in a curiously relaxed manner, moved troops on 10th October across the Niagara River and Black Creek towards the Chippewa battlefield. From fresh positions behind Street's Creek, he fired at the British outposts beyond, but made no attempt to cross. This was becoming a war of 'nearly battles', of skirmishes that never developed and of unenthusiastic watching of the enemy.

General Izard cannot really be blamed for this lackluster activity. On 10th September, Yeo had launched the 110 gun 'St. Lawrence' at Kingston, claimed, at that time, to be the largest warship in the world. Faced by the monster, Chauncey, outclassed and outgunned and as cautious as previously, chose to withdraw to the sanctuary of Sackets Harbor, and his sails were no longer seen on the open waters of Lake Ontario. Without naval support, Izard feared to be bold. On 16th October he wrote to Armstrong from his camp at Street's Creek to justify his reluctance to strike at the enemy. '*This* (Chauncey's withdrawal) *defeats all the objects of the operations by land in this quarter. I may turn Chippawa, and, General Drummond not retire, may succeed in giving him a great deal of trouble, but if he falls back on Fort George or Burlington Heights, every step I take in pursuit exposes me to be cut off by the large reinforcements it is in the power of the enemy to throw in twenty-four hours upon my flank or rear.*' On 1st November, faced by near mutiny of his unpaid militia, he withdrew his troops across the frontier and so ended America's last invasion of her neighbour. And it was he who ordered the evacuation of Fort Erie on the 5th, despite having command over the largest American army to assemble on the Canadian frontier. *'It commands nothing, not even the entrance of the strait,'* he rather unconvincingly commented in his orders to Brown that day.

Drummond's sword also remained in its scabbard. But, while George Izard's immobility was caused by a lack of nerve, the British commander was straitjacketed by a lack of troops and the inexplicable reluctance of Yeo to use his new giant on the lake. He pleaded with Prevost for two more regiments and with Yeo for the support of naval guns. Neither man responded. When Colonel James Fitzgibbon and the Glengary Light Infantry found the works of Fort Erie deserted, they were ordered back to Fort George at the very moment when America was most vulnerable. The high command of both sides had ceased to breathe the fires of war and retribution. British and American commanders alike now seemed content to await the outcome of talking in the Belgian city of Ghent.

Ironically, at this time of lassitude, Britain chose to put a more forceful man in Yeo's place. On 12th December Captain E.W. Owen took over from Yeo. In his personal baggage were fresh orders from London to adopt a firmer attitude on the lakes. But he, too, quickly caught the disease of indifference and failed to take any advantage of Chauncey's timidity. The sails of his vessels remained furled, gun ports stayed shut and the only sound on board the ships was the wind in the rigging and anchor chains rubbing against the hulls.

The war at sea lasted much longer—well beyond the declaration of peace. The transmission of news, even on land, was slow. Those at sea would have to rely upon messages from passing ships and, as a result, the two navies' guns were still in play three months after the war had ended. The actions that had taken place during 1814 had provided very little benefit for either side and most were personal affairs, which tested the muscle and inclinations of individual captains. America had built ambitiously that year. The frigate 'Guerriere', armed with 44 guns, was launched in Philadelphia in June. She was followed in August by the birth of her sister, the 'Java', at Baltimore. Then, in a radical departure from previous policy, the United States Navy began the construction of the first ships-of-the-line, the 74 gun 'Independence', which was launched in June in Charlestown, Massachusetts, and the equally well armed 'Washington', which came off the stocks at Portsmouth, New Hampshire, in October. Born too late in the tide of war to see service, the two ships formed the basis of the republic's future navy. By the end of 1814, Congress had made provisions for two more 74 gun ships-of-the-line, twelve additional frigates, nine of which would carry 44 guns, and three lesser armed ships with 36 guns. Almost ironically, the world's first steam powered frigate, 'Fulton the First', was built, not in Britain, but in New York. Designed by the marine engineer Robert Fulton, she was launched in October, but, like the men of war, she arrived too late to contribute much in the rapidly fading war. Her presence in the New York shipyard, however, apparently deterred the British from any plans for an autumn attack on the city. The resourceful engineer also developed a 'turtle boat', an early submarine designed to allow her crew to attach torpedoes to the hulls of British ships. In the spring of 1814 the crew of this minute craft submerged beneath the hull timbers of the powerful 'Ramillies' at anchor off the harbour of New London. The submariners successfully drilled a hole in the warship's copper sheathing, but unfortunately snapped the bolt that was to be used to fasten the explosives. Days later the turtle boat was washed ashore on Long Island and was spotted by British sailors. A party of marines rowed towards the shore, but were fired upon by American militiamen in the nearby dunes. The guns of the 'Sylph' and 'Maidstone', part of Britain's assembled fleet, were turned on the Americans, forcing the men behind the dunes to flee. Having inspected the strange craft, the captors blew it up. Despite this resourcefulness and the recent additions to the fleet, The United States started and ended the year at a clear disadvantage. Her frigate fleet had been ineffective, and most had either been sunk or contained throughout the year in their home ports by His Majesty's blockades.

Adams Blockaded in Chesapeake Bay until she slipped out to sea on 18th January 1814. Scuttled in Penobscot River 3rd September

Boston Burned by her crew on 24th August at Washington to prevent her falling into the hands of the British

Chesapeake Captured by HMS Shannon after a duel off Boston on 1st June

Congress Returned to Portsmouth, New Hampshire, on 14th December 1813 after a period at sea and remained in port throughout 1814

Constellation Blockaded in Chesapeake Bay throughout the war

Constitution Blockaded throughout the year, but sailed in December and achieved her moment of glory on 20th February 1815 (see later)

Essex Captured by HMS Phoebe and Cherub off Valparaiso on 28th March

General Greene Sheer hulk at start of war, but finally destroyed on 24th August when the British sacked Washington

John Adams lockaded until April, but then conveyed Henry Clay and Jonathan Russell, American peace negotiators, to Europe on 14th April. Returned to the United States on 5th September with dispatches from Ghent

New York Blockaded near Washington and burned by the British on 24th August

President After successful career in 1812 and 1813, she returned to New York in February 1814 and was blockaded there until 14th January 1815 and was captured the next day (see later)

The fates of the frigates of the United States during 1814

Three of her sloops, however, had hunted successfully in the Spring and Summer, their achievements placing a veneer of glory on the otherwise tarnished records of the American navy. The 'Peacock' had sailed south from New York in March. On 29th April she made contact with a convoy on route from Bermuda to Havana. A single brig-sloop, the 18 gun 'Epervier' had been assigned to protective duty, and, in a fight lasting for less than an hour, the 'Peacock' holed the Britisher in several places. Boarding their victim to accept surrender, the crew found more than $100,000 worth of gold specie in her hold. Spirited, the American crew took the 'Epervier' into Savannah and then sailed out into the Atlantic's rich hunting grounds. In October, she returned to New York after sinking several merchantmen.

The 'Wasp' was even more successful in her four months of hunting under the command of Johnston Blakely. On 1st May she sailed from Portsmouth, New Hampshire, intending to bait the British in their own waters. On 28th June, after destroying five merchant vessels in the English Channel, she encountered the brig 'Reindeer' and immediately engaged. Very few details of this fight have emerged, but it seems that, after only 19 minutes, the 'Reindeer' was captured and set on fire. The 'Wasp', however, had sustained considerable damage and was forced to dock in Lorient for extensive repairs.

The appetite of the predator, however, could not be dulled by a setback such as this. On 27th August she left the French port and on 1st September engaged the 18 gun sloop 'Avon' off Britain's south coast. The 'Avon's sister 'Castilian' unfortunately appeared in the closing minutes of the duel. Fearing that she might be the forerunner of a much larger force, Blakeley left the badly damaged 'Avon' to find her grave. The later career of the 'Wasp' is uncertain; she seems to have sailed out into a fog of oblivion. She was reported to have captured the brig 'Atlanta' on 21st September, after which nothing more is recorded. She was last seen by a Swedish ship 900 miles off Madeira in October 1814.

America's subsequent sea actions all occurred after the ink on the Treaty of Ghent had dried. During November 1814, not a single U.S. warship was actually at sea, but in December the frigate 'Constitution', commanded by Captain Charles Stewart and bottled up in Boston Harbor for most of the year, ran the gauntlet and set course for the Bay of Biscay. On 20th February 1815 she met the 22 gun frigate 'Cyane' and the 18 gun brig-sloop 'Levant' about 200 miles east-north-east of Madeira.

This was to be an evening battle, fought in the gloom of winter's twilight. By about 5.45 pm the two British ships had formed in line ahead on a starboard tack, with 'Levant' in the lead by about three ship lengths. At 6 pm, the 'Constitution' enjoying the weather gauge, came abreast of the 'Cyane' and opened with her full broadside. Believing that he had silenced the ship, Stewart sailed on to tackle the 'Levant' in the same manner. 'Cyane', however, was far from dead and luffed up to rake the American from astern, forcing Stewart to drop back and resume the action against the rearmost ship. 'Levant' sensing an opportunity, sailed downwind and the 'Constitution', choosing to follow her, turned across the Englishman's stern and loosened broadsides from her port guns. The American then took on both ships simultaneously, raking the 'Cyane' from astern with her starboard guns while her port battery continued to engage the 'Levant'. At 6.50 the 'Cyane', distressed and incapable, struck her colours. Placing a prize crew on board, Stewart sailed off to settle matters with the 'Levant', now several ship lengths away.

At about 10 pm. The 'Levant' too, hauled down her colours, outgunned and outclassed. Casualties were light, no more than 16 dead and 59 wounded on all three ships. The American frigate, however, would not be permitted to escape with impunity or lead her captives home. Followed from the moment of success by the 50 gun 'Leander', the 60 gun 'Newcastle', ships built specifically to match the United States navy's breed of spar-decked frigates, and the smaller 'Acasta' with 40 guns, she was surprised while at anchor off Porto Praya in the islands of Cape Verde.

Little gunfire was actually heard that day. Stewart, knowing that destruction must follow from any action, raised every available sail and fled west, ordering his crewmen on the 'Cyane' and 'Levant' to do the same. Favoured by God or the wind, the 'Constitution' already described as a '*most fortunate ship',* with the 'Cyane' in tow escaped and reached New York days after the war had ended. And she survives to this day as part of the fabric of America's self-pride. '*Let us keep' Old Ironsides' at home',* the National Intelligencer pronounced,' *in honourable pomp as a glorious Monument of her own, and our Naval Victories.'* The slower moving 'Levant' was seized by he former owners and she soon flew the Ensign again.

The frigate 'President', the captor of the schooner 'Highflyer' in a fight off Nantucket in the September of the previous year, had been blockaded in New York's Harbour since her return to the port in February 1814. Here, however, she remained beyond the captor's reach, a fact that frustrated Britain's captains, who, having taken the 'Chesapeake' in June 1814, longed to haul in another of the jewels of the United States fleet. '*We must catch one of these great American ships,'* Broke had recently written, '*to send her home for a show, that people may see what a great creature it is, and that our frigates have fought well, though unlucky.'* This, however, would not be achieved until early the following year, but, by then, a success like this would hardly be relevant to the outcome of a dying war.

In November, at about the time that Brown evacuated Fort Erie and the American Republic had become resigned to the lethargy and inactivity of a war without promise, the Navy Department, perhaps more in search of some additional bargaining chips than from any real attempt to wrongfoot the Royal Navy, ordered Commodore Stephen Decatur to prepare the 'President' for sea, run the gauntlet of the blockade and set out as soon as practical to raid Britain's commercial trade routes in the Atlantic.

The commodore busied himself assembling the most powerful flotilla yet convened by the United States. Accompanying Decatur in the 'President' were the 'Peacock', 'Hornet' and a supply ship, the 'Tom Bowline'. For weeks, the dockside heaved with activity as provisions were loaded, carpenters shaped and fitted timbers and new sails were made. For New Yorkers, this was like the sudden heave of a dying monster, an indication, perhaps, that America's war efforts had not completely collapsed. No-one had yet heard that peace had been born.

The 'President' was ready before her companions. Impatient to be away, Decatur decided to set out with the store brig 'Macedonian' as his only companion. Ordering his companions to meet him in the vicinity of Tristan da Cunha, he rounded Sandy Hook on 14th January 1815, eluded the blockaders in the winter mist, but then grounded on a shifting sand bar.

His barrel of luck drained away completely on the following day. He was spotted 70 miles south-east of Montauk Point, Long Island, by the crew of the 40 gun 'Endymion', the 56 gun 'Majestic' and her two 38 gun companions, the 'Pomone' and 'Tenedos'. Straining every sail, Decatur tried to escape. The 'Endymion', equally manoeuvrable', set off in pursuit and struggled to close the distance. Losing the race, she opened on the American with her bow guns, hoping to hole her sails or timbers. Instead of continuing to rely upon wind and canvas to aid his escape, Decatur, never one to refuse a challenge, turned back towards his tormentor and ordered his gun crews to engage.

Something, a notion of superiority perhaps or a lack of faith in his gunners, persuaded him to try to board the enemy. Lookouts on the 'Endymion' stared in disbelief as the frigate bore down towards them. The Royal Navy warship swung around and opened with every broadside. The 'President' was forced to respond, and a two hour battle of broadsides took place, during which the canvas and yards of the British ship were torn away and every mast splintered.

The other British ships, however, had now arrived, and the 'President' was forced to strike her colours at the very moment that the 'Endymion' herself was about to surrender. Decatur, ship and crew were taken. The frigate reluctantly joined His Majesty's fleet and served without distinction until 1818.

A week later, the 'Peacock', 'Hornet' and the little 'Tom Bowline' slipped out into the Atlantic and set course for Tristan da Cunha, expecting to find Decatur and his frigate at anchor. The 'Hornet', under the command of Biddle, outpacing her companions, reached the island on 23rd March and found a British brig-sloop, the 18 gun 'Penguin', waiting for her instead.

The ensuing action took place after the ink on Ghent's peace documents had dried. During a fifteen minute fight, the crew of the 'Penguin' tried to board the American, and considerable blood was drawn in the support of a war that had now ended. At some point, a British officer was heard to cry that the brig was prepared to surrender. Biddle, hearing the assertion above the noise, ordered his crew to stop fighting. Two British marines, seeing him on the deck, took aim and shot Biddle through the neck. Neither marine lived to take any credit for the deed. Fortunately, Biddle's injury was only slight and he would return home to receive the honour of being responsible for conducting the last naval battle of the war—and the last fight ever between a British and American man-of-war.

Scuttling the badly damaged 'Penguin' before he left and joined at last by his two companions, Biddle set sail on an indirect journey homeward, still in ignorance that peace had arrived. Parting company with the 'Peacock' somewhere on route, he clashed briefly with the 74 gun 'Cornwallis'. Anxious to escape, he offloaded supplies and stores in an effort to lighten his vessel and eventually reached New York on 9th June without even an anchor left to drop in the harbour. And here at last he learned that peace had been declared—even before he and Biddle had left New York on the outward voyage to Tristan da Cunha.

Captain Warrington, master of the 'Peacock', can have the credit for firing the last shot of the war. In mid-Atlantic, on 18th February 1815, he met another of Britain's brig-sloops, the 'Nautilus'. After firing a few broadsides and forcing the surrender of the brig, whose captain had apparently only fired back in self-defence, Warrington at last learned that the war was over. Of course, he felt obliged to let his prize go free. Ironically, in those last few days of war and first few days of peace, America had achieved more than she had done in the entire two years preceding.

CHAPTER 16

'You have not even cleared your own territory of the enemy'

'You cannot, then, on any principle of equality in negotiation, claim a cession of territory excepting in exchange for other advantages which you have in your power . . . . You can get no territory, indeed, the state of your military operations, however, creditable, does not entitle you to demand any.' The Duke of Wellington had warned in November 1814 in a letter to Lord Liverpool. His realistic assessment of Britain's likely negotiating strength was widely shared, and few politicians or administrators would have openly offered a more optimistic assessment. Opinion in Britain had swung dramatically since the Spring, when even the generally objectively-minded 'Times' newspaper had declared, *'Strike! Chastise the Savages, for such they are!'* British shipping interests and the entire trading community were anxious to see the war ended; American privateers and warships had caused insurance rates to rocket. Landowners, faced by further rises in the land tax, vociferously opposed continuing hostilities. Dominating Parliament, they might howl down any Administration that failed to search for peace.

In short, Britain had grown tired, disillusioned or perhaps just bored with a probably interminable war. Unlike the great European war, in which vast swathes of territory had been wrested from the opposing side, the American war had operated within local horizons and with no declared intention of permanently occupying those strips of land taken during a campaign. The capture of the enemy's capital usually tips the scales of advantage in the favour of the captors. But Washington had been vacated within hours of its taking. *'You have not been able to carry it into the enemy's territory, notwithstanding your military success and now undoubted military superiority, and have not even cleared your own territory of the enemy,'* the great duke had said in judgment of his country's efforts in his letter to the Prime Minister—as if the latter had any need to be reminded of Britain's puny efforts.

Leading politicians on the other side of the Atlantic had come to the same conclusions and advocated peace as the only alternative to continuing a war which must result in mutual exhaustion. When Czar Alexander proposed in March 1813 that Russia act as mediator in the quarrel, President Madison eagerly agreed. He immediately appointed three delegates; the pacifically minded Senator James Bayard, who had spoken out in opposition to the war during senatorial debates, Albert Gallatin, the Swiss born Treasury Secretary, and John Quincy Adams, already serving in St. Petersburg as his country's minister to the Russian Court. The two men reached Russia's capital on 21st July 1813. And here they were to remain for a year, armed with instructions from Washington and hoping for eventual confirmation from London that Britain would be prepared to negotiate.

The Czar's offer of mediation came to nothing, ultimately rejected by King George's government who, in the Spring of 1814, stated that only face-to-face discussions between representatives of the two belligerents would be acceptable. The war in North America, the Ministers in London argued, was a family affair and did not require the involvement of an outsider.

The mediation would probably have failed anyway—for the American delegation came to St. Petersburg overloaded with pre-conditions. Foremost amongst these were the demands that Britain unequivocally renounce the practice of impressment and relinquish all the trading concessions granted to Canadian fur traders. Attached to this was a demand that Canadians should abandon trading with Indians living in American territory and keep their vessels out of America's inland waters. Even more controversially, the delegation in Russia later received instructions to impress upon the British '*the advantages to both countries* (of a transfer) *of the upper parts and even the whole of Canada to the U.S.'* This fantastic request would, Washington argued, relieve Britain of a considerable financial and political burden, particularly in times of warfare.

And so the bookish Adams, who felt irritated if his diplomatic duties prevented him from spending at least 5 hours a day in private study, and his two colleagues prepared to travel to Gothenburg, mutually chosen as a venue for discussions. The trio failed to gel from the very start. Gallatin, likely to be the most persuasive of the three, was more socially inclined and less given to seeking his own company than Adams or Bayard. By now, he was hardly on speaking terms with either, and the chances of speaking with one voice seemed remote. Partly for this reason, two new delegates, the hawkish Henry Clay and Jonathan Russell, were sent from America on board the frigate 'John Adams' to join the long standing delegation. Ghent, however, was then chosen as the place for the meeting of minds. By 6th July all five American delegates had taken up residence in the Belgian city and awaited the arrival of those with whom they were expected to deal.

Britain's choice of delegates was apposite: a naval officer, a politician and an expert in maritime law. Vice-Admiral Lord James Gambier, a desk bound officer with relatively little experience of the sea, was the leader of the delegation. Dr. William Adams, a stuffy legalist, might have considerable knowledge about the niceties of mercantile law, but was such a nonenity—and a bore—that it was said that the Earl of Liverpool could not even remember the man's name. Henry Goulburn, under-secretary to Lord Bathurst in the Colonial Office and only thirty years old, had something of a silver tongue, but his clear hatred of all things American made him an odd choice. Robert Stewart, Viscount Castlereagh, the Foreign Secretary since 1812, by insisting that the details of every discussion were referred back to him,clearly regarded the three men as nothing more than his messenger boys.

On 8th August 1814 the two delegations met for the first time and laid out their conditions for peace. Goulburn, less keen for a successful settlement and certainly less diplomatic than anyone else at the table, raised the issue of impressment, but then teasingly refused to discuss this until two other contentious areas had first been aired. He identified these as a revision of the 1783 international boundary and the planned establishment of a separate Indian state to exist as a buffer between the two countries. The delegates shifted uncomfortably in their chairs, aware of the huge burden of responsibility that had been laid upon their shoulders, and each felt unprepared to offer too many concessions out of fear that they might be regarded as weak.

An adjournment followed the opening round of talks, while both sides reflected and prepared reports for their respective heads of government. During the next session on the 19th, Gambier announced the precise details of British plans for the American Indians and the proposed buffer state. Emboldened by apparent American quiescence on the issue, the British delegation made even greater demands: free navigation rights on the Mississippi, a corridor of land in Maine to enable a road to be built from Halifax to Québec, and, most inflammatory of all, British control of the Great Lakes and the right to build forts along the lakes' southern shores. America, by contrast, would be denied any right to maintain naval vessels on the lakes.

Such proposals, far from settling any of the issues which had caused the present war, were nothing less than intolerable challenges to the sovereignty of the United States and would never be accepted. The Americans, in a genuine effort to be conciliatory, had dropped all their pre-conditions on impressment and compensation, and Monroe's demand for the cession of the two Canadas to the United States. Seen in this context, Britain's dictation of terms is more than unreasonable. Another adjournment followed while the five delegates considered their weighted reply. Finally, on 25th August, the night of the burning of Washington, Britain's humiliating terms were rejected and the delegation prepared to go home.

But Britain's hard line was more of an opening bid than any set-in-stone declaration of non-negotiable pre-conditions. Lord Liverpool and Castlereagh feared the collapse of talks and the political hornets' nest that this would arouse in London. Britain therefore began to indulge in a disingenuous attempt to keep the Americans in their chairs at the conference table, hoping that British forces still at war in America would win late victories and pressure Madison into even more humiliating terms than those now tabled. Moreover, Britain's Foreign Secretary considered that the parallel peace talks aiming to terminate the European war were far more important. What happened at Ghent, by contrast, was a mere sideshow. To keep those talks in progress, Castlereagh instructed his delegates at Ghent to drop the earlier demands for a buffer state for the Indians and for military control of the lakes. London demanded instead that the Indians be granted the territories, rights and privileges that they had enjoyed before the start of the war. On 8th October, Gambier's note to the Americans embodying this new proposal was accepted. Britain and America had made an agreement on one point.

Settlement of the international boundary was bound to be more contentious. The livelihoods of white men newly arrived on the frontier were felt to be far more valuable than the rights of the original inhabitants. Furthermore, Britain was in occupation of several posts within the United States; Prarie du Chien, Fort Niagara and Michililmackinac—with even more recent acquisitions in N. Maine. America, by contrast, held very little on Canadian soil, apart from Forts Malden and Erie—and the latter would soon be abanoned. In exchange for newly won Castine and Machias, Britain expected to retain the islands of Passamaquoddy Bay and all of Maine from the Penobscot north to the Aroostook River.

The five Americans, boosted by reports on 17th October of victories at Baltimore and Plattsburgh, refused to concede even one inch of sovereign American territory. And Britain, in continuing mischief, began to raise more peripheral issues—the American practice of curing fish on Canadian shores and fishing in Canada's waters, to name but two. Then London reaffirmed Britain's right, confirmed by the treaty ending the War of Independence, to free navigation of the Mississippi River. Clay and his colleagues must have been patient men indeed to remain at the table in the face of such provocation.

A probable realignment of the Great Powers in Europe broke the deadlock at Ghent. Russia and Prussia had reached a mutual agreement over the future of Poland and Saxony and, in so doing, aroused the concerns of Austria and Britain, who began to brew a counter-alliance. In such a situation and with a renewal of war a possibility, Britain's ministers suddenly became keener to settle with the Americans and bring their soldiers home.

Bathurst's next message to his commissioners in Ghent was consequently straighforward and realistic. *'Although our peace will not be very creditable compared with our overture, yet it will be the best thing that can happen, particularly if it is soon concluded.'* The peacemakers of both sides met on 1st December for their first full meeting since October to thrash out the remaining areas of disharmony. Much was said in heated exchanges, even more was thought but never aired, and the eight men, now no longer strangers to one another, maintained an atmosphere of gravitas and social distance. The members of each side studiously assessed the qualities of the other, noting every mannerism, strength and foible, and trying to avoid being too antagonistic. Winter sunlight, shafting across the table from the unshuttered windows, revealed the contours of stress on the delegates' faces. '*From Mr. Goulburn, we have endured much,*' Quincy Adams wrote. '*But I do not recollect that one expression has escaped the lips of any one of us that we would wish to be recalled.*' Of his fellow delegates, he was even more critical. '*There is the same dogmatical, overbearing manner, the same harshness of look and expression, and the same forgetfulness of the courtesies of society in both,*' he commented in his assessment of the qualities of Clay and Russell. And yet, in this charged atmosphere of bitterness and mistrust, the path to peace was somehow trodden. On Christmas Eve at 4 p.m., the eight men sat down at their customary places, read the 2250 word document and solemnly signed. On the following day, in more seasonal mood, they dined on beef and plum pudding while an orchestra played 'Yankee Doodle' and 'God Save the King'. At 2 p.m. the city's church bells were heard to ring.

And what had these men produced during those long hours of deliberation? Very little indeed. The document to which they had attached their signatures said nothing about impressment, fishing rights, navigation of the Mississippi, international boundaries or control of the lakes. In fact, it emptily re-stated that the situation that had existed before the war would be the basis for any settlement and left all the contentious issues to be resolved in future discussions. All conquered territory would be restored '*without delay, and without causing destruction,*' and those regions where ownership had been disputed before the war would be referred to special commissions. On the subject of the Indians, the treaty was almost silent—apart from a stipulation that neither side was to employ them in any future war against the other.

For the British, however, this almost worthless settlement was an example of peace purchased at any price. It was almost immediately referred to by one French diplomat as a '*Treaty of Omissions.*' It had been purchased with English blood and shattered lives, but the benefits that the treaty conferred, nothing more than a cessation of hostilities, had been zero. And, in addition to this price measured in terms of the numbers of dead, there had been an intangible price, too: the loss of Britain's self-esteem, reputation and her dominance of the non-European world. The peace at Ghent had been hastened, more by the threat of a renewal of war in Europe, than by any real desire to come to terms with the American people.

If wars are caused by trivialities, a fresh war between Britain and the United States might have broken out at almost any time during the next thirty years. Although most of the border forts near the Great Lakes reverted to their former owners during the summer of 1815, the scars papered over by the treaty makers were sometimes rubbed to soreness by the activities of the discontented. Andrew Bulger set fire to the fort at Prairie du Chien and returned to Michilimackinac with the captured American guns, but McDouall refused to evacuate the latter fort without expressed orders from London to do so. America reacted by holding onto Fort Malden and keeping the fort's guns ready. On 18th July, however, Britain gave way—and a few days later, both forts were back in the hands of their former owners.

On the east coast, however, reversion to the pre-war borders and status quo took a little longer to achieve. British troops were withdrawn from the Penobscot Bay region before the Spring of 1815, but Major-General Gosselin returned to Halifax with £11,000 that had been collected in customs duties in Castine during the months of British occupation. Ownership of Passamaquoddy Bay remained in dispute until 1818, and British troops did not leave Eastport until June of that year when the boundary was finally decided. Less easy to resolve, partly because many of the locals felt allegiance to the British Crown, was ownership of mainland Maine as far as the Penobscot River, an area of the American nation on which the Treaty of Ghent had dared not pronounce. The region remained in Britain's hands until 1838, after border disputes along the Aroostook River caused the dispatch of regulars from Halifax. Winfield Scott and Sir John Harvey, who had faced each other during the 1812 war, nearly came to blows, and young Victoria seemed about to order her troops to war. Good sense, however, prevailed and the boundary between Maine and New Brunswick was finally defined in 1842 by the cool diplomacy of Daniel Webster and Lord Ashburton.

Article 1: '*All territory, places and possessions whatsoever taken by either party from the other during the war . . . . shall be restored without delay.*' The clause specifically excluded the islands of the Bay of Passamaquoddy.

Article 11: '*Orders shall be sent to the armies, squadrons, officers, subjects and citizens of the two Powers to cease from all hostilities . . . all vessels . . . . shall be restored on each side.*'

Article 111: '*All prisoners of war . . . shall be restored as soon as practicable . . . . on their paying the debts which they may have contracted during their captivity.*'

Article 1V: Referred to the boundaries as laid down in 1783 and stated that disputed claims '*shall be referred to two Commissioners . . . one Commissioner shall be appointed by His Britannic Majesty, and one by the President of the United States, by and with the advice of the Senate . . . the said two commissioners so appointed shall . . . . decide upon the said claims.*'

Article V: Referred specifically to the contentious area of Maine '*from the source of the River St. Croix directly north to the north-west angle of Nova Scotia.*' Reaffirmed the arrangement in Article 1V to appoint commissioners to determine the boundary.

Article V1: Appointee commissioners to re-consider the boundary passing through the Great Lakes.

Article V11: Also dealt with the great Lakes.

Article V111: Appointee a secretary for the commissioners and established the amount of remuneration to be paid to the commissioners.

Article 1X: Both sides were to agree to put an end immediately '*to hostilities with all the tribes or nations of Indians with whom they may be at war at the time of such ratification . . . and forthwith to restore to such tribes or nations . . . all the possessions . . . .*

Article X: Committed both sides to use their best endeavours to end the traffic in slaves.

Article X1: Committed both sides to ratify the treaty within four months. The names and seals of all those involved in the negotiations were attached.

Summary of the articles of the Treaty of Ghent

The issue over naval control of the Great Lakes was also settled by diplomacy—but only after a number of incidents on or near the waters had threatened the peace. The seizure of the British schooner 'Julia', the determination of the Americans to hold Bois Blanc Island opposite Fort Malden, and the aggressive rantings of Lewis Cass, who considered that every movement and utterance of the British on the Ontario frontier was evidence of a wish, *'if not to make open war, at least to break the peace which has so happily been accomplished,'* made a renewal of war quite possible. The building of the mighty 3 decker warships, Canada, Wolfe and Saint Lawrence, and the supporting utterances of one of the Lords of the Admiralty in a speech to the Commons that *'Englishmen must lay their account for fighting battles in fleets of three-deckers on the North American lakes,'* caused more than a minor flutter of alarm in Washington breasts. James Monroe pressed home this matter in letters to Castlereagh and, rather surprisingly, found the latter receptive to discussions. During the summer of 1816, the American Secretary of State discussed the issue with Sir Charles Bagot, the British Minister in Washington, but frustratingly made little progress. Almost another year passed, a presidential election took place, and still the two sides could not agree on the arrangements for a disarmament on the lakes. In April 1817, a few months after the inauguration of Monroe as America's fifth president, an agreement was finally reached. Negotiated by Bagot and Richard Rush, the acting Secretary of State, the new treaty limited the naval forces of both sides to a total of 4 vessels each, 1 vessel on Lake Champlain and Lake Ontario, and 2 vessels each on the other lakes—and none of these were to exceed 100 tons or carry more than a single 18 pounder gun. All ships of war still on the stocks were to be disarmed and, either 'housed over' or sunk in deep water, from where they could be raised again if the need arose. Rigging, cordage, anchors and guns were generally stored, ready for use if a deteriorating situation required.

Saint Lawrence 112 guns launched September 1814 laid up in 1815 and sunk during a storm in 1832

Wolfe 112 guns still building in 1815 when construction abandoned

Canada 112 guns

Prince Regent 56 guns launched April 1814

renamed 'Kingston' in December 1814—laid up in 1815 and sold in 1832

Psyche 56 guns launched December 1814 and never completed sold 1837

Princess Charlotte 42 guns launched April

1814—renamed 'Burlington' in December and soon after disarmed—sold 1833

Royal George 20 guns (sloop) launched July 1809—renamed 'Niagara' in January 1814—converted to transport use in 1815 and sold in 1837

Wolfe 22 guns (sloop) launched May 1813—renamed 'Montréal' in January 1814 and sold in 1832

Earl of Moira 16 guns (brig sloop) launched May 1805—renamed 'Charwell' in January 1814—hulked in early 1816 and sold 1837

Melville 14 guns (sloop) launched July 1813—renamed 'Star' in January 1814—converted to transport use in early 1815 and sold in 1837

Fates of the larger British war vessels serving on the Canadian lakes

The Rush-Bagot agreement of 1817 might have made Americans feel a little more secure, but did nothing to remove the mistrust that separated the two nations—something that only time, and the evolution of a common interest could remove. Moreover, the agreement could be annulled by either side after a period of six months and, even more alarmingly, it did not extend beyond naval defence. In the years following, Britain spent extravagantly on land fortifications along the border: Fort Henry, Fort Lennox and the citadel at Quebec to name just three. More of concern to Canadian politicians was the fact that the 1817 pact was made between the United States and Great Britain, and not with Canada. At the time, this might not have accounted for much. But, as the disparity between the two American neighbours in men and resources grew greater, and Canada took responsibility for her own security, Canadian government concerns began to grow as well. Even today, Canadians remain a little uncomfortable with a world superpower as their neighbour. And they, looking back at the war, even from the perspective of 1817, could see no benefits. The feeling of vulnerability, that an easily annulled treaty could never remove, extended to the governed as well as the governing. Those living in Upper Canada, many of whom had taken up arms in Britain's cause, felt let down and even betrayed by the Treaty of Ghent that had won them nothing.

On 15th February 1815, the United States Senate ratified the treaty by 35 votes to nil, finding little fault with the men who had negotiated the peace. America, unlike Canada and Great Britain, had gained in prestige, an intangible gain more valuable than the acquisition of territory. And she had forced her old enemy to cease her bullying, hectoring ways and accept the republic as her equal on the international stage. The war and the treaty had elevated the image of the United Sates in the opinion of other nations, too, and, had, as Albert Gallatin later wrote. '*renewed and reinstated the National Feelings and character which the Revolution had given . . . the people now have more general objects of attachment with which their pride and political opinions are concerned. They are more American; they feel and act more as a nation, and I hope that the permanency of the Union is hereby secured.*' [7] When President Monroe announced in 1823, in his now famous Doctrine, that European nations would not be permitted to interfere in the affairs of the New World, the Old World accepted his stance and raised hardly a murmur of protest.

CHAPTER 17

'Astride the alligator's scaly back'

Jackson's Creek War of 1813, judged at the time to be a sideshow and no part of the struggle with Britain, had ironically produced one of the war's better known battles and nearly involved another European nation in the conflict. Jackson's defeat of the Red Stick Creeks and his imposition of terms on these people had merely fuelled their discontent and spawned the potential for another war. Yet, disorganised, broken and leaderless, it would be hard to see how these dispirited people could have resisted the power of the regular soldiers of the United States or claimed back for themselves what America had previously refused to concede.

British mischief provided the match that ignited this tinder box of resentment. Capitalising on this unrest, His Majesty's commanders in America recognised that these aggrieved tribesmen might prove to be effective allies and only needed the gentlest of shoves to send them rushing against the barricades of Alabama's and Louisiana's strongpoints. Mobilised, bribed and charismatically led, the warrior bands would be unstoppable. Charles Cameron, the British Governor of New Providence Island, was amongst the earliest to recognise the value of the Creeks as allies. Before the end of 1813, he was in communication with their chiefs and was soon promising powder and a variety of bribes to purchase their support. While this intrigue was taking place, local British commanders scouted the coast and eventually identified the mouth of the Apalachicola River as the most suitable point to make contact with any Creek, Choctaw and Cherokee warriors that might be willing to rise against their overlords.

The sponsoring of an Indian uprising, however, was regarded as secondary to a British attack on New Orleans and the Mississippi delta. The two objectives soon became intertwined, and plans were put in hand to involve the assistance of Indians, negroes and even pirates in the push against America's southern jewel. On 10th May 1814 H.M.S. 'Orpheus', under the command of Captain Hugh Pigot, anchored off the Apalachicola River. On board the 36 gun ship were 2000 muskets, 3000,000 musket balls and British uniforms, intended for distribution to any individual willing to serve in Britain's ranks.

Great Britain then embarked on some very dubious diplomacy, employing reprehensible characters as her ambassadors amongst the tribes. George Woodbine, of whom little is known, promised restoration of tribal lands, instructed the warriors in the use of firearms, fed the starving and bribed the less hungry. The grateful Creek and Choctaws, professing that they had always been Englishmen, enlisted in their hundreds, many quarreling with each other over the limited number of red tunics available. By July, an entire battalion had emerged from the swamplands of Pensacola. It was entered upon the British Army's supplementary list as the Third Battalion of Royal Marines and placed under the command of an experienced officer of the marines, Lieutenant-Colonel Edward Nicolls. Two 6th rate warships, the 'Carron' and 'Hermes' were assigned to convey this newly raised unit to wherever it might be required. Jackson's treaty with the Creeks in August swung many more Creeks in Britain's direction. Lord Bathurst in London, having won over the doubters in Liverpool's Cabinet, now gave Admiral Alexander Cochrane, the undoubted architect of the plan to hit New Orleans, full authority to proceed.

To the Cabinet in London, September 1814 appeared like brilliant sunshine after months of dismal mists. Napoleon had been banished, America's capital humiliated and General Prevost was in command of just about the largest army ever assembled in North America. Liverpool, Bathurst and Castlereagh basked in the golden glows of success, convinced that they had personally steered Britain through the uncertain thornland of warfare towards a peaceful horizon ahead. But, in their heady optimism, they nearly overlooked a highly significant fact. For Pensacola, which Cochrane intended to use as his base of operations, was Spanish territory. Choosing to ignore this fact could involve Britain in a tussle with Spain, the nation that the British had recently worked so hard to liberate.

The Spanish governor of Pensacola's recent experience of American aggression had divested him of any love for the American nation. When this is added to his appreciation of Britain's help in driving French troops out of his homeland, it is hardly surprising that Senor Mateo Gonzales Manrique saw little reason to object to Nicoll's request to station British forces there. On 29th August the two British warships, now supported by the 18 gun 'Sophia' and the recently captured American privateer 'Anaconda', appeared off Pensacola and disgorged a token force of 100 men, which had been given permission by the Governor to take up residence in nearby San Miguel Fort and place troops in nearby Fort Barrancas.

Nicoll's actions in the days following were probably unauthorised. His public language was petulant and phrased in a way that would provoke an American reaction. In an appeal aimed at the residents of Kentucky and Louisiana, he claimed that he came to relieve them '*from the chains which the Federal Government was endeavouring to rivet upon them.'* He described the government of President Madison as a '*faithless, imbecile government*' that oppressed the honest and hard working men of America. He was reputed to have offered his Red Stick recruits a dollar for every scalp they took, regardless of whether it was that of a man, woman or child.

His plans, even without such verbal abuse of his enemy, were starting to unravel. For, as he spoke, the American authorities in Alabama were negotiating agreements with the Choctaws, Cherokees and Chickasaws, leaving only the Florida Indians and the Red Sticks in the camps of the British. And, even more dangerously, Andrew Jackson had now declared publicly his intention of driving the British from the Gulf.

Cochrane felt that the capture of Mobile would be the key to unlock the route to New Orleans. From the start of the campaign in September 1814, Britain's commanders underestimated the determination and the ability of America to hold the town, and the force sent to wrest the place from America's clutches would be quite inadequate for the task. Situated on the tip of Mobile Point was the impressive Fort Bowyer, manned by

120 regulars under the command of Major William Lawrence. Perched on high bluffs, the fort could comfortably dominate any attacking force arriving in the bay. Sailing the 40 or so miles from Pensacola, Nicolls landed an assault party on a beach south of the fort on 12th September 1814, while Captain Henry Percy and his four ship flotilla rounded the tip of Mobile Point on the 15th and prepared to bombard the strongpoint from the waters of the bay.

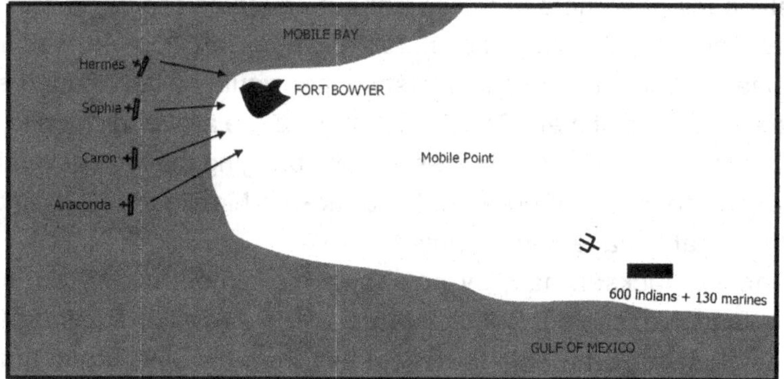

The bombardment of Fort Bowyer

A four hour bombardment failed to subdue the fort. Anchored in an exposed position and uncomfortably within the range of the fort's guns, the four British ships suffered far more than the defenders in the fort on the cliffs. The 'Hermes' was so badly damaged that Percy felt obliged to set the boat on fire and consign her to a grave. The 'Sophia' only just survived. Major Lawrence lost only four dead and the same number wounded. Percy, by contrast, counted 162 corpses lying on his decks and 72 more wounded. And, sadly, Nicolls on land, despite the support of a howitzer and a 12 pounder gun, could make no progress against Fort Bowyer's land facing defences. Twenty-four hours later the two men withdrew their forces to Pensacola with their tails between their legs.

In the hiatus following, Jackson was able to snatch the initiative. Appointed to succeed Flournoy in the command of the 7th Military District in May, he had arrived at Mobile in late August to take up his new post and prepare Louisiana for what might be coming. He had been there less than three weeks when the British assaulted Fort Bowyer: he probably had less than 1000 men under his direct command at the time.

Fort Bowyer's robustness fortunately saved Mobile and probably Jackson's reputation as well. It is sterile to conjecture on what might have happened if the fort had fallen, for the outcome would have been just as certain. Sooner or later, there would have been a climactic battle, whether at New Orleans or elsewhere, and it would undoubtedly have been an American victory.

Spared an embarrassment at Mobile, Jackson appealed to Monroe to call on the governors of the neighbouring states to furnish him with troops. The appeal to his old comrade-at-arms, John Coffee, was more personal and direct, couched in a style that would have softened even the least patriotic of men. On 25th October Coffee arrived at Mobile with a newly raised brigade of Tennessee men, bringing the total assembled in the town to nearly 4000. A British attack on Mobile at this later date would probably have been repulsed.

Andrew Jackson had, by now, become almost obsessed in his determination to snap at British throats, and not even prohibitions from Washington would be able to deflect him from his aim. Afraid that an attack on Pensacola would involve the United States in an unnecessary war with Spain, Monroe hurriedly wrote to Jackson on 21st October, forbidding him to attack Pensacola or cross into Spanish territory. The letter, however, did not reach him for several months—or was it conveniently ignored by a man with an unstoppable sense of mission? '*I well know that every man whose soul beats high in the proud title of freeman . . . . will rally round the eagle of Columbia.*' He eloquently proclaimed in his public response. Nicolls at Fort San Miguel possibly sensed the passions of his rival. The attempted enlistment of Indians had not brought in the numbers for which he had hoped and, even before his futile attack on Fort Bowyer, he had looked for other sources of manpower in the swamps and etangs of the Gulf's ill-defined coast. On 29th August, he scraped the barrel of desperation, attempting a policy of recruitment that few respectable men could ever condone. For, on that day, the brig 'Sophia', the ship that would be almost sunk a few days later off Fort Bowyer, visited the pirate stronghold of Barataria on the Mississippi delta, where savage Jean Lafitte held court over an army of more than 800 buccaneers. Captain Nicholas Lockyer, brought before the pirate king, tried to buy the ruffian's support, promising him the earth and more in return for their sweat and muscle. The wily man stalled their offer and held the captain and his party virtual prisoners while he held talks with the Americans to see if he could sell his services to them for an even higher price. Honourable America refused—and, anxious to rid sovereign American territory of the pirates' presence, the Administration sent a naval detachment under the command of Commodore Daniel Patterson to destroy the island stronghold.

Jackson was now dictating the timetable of events in the south. Feeling that he had sufficient men to flush the British from the forts of San Miguel and Barrancas, he set out from Mobile on 3rd November with his Tennessee brigade and two regiments of regulars, arriving in front of the walls of the town during the night of the 6th. He intended to pursue his aim of evicting the British from the forts, even if this triggered a war with the Spanish.

He sent in a formal summons for the surrender of the forts. The messenger carrying the demand was unsportingly fired upon, probably by the British. When finally delivered to the governor, it was unhesitatingly refused. Senor Gonzales, the man who had invited the British to man the forts, had honorably adhered to his agreement with the British, despite the fact that the American demand had not required him to surrender the town. Jackson reacted like a goaded bull. On the morning of the 7th, as the sun rose, he took his forces around to the east side of Pensacola to avoid gunfire from San Miguel, and arranged his men in three columns. His face furrowed and his expression became ashen grey, according to one of his aides. This was to be his first encounter with European soldiers, and he was conscious that he might be the instigator of a war with Spain.

The battlefield in front of him was hardly favourable. The sands of the beach on which he was forced to deploy were too soft for his wheeled artillery, and the Spanish battery and muskets had probably already picked out their intended targets. Jackson's troops moved forward; two guns in the centre of the main street opened on his lines, and volleys of musket fire from the buildings added to the carnage. This was a match between two untested forces and a struggle for national honour. For these reasons, Jackson, piqued by Spanish resistance when he expected none, immediately sent his men forward again, this time at a charge. Within minutes, the Americans had overwhelmed the two gun battery and searched for the men in the buildings and doorways who had caused them injury. But the flag of truce was already waving. Senor Gonzales had done all that national honour required and was now willing to accept America's terms.

This, of course, included the surrender of San Miguel and Barrancas. The former held out for a while in defiance of Senor Gonzales' orders, but surrendered when Jackson's troops seemed on the point of attacking. The British commander of Barrancas preferred to slip away instead. Blowing up the fort, he and his men pulled back to Prospect Bluff on the Apalachicola River, the position that Nicolls had chosen in case of a defeat that he had never expected.

Although Bathurst and Liverpool had stamped their approval on the plan to strike America in the south, Cochrane, the architect of the strategy, had not yet received confirmation of the decision and was consequently in the situation of having nothing very useful to do. The hurricane season was now in full fury, and he therefore felt that the attack on New Orleans would have to wait until that dreadful period of winds had passed. In the interval, an attack on Rhose Island seemed appropriate—for it would serve to draw away American military resources from the south.

In London, the King's ministers were still under the illusion that they were plucking victories by the handful in America. Reports of the sacking of Washington only reached them on 27th September, four weeks after the event, and news of Plattsburgh would not arrive until much later. And nobody in Britain or America seemed to have any confidence in the current negotiations at Ghent, which seemed more like an irrelevant theatrical sideshow staged in the street outside a grand theatre where a major drama is playing. Elated at the news of the flames in Washington, the ministers sent off messages of congratulation to General Ross for a job well done, ordered another 5000 men to be despatched as soon as possible and selected two major-generals to serve as his subordinates in the campaign in the south.

John Keane, the first of these, a black-whiskered Irishman who enjoyed the personal recommendation of the Iron Duke, would carry instructions from London to help the inhabitants of Louisiana to return to Spanish rule. He was expressly forbidden to foster or support any move to claim the territory for the British Crown. The second of these senior officers was John Lambert, another of the Peninsula officers.

He had a methodical mind and was capable of developing original strategy, not merely implementing the ideas of others. The euphoria created by a job well done was suddenly blown away by the sad news of the death of General Ross. For a while, black clouds of despondency blotted out the sunlight shining across Whitehall's desks.

A search for a replacement was immediately necessary—and even those at the pinnacles of accomplishment were included in the list of possible candidates. Arthur Wellesley, the Duke of Wellington, felt reluctant to go, arguing that his place was in Europe. '*It will be for you to consider whether I can be more useful to you there, here or elsewhere,*' he rather unhelpfully said to his political masters. His brother-in-law, Sir Edward Pakenham, was the Prince Regent's choice, and it was he who ultimately received the call.

Admiral Cochrane, receiving confirmation at last that British military resources were to be concentrated for an attack on the 'Crescent City' and assuming that this meant that campaigning would cease elsewhere, asked Prevost to send him the 1st battalion of the Royal Marines, but was refused. He immediately abandoned any thoughts of an attack on Rhode island and focused instead on Negril Bay, Jamaica, the chosen assembly point for the forces involved. In an effort to divert America's eyes from his true intentions, he ordered Sir George Cockburn and 1500 men to land on Cumberland Island, Georgia, and nurture the impression that subjugation of that state was Britain's single objective.

The build-up of forces at Negril Bay was rapid. Arthur Brooke and the army from Chesapeake Bay reached Jamaica on 19th November. Five days later, Keane arrived from England, bringing with him some 2000 additional men. On the following day, Cochrane and Keane sailed for the Gulf and sought out Nicolls at Prospect Bluff, leaving Rear-Admiral Pultney Malcolm to follow with the army. Not far from shore, the two men penned their own appeal to the Creeks, a proclamation that possessed neither merit nor sincerity. '*The same principle of justice which led our Father to wage a war of twenty years in favour of the oppressed Nations of Europe, animates him now in support of his Indian children. And, by the efforts of his Warriors, he hopes to obtain for them the restoration of those lands of which the People of Bad Spirit have recently robbed them.*'

Jackson, meanwhile, had fended off the unkind blasts of those who branded him, not as a national hero, but as an untamed war hawk. Milder critics regarded his attack on Pensacola as unnecessary and doing nothing to prevent the British from pursuing their real objective. On 11th November he returned to Mobile from Pensacola, working on the assumption that the redcoats would attack this latter town before moving against the city on the Mississippi delta. As soon as the hopefully reliable James Winchester arrived on the 20th, sent there by the Washington Government, Jackson split his forces, leaving about 3000 men under Winchester at Mobile, while he set out on the 21st to assume responsibility for the defence of treasured New Orleans.

He arrived there on 2nd December. Those in New Orleans unfamiliar with the man of the saddle and hardened ways might have been surprised to see an untidy and emaciated figure, with no visible manifestations of charisma and generalship, apart from the penetrating stares that he dealt out to those who opposed his views. He had been suffering from dysentry for days, probably even longer, and would eat nothing but boiled rice. The gaunt man reviewed the city's volunteer companies, mainly composed of negroes, that afternoon and began his assessment of the city's defensive capabilities. Britain, he suspected, would throw everything available against New Orleans, but for reasons which, at the moment, he could only guess at.

Monroe now actively threw his weight into the requisitioning of men and supplies. No hints of any likely success at Ghent had yet crossed the Atlantic, and, without this avenue to peace, the Administration felt committed to pursuing the only alternative route—total and unquestioned victory over Britain's armies. Yet, as usual, the machinery of requisitioning did not work well, and the burden fell on Kentucky and Tennessee. Governor Willie Blount of the latter state managed to dispatch 2500 men from Nashville, but the Kentucky authorities failed to find sufficient vessels to convey the men down river, and men sat idly at Louisville, waiting for Federal transports to ship them down the Ohio and Mississippi. Eventually, an enterprising Kentucky officer borrowed funds and hired a quantity of flatboats. These, however, leaked like sieves and needed to be repaired almost daily, and the journey was tediously slow. Four thousand muskets shipped from Pittsburgh at Federal expense were also travelling just as slowly, and these were still on their way on 26th November, the day that the British armada set sail for New Orleans.

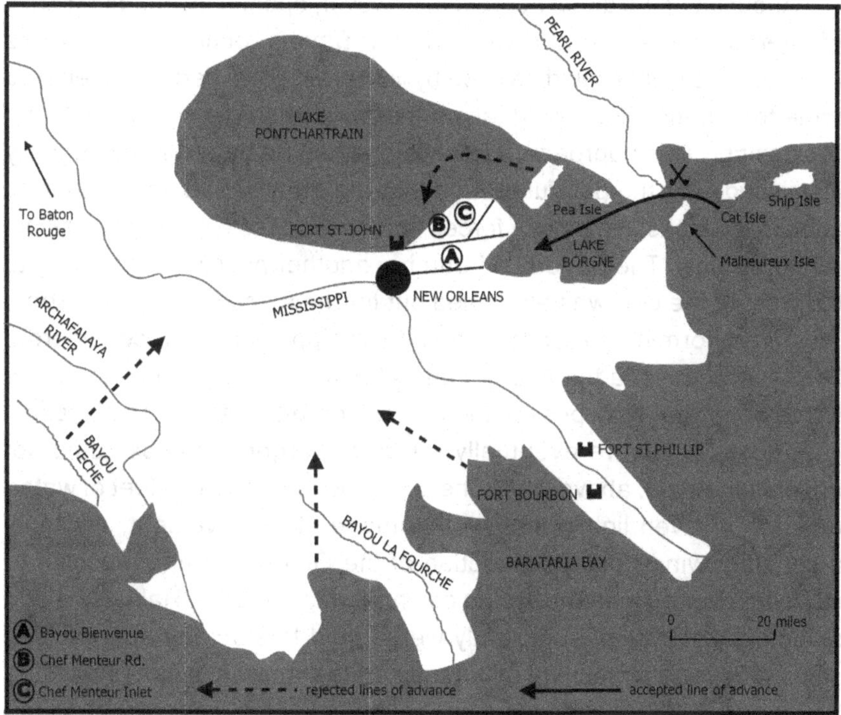

The Mississippi Delta Lands

The direction of the British approach would be difficult to predict—and perhaps just as difficult for Cochrane to choose. The land behind Mobile, drained by the Pearl River, was studded with good roadways and small open woodland. One obvious route would be an indirect movement into the interior of Mississippi Territory towards the town of Natchez. If accomplished, this would place the entire lower valley of the Mississippi River in British hands and so prevent the transport of supplies down river for the sustenance of New Orleans. Cochrane and Keane briefly contemplated this line of approach, but discounted it quickly for three very logical reasons. Firstly, the line of communication would be dangerously exposed. Marching through a hostile landscape is never advisable and should be avoided if an alternative strategy is possible. Secondly, being an indirect route, it would inevitably take longer to reach New Orleans—and time was a resource as limited as manpower and munitions. Finally, Cochrane felt that he had no need to pursue such a circuitous movement when he had the vessels to strike at New Orleans from the sea.

Adoption of the direct approach, however, opened up another galaxy of alternatives. Far to the west lay the Bayou Teche, a water route towards the city that could be used by light craft. From here, an open land route for ninety miles would take the army across the Atchalafaya and Mississippi. This approach, when weighed in the balance, was quickly dismissed—for the painful reason that the army would be exposed to attacks by Jackson's mobile forces, and the crossing of the Mississippi would be slow. The Bayou La Fourche, another possible route lying to the west of the city, was also ruled out for the same strategic reasons. The rivers forming the delta of the Mississippi were then considered. For several days, admiral and general poured over the limited charts of the delta that they possessed and pondered on the possibilities.

These, too, were eventually rejected. Larger warships could not traverse the bars, above which there was no more than 15 feet of water. Adverse or even light winds would impede the movement, and only a constant wind from the direction of the Gulf would enable ships to move up river against the strong down flowing currents. Half-way along stood Fort St. Philip, sufficiently well-armed to stop any approaching ships. Just one possibility still remained: an approach from Barataria Bay through a series of lakes and bayous towards a canal that ended only a mile from the city.

This was quickly dismissed—for it was assumed that the route would be heavily guarded. If the British had secured Pirate Lafitte's support, this line of approach would have been far more feasible. Cocharane's options had become limited—and he turned, therefore, to look at possibilities further east. The approach through Lake Pontchartrain was heavily canvassed by his officers. But the channels and roadways from the lake were no more than 8 feet deep, and a well-positioned fort, Petites Coquilles, together with a family of batteries, and Fort St. John on the southern shore of the lake, seemed likely to hamper an advance from this direction.

It was in an almost negative frame of mind, therefore, that the two commanders, Cochrane and Keane, eventually chose the route through Lake Borgne, the most direct of all the approaches and the one least obstructed by sand bars. The little Isle aux Pois (Pea Island), half way along the coast from Mobile, was chosen to serve as their intermediate base. From here the Lake Borgne route could be surveyed more closely and the final details of the plan could be decided.

The two men had chosen to disregard the flotilla of 5 gunboats that patrolled the lake. They certainly underestimated the tactical qualities of Lieutenant Thomas Ap Catesby Jones, the man in command. On 10th December Jones spotted the British fleet at anchor between Cat and Ship Island, only 80 miles from New Orleans. Knowing that his fragile craft would be vulnerable in the open waters, he headed for the sheltered waters of Bay St. Louis, from where he could safely observe the eastward transit of the British fleet.

The lieutenant's extensive capabilities were revealed in the days following. When he saw the British ships moving towards Lake Borgne, he tried to block the opening with his gunboats, but unfriendly winds prevented him anchoring in line, and he retired towards the shallow waters of Malheureux Island, knowing that the British would be bound to follow. On the 14th, he anchored his 5 boats in a line facing northwards between the island and Point Claire on the mainland. Springs on the boats' cables would enable the men to rapidly swing the boats around if required and bring the port guns into action.

At 10.30 a.m. the three columns of rowing boats carrying Britain's invading force, perhaps 60 boats in all, and each with about 20 men in each and with a carronade mounted in the bows, were seen moving towards the gunboats. Standing behind the carronades, the gun crews were dangerously exposed to the still silent American guns. Few soldiers in a line of combat on land could have felt so vulnerable. And yet the British boats came on, and the passionless eyes of the British gunners, knowing that very soon the American guns would pour out their shot, never flickered. Behind them, only slightly less exposed, sailors heaved at oars—but with their backs to the enemy.

Jones's guns roared out. The carronade operators in the nearest boats were felled instantly, and hardly a British weapon was able to respond. America's gunners reloaded, British backs were smashed and, for a while, oars were unmanned. One final discharge from the gunboats' weapons followed, the rowing boats closed in, and, like angry ants, the British sailors swarmed aboard. By noon, the 5 American vessels had been taken and their flags torn down. Amongst the severely wounded of the day were Jones and Captain Lockyer, the commander of the British row boats. '*Our men performed their roles with verve and enthusiasm,*' one of Lockyer's officers clinically testified to the Admiralty in London on his return. Six Americans had been killed and 35 wounded. Britain had lost far more: 17 killed and 77 wounded.

Poor Lieutenant Jones, nursing his injuries, was later severely criticised for taking on the enemy and sacrificing his valuable craft. Jackson would now only have the services of the schooner 'Carolina', the sloop 'Louisiana' and a solitary gunboat. But Jones had succeeded in delaying the British advance for 6 days and purchased time for Jackson to improve the defensive capabilities of the City of New Orleans.

Seahorse (schooner)	Aligator (tender), gunboats 5, 23,156, 162 and 163
Destroyed	Taken

U.S ships destroyed or taken at the Battle of Lake Borgne

The British began to disembark on the Isle aux Pois on 16th December, during a period of intense cold. The ice on the water tubs lay an inch thick, and even the admiral, accommodated in a thatched shed, shivered miserably at night. From the island, he sent out two scouts, officers named Peddie and Spencer, to identify the best route through Lake Borgne. Disguising themselves in blue smocks, the pair landed on the mainland and soon found a 100 yard wide waterway, the Bayou Bienvenu, that drained from the lake. Discretely following its course and making mental notes as they travelled, the two scouts eventually found themselves standing on a road only 8 miles from New Orleans. When they returned to Pea Island with their positive report, Cochrane and Keane enthusiastically accepted their recommendation.

Jackson, meanwhile, was reviewing his troops. On the 18th, in an almost carnival atmosphere, his men paraded in the Place d'Armes, watched by the belles of the town, who had dressed in their prettiest frocks. The general from Tennessee was being forced to guess from where the British attack might come. He had long before suspected that the Chef Menteur roadway and channel or Lake Pontchartrain would be the most likely arteries for advance, but, until the 15th, when reports of Jones' defeat reached him, he had received not a single hint of British intentions. To Coffee at Baton Rouge, he had sent a messenger that night: '*You must not sleep until you reach me or arrive within striking distance*'. The faithful subordinate responded mercurially. On the 20th he rode into New Orleans at the head of 850 unshaven men adorned in raccoon-tailed hats, and each with a tomahawk in his belt. They had ridden 135 miles in 3 days. The following day, William Carroll's Tennessee brigade rode in. Few, probably only one in ten, had left home with a rifle in his hands. But, more by chance than design, they had caught up with the leaking flatboats and their cargo of weapons—and the needs of every man had been instantly met.

The British advance was rapid, and its route of approach was becoming crystal clear. Leaving the Isle aux Pois at 10 a.m. on the 22nd, the advanced column, led by Lieutenant-Colonel William Thornton and consisting of the 4th, 85th and 95th Foot, about 1850 men, landed, as soon as darkness fell, at Bienvenu. Here they were guided and advised by fishermen, and it was they who informed Thornton of the existence of a tiny detachment of American soldiers posted in a nearby village. Scattering the surprised unit with ease, Thornton and Keane, who had accompanied the vanguard, reached the head of the Bayou Mazant and began the search for Peddie's and Spencer's recommended routeway. Ahead lay the 8 mile long Villere canal, one of the few maintained waterways that laced this section of the New Orleans environment. It led directly to the Chef Menteur road, and the entire force toiled in swampy conditions to reach the city's approaches before America was able to respond.

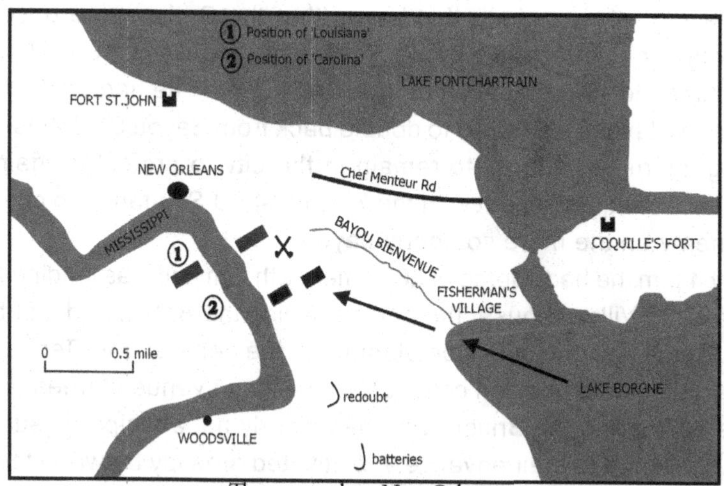

The approach to New Orleans

But any hope of surprise was punctured in the hours following. A tiny detachment of militiamen, probably no more than 30 in total, was stationed in a house nearby. Roused by the British while they were resting, the commander and some of the men jumped out of a window and raced back to New Orleans with reports of the British presence.

Slight dissension at the tables of the British command purchased Jackson a few more valuable hours. Thornton was anxious to make an immediate advance on the city, but Keane, accepting the word of Joseph Ducros, a prisoner, that 10,000 men stood in defence of the Mississippi River city, preferred to wait for the rest of the British army to arrive. Jackson had already positioned Major Jean Baptiste Plauche and his battalion of Creoles on the Bayou St. John to the north of the city. At nearby Fort St. John, a fortification which the British would have to take before they could subdue New Orleans, a force of regulars stood watch. Jackson consequently had few concerns for his northern front. Only a day or two before the arrival of Keane on the Chef Menteur road, he had sent Jean Lafitte and his Baratarian pirates, despite the fact that he had publicly denounced the men as '*hellish banditti,*' to the bayou as reinforcements.

The British, so close to the city's northern edges, were still looking. It was probably only late on the 22nd that Keane surveyed the course of the Bayou Bienvenu and discovered that it extended almost to the Mississippi, just a few miles south of New Orleans. Moreover, to his surprise and delight, the major-general also found that it had been left undefended. It was along this bayou that the British were observed marching that afternoon by Jackson's mobile units. 'Old Hickory' determined to stop them in their tracks. By 1 p.m. he had sent hurried orders to Plauche's Creoles to double back from Bayou St. Johns, and, having instructed Carroll to remain in the city to protect it against a surprise attack, he set out with the 7th and 44th U.S. infantry to confront the enemy on the more southerly bayou.

By 4 p.m. he had a force of 2000 men with him and was leading them towards the Villere house, the point at which the British had last been seen. At the nearby La Ronde plantation, the general from Tennessee calmly selected a position concealed by a long avenue of trees. A mile to the east stood the British, who had clearly not anticipated such an early challenge to their advance. A cultivated area lay between the two forces. Flat and open, it was bounded on the north by swampland and by the Mississippi in the south. John Coffee, with 730 men, took up a position close to the swamp on the left of the American line. With him were Beale's Mississippi dragoons and some of the city's volunteer riflemen. Next to him were the 465 regulars of the 7th U.S. Infantry and the similarly sized 44th. Forming closest to the river was Plauche's unit and an amorphous and militarily questionable unit of refugees from Santo Domingo under the command of Louis Daguin. At about 7 p.m. the schooner 'Carolina', with its 14 guns, anchored in the river, positioned to enfilade the British left.

The first of the two battles near New Orleans commenced that night in the near darkness of a winter evening. Thornton, blissfully unaware of Jackson's intentions to attack that night, had pitched camp, and his men were preparing supper. Crewmen on the American schooner could see the campfires and the silhouettes of men, some lying, some sitting, the thoughts of most weighed down by what might happen to them on the morrow.

At 7.30 p.m. the schooners guns suddenly pierced the silence, throwing the camp into total confusion. Discipline, the structure on which the British army had always depended, was shattered in those opening minutes, and the liquid mass of men would probably have been quickly overcome if the American troops had immediately attacked. Thirty minutes of bombardment followed, however, and, during that time, the British fighting form was restored.

At 8 o'clock, Coffee and Beale, crouching on the fringes of the swamp land in the north, moved forward through a cane field, their intention being to cut off British communications with the Bayou Bienvenu or, if the opportunity really arose, break the enemy's right flank. At almost the same moment, General Jackson ordered his lines forward, the men stealing over the darkened ground as though they were in a devious alliance with night.

Britain had, by now, recovered from the rudeness of the surprise. Suppers were left uneaten as soldiers stamped out campfires and formed in line. Colonel William Thornton himself led the defence on the left, and his energetic counter-attack almost overran the artillery pieces which Jackson had positioned there. Seeing the danger, the American personally exhorted the artillery men to continue firing, despite the growing threat to their valuable guns. Plauche and Daguin's rough troops were easily forced back by the pressure of the British regulars, but the late arrival of the two American infantry units, the 7th and 44th, who lent their support at the critical moment, eventually forced Thornton into a retreat. Simultaneously, Coffee dismounted his horsemen and led them in a direct assault on the British camp. The ensuing hand-to-hand combat was intense, fuelled by an ardour in the American ranks which is only generated when men are fighting to save their homelands. Britain's soldiers, the invaders, by contrast, fought with textbook precision but with far less passion. Yet, after nearly two hours of sustained close-haul combat, they managed to force back the hot-headed men of Tennessee and salvage their reputation. It was now 9.30 p.m.

Fog apparently brought the action to an end soon afterwards, although some reports contend that fighting continued until nearly three o'clock in the morning. Another colourful report centres on the impatience of Brigadier-General David Morgan's Louisiana militiamen who, stationed at the English Turn a few miles to the south, heard the sounds of gunfire and were eager to be involved. They hurried to the battlefield, but could not distinguish friend from foe and so found themselves in the role of an audience forced to listen to a discordant orchestra. One fact, however, is indisputable: in the closing minutes of the action, the British 93rd Regiment of Foot arrived on the field. Less confused than Morgan's Louisiana men, they joined their comrades in repelling one of the final U.S. assaults.

The casualty rate was out of proportion to the numbers involved: 46 British killed and 167 wounded out of a force of barely 1600. America lost less—perhaps 24 dead and 115 laid low with injuries out of a total of 2100 men known to have been on the field. Sadly, it was not the decisive battle that some had anticipated. Britain's main field force had not yet disembarked, and New Orleans, the objective of the campaign, still flew American colours.

That climax could have occurred two days later on the 24th. For the whole of the 23rd, the opposing sides stayed on the field, Jackson remaining to shield the city, and the British generals out of uncertainty about what to do next. Thornton argued for an immediate drive towards New Orleans, but the more cautiously minded Keane felt the need to await the arrival of Britain's strength. Yet, even when the British forces swelled in number to 4700 on the morning of Christmas Eve, Keane still delayed and so lost his golden chance.

Jackson imposed a curfew on the city that evening and then conducted an orderly 3 mile withdrawal to a position behind the Rodriguez

Canal, a semi-dry ditch about 4 feet deep and 20 feet wide than ran at right angles to the Mississippi. Here the frontage between the river and the swamp was at its narrowest and afforded the best position from which to hold off a British frontal assault. Thirty or so yards behind the canal, American soldiers, slaves and civilians laboured to construct a 3 foot high earthwork and supporting trench. Keane's hesitancy gave them the time they needed While the excavation took place, American snipers made life uncomfortable for the soldiers in Britain's forward positions. Every redcoated activity, move or gesture was observed by marksmen, and even the most casual and insignificant of gestures would place a bullet in a soldier's chest.

Christmas Day came and went without festive mood or celebration. For the Americans, this was the most galling of occasions. Food was fortunately not in short supply, but the normal wish to eat was washed away by pangs of excitement and anticipation. For the British, the pre-battle hours were normal, part of the routine which had carried them through the war on the Peninsula of Spain to victory over France. On the 26th, Lieutenant-General Sir Edward Pakenham arrived to take over supreme command, his arrival announced by loud cheers that were heard in the American lines.

Heated exchanges took place that night in the parlour of the Villere mansion. One look at the British position had convinced Pakenham of Keane's lack of strategic judgement. Conjecture and fanciful imagination have taken the place of precise reporting of what happened that night. It is hinted that Cochrane joined in the censure of Keane and Thornton. He apparently claimed that the navy could have done a better job and is supposed to have offered to lead his sailors and marines in an assault on New Orleans. The army, he mockingly said, could take on the less demanding task of conveying the baggage!

The acrimony, if it did take place, certainly slowed down Britain's movements for even longer. It allowed Jackson time to post two 6 pounder guns near the levee on his right flank and to position the 'Louisiana' and 'Carolina' in support nearby. Throughout the night of the 26th, while the arguing went on in the dimly lit parlour of the mansion, Jackson's men moved and prepared, determined that the battle would occur at a time and place of their choosing.

Pakenham would have to comply. Only a withdrawal would prevent this stretch of land on the east bank of the Mississippi from being the place of decision But he would then need to find an alternative avenue of approach, but, as one of his officers remarked:, the only other routes would be on the back of a *'bird of prey or astride the alligator's scaly back.'* The newly arrived officer had no choice but to continue with Keane's imprecise strategy and somehow force the earthen defences that were growing along his front.

Planning the destruction of the 'Carolina' occupied the next few hours. While the army awaited the late arrival of the artillery from Pea Island, a furnace was built, and on the morning of the 27th, just after the artillery had lumbered in and been installed, hot forged metal shot from the cannon rained down on the 'Carolina' and blew the vessel up. The 'Louisiana', with her 22 guns, had anchored a little further up river, and she now became the target of Britain's vengeful batteries. She was soon withdrawn to a safer position and so was spared a similar fate. One-third of Britain's entire supply of artillery ammunition was used up in the punishment of the ships.

Jackson, in an attempt to restore his advantage, now sought nature's assistance. Hoping to inundate the land over which the British would be advancing, he ordered the levees to be cut. The river, unfortunately, was too low, and the strenuous effort of breaking down the banks merely tired out his men at a time when they needed to be fresh. But the other prominent feature of the landscape was used to full advantage. Extending his earthwork for a quarter of a mile into the swamp, he turned it northward in an effort to prevent envelopment. Behind, ranged along a 1500 yard front stretching from the river on the right were 24 guns arranged in 8 batteries and an army of nearly 4000 men. Throughout the night of the 27th, the American artillery and small arms teased the British, robbing the redcoats of sleep. Pakenham and Keane, used to the tasteful standards of a European war, regarded this as a breach of manners and military etiquette—and made a point of informing the Americans of this unacceptable flouting of military conventions.

Jackson, in those closing minutes of the 27th, now faced discomforting reports that might have unnerved a less steely general than he. Members of the Louisiana legislature were apparently preparing to come to terms with the invaders. Andrew Jackson, a man who always found it difficult to distinguish the political from the military, arrived with soldiers to eject the legislators in Cromwellian fashion. They, in turn, accused him of aspiring to become a military dictator. Within two days, however, the assembly was back in session, but a seismic rift had unfortunately been caused. Completely impervious to their claims, Jackson returned to the Macarte plantation battle positions and continued with his preparations. Morgan's Louisiana men, joining him that day, were sent across the river to form an extension of the line on the west bank. Lafitte's pirates were there, too, their undisciplined and loud behaviour reinforcing the redcoats' dismissal of the quality of Jackson's fighting machine.

Pakenham, thinking conventionally, had positioned his army to confront the lines of Americans drawn up behind the canal. Keane, with the 1200 men of the 93rd and 95th Foot, formed the left of the British front, established in 4 lines nearest the Mississippi. Major-General Sir Samuel Gibbs, who had arrived in America with Pakenham, the 'Hero of Salamanca', occupied the positions nearest the swamp, placing his 2600 men to match those of General Keane. Lambert, who had still not arrived with his troops, would be held in reserve. Thornton, with another 1400 men, guarded the river's bank, well to the rear of Keane.

The second of the Battles of New Orleans took place on the 28th, when Gibbs ordered Colonel Rennie to lead a detachment through the swamp in a bid to engulf the American left flank. Keane, to distract the enemy, also advanced, firing rockets as he moved. An air of over-confidence advanced with the lines, and the men moved forward almost as if no enemy lay beyond. Exposed to the full anger of American muskets and artillery, Keane's men soon broke, shattering any pre-held belief that the Louisianians might have held that Britain's soldiers were as impervious to fear as the heroes of the Trojan War. On Britain's right, Rennie's men came up against Carroll's men of Tennessee, fighters that excelled at the sort of skirmishing that was now required. Both sides tried to outflank each other and here, on the margins of the swamp, the fighting was intense and personal, skill matching discipline, but with British numbers gradually dominating. But General Gibbs, despite his emerging advantage, had seen Keane retire and concluded that he should do the same. The morning's fight had cost the United States just 17 men. Britain, by contrast, had lost 150.

Pakenham, having seen for the first time the battle tenacity of America's forces, regular and irregular, was openly impressed and would henceforth be less dismissive of America's ability to resist. In the period of inactivity following this skirmish, Jackson ordered the men on the left to build floating platforms of logs and so extend his left wing well out into the swamp. Here he also placed 4 supporting guns, one of which was a heavy 18 pounder. For Pakenham, keenly watching, this was a completely new dimension of warfare, unlike anything that he had experienced on the Peninsula of Spain. A conventionally minded general was being obliged to fight an unconventional battle—and Britain was consequently at some disadvantage.

Jackson was also busily building up his strength on the Mississippi's other bank. The heavier guns of the 'Louisiana' were offloaded and placed near Morgan to fire obliquely across the river. Britain's sailors, too, were landing guns. Between the 28th and 31st, 24 naval guns, a mixture of 18 and 24 pounders, were rowed ashore and incorporated in 4 batteries. One of these was positioned to fire upon the enemy's positions on the river's west bank while the other three assisted the army's guns on the main battle front. The platforms on which the guns were mounted, however, were so light that the structures shook when the guns fired, reducing the accuracy of the weapons and aggravating the recoil.

1stbrigade (Lambert)	2nd brigade (Gibbs)	Keane's brigade
7th Foot	4th Foot	93rd Foot
43rd Foot	21st Foot	95th Foot
14th Light Dragoons	1stW.India Regt. (part)	1st W.Indian regt. (part)
5th W.Indian Regt.		

Rennie's force: Thornton's force:

1 company from each of the 7th, 43rd, 93rd and 85th Foot and 100 Royal Marines

1 co. of 1st W.Indian regiment

British forces at the Battle of New Orleans

During those three days of tension, a battle of nerves was staged, almost as distressing for those involved as any battle with guns. Overall, the British suffered most, subjected to harassment by night and day. Knifemen from Tennessee were active at night, creeping towards the British lines and silently slitting the throats of sleeping Englishmen as if they were nothing more than rabbits. Here was another breach of etiquette, about which the redcoat officers could do very little. Only one and a half miles separated the two sides—and nocturnal visits would remain viable.

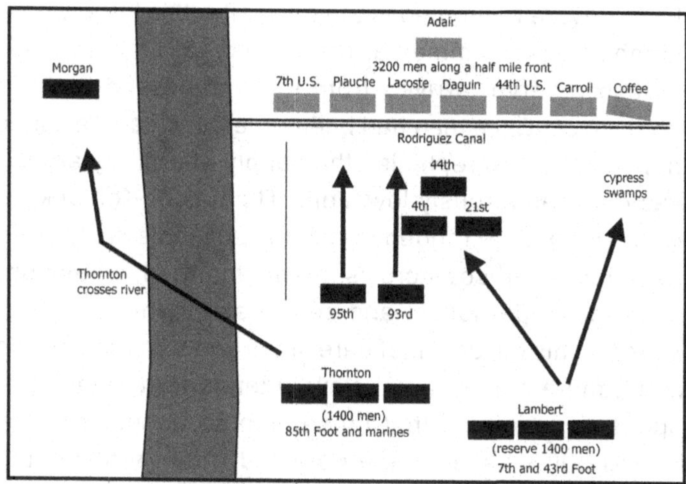

The Battle of New Orleans

On the 31st, in heavy fog, Pakenham moved his forces forward by several hundred yards, making his sleepers even more vulnerable! The opening of another trial of strength on 1st January 1815 probably came as a relief. Men asleep are far more vulnerable than those awake. Every soldier was consequently awake and ready before dawn, many choosing to wash and shave on a day when such niceties hardly mattered. British guns, many protected by hogsheads of sugar placed in front, opened soon afterwards, hoping to soften the American defences prior to an infantry attack. The artillery of the United States quickly opened in response, and, within 40 minutes, during a dialogue which seemed to prove the superiority of the American gunners, they destroyed 5 British guns and dislocated 8 more. Britain learned that a better substitute for sand would need to be found. More volatile than sand, the sugar had flown out of the punctured hogsheads and rained down on the gunnery teams. At some stage during the artillery fight, Pakenham ordered the infantry to advance against Coffee on America's left. But the fortunes of war remained solidly on America's side, and the attack was driven back. By 1.30 p.m. the last of Britain's guns fell silent The older nation had been outclassed by the younger, despite the numerical superiority in the number of guns. (24 British to 15 American)

Both sides were reinforced in the days after this largely one-sided battle. Lambert's two regiments, the 7th and 43rd, intended to serve as the British reserve, arrived from Pea Island and took up their appointed position. Each man had been ordered to carry a cannon ball in his knapsack to help replenish the supply of artillery ammunition, which was now dangerously low. John Thomas of Kentucky arrived on the 4th, leading 2250 ragged men into Jackson's camp. Here was a force of semi-naked scarecrows, many unarmed, whose only real strength was their patriotism and zeal. Pakenham, if he had been able to observe this collection of bare limbs and torn hats, would have instantly felt more comfortable. New Orleans fortunately produced the weapons and clothing that these men so desperately needed. An additional 500 muskets were obtained within a few hours from the citizens of the town. The ladies, meeting in groups, bent over their sewing baskets and made jackets to cover the cold muscles of Kentucky. Clothed, the men were sent to join Morgan's ranks on the far side of the river. Only 250, for various reasons, actually managed to cross.

British strategy for dealing with Jackson's lines was as unclear as the winter fogs that clouded the Mississippi for the next few days. For a while, General Pakenham focused on the river's west bank, perceived to be the weakest point in the American line, and gave Thornton the responsibility for dealing with Morgan's untidy force and silencing the batteries there. Transporting the troops across the river to the opposite bank would require the assistance of the navy. Cochrane, however, seemed intent on reducing Fort St. Philip, almost 40 miles to the south, and the navy's energies were diverted in that direction. Operating largely on his own agenda, the admiral sent 6 ships to the delta of the great river with orders to force the river's passage and attack the fort. Deprived of naval help, Thornton was forced to call up the bateaux lying at the mouth of the Bayou Bienvenue and arrange for them to be brought to the Mississippi's eastern bank.

Digging a canal from the bayou to the river was felt to be the only way. In an area of interlaced watercourses and easy flooding, a shallow canal could be constructed in days, theoretically enabling the 50 bateaux, supplies and provisions to be transported by water with minimal effort. But theory and practice annoyingly moved in opposite directions. The hastily built dam and walls collapsed and only 18 inches of water graced the bed of the new canal. The few boats that reached the Mississippi were then carried down river by the current to a point several miles below the intended points of embarkation and landing.

Jackson, with all his expected troops now in place, was less inclined to experiment with nature. Unconcerned by Britain's efforts, he formed two new lines of defence; the line Dupre and the line Montreuil, the former a mile and a half behind the Rodriguez Canal and the latter just beyond the city's eastern outskirts.

Pakenham's plans for the 8th, his intended day for the assault on Jackson's lines, emerged from the fogs of obscurity late on the 7th,when he believed that Thornton might at last be ready. Gibbs and Keane were instructed to be ready to commence their advance when they received a signal from Thornton to confirm that he and his 1200 men had successfully crossed and taken up offensive positions on the far bank. Gibbs would then order an advance, sending the 44th Foot out in front to fill the ditch with fascines (bundles of tied wood). The other two regiments would follow with ladders and do their best to top the ramparts along the eastern end of Jackson's line. Keane, holding back, was to wait until it seemed that Thornton had silenced the artillery on the opposite bank and then advance along the river's shoreline to hit the defenders in front of the Macarte House. In textbook terms, the plans for the attack seemed flawless and comprehensive.

These plans were very soon in danger of becoming unstitched. The crossing of the river, already hindered by the current, thick fog and the lack of boats, proceeded too slowly and only 450 men crossed. Landing a mile downstream and passing through an orange grove, Thornton met a force of 250 Kentucky riflemen in an exposed and forward position. Although he managed to throw them back with very little effort, he found Morgan's main line as solid as a buffer, and the Britisher was obliged to forge a counter strategy.

He managed this rather well. Seeing small redoubts near the river, he decided to strike at the right of the line, which he judged to be weaker. Sending 100 sailors and a company of the 85th to make a demonstration against the redoubts, he advanced at the head of another two companies of the regiment against the untested centre, leaving his second-in-command, Lieutenant-Colonel Gubbins, to lead the rest of the regiment against the enemy's right.

By now, the attack on the Rodriguez Canal positions on the other bank had commenced. Gibbs and Keane never heard Thornton's signal—and it remains doubtful whether it was ever given. Pakenham rose at 5 a.m., took a light breakfast and listened in vain for evidence of success on the western bank. Knowing that he was now committed to action, whatever the situation across the river, he ordered Gibbs forward soon afterwards and prayed that the fog would blanket his advance.

Further unstitching of his hopefully seamless plans followed. The 44th advanced without the fascines to fill the ditches and the ladders to scale the works, and the fog began to lift. Exposed to the fire of the American batteries, Gibbs's other two regiments, the 7th and 43rd, moved obliquely in columns 60 men wide towards the swamp, aiming at the point on the canal that lay between Carroll and Coffee. The Tennessee rifle, a particularly effective weapon, now joined with the artillery in firing on the British, and the stability of the redcoat columns immediately wavered. A few of the attackers reached the American breastworks, but their bodies soon lay sprawled and distorted for all to see. Those more inclined to save their lives, the majority, eagerly retreated when the recall was sounded. Amongst these were 900 kilted men of the 93rd, part of Keane's command. Only freshly arrived from service in South Africa, they had been detached by Keane to assist Gibbs when it was clear that the attack was wavering. Caught in the oblique fire from the naval batteries on the other side of the river, 670 of the 93rd fell during the advance and retreat, a frightful casualty rate to be sustained in the course of only a few minutes. Gibbs was amongst the fallen. Conspicuous on his mount, he had been shot in the left hand during the opening moments. Minutes later, his horse was killed. A subsequent bullet then claimed the general's life. The situation was a little more favourable for Keane—at least in the early stages of his advance. Subjected, like Gibbs, to the fire from across the river, he, too, angled his approach towards the American left, leaving Colonel Rennie's 4 companies to tackle the US. 7th Infantry and the batteries nearest the river.

They were the only units to achieve any success that day on the Mississippi's east bank. Reaching the Rodriguez Canal earthworks, Rennie's men drove out Beale's riflemen manning a bastion forward of the 7th Infantry's main line and planted the colours of the 3 regiments involved. Immediately, the American regulars struck out, rushing towards the bastion in a fit of enraged patriotism. In violent hand-to-hand fighting, Rennie was killed and the bastion re-taken. And still the guns taken ashore from the 'Louisiana' fired on, sending balls diagonally across the battlefield. On Britain's right, Carroll's and Coffee's men were in motion now, moving through the swamp to outflank Britain's exposed right. Betting men might now have risked placing wagers on the battle's final outcome.

Devastating disaster now wrenched the heart from Britain's army. Pakenham, posing a dazzlingly conspicuous target, wrenched his shoulder when his horse was shot dead. He mounted another, but it, too, was killed. Bemused, dazed and injured, he was being led from the field to recuperate when a shell exploded close by. A fragment lodged in his thigh and severed an artery. Before he died from loss of blood, he ordered Lambert to move in with the reserve and sustain the attack, whatever the cost.

Lambert, of course, was hesitant and set out to confer with Keane, the only other general of similar rank. But Keane was also amongst the wounded and was in no fit state to give an opinion. Left with the onerous responsibilities of command weighing on his inexperienced shoulders, Lambert halted the attack on the left bank and sent Lieutenant-Colonel Dickson across the river to report back on the situation in Thornton's sector of the field.

Regular forces (total 1026 men)	U.S. Regular Light Artillery (Capt. Enoch Humphries)
	7th U.S.Infantry Regt.
	44th U.S.Infantry Regt.
	1st U.S.Dragoons—2 troops
Irregular forces: (total 4374 men)	Plauche's Uniformed Militia
	Daguin's Free Men of Colour and 36 Baratarian pirates
	Jugeat's Choctaws
	Lacoste's Free Men of Colour
	Mississippi Dragoons (Col.Hind
	Kentucky Riflemen Regt. (Col. Adair)
	Harrison's Kentucky Militia
	Jesse Bean's Co. of Tennessee Mounted Spies

Hand's Mississippi Dragoons
<u>William Caroll's Brigade:</u>
1st Regt. of W.Tennessee Militia (Col. Metcalfe)
2nd Regt. of W.Tennessee Militia (Col. Cock)
3rd Regt. of W.Tennessee Milita (Col. Paulston?)
<u>John Coffee's Brigade</u>:
1st Regt. of W.Tennessee Mounted Volunteers (Col. Dyer))
2nd Regt. of W.Tennessee Mounted Volunteers (Co. Williamson)
<u>Colonel Morgan's Force on the west bank</u>: (1076 men)
Naval battalion and 16 guns incl. 1x24 pdr and 2x18 pdr guns. Kentucky militia Regt (Lt.Col. John Davies)
1st Louisiana Militia Regt.
2nd Louisiana Militia
6th Louisiana Militia Regt.
Natchez Volunteer Riflemen
Col.Dijean's Militia Regt.

American forces at the Battle of New Orleans

Colonel Thornton had scored the only real British success of the day. The Kentuckians under the command of Philip Caldwell instantly broke when Gubbins charged. Louisiana men in the centre were just as keen to depart when Thornton's companies moved in. Swinging inwards towards the naval batteries on the river bank in order to neutralise the guns which had caused so many casualties on the river's other bank, he overran the 16 guns, although the gunners had time to spike the weapons before making their escape. Thornton had lost just 6 killed and 76 wounded.

The trend on the main field of battle was moving very differently. Gibbs, Pakenham and hundreds of men lay dead or dying, and the sting of the redcoat army had been removed. If Thornton had been able to move faster and with greater numbers, the outcome of the Battle of New Orleans might have been quite different. But the British colonel, conducting his own little battle, was unaware of the trend of events on the bigger field of battle and moved only at the speed necessary to capitalise on his success. Morgan was in full retreat and falling back to his reserve positions, the so-called Line Boisgervais. The back door to New Orleans seemed to be opening.

It was at this moment that Dickson arrived with reports of the disaster in the east. While Dickson and Thornton deliberated, America's west bank commanders began to argue. General Jean Humbert, a New Orleans officer and protégé of the Louisiana Assembly, had come out from the town during the height of the fighting and calmly informed Morgan that Jackson had sent him to take command. Morgan, naturally upset at his apparent demotion, refused to yield until he had seen an order of transfer written in Jackson's hand. The two men were still wrangling when the retreat began and the need for any command at all on this front was swept away. But Thornton, or Dickson, would not be following the fugitives towards the town. For Lambert, despite some opposing voices in his council, had decided to end the fighting and ask Jackson for an armistice to last for a day.

U.S.force present: about 8400	British force present: 1500 marines and 7450 Regulars
U.S.casualties: 57 killed, 186 wounded 93 missing	British casualties: 378 killed, 1518 wounded 548 missing

Statistics of the Battle of New Orleans

So ended the Battle of New Orleans, an action fought two weeks after the signatures on the Treaty of Ghent had dried and the war had officially ended. No heroes, posthumous or otherwise had been created, but victims of the verbal war that followed would be plentiful. Pakenham, of course, would hear none of the criticisms levelled at his leadership. His body, cleaned of blood, was placed in a cask of spirits and taken on board ship for the journey home Poor Lieutenant-Colonel Mullins of the 44th Foot was court-martialled for his failure to arm his men with the fascines and ladders and was forced to carry the blame for the regiment's colonel, Arthur Brooke, who had failed to fight on the grounds that he was officially on leave! Admiral Cochrane, youngest son of the Earl of Dundonald, was also strongly criticised for arguing for an assault on the American south. '*A piece of folly so childish that it ought to have warned the British ministers against listening to any of his projects,*' Fortescue, the military historian concluded.

The admiral had completely failed in his attempt to deal with Fort St. Philip, New Orleans' protective fort to the south. Twenty-nine 4 pounder guns lined its walls in addition to mortars and supporting pieces, making it one of the more formidable fortresses of the American south.

In December 1814 a Major Overton had taken on the command here, only days before some of Cockburn's ships arrived. On January 9th Cochrane's marines, supported by his two bomb craft, the 'Herald' and the 'Sophia', landed nearby and occupied a signal station close to the fort. For more than a week, British guns hammered at the place, causing damage to the flagpole but very little more. Anxious to restore the Stars and Stripes to its rightful place, an American sailor had climbed to the cross tree and repaired it while under fire. He climbed down unhurt ; several of the garrison, who had been sheltering from the guns and were never exposed to the guns, were injured by splinters, some quite seriously! The Battle of New Orleans had been fought and lost during the period of the siege, and Britain's land forces were beginning to pull back towards Lake Borgne. On the 20th, Overton found that he was no longer under threat. The last of the besiegers could be seen returning to the boats. Further out to sea, Cochrane's larger ships were full of sail, indicating that they were intending to withdraw. It was quite late in the evening that Overton discovered the reasons for the withdrawal.

Jackson would be particularly fulsome in his praise of Overton, far more generous than he would ever be in his comments about those who had stood with him in the lines at New Orleans. '*The conduct of that officer and of those who acted under him, merits, I think, great praise. They nailed their own colours to the standard and placed those of the enemy underneath them, determined never to surrender the for.t'* Another officer, who left a detailed account of the siege, was less appreciative of the American war effort and the administration that provided the munitions: '*Perhaps the duration of the siege would not have been so long had the fuses, sent from the northward, been of a good quality; for several days the mortar, with which only there was any probability of reaching the enemy, was entirely or nearly useless.*'

80 guns:	Tonnant				
74 guns:	Royal Oak	Norge	Bedford	Asia	Ramillies
50 guns:	Dictator				
44 guns:	Gorgon				
38 guns:	Annide	BellePoule			
35 gubs:	Sea Horse				
	Other vessels: 9 ships carrying 32-38 guns; 5 ships with 16 guns, 2 bomb craft (Herald and Sophia) and 11 transports				

Admiral Cochrane's Gulf coast fleet

General Jackson was translated overnight into the hero of the nation. Yet he did not escape criticism entirely. Mildly censored for his neglect of the river's right bank, he would proceed to blame Morgan and the men of Kentucky for the disaster that had occurred there. For this, he was never forgiven, and Jackson's popularity in Kentucky would not achieve the levels that were reached elsewhere.

The deaths and injuries of the campaign in the south need never have occurred. It is estimated that Britain had lost 378 killed, 1518 wounded and 548 missing in the actions since the day before Christmas Eve. The United States of America had lost just 57 dead, 186 wounded and 93 missing.

News of peace landed on America's eastern seaboard at about the time that General Lambert, now in charge of an army of fading hopes, pulled back from contact with the enemy and retreated to Bayou Mazant. While bells rang in distant Boston, Philadelphia and New York and messengers sweated to carry the news to the Gulf, the saddened British army laboured to produce a strongpoint a mile from Lake Borgne, unaware of the sweet turn of events. Not a word, nor a whisper, of the ending of hostilities had reached Lambert, nor would it do for days to come. Like the welcome arrival of warm air after a winter of hard ice, reports that the two countries were at peace would take time to travel across the wilderness nation and only reached the citizens of New Orleans after the British army had begun to re-embark on 27th January.

Adverse winds, blowing on shore, kept the army's transports in Lake Borgne until 4th February, but still not a sigh or sound of peace was carried on that wind from the east. And, it was in this continuing spirit of ignorance that Lambert, trying to win some personal credit, made Britain's second attempt to take possession of Fort Bowyer. First establishing a staging point on Dauphine Island, the navy's vessels fanned out west, north and south of Fort Bowyer in virtual repetition of what they had done before. On 8th February, 5000 men were landed just over 2 miles east of the fort. Siege works sprung up, almost as quickly as toadstools after warm wet weather. By the 11th, the siege lines had approached to within 40 yards of Bowyer's walls, and the navy's guns spoke out. The following evening William Lawrence surrendered the fort after little more than a token resistance. The Union flag flew for a few hours only. A dispatch boat brought news of peace the following day and Bowyer was unceremoniously returned to its rightful owners.

Admiral Cockburn, in his own theatre of war well to the east, was another of those wallowing in ignorance of the facts. Conducting a campaign designed to inflict awe and draw away support from New Orleans, he had landed a contingent of marines on Cumberland Island off the Georgian coast on January 10th. Three days later the marines crossed to Point Petrie on the mainland and destroyed a small battery situated there. From here the British moved on and occupied the settlement of St. Mary's. Aware that Edward Nicolls was somewhere within the interior of Georgia, Cockburn dispatched a party up the St. Mary's River to link with Nicolls and carry war as far as Savannah.

Britain	United States
Killed: 1600	Killed: 2260
Wounded: 3679	Wounded: 4505
Deaths from disease: etc.: 3321	Deaths from disease etc. 4535
Civilian dead: N/A	Civilian dead: c.500
Troops involved:	Troops involved:
At war's start: 5520 regulars	At war's start: 7000 regulars
At war's end: 48,100 regulars	At war's end: 35,800 regulars
Irregular forces:	Irregular forces:
Rangers: less than 300	Rangers: 3049
Militia: c. 4000	Militia: 458,463

Casualties and manpower statistics of the 1812 War
Source: Wikipedia

The motive for this isolated invasion of Georgia seems to have been the product of highly emotive military thinking combined with pure vindictiveness, and was clearly an attempt to undermine American nationhood in the south. Cockburn and Nicolls openly incited the slaves to revolt, something, which if successful, would tear at the fabric of southern society and destroy its commercial prosperity. Peace fortunately stilled both men's hands. I have found no record of what the pair now did, nor how they reacted to the realisation that their efforts were no longer required. Their withdrawal from American territory would follow almost immediately and was, of course, largely unimpeded.

They left behind a nation embittered by the foreigners' aggression. A whole chapter, or more, could be written about the impact of the war on the American people, but a few statistics will have to suffice. The value of damage to property and buildings, private and public, has never been accurately assessed, but seems to have been about 3% of the total calculated value of the national estate at the time. The impact on trade and commerce is less easy to estimate. The value of U.S. exports, which had risen continuously during the first decade of the 19th century, fell from $76 million in 1812 to less than $58 million in 1814. Much of this fall is attributable to the embargo on trade imposed by Madison's Administration, and might not entirely be the result of the British blockades. Imports fell by almost 13%, from $92 million in 1812 to less than $81 million in 1814, a surprisingly small decline for such a prolonged period of war. American ports suffered little long-term damage. The value of manufactures actually rose, fostered by a greater need for self-sufficiency and by the demand for guns, tools and ammunition. The United States would require another century to emerge as a great trading and manufacturing nation, but the seeds of industrialism were sown during the period of national assertiveness between 1776 and 1814.

In terms of blood spilt, this had not been a war of calamitous proportions. Reliable figures indicate that only 2260 American soldiers and 500 civilians were killed in the two and a half years of fighting. Estimates of the numbers of wounded fluctuate between 4505 and 6765, a figure similar to the estimates of the number dying from the ravages of disease (4535). Britain, in comparison, lost just 1600 killed in battle, 3679 wounded and a further 3321 from war associated conditions. Casualties greater than this had occurred in a single battle in the Peninsular War.

The war had brought increasing numbers of men to the battle front, regulars and militia. The 17 U.S. regiments of infantry, 1 rifle regiment, 2 regiments of dragoons and 4 artillery regiments existing at the war's start housed about 7000 men in total. By the end of 1814, at least 45 American regiments of regular infantry existed, serviced by 39,800 professional soldiers. In addition, there were 3049 rangers under arms, distributed amongst 16 companies. The total number of American irregulars serving their country is difficult to calculate with any degree of accuracy. 458,463 names appear on the militia muster rolls, but many of these appear several times. The truer figure for the number of militia men fighting is nearer 100,000, a tiny percentage of the population of nearly 8 million.

Psychologically, however, the war had far more impact. The folk of New York, Michigan, Ohio and the Gulf saw foreign boots turning their tracks and roadways to mud. Settlements on both sides of the frontier suffered, York and Buffalo in particular, and homesteads were undoubtedly ruined. But, like vegetation after a forest fire, new shoots soon appeared. Congress, surveying the blackened shell of the Capitol, transferred their meetings initially to the Patent Office, formerly Sam Blodget's Hotel, and then to the 'Brick Capitol'. In 1819 Congress moved back to the newly rebuilt Capitol building. Throughout the United States the damaged infrastructure of war would soon be replaced and the ephemeral scars of war were surfaced over.

Every one of these scars, physical and emotional, has now been removed. How many Americans are still angered by the stories of Sir George Cockburn's actions at the sacking of the Capitol? Britain today feels little embarrassment by what she did to America's capital city.

It would take a greater and more dedicated observer of North American society than I to comment on the present relationship between Canada and her more powerful neighbour to the south. Tensions have periodically flared along the border, but the perceived subservience of the more northerly country to the republic seems more myth than fact. A common Anglo-Saxon identity has helped to bind the two nations together throughout most of the 19th and 20th centuries, and it is only recently that multi-cultural tensions and the demands of world affairs seem to have loosened these mutually tightened bindings.

It is one of the great ironies of history that Britain's two protagonists in the three wars fought in North America between 1756 and 1815 have become her greatest allies. 1814-15, the year of peace in Europe and America, saw the start of the long process by which former enemies became eventual partners in the two great wars of the 20th century. For both, France and the United States, the process of alliance with the British was never easy, and the path was strewn with the thorns of distrust and justifiable anglophobia. Britain, sometimes the aggressor and sometimes the aggrieved, has found herself on the brink of war with both nations from time to time. Yet, faced by external threats, first from Tsarist Russia and then from Imperial and Third Reich Germany, France and Britain began to pull at last in the same direction and paint on a canvas of a common destiny. Since 1904, that common identity has been more real than merely desirable. 'Perfidious Albion', the real bain of all things Gallic, has become the idiosyncratic but well-meaning neighbour, with a reputation for poor cuisine, mild xenophobia and an inability to do well in sport.

America's path to co-habitation with the British has been tempered by the geographical distance between the two and the fact that, unlike France, their cultural backgrounds and aspirations have been almost identical. For most of the 19th century, the United States, wrapped in her own massive world of the Western Hemisphere, refused to step onto the world's diplomatic stage. For the Americans, the Monroe Doctrine of the 1820's awarded the nation pre-eminence in this trans-Atlantic world and things European were of no consequence. A global view was forced upon the young republic by events, not policy. Entry into the two great wars was not universally popular. America, acclimatising herself to the fact that she had become the defender of freedom and democracy, initially shuddered at the prospect.

And so the 'special relationship' between Britain and the United States was born. Spurious, artificial, but venerated, this relationship seems to have been accepted by British statesmen as though it had been pre-determined by the gods, and as self-evident as the fact that the Earth is round. Molded out of fear of communism and, more recently, terrorism, it has become enshrined in Britain's political culture, and few politicians have dared to suggest that this marriage of unequals should be abandoned. No further comment is necessary. The likely consequences of events in today's world, Iraq, Iran, Afghanistan and elsewhere can be interpreted as they unfold. Yet the inescapable fact remains: Britain, having given birth to a determined and wayward child and having failed to discipline it, has now been obliged to accept that the child, growing round and healthy in the pastures of freedoms, has forced a reversal of the former roles.

APPENDIX1

Ships of the Royal Navy lost in American waters or in action with American vessels

Note: only vessels known to have been captured or sunk by American ships in international or North American waters are included in this list.

Alert (ex-collier)—captured 13.8.12 by USS Essex
Avon brig-sloop—sunk 27.8.14 in English Channel while in action with USS Wasp
Ballahou schooner—captured 29.4.14 by US privateer 'Perry' off coast of the United States
Boxer gun-brig—captured 5.9.13 by USS Enterprise off Maine
Caledonia brig—captured 9.10.12 on Lake Erie
Chippeway schooner—captured 10.9.13 on Lake Erie
Chubb schooner—captured 14.8.12 off Halifax
Confiance schooner—captured 5.10.13 on Lake Erie
Confiance 5th rate—captured 11.9.14 on Lake Champlain
Crane brig-sloop—foundered 30.9.14 in the West Indies
Cyane 6th rate—captured 20.2.15 by USS Constitution in mid-Atlantic
Detroit—brig (ex-USS Adams) recaptured by America 9.10.13
Detroit sloop—captured 10.9.13 on Lake Erie
Dominica schooner—captured 5.8.13 by American privateer off Charlestown (recaptured 22.5.14)
Eagle brig—captured 4.7.12 (recaptured 9.13 and renamed Chubb)
Epervier brig-sloop captured 29.4.14 by USS Peacock off East coast of N.America

Fairy Queen schooner—captured 19.11.81 by Spanish off the Orinoco
Finch brig—(ex-USS Growler captured from Americans 9.13 on Lake Champlain but then recaptured 11.9.14 by former owners
Gloucester brig—captured 24.4.13 at York (subsequently destroyed by British 20.5.13 at Sackets Harbor)
Guerriere (ex-French)—captured by USS Constitution 19.8.12
Hermes 6th rate—grounded 15.9.14 at Mobile
Highflyer schooner (ex-American) recaptured by USS President 8.9.13 off Nantucket
Hunter brig—captured 10.9.13 on Lake Erie
Java 5th rate (ex-French)—captured 29.12.12 by USS Constitution off San Salvador
Lady Prevost schooner—captured 10.9.13 on Lake Erie
Laura schooner—captured 8.9.12 by French privateer off North America
Levant 6th rate—captured 20.2.15 by USS Constitution—returned to Britain at end of war
Linnet brig—captured 11.9.14 on Lake Champlain
Little Belt 6th rate—captured 16.5.11 by USS President, but then returned
Little Belt sloop—captured 10.9.13 on Lake Erie
Lord Nelson brig—captured 6.1812 by American schooner
Macedonian 5th rate—captured 25.10.12 by USS United States
Mary schooner—captured 1813
Nancy schooner—burnt 14.8.14 by US forces
Nautilus brig sloop—captured 18.2.15 by USS Peacock
Peacock brig sloop—captured 24.7.13 by USS Hornet
Peacock (ex-USS Wasp) foundered and lost July 1814 off Virginia Capes
Penguin brig sloop—captured 23.3.15 by USS Hornet
Pictou brig sloop—captured 14.2.14 by USS Constitution
Queen Charlotte sloop—captured 10.9.13 on Lake Erie
Reindeer brig sloop—captured by USS Wasp 28.6.14 in English Channel
St. Lawrence schooner (ex-USS Atlas)—captured by US privateer in the West Indies
Sir Isaac Brock 6th rate—destroyed 27.4.13 on stocks at York

Sir Sidney Smith (renamed Magnet) brig—burnt 5.8.14 to avoid being taken by Americans

Southampton 5th rate—wrecked 27.11. 1812 off the Bahamas

Whiting schooner—captured 22.8.12 by French privateer off North America

APPENDIX 2

Warships of the United States of America serving in the War of 1812-14.

The names are followed by the year in which the ship was commissioned or acquired. Names shown in bold identify those lost (captured or sunk) during the war. Ships with * survived the war

Ships of the line (74 guns)
Independence 1814
Washington 1814
Franklin 1815
New Orleans 1814 (87 guns) planned for service on Great Lakes, but construction halted 1815

Frigates:
Adams 1799 *scuttled in the Penobscot River in September 1814*
Boston 1799 *burnt by her crew in August 1814 to prevent capture by the British*
Chesapeake 1800 *captured by HMS Shannon in June 1813 off Boston*
Congress 1799 *
Constellation 1797 *
Constitution 1797 (fondly known as 'Old Ironsides' and preserved) *
Cyane (captured from British in 1815) *
Essex 1799 *captured by HMS Phoebe off Valparaiso in March 1814*
General Greene 1799 *burnt in August 1814 when British attacked Washington*
Guerriere 1814 (commissioned after cessation of hostilities) *

Java 1814 (commissioned after cessation of hostilities) *
John Adams 1799 *
Macedonian (captured from British in 1812) *
New York 1800 *burnt by British in August 1814 near Washington*
President 1800 *captured by HMS Endymion, Pomone and Tenedos in February 1815*
United States 1797 *
Mohawk 1814 built for service on the Great Lakes *
Superior 1814 built for service on the Great Lakes *

Schooners:
Alligator 1809 *attacked and run aground January 1814 in the Stone River, S.C.—subsequently refloated—sunk in Port Royal Sound in July 1814 during heavy storm, but again refloated* *
Ariel 1813 *possibly burnt December 1813 by British on Lake Erie*
Asp (1) 1813 *captured in Yeocomico River July 1813 by marines from HMS Contest and HMS Mohawk*
Asp (2) (British merchant vessel 'Elizabeth' captured in April 1813 by U.S. ship 'Growler' on Lake Ontario)*
Carolina 1812 *destroyed in December 1814 during Battle of New Orleans*
Chippewa (captured from British in September 1813 on Lake Erie) *burnt by British in December 1813 after being driven ashore at Black Rock*
Comet 1810 *
Confiance *(British schooner captured in October 1813 on Lake Erie)
Conquest 1812 *
Despatch 1814 *
Enterprise 1799 *
Epervier 1812 (British ship captured in April 1814) *disappeared without trace in July 1815 near Gibraltar*
Hornet 1814 *
Julia 1812 *captured August 1813 by British on Lake Ontario and briefly renamed 'Confiance'* (recaptured October 1813 by U.S.) *
Lady of the Lake 1813 *
Lynx 1812 *captured March 1813 by British in Chesapeake Bay*
Nautilus 1799 *captured July 1812 by British off New Jersey—the first capture of the war—*

Nonsuch 1813 *
Ohio 1812 *captured August 1814 by British during siege of Fort Erie*
Ontario 1813 *
Porcupine 1813 *
Ranger 1814 *
Raven 1813 *
Scorpion 1812 served as floating battery *burnt August 1814 by Americans in Potomac to prevent capture by the British*
Scorpion 1813 *captured September 1814 by British on Lake Huron*
Scourge 1812 *capsized and sunk August 1813 during storm on Lake Ontario*
Seahorse 1812 *burnt December 1814 at Battle of Lake Borgne to prevent capture*
Somers 1812 *captured August 1814 by British during siege of Fort Erie and renamed HMS Somers*
Spitfire 1814 *
Sylph 1813 *
Ticonderoga 1814 *
Tigress 1813 (ex-schooner 'Amelia')*captured September 1814 by British on Lake Huron and renamed HMS Surprise*
Tom Bowline 1814 *
Torch 1814 *
Vixen 1803 *captured November 1812 by HMS Southampton and wrecked off the Bahamas*
Vixen 1813 *captured December 1813 by HMS Belvidera*
Wasp 1807 *captured October 1812 by HMS Poictiers—briefly renamed Loup cerviers before further renaming as HMS Peacock*
Wasp 1810 *

Sloops and brigs:
Alert (captured from British in August 1812)
Alligator 1813 (converted to gunboat) *captured December 1814 at the Battle of Lake Borgne*
Arab 1812 *captured April 1813 in the Rappahannock River*
(1)Argus 1803 *captured in August 1814 by HMS Pelican off British Isles*
(2) Argus 1813 *burnt by Americans in August 1814 near Washington to prevent capture*

Buffalo 1813 *
Camel 1813 *
Detroit *(ex-British 1812 captured by U.S. in Battle of Lake Erie)
Dolphin 1812 *captured April 1813 on the Rappahannock River and taken into British service*
Eagle 1812 *captured June 1813 by British on Lake Champlain and renamed HMS Finch* (recaptured by US in September 1814) *
Eagle 1814 * (holed 39 times during the Battle on Lake Champlain)
Erie 1813 *
Fair American 1812 *
Frances 1813 (returned to owner in 1814)
Frolic 1813 *captured in April 1814 by HMS Orpheus and renamed HMS Florida*
Gallatin 1807 *caught fire and exploded April 1813 in Charleston, S.C.*
General Pike 1813 *burnt before launch during attack on Sackets Harbor May 1813 but subsequently completed and launched to serve on Lake Ontario* *
(1) Growler 1812 *captured August 1813 by British on Lake Ontario, but recaptured October 1813 by USS Sylph—retaken by British May 1814 at Oswego and renamed HMS Hamilton*
(2) Growler 1812 *captured June 1813 near Ile aux Noix (L.Champlain)—briefly named Shannon by British, then renamed Chubb—captured by USS forces September 1814 during Battle of Plattsburgh*
Hamilton 1809 *capsized during storm August 1813 on Lake Ontario*
Highflyer date unknown *captured in January 1813 by HMS Poictiers*—retaken by USS President in September 1813 off Nantucket
Hornet 1805 *
Jefferson 1814 *
Lawrence 1813 deliberately sunk at end of war to preserve her timbers
Louisiana 1812 guns removed during Battle of New Orleans—final fate obscure
Linnet (ex-British captured by US September 1814 at the Battle of Plattsburgh)
Lynx 1812 *captured April 1813 in the Rappahannock River and taken into British service as HMS Mosquidobit*
Madison 1812 *

Montgomery 1813 *
Niagara 1813 *
Oneida 1810 *
Patapsco 1806 no details
Peacock 1813 *
Pert 1812 *
Preble 1813 *
President 1812 *captured in 1814 on Lake Champlain and renamed HMS Icicle*
Racer 1812 *captured April 1812 in the Rappahannock River and taken into service as HMS Shelburne*
Rattlesnake 1813 *captured June 1814 off Cape sable by HMS Leander*
Queen Charlotte (ex-British captured by US September 1813 at the Battle of Lake Erie) *
Saratoga 1814 *
Spark 1813 *
Syren 1803 *captured July 1814 by HMS Medway*
Trippe 1812 *burnt December 1813 by British on Lake Erie*
Tickler 1812 *
Viper 1806 *captured January 1813 by HMS Narcissus and renamed HMS Mohawk*
Viper 1814 (galley) *
Wasp 1813 returned to owners in 1814
Wasp 1814 lost November 1814 during storm

Others: list includes a number of privateers captured by the British and other armed vessels that played a prominent part in the war
Anaconda (privateer) *captured July 1814 by British in Chesapeake Bay—became HMS Anaconda*
Active 1812 *
Curlew *captured 1813 by HMS Acasta—became HMS Columbia*
Caledonia 1812 (ex—HMS) (captured by U.S. October 1812 on Lake Erie but *burnt by British a few days later)*
General Armstrong (privateer) *captured September 1814 in Fayal (Portugal) by HMS Rota and Plantagenet*
Ilsley (privateer) *
Independence (privateer) *captured November 1812 by British*

Little Belt 1813 (ex-British captured by U.S. schooners Scorpionand Chippeway September 1813 at Battle of Lake Erie) *driven ashore at Black Rock December 1813 and burnt by British*
Marietta 1803 (galley) *
Oneida 1808 *
Prince de Neufchatel (privateer) *captured December 1814 by British*
Superior 1814 (64 gun ship launched on Great Lakes)
Teazer 1812 (privateer) *boarded and burnt December 1812 by crew of HMS San Domingo*
Tickler 1812 *
William Bayard (privateer) *captured March 1813 by HMS Warspite—became HMS Alban*

APPENDIX 3A

The United States Army 1812-15

Note: successive re-organisations and re-numbering of the constituent regiments since 1815 has made it far from easy to identify which of today's regiments were engaged in the battles of the war. What follows is a simplified explanation of the regiments formed before or during the war and their subsequent consolidation in the peacetime restructuring of 1815

Infantry:

The development of the army's infantry commenced with the creation of the-

1st American Regiment: formed by Congressional Act in 1784 and placed under the command of Lieutenant-Colonel Josiah Harmer ⇒ 1st Infantry regiment in 1791.

2nd American Regiment: formed 1791—912 regulars supported by 2000 shorter-term volunteers were raised and placed under the command of Major-General Arthur St. Clair.

Both of these regiments were organised into ten companies, each of 76 men.

Subsequent regiments: In March 1792, following setbacks in the war with the Indian tribes on the Ohio frontier, Congress provided for the raising of three more regiments, each enlisted for a period of three years. These were formed into the 'Legion of the United States', which was then organised into four 'sub-legions of 1280 men apiece, infantry, artillery and supporting dragoons.

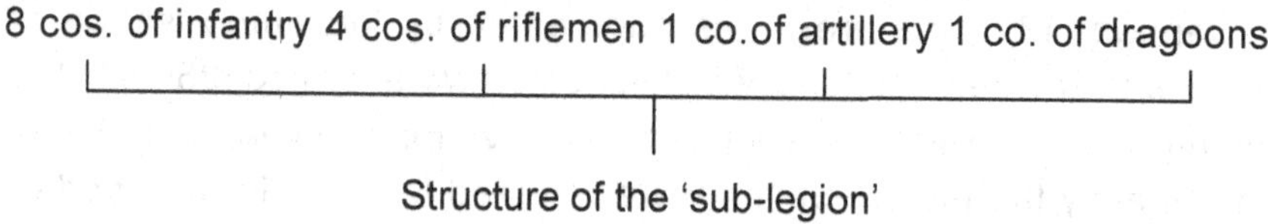

Structure of the 'sub-legion'

In October 1796, following success in wars with the Indians, Congress abolished the legion and cut back the number of infantry regiments from five to four. Only two companies of dragoon were retained. The size of the army was consequently reduced from 5000 men to 2000.

In May 1798, fuelled by the possibility of war with France, Congress set up a 'paper army' of 12,000 men, formed into twelve regiments of infantry and six troops of dragoons. Settlement of the dispute with the French Revolutionary government ensured that these regiments were never actually formed. In 1800 the United States Army still consisted of just four regiments of infantry. The new administration of Thomas Jefferson reduced the strength of the army still further in 1802, leaving a skeletal force of just twenty companies of infantry and artillery and abolishing the cavalry force entirely.

In April 1808, during an era of uncertainty created by growing resentment against Britain, Congress called for the formation of 5 more regiments of infantry, one regiment of Riflemen and a regiment of Light Dragoons, the so-called 'additional force'. (3rd,4th,5th 6th and 7th US Infantry). Each regiment consisted of ten companies, with 78 men in each company.

In January 1812, a further ten regiments of foot were commissioned (8th-17th US Infantry, each with eighteen companies of 110 men, arranged in two battalions) followed in June by the raising of ten more regiments, although only eight of these were actually raised in time for the start of hostilities (18th-25th US Infantry). The United States Army, in the summer of 1812, theoretically consisted of 27,000 officers and men, but the actual number in uniform or training was no more than 12,000. It was also decided to establish a uniform structure for all existing regiments—ten companies, each consisting of 102 men.

In January 1813 the army was augmented by the authorisation of another twenty regiments, of which nineteen were formed (26th-44th US Infantry). These were initially raised to serve for one year, but almost immediately the men recruited were required to serve for a period of five years or for the duration of the war, whichever was the longer of the two periods.

The final bout of recruitment took place in early 1814 when four more regiments of infantry

(45th-48th US Infantry) and three more rifle regiments were raised. Later that year, four undermanned regiments (17th, 19th,26th and 27th) were consolidated to form two new regiments—the 17th and 19th US Infantry. At the same time, the 47th was renumbered as the 27th and the 48th as the 26th.

These, then, were the regiments of infantry that fought the war of 1812-14. By September 1814 there were 38, 186 listed in the American army ranks. At its largest size, the army numbered just 57,000 men in December 1814. These regulars, however, were supported by 3,049 rangers, 10,110 volunteers and 458,463 militia men.

The restructuring of 1815: Peacetime called for reduction in the size of the army. The 35 remaining regiments were consolidated as follows:
New regiment: formed from:
1st US Infantry 2nd, 3rd, 7th and 44th
2nd US Infantry 6th, 16th, 22nd, 23rd and 32nd
3rd US Infantry 1st, 5th, 17th, 19th and 28th
4th US Infantry 14th, 18th, 20th, 36th and 38th
5th US Infantry 4th, 9th, 13th,21st, 40th and 46th
6th US Iinfantry 11th, 25th, 27th, 29th and 37th
7th US Infantry 8th, 24th and 39th
8th US Infantry 10th and 12th

Rifle Regiments: In April 1808 Congress called for the recruitment of a regiment of rifles (1st *Regt. of Rifles)* and this unit served throughout the war under the commands of Col. Alexander Smith (until July 1812) and then under Col T.A.Smith (until January 1814).
Three more regiments of rifles were formed in February 1814:

2nd Regiment of Riflemen (Col. Anthony Butler)
3rd Regiment of Riflemen (Col. William King)
4th Regiment of Riflemen (Col.James Gibson until Sept. 1814, Col. James McDonald until the war's end)

Rangers: The January 1812 orders called for the establishment of six companies of rangers to be recruited for one year. In July 1812, a further company was added and the existing companies were formed into three battalions. In February 1813 ten additional companies were raised.

Dragoons:
The four regiments of dragoons which had served during the War of Independence had all ceased to exist by the end of 1783. The first regular units of cavalry emerged in 1784 when two troops of cavalry, each consisting of 60 men, were attached to the 1st American Regiment of 1784. As stated above, the 'Legion' formed in 1792 was supported by four companies of dragoons. Requiring a distinct form of training, these four companies were actually kept separate from the infantry and placed under the command of Lieutenant Robert Campbell. The subsequent reduction in the cavalry force in 1796 and 1800 has been outlined above.
When the additional five regiments of infantry were created in the 1808 Congressional legislation, a Regiment of Light Dragoons, consisting of eight companies, was also established and placed under the command of Colonel Jacinth Laval. In January 1812, another regiment, the 2nd U.S. Light Dragoon Regiment, twelve companies strong, was added to the establishment. James Burn of South Carolina, who had served in the Charleston Volunteer force since 1790, was given the command of this unit. In early 1814 these two regiments of Light Dragoons were merged.

Artillery:
Legislation in 1802 had authorised the creation of a regiment of artillery consisting of 20 companies. ⇒ 1st Regiment of U.S, Artillery. A further act in 1808 created a 10 company regiment of 'Light Artillery. The January 1812 legislation, as well as creating ten new regiments of infantry, also set up two more artillery regiments and these were numbered 2nd and

3rd U.S. Artillery regiments. In 1814 the 3 regiments were combined into the Corps of Artillery, a unit consisting of 12 battalions, each with 4 companies. The involvement of these units in the main battles of the war is shown below:

	1st Art.	2nd Art.	3rd Art.	Light Art.	Corps of Art.
Maguago	♦				
Queenston		♦		♦	
York			♦	♦	
Fort Meigs				♦	
Fort George		♦	♦	♦	
Stoney Creek		♦		♦	
Crysler's Farm		♦	♦	♦	
Fort Oswego			♦	♦	
Chippewa					♦
Lundy's Lane					♦
Plattsburgh					♦
Baltimore					♦
Fort Erie					♦

U.S.Army regiments existing at the end of the war: 1 regiment of cavalry, 45 regiments of infantry, 4 rifle regiments and 42companies of artillery.

APPENDIX 3B

The British Army in North America 1812-15

Britain began the war with 5200 redcoated regulars serving in the 4 regiments based in Canada. These were: 8th Foot,—posted 1810 (1st battalion only)

41st Foot	1799
49th Foot	1802
100th Foot	1805

During 1812 the 1st Foot, the 2nd battalion of the 8th Foot and the 103rd Foot arrived, swelling the number of regulars in Canada to 12,655.
During 1813 three squadrons of the 19th Light Dragoons were posted for service. These were followed by the arrival of the 13th, 64th, 70th, 89th and 101st Regiments of Foot., bringing the total to 19,477 men.
1814 saw the arrival of many of the experienced Peninsular War veteran regiments. These were the 3rd, 4th, 5th, 6th, 9th, 16th, 21st, 27th, 29th, 37th, 39th, 44th, 57th, 58th, 60th, 62nd, 76th, 81st, 82nd, 85th, 88th, 90th, 97th, 98th, 99th and 102nd Regiments of Foot, swelling the final strength of the redcoats at the end of the war to 48,160 regulars.

Regular regiments on the Canadian Establishment:
The involvement of these units, with the exception of the Royal Nova Scotia Fencibles (which was involved in no actions), the small regiment of the Michigan Fencibles and the Royal Veterans' Battalion, and the West Indian Regiment are shown in Appendix 5.
Royal Nova Scotia Fencibles—formed 1803—became part of the 104th Foot (Regular establishment) in 1810
New Brunswick Fencibles—formed 1803—became part of the 104th Foot

Canadian Fencible Infantry—formed 1803—became part of the 104th Foot—recruited largely from French speaking settlers.

Royal Newfoundland Fencible Infantry—formed 1803—became part of the 10th Foot—at its maximum strength, this unit consisted of 556 men.

Glengarry Light Infantry—formed in 1812 from Scottish immigrants—the originally recruited force grew from an establishment of 376 to more than 600 men by 1814. Initially commanded by Colonel George MacDonnell of the 8th Foot, the regiment was later under the command of Colonel Edward Baynes. Officially part of the British Army establishment from October 1812

Provincial Corps of Light Infantry (Voltigeurs)—formed in 1812 from French-speaking settlers and commanded by Lt.Col. Charles de Salaberry. Recruits were promised 50 acres of land on discharge.

Michigan Fencibles—formed in 1813. The unit numbered no more than 45 men and served in the actions at Fort Mackinac and the Siege of Prairie du Chien

10th Royal Veterans' Battalion—raised in the Isle of Wight in 1806 from British army veterans—arrived in Canada in 1807 and formed garrison of Fort St. Joseph—the regiment was responsible for the capture of Fort Mackinac—renumbered 4th Veteran Battalion in 1815.

1st West Indian Regiment—raised in 1795 by recruiting freed slaves—the regiment served at the Battle of New Orleans.

Regiment de Meuron—formed in Switzerland in 1781 as a mercenary unit. Entered British service in 1798—served in Spain until the unit's transfer to N. America in 1813.

Regiment de Watteville—formed in Switzerland in 1801 as a mercenary unit. Like the above regiment, the unit was transferred to the British establishment and was posted to Canada in the spring of 1813. The unit saw its most concentrated action at the attacks on Oswego and Fort Erie.

Militia regiments: details of the larger or more significant units are provided.

Frontier Light Infantry—two companies of English speaking volunteers, which are usually listed as the 9th and 10th companies of the Voltigeurs.

Select Embodied Militia—six battalions had been formed by 1813, most members signing up for one year service. Featured prominently at the battle of Chateauguay.
Incorporated Militia Battalion—formed in 1813. Saw service at York and Lundy's Lane.
William Caldwell's Western Rangers—a unit consisting of no more than 50 men serving throughout the war, particularly at Moravian Town (The Thames), Longwoods and Lundy's Lane.
William Merritt's Provincial Dragoons—a unit of perhaps 100 men which assisted the British Crown forces on the Niagara peninsula.
Mississippi Volunteers—a spontaneous assembly of Ohio and Michigan traders, who took up arms during the attack on Prairie du Chien.
Québec Volunteers—a small unit, perhaps no more than 65 men, set up purely for the defence of the city and Lower Montréal. The unit became part of the 6th battalion of the Select Embodied Militia.
Dundas, Glengarry, Grenville, Leeds, Stormont and York militia regiments—formed within the counties of those names, the numbers of regiments fluctuated, but all saw major service during the principal campaigns of the war.
Loyal Kent Volunteers—set up in the Spring of 1814 for defence of the Lakes Peninsula. The unit took a prominent part in the skirmish of Longwood(s).
Loyal Essex Volunteers—also set up in the Spring of 1814 for the defence of the Lakes Peninsula.

British army strength at the end of the war: 2 cavalry regiments, 84 infantry regiments and 31 companies of artillery.

APPENDIX 4

Land Battles of the War of 1812

Source: Niles' Weekly Register, 1816

Battle	Date	U.S. commander	Details of US force	number	k.	w.	m.	c.
Brownstown	4.8.12	. Vanborn	Riflemen/ militia	200	17	30		
Magawgwa	9.8.12	. Miller	Riflemen / militia	600	18	58		
Detroit	16.8.12	Hull	Infantry / volunts.	340/2000	1		50	2300
Queenston	12.10.12	Rensellaer	Infantry / militia	300/700	90	160		700
French town (1)	18.1.13	. Lewis	Volunteers	?	12	55		
French town (2)	22.1.13	Winchester	Volunteers	1000	357	64	42	537
York	27.4.13	Dearborn	Infantry/Rifles	1300	66	203		
Fort Meigs	5. 5 13	. Harrison	Infantry/volunts.	300	61	121		
Rapds/Miami	8.5.13	. Dudley	Militia	800	80	100		700
Fort George	27.5.13	. Dearborn	Infantry/Art/Rifles	4000	39	121		
Sackets' Harbor	29.5.13	. Brown	Militia	600	21	84	26	
Stoney Creek	6. 6. 13	. Chandler	Infantry	2000	17	38	100	
Craney Island	22.6.13	. Beatty	Infantry/sailors/art.	450/150/150	?	?		
Beaver Dams	24.6.13	. Boerstler	Infantry/art.	335	25	50		460
L.Sandusky	2.8.13	Croghan	Infantry/volunts.	160	1	7		
Moravian Town	5.10.13	Harrison	Infantry/vol/militia	120/1500/1500	7	22		
Williamsburg	11.10.13	. Boyd	Cavalry/infant/art.	1800	102	237		
La Cole Mill	30.3.14	Wilkinson	Infantry	4000	8	66		
Oswego	6.5.14	. Mitchell	Artillery	300	6	38	25	
Sandy Creek	30.5 14	. Appling	Rifles/Indians	150/ 125	1	3		
Chippewa	5.7.14	. Brown	Infantry/Art/ militia	Unspecified	60	244	19	
Niagara	25.7.14	. Brown	Infantry/Art/militia	Unspecified	171	572	117	
Conjetta Creek	3.8.14	. Morgan	Riflemen	240	2	8		
Fort Erie	15.8.14	. Gaines	Infantry/Art/militia	unspecified	17	56	11	
Bladensburg	24.8.14	. Winder	Militia/art/ marines	6000	30	40	120	120
Moore's Fds.	30.8.14	. Read	Militia	170		3		
Plattsburg	11.9.14	. Macomb	Infantry/militia	1500 in total	37	62		
Baltimore	13.9.14	. Smith	Volunteers/militia	3200	24	139	49	49
Fort Erie	17.9.14	. Brown	Infantry/Rifles/militia	1000/1000	79	216		
Fort Bowyer	18.9.14	.Lawrence	Infantry/Rifles	?	4	5		
Cook's Mills	19.10.14	Bissel	Infantry/ Art,/ militia	900	11	54		1
New Orleans(1)	23.12.14	A.Jackson	same	1500 in total	24	115	74	
New Orleans(2)	28.12.14	A.Jackson	same	3382 in total	7	8		
New Orleans(3)	1.1. 15	A.Jackson	same	3961 in total	11	23		
New Orleans(4)	3.1. 15	A.Jackson		4593 in total	13	39	71	
Totals					1422	3044	555	4867

Descriptions and figures in bold identify regular units involved

APPENDIX 5

Involvement of British regiments in land battles of the war

No. of regiment 1	1	3	4	5	6	7	8	9	13	16	21	26	27	29
Action														
Maguago 9.8.12														
Detroit 16.8.12														
Fort Erie 9.10.12	♦													
Queenston 13.11.12														
Niagara 21-27.11.12	♦						♦							
Frenchman's Crk. 28.11.12														
Ohio Front 16.9.12														
Frenc town 18.1.13														
Ogdensburg 21.2.13							♦							
York 27.4.14							♦							
Fort Meigs 1-8.5.13														
Fort George 26.5.13	♦						♦							
Sackets Harbor	♦						♦							
Ile-aux—Noix 3.6.13														
Stoney Creek 6.6.13							♦							
Craney Island 22.6.13														
Beaver Dams 24.6.13							♦							
Lake Champlain 29.7.13									♦					
Fort Stephenson 31.7.13							♦							
Moravian Town 5.10.13														
Chateauguay 25.10.13														
Crysler's Farm 11.11.13														
St. Lawrence 11.13—2.14														
Fort Niagara 18.12.13	♦				♦		♦							
Lacolle Mill 30.3.14							♦		♦					
Oswego 5.5.14														
Chippewa 5.7.14	♦						♦							
Lundy's lane 25.7.14	♦						♦							
Fort Erie 15.8.14—17.9.14	♦				♦		♦							
Castine														♦
Machias														♦
Penobscot														
Bladensburg 24.8.14			♦								♦	♦		
Plattsburgh 11.9.14		♦		♦					♦	♦			♦	♦
Baltimore 13.9.14												♦		
Fort Bowyer 18.9.14			♦			♦								
Mobile			♦			♦								
New Orleans 12.14—1.15			♦			♦					♦	♦		♦

No. of regiment	37	39	40	41	43	44	49	57	58	59	60	62	64	70
Action														
Maguago				♦										
Detroit				♦			♦							
Fort Erie				♦										
Queenston				♦			♦							
Niagara							♦							
Frenchman's Creek				♦			♦							
Ohio Front														
Frenchtown				♦										
Ogdensburg														
York														
Fort Meigs				♦										
Fort George				♦			♦							
Sackets Harbor														
Ile-aux-Noix														
Stoney Creek							♦							
Craney Island														
Beaver Dams							♦							
Lake Champlain														
Fort Stephenson				♦										
Moravian Town				♦										
Chateauguay														
Crysler's Farm							♦							
St. Lawrence														
Fort Niagara				♦										
Lacolle Mill														
Oswego														
Chippewa														
Lundy's Lane				♦										
Fort Erie				♦										
Castine											♦	♦		
Machias														
Penobscot											♦			
Bladensburg						♦	♦							
Plattsburgh		♦					♦		♦	♦				
Baltimore						♦								
Fort Bowyer														
Mobile			♦			♦								
New Orleans			♦		♦	♦								

No. of regiment 76	76	81	82	85	88	89	90	93	95	14ld	19ld	97	98	99
Action														
Maguago														
Detroit														
Fort Erie														
Queenston														
Niagara											♦			
Frenchman's Creek														
Ohio Front														
Frenchtown														
Ogdensburg														
York														
Fort Meigs														
Fort George						♦					♦			
Sackets Harbor														
Ile-aux-Noix														
Stoney Creek														
Croney Island														
Beaver Dams														
Lake Champlain														
Fort Stephenson														
Moravian Town														
Chateauguay														
Crysler's Farm						♦								
St. Lawrence														
Fort Niagara			♦			♦					♦			
Lacolle Mills						♦								
Oswego														
Chippewa														
Lundy's lane						♦								
Fort Erie			♦			♦								
Castine											♦			
Machias											♦			
Penobscot			♦											
Bladensburg				♦										
Plattsburgh	♦				♦				♦		♦	♦		
Baltimore				♦										
Fort Bowyer														
Mobile														
New Orleans				♦			♦	♦	♦	♦	♦			

No. of regiment	100	101	102	103	104	RM	RW	RN	CF	GL	NB	V	MF	Mar.
Action														
Maguago														
Detroit								♦						
Fort Erie														
Queenston			♦											♦
Niagara														
Frenchman's Creek														
Ohio Front														
French town								♦						
Ogdensburg								♦		♦				
York								♦		♦				
Fort Meigs								♦						
Fort George					♦			♦		♦				
Sackets Harbor	♦				♦			♦		♦	♦	♦		
Ile aux Noix	♦													
Stoney Creek								♦						
Craney Island			♦											♦
Beaver Dams					♦					♦				
Lake Champlain	♦			♦										♦
Fort Stephenson														
Moravian Town								♦						
Chateauguay									♦			♦		
Crysler's Farm									♦	♦		♦		
St. Lawrence														
Fort Niagara	♦			♦	♦					♦				
Lacolle Mill	♦								♦			♦		♦
Oswego							♦			♦				♦
Chippewa	♦													
Lundy's lane				♦	♦					♦				
Fort Erie	♦			♦	♦		♦	♦		♦				
Castine														
Machias														
Penobscot														
Bladensburg														♦
Plattsburgh						♦								
Baltimore														
Fort Bowyer														
Mobile														
New Orleans														

Explanation: number at top of column identifies the regiment e.g. 7 is 7th Foot.

Numbers in bold identify the two regiments of Light dragoons

Abbreviations: RM =Regiment de Meuron RW= Regiment de Watteville RN= Royal Newfoundland Fencibles CF = Canadian Fencibles GL= Glengarry Light Infantry

NB= New Brunswick Fencibles V= Provincial Corps of Light Infantry (Voltigeurs)

MF= Michigan Fencibles Mar= Royal marines

Official Battle Honours were awarded at:
Detroit August 1812: 41st Foot
Quuenston October 1812: 41st and 49th Foot
Miami January 1813: 41st Foot
Niagara December 1813 to: 1st, 8th, 41st, 89th, 100th, 103rd m104th Foot
19th Light Dragoons and the Glengarry Regiment
Bladensburg August 1814: 4th, 21st, 44th and 85th Foot

APPENDIX 6

Involvement of U.S.Regular regiments in the main engagements of the war

No. of regiment	1	2	3	4	5	6	7	8	9	10	11	12	13	14	15	16
Action																
Tippecanoe 7.11.11				♦												
Brownstown 4.8.12																
Maguago 9.8.12				♦												
Detroit 16.8.12				♦												
Queenston 12.10.12					♦	♦						♦	♦	♦		
French Town 18.1.13																
York 27.4.13					♦	♦								♦	♦	♦
Fort Meigs 5.5.13	♦		♦													
Fort George 27.5.13					♦	♦						♦	♦	♦	♦	♦
Stoney Creek 6.6.13																
Craney Island 22.6.13																
Beaver Dams 24.6.13						♦										
Ft.Stephenson 31.7.13	♦		♦													
Moravian T. 5.1.0.13																
Chateauguay 25.1.0.13				♦												
Crysler's Fm. 11.11.13									♦		♦	♦	♦	♦		♦
Lacolle Mill 30.3.14				♦		♦										
Oswego 6.5.14																
Sandy Creek 30.5.14																
Chippewa 5.7.14			♦		♦	♦			♦		♦					
Lundy's Lane 25.7.14	♦		♦		♦				♦		♦	♦	♦	♦		♦
Fort Erie 15.8.14									♦		♦	♦				
Bladensburg 24.8.14																
Plattsburgh 11.9.14				♦	♦	♦			♦		♦	♦			♦	♦
Baltimore 13.9.14																
Cook's Mills 19.10.14																
New Orleans 1.1.15		♦					♦	♦								

2nd and 8th U.S.Infantry served in the south throughout the war. The 10th U.S. Infantry was positioned in defence of Georgia

No. of regiment	17	18	19	20	21	22	23	24	25	26	27	28	29	30	31	32
Action																
Tippecanoe																
Brownstown																
Detroit			♦													
Queenston				♦			♦									
French Town																
York					♦											
Fort Meigs	♦															
Fort George				♦	♦	♦	♦		♦							
Stoney Creek																
Craney Island																
Beaver Dams																
Ft. Stephenson	♦															
Moravian T.	♦							♦		♦	♦	♦				
Chateauguay																
Crysler's Fm.					♦				♦							
Lacolle Mill																
Oswego																
Sandy Creek																
Chippewa				♦	♦	♦	♦		♦							
Lundy's Lane	♦		♦		♦	♦	♦		♦	♦						
Fort Erie						♦	♦		♦							
Bladensburg																
Plattsburgh					♦	♦			♦				♦	♦	♦	
Baltimore																
Cook's Mills																
New Orleans																

18th U.S.Infantry was placed in defence defence of South Carolina defence of South Carolina, particularly Charleston

No. of regiment	33	34	35	36	37	38	39	40	41	42	43	44	1R	2R	3R	4R
Action																
Tippecanoe																
Brownstown																
Detroit																
Queenston													♦			
French Town																
York													♦			
Fort Meigs																
Fort George													♦			♦
Stoney Creek																
Craney Island																
Beaver Dams																
Ft. Stephenson																
Moravian T.																
Chateauguay																
Crysler's Fm.													♦			
Lacolle Mill																
Oswego																
Sandy Creek													♦			
Chippewa																
Lundy'sLane													♦			
Fort Erie																
Bladensburg				♦		♦								♦		
Plattsburgh	♦	♦											♦			
Baltimore																
Cook's Mills																
New Orleans												♦			♦	

39th U.S. Infantry was primarily responsible for conducting the war against the Creeks in Alabababa

BIBLIOGRAPHY

Primary sources: Amongst the most accessible primary resources are the following, many of which have been reprinted several times.

Claiborne, William *Letterbook*

Dunlop, William *Recollections of the American War, 1812-14*

Latour, A. *Historical Memoir of the War in W.florida and Louisiana*

Lossing, Benson J. *The Pictorial Field Book of the War of 1812*

Niles' Register

Richardson, John *Richardson's War of 1812*

Scott, Winfield *Memoirs of Lieut-General Scott, Written by Himself*

Wellesley, Arthur *Supplemantary Correspondence and Memoranda*

Wilkinson, James *Memoirs of My Own Times*

Wood, Eleazer *Journal of the Northwestern Campaign*

Secondary Sources:

Campaigns and general reference:

Adams, Henry *History of the United States of America during the First Administration of James Madison*

Barbuto, Richard *N francisiagara 1814*

Beirne, Francis *The War of 1812*

Berton, Pierre *The Invasion of Canada*

Berton, Pierre *Flames Across the Border*

Burt A. *The United States, Great Britain and British North America*

Cruikshank, C. *The Documentary History of the Campaign upon the Niagara Frontier in the year 1812*

Cruikshank, C. *From Isle aux Noix to Chateaugay*

Cruikshank, E.A. *The County of Norfolk in the War of 1812*

Elting, John *Amateurs to Arms: A Military History of the War of 1812*

Engelman, Fred *The Peace of Christmas Eve*
Finan, P. *An Onlooker's View*
Frederiksen, John *War of 1812:Eyewitness Accounts*
James, I. *Border Captain*
Latimer, John *1812*
Lord, Norman *The war on the Canadian Frontier 1812-14*
Lucas, Charles *The Canadian War of 1812*
Malcomson, Robert *Historical Dictionary of the War of 1812*
Mahan A.T. *Sea Power in its Relation to the War of 1812*
Tucker I. *Poltroons and Patriots*
Updyke, Frank *The Diplomacy of the War of 1812*
Wood, William *Select British Documents of the Canadian War of 1812*

Army organisation:
Frederiksen, John and Barbuto, Richard *The United States Army in the War of 1812*
Heitman, Francis *Historical Register of the United States Army*
Quimby, Robert *The U.S.Army in The War of 1812(2 volumes)*

More recent publications: (with dates of publication and names of publishers)
The following are particularly recommended:
Benn, Carl *The War of 1812* (2002 Osprey)
Borneman, Walter *1812: The War That Forged a Nation* (2005 Harper Collins)
Coggelshall, George *History of the American Privateers and Letters of Marque* (2006 University of Michigan Press)
Elting, John *Amateurs To Arms: A Military History of the War of 1812* (1995 Da Capo Books)
Frederiksen, John *Free Trade and Sailors' Rights: A Bibliography of the War of 1812*
(1985 Greenwood)
Frederiksen, John *War of 1812: Eyewitness Accounts* (1987 Greenwood)
George, Christopher *Terror on the Chesapeake: The war of 1812 On the Bay* (2000 White Mane Books)

Gleig, George *The Campaigns of the British Army at Washington and New Orleans* (2007 BiblioBazaar)
Hickey, Donald *The War of 1812: A Forgotten Conflict* (1995 University of Illinois Press)
Katcher, Philip *The American War 1812-14* (1990 Men-at-Arms)
Malcolmson, Robert *Lords of the Lake: The Naval War on Lake Ontario* (2003 Chatham Publishing)
Pitch, Anthony *The Burning of Washington: The British Invasion of 1814* (1998 Naval Institute Press)
Remini, Robert *The Battle of New Orleans: Andrew Jackson and America's First Military Victory*
(1999 Viking Penguin)

GENERAL INDEX

Entries for forts are listed under names of forts. Where practical, the names of battles and campaigns have been placed beside an entry. Names of today's states are given.

Appendices 1 and 2 give a fuller coverage of ships involved.

INDEX OF ACTIONS, BATTLES AND ENGAGEMENTS

The major actions at sites which play a significant role are shown in bold at the end of the list of entries for that place. This list does not attempt to name all the places mentioned in the text. It merely identifies those at which an action is known to have occurred.

O

P

Q

R

S

T

W

Y

INDEX OF PERSONS

The list does not attempt to include all those mentioned in the text, many of whom played only local or brief roles.
Only those with a significant or continuous role are listed.

T

V

W

Y